A Bibliography of British Municipal History

CHARLES GROSS

A BIBLIOGRAPHY OF

BRITISH
MUNICIPAL HISTORY

including
GILDS AND PARLIAMENTARY
REPRESENTATION

Second Edition with a Preface by
G. H. MARTIN

LEICESTER UNIVERSITY PRESS
1966

First published as Volume V of Harvard Historical Studies by Longmans, Green and Co., New York, 1897

Second edition, 1966, reprinted photographically from the sheets of the first edition by Lowe and Brydone (Printers) Ltd., London, and published by Leicester University Press

PRINTED IN GREAT BRITAIN

CONTENTS.

NOTE ON PAGE NUMBERS

From page xi onwards the pagination in this edition corresponds exactly with that of the first edition. In the preliminary matter, however, the order of preface to the first edition and of the table of contents has been transposed. The table of contents, which was set as page ix of the first edition, now appears as page v; and the preface by Charles Gross to the first edition, formerly occupying pages v, vi and vii, is now found on pages vii, viii and ix. In order to avoid disturbing further the original pagination, the preface to the second edition by G. H. Martin is numbered [i]–[xvi] and is inserted between pages vi and vii.

PREFACE TO THE SECOND EDITION
by G. H. Martin

Charles Gross's *Bibliography of British Municipal History* is that rare and excellent thing, a bibliography that is itself a contribution to the subject that it illuminates. The seventy years that have passed since its publication have added many books to the written history of British towns, and have seen great changes in the emphases of historical scholarship, but they have not blunted the shrewdness with which Gross assessed his material, nor have they invalidated many of his assumptions about the ways in which later scholars would study municipal history. Any competent bibliography has an historical interest of its own, but this is one that has maintained its usefulness as a work of reference and a guide to thought for the greater part of a century. It is intelligently constructed, comprehensive, and remarkably accurate: the work of a patient, discriminating, widely-read man. These are qualities that make it an excellent and even a necessary foundation for any new bibliography of the history of British towns, for merely to edit Gross would entail excising matter that is still relevant in order to make room for an arbitrary selection of more recent work. The whole book is therefore reprinted here as the first volume of a series that will extend Gross's work, in as fully comprehensive a fashion, to the present day. It is not inappropriate that the consequent division of the bibliography at 1897 will lend a special emphasis to Charles Gross's own contribution to municipal studies.

Quite as much as any creative work, a bibliography is a product of its age and of its editor's personality. Gross thought and wrote as he did as a man of his time, and an American of wide education. As a scholar he was sensitive to the intellectual excitements of the late nineteenth century; as a foreign student he was more conscious of the unity of British history than of the differences between one part of the United Kingdom and another. He was also a man who, before he enjoyed distinguished success as a teacher, had endured and overcome personal disappointments, who had spent several years in solitary study, and whose scholarly instincts and methodical habits of mind were enhanced by his knowledge and love of books.

Charles Gross was born at Troy, in Rensselaer County, New York, on 10 February 1857. His parents, Louis and Lotty Gross, were Jewish, and his father had a clothing business, one of Troy's many, which Charles was narrowly saved from joining at a low point of his academic fortunes. Educated in Troy and at the neighbouring Williams College, in Massachusetts, he studied in Europe after taking his bachelor's degree in 1878. He proceeded to his M.A. in 1881, and in 1883 received the degree of Ph.D. at Göttingen University for a thesis that was published in that year under the title of *Gilda Mercatoria: ein Beitrag zur Geschichte der englischen Städteverfassung*. The thesis declared his chief interest for the rest of his life: medieval institutions, and particularly those exemplified by English municipal history. From 1883 to 1888 Gross worked in libraries and muniment rooms in Britain, and tried unsuccessfully to secure a post as a teacher in a university. In 1887, when he delivered a substantial paper at the Anglo-Jewish Exhibition on the 'Exchequer of the Jews of England in the Middle Ages', he came to despair of his modest ambition, but just at that time a chance meeting in the

British Museum with Bliss Perry, a friend from his days at Williams, moved him to apply for a post at Harvard. President Charles Eliot of Harvard sensed the quality of the unknown applicant, and offered him a year's instructorship "as an experiment" in 1888.

The instructorship was extended in 1889, and became an assistant professorship in 1892; in 1901, as the leader of a distinguished school of medieval studies, Gross became Professor of History. During that time he developed his doctoral thesis into an authoritative work upon the gild merchant and its part in British town life both in the Middle Ages and later. *The Gild Merchant*, published in 1890, has been twice reprinted, and has decisively influenced the study of gilds and of the medieval borough ever since its first appearance. In his preface to the book, Gross referred to "a comprehensive bibliography of British municipal history, comprising about 4,000 titles with a critical survey of the whole literature," which he had "almost ready for the press." Its future depended, he said, upon the succcess of *The Gild Merchant*, but although that work was well received, the bibliography was not published until 1897, when it appeared as Volume V of *Harvard Historical Studies*, the first work on British history to figure in that series.

The *Bibliography* received a short but percipient notice in the *English Historical Review* from Frederic William Maitland, who commended its thoroughness, and recognized it as an indispensable aid to anyone "who means to study town life, or any aspect of town life." Even so, Maitland was not entirely content to see Gross's talents devoted to mere aids to study, and in praising the introduction he expressed his regret that its author had spent "his time and powers on this catalogue rather than on a history of our municipal institutions," a history that Gross was evidently well qualified to write. However, Gross was a modest man, despite his learning, and at the age of forty he was still a young man, who apparently had time enough to pursue his municipal studies; in the meantime he felt that he had more bibliographical work to do. In 1900 he published an even more remarkable compendium, which has also worn well for more than half a century: *The Sources and Literature of English History, from the Earliest Times to about* 1485.

Like the *Bibliography of British Municipal History*, the new work was in part a product of Gross's mild exasperation over the untidiness of British historical studies, and his instinctive desire to impose a useful order upon them. Although British scholars have been grateful for both works, they have not been readily stirred to emulate him. The ground work of *The Sources and Literature of English History* lay in Gross's lectures at Harvard, but although the book had been projected as early as 1893, it was not until 1897 that he was free to concentrate upon it. By that year he had completed and published a volume of texts for the Selden Society, *Select Cases from the Coroners' Rolls*, which appeared in 1896, and he also undertook a second volume, *Select Cases concerning the Law Merchant*, which was published in 1908. He was then able to turn to the comparative study of English municipal institutions for which Maitland had called several years before, but on 3 December 1909 he died, and the work was left unfinished. *The Sources and Literature of English History*, which Gross had been correcting and revising, was prepared for a second edition and re-published in 1915 by a small committee of his colleagues, but there was no one to take up his work on towns.

When the *Bibliography of British Municipal History* appeared the early history of the English borough was the subject of a wide and lively debate among scholars, and it may well have seemed to Gross that his careful compilation would soon be outmoded, as new evidence was published and new theories propounded. He had himself made a large contribution to the subject by his work upon the gilds. In 1897 Maitland delivered the Ford Lectures at Oxford, and published them the next year in the most felicitous and illuminating of his books, *Township and Borough*. At the same time he inaugurated a new controversy over the origins of boroughs with the theories that he propounded in *Domesday Book and Beyond*. Although the learned world eventually rejected Maitland's suggestion that the borough grew out of a communal fortress garrisoned by the shire, the argument roused new voices. The garrison theory was developed, rather too enthusiastically, by Adolphus Ballard, but Ballard then went on to do invaluable work on borough charters. Mary Bateson began a detailed edition of the medieval records of Leicester, traced the influence of the customs of Breteuil on Anglo-Norman boroughs, and prepared a definitive survey of borough custumals for the Selden Society, published in two volumes in 1904 and 1906. A decade of such activity did much to redress that neglect of municipal history of which Gross and others had complained, and the borough seemed to have passed at length from the hands of the amateur historian to those of the professional. The first decade, however, proved to be the last. Mary Bateson died in 1906; Maitland, saddened by the sudden loss of a brilliant pupil and one whose scholarly interests had come very close to his own, wrote an obituary in which he said: "If we have to think of promise, we can also think with some comfort of performance. For much more we confidently hoped, but we have much that cannot be taken away." Within the month he too was dead, and it was as though he had written of himself. Maitland was only fifty-six; Gross died at fifty-two: he had begun to shape the work of a promising pupil, M. de W. Hemmeon, but Hemmeon lived to write only one book, *Burgage Tenure.* It cannot be said that municipal history came to a stop at this wall of catastrophes, for Ballard's work on charters was ultimately bequeathed to James Tait, and Gross lived to commend burghal studies to the young Carl Stephenson, but a great deal died with the distinguished company that was at work in 1900, and had been scattered by 1910.

At the present time, therefore, Gross's *Bibliography* ranks as one of several stimulating works that promised a swift and impressive advance in municipal history, and yet have come down to us with the promise still largely unfulfilled. Like *The Sources and Literature of English History*, its quality would have earned it an honourable place in Anglo-American historiography, but it has instead kept a curious, and perhaps unique, immediacy as an earnest of its author's intentions. As Maitland said it would, the *Bibliography* at once took its place as a necessary aid to research, but the fitful progress of that research has made it a boundary mark rather than a milestone. The edition of 1897 was a comparatively small one, and for most of the time since then the *Bibliography* has been excessively rare, a collector's prize rather than an ordinary piece of scholarly equipment. It has, also, perhaps consequently, been an institution to be admired rather than an exercise to be emulated or excelled.

For a country thickly studded with towns, and not ill-provided with historians, England has produced very few town histories of any distinction, and little work upon municipal institutions. Although it is only in the last century that a majority of Englishmen have been town and city dwellers, the towns have long played their part in shaping English society.

The close connection between the boroughs and Parliament has ensured them some attention from historians, but that only as constituencies, not as communities. In the same way, relations between the boroughs and the central government have usually been considered from the Crown's point of view. Even today, after the study of history has been professionally directed for almost a century, a great part of our municipal archives, funds of extraordinary richness, remain unexploited, and we know little in detail, for most of the phases of their long existence, of the economy and society of our towns, of the origins and development of their forms of government, or of their contribution to the enduring traditions of an orderly national life. That is in part an English failing, and there has certainly been a very English reluctance to classify and compare municipal types. Scotland has had better-defined urban communities, and the early records of the Scottish burghs were published in an exemplary manner well before 1900, but the special problems of Wales and Ireland have not been as energetically expounded to an English audience as they ought to be, and the final discussion of what is peculiarly British in the urban history of the United Kingdom has to wait upon these and other preliminaries. Meanwhile the picture is generally one that Charles Gross and his fellows would find depressingly familiar.

The rapid growth of cities and large towns was a commanding feature of British life in the nineteenth century just as it is today, and it was undoubtedly connected with the surge of interest in urban history which came at the end of the century. The way in which the subject grew with the towns themselves can be illustrated by the difference between Robert Vaughan's *The Age of Great Cities* (1843), which discusses the moral effects of urban growth, with due reference to the cities of classical antiquity, and a work like F. H. Spencer's *Municipal Origins* (1911), which is an historical essay on the role of the Private Bill in local government. By the 1890s the study of history was too sophisticated a business for the connexion with modern politics to be a very blatant one, although Alice Stopford Green's *Town Life in the Fifteenth Century*, published in 1894, was powerfully flavoured by her radical interest in Irish politics. Just as import-ant as the current topicality of local government and the inde-pendence of small communities in the centralized state, was the great advance in historical method that characterized the later nineteenth century: an intellectual dividend from the wealth of an industrial society and a movement of which Gross and his contemporaries in Britain and America were the product. That advance was particularly marked in the study of medieval history, a field that the nineteenth century thought congenial on æsthetic grounds, and that offered attractive and stimulat-ing technical problems.

The task before Gross was first to define his subject, to survey its general materials, both in the form of primary sources and of commentaries and comparative studies, and then to select the best and most informative among the many local histories that made up the bulk of the literature. These last would depend partly upon his definition, but they were a large company, for there has been a long tradition of local studies in English historio-graphy. The great problem was to decide at the outset what constituted a town, and that was one that had long vexed kings and their advisers before it came to concern scholars. Gross's own interests lay primarily, but by no means exclusively, in legal and constitutional history, and so in institutions rather than in urban society or economic affairs, and he chose a prag-matic definition of municipalities which accepted the past or

present formal status of a city or borough, and certain historic characteristics of boroughs, such as control of a market, without further question. He was then able to include those places which had acquired charters in his own lifetime, as well as those which had once enjoyed the title of borough but had lost both substance and title under the pressures of industrial development and political reform. The *Bibliography* therefore covers the cities and major towns of nineteenth-century England as well as many places that had enjoyed importance or some potential in the past, but not those towns of recent growth that fell short of corporate status, such as the Urban Districts of 1894. The final test for inclusion, however, was the existence of some history of the place which referred to its municipal institutions, or threw an incidental light upon them. On that principle Croydon figures in the list, on the strength of a charter granted in 1883 and a commemorative account of the borough's first election, but Ashton-under-Lyne, chartered in 1847, and Tunbridge Wells, incorporated in 1889, do not. Similarly Torquay, which had a charter in 1892, is represented by J. T. White, *The History of Torquay*, which was published in 1878, when there was no municipality although there was a community to describe, but Blackpool and Bournemouth, chartered in 1876 and 1890 respectively, are absent.

The bibliography is consistent in its principles, and it is a bibliography and not a directory. It may nevertheless disappoint both the student of nineteenth-century municipal history, and also the student of modern urban history, who will wish to ask questions of much wider import than those about constitutional forms and public law that exercised the nineteenth century. Both those and other readers, however, still find it a useful primary guide. In 1897 the records of the reformed cor-

porations were still closed to students, but Gross was aware of
the problems of modern municipal organization, and aware
that they would in time become historical problems; he was
therefore at pains to include foreign works on modern English
local government as well as the works that he found in English.
The historian's difficulties here arise in part from a contemporary political and social problem, for the bitterness of the struggle
for municipal reform earlier in the century inhibited municipal
enterprise of any kind until much too late an hour. For the
greater part of Victoria's reign civic virtue was commonly
supposed to reside in inactivity, for it was better to spend no
public money at all than to be suspected of spending public
money improperly. As for urban history in the widest sense,
Gross had an eye for intelligent writing, and his comments are
generally as shrewd as his range was wide, but he was occasion-
ally led into severity by his terms of reference. John Glyde's
*The Moral, Social, and Religious Condition of Ipswich in the
Middle of the Nineteenth Century*, published in 1850, is dismissed
as "of little value" because its historical section is scant and
shaky, whereas to modern eyes it presents an interesting picture
of the society of a provincial town. Gross knew the risks that
he ran in attempting to evaluate the books that he listed, and
he quite rightly thought that the advantages of a critical bibliography outweighed its natural failings. A man may be forgiven
if he fail to recognize in the industrial towns and seaside resorts
of his own day all the preoccupations of the next generation's
historians. Even so, the absence of any reference to the decen-
nial Census, or to demographic matters in general, is a reminder
of one difference between the nineteenth-century and the
modern historian of towns.

The student of early town history is naturally better served.

In the Middle Ages and for some time afterwards written evidence is less abundant than it becomes in a more nearly literate society, and the semantic problems raised in interpreting it, together with the uncertain definition of early institutions, make it more difficult for the municipal historian to take a narrowly specialized view of his subject. From the middle of the nineteenth century the publication of competently edited texts, and still more the growing popularity of history as a subject of study in the universities, transformed the accepted notions of medieval government and society. Little direct attention had been paid to medieval towns before Gross began his own academic career, but the emphasis upon constitutional history drew attention to the prescriptive and chartered privileges of the boroughs, just as the political debate on their reform earlier in the century had provoked both critics and defenders to antiquarian research and historical arguments. Probably the most important contribution made to municipal history before the last years of the century came from the investigations of the Historical Manuscripts Commission, which from 1870 onward inspected and published historical material from the collections of private and corporate owners. The inspectors' reports to the Commission revealed the extraordinary range and wealth of English municipal archives for the first time, although the Scottish Burgh Records Society had been publishing Scottish material since 1868. At a time when London alone had a municipal archivist, and only a handful of towns had published lists of their records, or even had any clear idea of what their records might comprise, the Commission's reports marked an enormous addition to the historical repertory, and were a great stimulus to further exploration.

What was lacking when Gross began his work was systematic

order, and that he was well able to provide. The existing bibliographies were either concerned with particular localities or were, as he says, merely booksellers' guides; no one had attempted before to analyze and arrange either the general or local literature. In Part I of the *Bibliography* Gross marshalled the general authorities, ranging from Robert Brady's *Treatise of Boroughs* of 1690 and Thomas Madox's learned *Firma Burgi* to the Parliamentary Papers and commissioners' reports of his own day. Here as nowhere else the student has laid before him the entire apparatus of printed sources, a detailed, orderly guide to every substantial commentary on municipal institutions as they had impinged upon public life in Britain. It is followed in Part II by a catalogue of works on 407 towns in England, Ireland, Scotland, and Wales, with many of the titles annotated sanely and pungently on the basis of Gross's own wide and purposeful reading. Either part of the book would have been a valuable addition to historical knowledge; together they make a quite remarkable work of scholarship.

In his introduction to the volume Gross dwells particularly upon the deficiencies of the subject as they were revealed in his own researches and in preparing the bibliography. He noticed particularly the want of systematic analysis and of an effective general treatise, even in Scotland, where the scope of municipal history was certainly easier to define than it was elsewhere in the kingdom. He also pointed to the contemporary neglect and past misuse of the borough's own archives, and that state of mind in many corporations which, whilst it did nothing to hinder scholarly investigation, certainly did nothing to promote it. Above all he was bemused, as a foreign observer might well be, by the vagaries of the amateur tradition that was strong, as it still is, in the writing of local history. As a fair-minded and a learned man he would readily praise what he found to admire, but he could not subdue a rasping note of wonder that some things should have passed unremarked by others. "The mania for copying sepulchral inscriptions is not so prevalent as it used to be," is surely a cry from the heart; so, though less plangent, is a following stricture upon "vague conjectures . . . together with a heavy padding of generalities concerning the Celts, Romans, and Anglo-Saxons." Thomas Madox he quotes with entire approval; the two men would probably have enjoyed much common ground.

Time has not aged Gross's Introduction as much as he might have hoped. The present century has made some notable additions to his catalogue, but there is still no study of a British town truly comparable with such European works as Georges Espinas's *La Vie Urbaine de Douai au Moyen Age* (1913), and the amateur and antiquarian traditions die hard. There have been no great discoveries of manuscripts since 1897, although there is some surprising material to be found in the muniment rooms, and the growth of municipal responsibilities since the late nineteenth century has added enormously to the historical material stored in our town halls, making both the preservation and the arrangement of the modern archives a serious problem. That material is still hardly touched by historians, but medieval studies have made some progress. Since 1909 the analytical work that Ballard began on borough charters has been extended by James Tait and Martin Weinbaum, an American scholar, but the burgesses' own contribution to the framing of their charters remains to be explored. Besides that large work, the chief advance has been in the publication of the ordinary administrative records of the boroughs, both by the corporations themselves, and by the efforts of record societies.

The one section of his Introduction that Gross might later have sought to revise is that on town chronicles. He was familiar enough with examples from the Continent, especially from Germany, to recognize the general inferiority, as well as the paucity, of those in England, but there are a few more than he refers to, whilst the mayoral lists and calendars that he discusses under the same heading are for the most part late antiquarian productions rather than contemporary *fasti*. The true medieval chronicles, those like the brief and imaginative annals in the Oath Book of Colchester, are too slight and rare to lend themselves to such a discussion of townsmen's beliefs and attitudes as Dr Heinrich Schmidt has recently essayed for German towns in *Die deutschen Städtechroniken als Spiegel des bürgerlichen Selbstverständnisses im Spätmittelalter* (1958), but they open some interesting questions about the dissemination both of news and of historical information. In that connexion too there is much to be discovered about the spread of literacy in medieval towns, and the growth of a professional administration there.

Of all things, it is the essential quality of urban life in the past that we still have to determine. We suppose ourselves familiar with the purpose and advantages of town-dwelling in an industrial society, although motor-transport and electrical power have begun to modify its patterns just when we have begun to count its cost. We are still ignorant even of the purely municipal history of our modern industrial cities, and we know lamentably little about the quality of town life in earlier periods, where we have investigated formal municipal institutions more carefully. In England we have been careless in our definition of our towns, and on occasions we have been reluctant, perhaps for the same reasons, even to confess to their existence. The consequence has been cities allowed in recent times to grow like huge untidy hamlets, and for a rather longer time histories that are written as though towns were country parishes. Yet the historic towns of Britain have their own distinctive traditions, and from age to age they have enriched the nation's life. Their history is a large part of national history, and it deserves to be explored most patiently, from its origins and the emergence of corporate communities in the Middle Ages, to the full tide of urban growth in the nineteenth and twentieth centuries. The history of municipal institutions, of the contrivances by which towns won and exercised their autonomy under the common law, is only one strand, but a vital one, of the whole story. At present, as in Gross's day, it is a fragmentary tale, partly reconstructed for the Middle Ages, but later illuminated only when it touches national politics, as it does under the later Stuarts, or during the struggle over Parliamentary reform in the early nineteenth century.

Municipal history cannot be studied in isolation; it demands constant reference to economic affairs and the development of society. The failure of some towns to achieve a formal municipal status, or the ways in which they fashioned substitutes for it, also belong to the enquiry, although their relevance has not always been recognized. Gross's work points the way to these and other investigations; it was the first, and a highly successful, effort to take stock of the literature, and to show what remained to be done by imposing coherence upon what had been accomplished.

Our debt to Charles Gross is still a large one, and the time has come to discharge some part of it by continuing his work. A new bibliography on the firm basis of his own might stimulate us to complete or improve upon the other investigations that his generation began and that have since lain neglected. Certainly the *Bibliography* is still as useful to modern scholars as it was to their predecessors, and many of the enquiries that Gross planned or envisaged will have to be completed before it can itself become merely an historical document. If that day does eventually come, the *Bibliography of British Municipal History* will not look any less remarkable to the discerning student of late-Victorian historiography than it does now to the student of the history of towns. If it is easier today than it was some few decades since to do justice to the nineteenth century, it is still salutary to be reminded, as the *Bibliography* reminds us, of the energy and resourcefulness of that astonishing time. Charles Gross's contribution to its acts and monuments was a worthy one.

PREFACE.

———•———

THIS Bibliography comprises books, pamphlets, magazine articles, and papers of learned societies, relating wholly or in part to British municipal history; in other words, to the governmental or constitutional history of the boroughs of Great Britain, including gilds and parliamentary representation. Town histories which do not deal with any of these topics, purely topographical works, and parish histories are omitted.[1]

The Introduction gives a brief survey of the principal categories of sources (the public and local records and the town chronicles) and a critical account of the modern literature. Part I. contains the titles of the general authorities, while Part II. is devoted to works concerning particular towns. The notes appended to the titles in Part I. should be useful to students interested in the history of any particular borough, who are often inclined to neglect the public records and other general authorities; they will find all the references to a given town, in both parts of the book, indicated in the Index under the name of that town.

An attempt has been made to give some estimate of the value and character of the most important books. This is a hazardous undertaking in a bibliography comprising so many

---

[1] Some idea of the extent of the whole local literature relating to boroughs may be obtained from vol. iii. of Hyett and Bazeley's *Manual of Gloucestershire Literature*, in which 337 large octavo pages are devoted to Bristol.

titles; but the brief critical notes, however fallible and incomplete, may prove helpful in guiding students through the labyrinth of material.

The British Museum has the largest collection of works relating to municipal history, including many valuable manuscripts; but this collection is far from complete, lacking especially many privately printed books. In the *Reliquary* (1882, xxiii. 60), it is affirmed that the British Museum does not contain one tenth of the topographical literature of Great Britain. It would perhaps be nearer the truth to assert that it does not contain more than three quarters. Many local publications which are not in the British Museum, will be found, in London, in the Gildhall Library and in the Library of the Society of Antiquaries. Many histories of Scotch burghs are accessible only in Scotland, especially in the Advocates Library and in the Signet Library. The best American collections of British topographical literature are those in the Harvard College Library and the Boston Public Library.

The preparation of this Bibliography was begun in 1886. A selection, entitled " A Classified List of Books relating to British Municipal History," was printed in 1891, in the " Bibliographical Contributions of the Library of Harvard University," No. 43; and another selection, " Town Records of Great Britain," in the *American Historical Review*, 1896, ii. 191–200. It is unnecessary to rehearse the difficulties encountered in making this compilation, — to enumerate the many libraries, public and private, which had to be visited, the numerous catalogues, bibliographies, periodicals, publications of learned societies, and other devious by-ways which had to be explored. Despite all this labor, I am conscious that the work is incomplete, especially as regards the pamphlet literature. What I have aimed to do is not to furnish book-sellers and book-buyers with an exhaustive catalogue of books, but to make the material which is most useful for the study of municipal history more accessible to historical students, and thus to help prepare the way for a better understanding of the development of town life in Great Britain.

Among those who have kindly aided me, I wish to thank especially the late Mr. W. H. Overall, for facilitating my work in the Gildhall Library, London; Mr. F. T. Barrett, of the Mitchell Library, Glasgow, and Mr. Frederic Boase, of the Library of the Incorporated Law Society, for similar favors; Mr. A. W. Robertson, of the Aberdeen Public Library, for information concerning Aberdeen books; my colleague, Professor J. W. Platner, for the tedious labor of reading my proof-sheets; and Mr. George Stronach, of the Advocates Library, whose generous aid has been of inestimable value in enriching the lists relating to Scotch burghs.

C. G.

September 4, 1897.

NOTE.

A dagger (†) is prefixed to titles of works which the compiler has not been able to examine. An asterisk (*) is prefixed to titles of works which are particularly valuable.

Most of the abbreviations used are doubtless sufficiently intelligible, but the following may require explanation :

Archæol. Journal. The Archæological Journal, published by the Royal Archæological Institute of Great Britain and Ireland.
Hist. MSS. Com. Reports of the Historical MSS. Commission.
Record Com. Record Commission.

INTRODUCTION.

———•———

N O country of Europe has a soil more congenial to the study of history than England. The genesis of her present institutions, their foundation in the remote past, the unbroken continuity of their development, the interest that the present awakens in the past and the past in the present, the urgent necessity of carefully studying the past in order to know and improve the present, — all should form a strong incentive in England to the study of history. Moreover, owing in great part to this very continuity of development, England has a collection of public records unequalled in richness by those of any other country of Europe. Thousands of well-preserved parchment rolls, easily accessible and full of valuable material, invite investigation. Nevertheless, England remains far behind some of her neighbors in the study of the past. This is particularly true of the study of municipal history. The object of this Introduction is to consider briefly the scope and value of the original sources and of the modern literature relating to the history of the English municipalities.

§ 1. Public Records.

Our records begin with a few passages in the Anglo- Saxon laws and Domesday Book. Though the entries relating to towns in the Conqueror's great survey are not copious, they throw some welcome gleams of light on the internal affairs of the boroughs. For the twelfth century we must depend mainly upon a few town charters [1] and upon the meagre data of the Pipe Rolls. [2]

Charter and Patent Rolls.

In the first half of the thirteenth century the public records multiply, and thenceforward afford us much assistance. The Charter and Patent Rolls,[3] which contain the privileges granted to towns and gilds, are particularly valuable, and are supplemented by the Confirmation Rolls, in which all the grants made by the crown to a borough since the twelfth century are often recited in a single document.[4] The early town charters are worthy of more attention than they have as yet received. They are valuable not merely for the history of municipal institutions, but also as a repository of old Anglo-Saxon legal ideas. For the boroughs, however progressive in other directions, still clung tenaciously to certain Anglo-Saxon traditions long after the Norman Conquest.

Rolls of Parliament and other records.

Next to the charters in importance are the Rolls of Parliament, together with their prolific modern progeny, the Journals of the Commons, the Journals of the Lords, and the Parliamentary Papers.[5] The material relating to towns in the Statutes, Plea Rolls, Hundred Rolls, Close Rolls, and other public records

---

[1] See below, Nos. 78, 118, 124, 136, 1199, 1485, 2860–1, 3086.

[2] No. 129.

[3] Nos. 119–21, 130, 133, 709–12, 714. The charters were merged in the patents in 8 Henry VIII. There is a valuable collection of transcripts of charters and letters patent in the Inner Temple Library, Petyt MS. 536, vols. xiii.–xiv., from which Merewether and Stephens (No. 79) obtained many of their documents.

[4] Historians have made little use of these valuable Confirmation Rolls, which extend from 1 Richard III. to 1 Charles I. Before 1 Richard III. the confirmations are entered on the Charter and Patent Rolls, and after 1 Charles I. on the Patent Rolls.

[5] Nos. 44, 134, 287, 288.

is scattered about in divers parts of the huge folio volumes of the Record Commission and in the ponderous rolls of the Public Record Office; [1] from them, by patient, laborious investigation, much information may be obtained, especially regarding the relations of the boroughs to the crown.

§ 2. Town Records.

The town records form the main source for the study of internal municipal affairs.   A few boroughs possess charters of the twelfth century.   In a somewhat larger number the town records begin early in the thirteenth.   But in most boroughs the oldest muniments are of later date, the collective volume of material steadily increasing as we advance toward the close of the Middle Ages and into modern times.   In many archives we find municipal charters, chamberlains' accounts or other *compotus* rolls, assembly rolls or council books (i. e., minutes of the burghal council), court rolls, rolls of a gild merchant, and books (with such designations as White Book, Red Book, Black Book, Oak Book, Chain Book, etc.)[2] containing ordinances and miscellaneous matters.

Their age and scope.

Many town archives have suffered much in the past from the negligence of their custodians.   We are thankful that the Black Book of Winchester and a Domesday Book of Ipswich are accessible in the British Museum, which has perhaps rescued them from destruction; but if they had been properly safeguarded, they would now be in their old homes at

Losses through negligence, at Winchester and Ipswich;

---

[1] Below, pp. 13, 22–9.

[2] See below, Index, under "Town Records." For a detailed account of the archives of various boroughs, see No. 62. For some records of the thirteenth century, see below, pp. 211, 262, 273, 287, 330, 389, 409, 417, 424.

at Hereford; Winchester and Ipswich.[1]   A woman who had charge
of the town-hall of Hereford early in the present century sold the oldest existing council registers as waste
at Weymouth; paper.[2]   Most of the ancient records of Weymouth
and Melcombe Regis came into the possession of Mr.
James Sherren, of Weymouth, who received permission
to remove them " from a stable in which they were
then [3] deposited as so much rubbish, and so had the
good fortune to rescue them from the housemaid and
fire-grate, to whose tender mercies a considerable
portion of them had been already consigned." [4]
at Yarmouth; Manship says that the muniments in the Gildhall of
Great Yarmouth, in 1612, " did not onely lye dispers-
edly but also very disorderly." [5]   Of the two hundred
and ninety-two writings mentioned in an inventory
made for the corporation of that borough early in the
seventeenth century, only twenty-eight could be found
at Plymouth; in 1853.[6]   We are informed that when the new Gildhall of Plymouth was ready for occupancy early in the
present century, the records " were thrown into heaps
in the streets and carted off, and whoever cared to do
at Hedon.   so helped themselves at pleasure." [7]   Poulson gives
the following vivid description of the archives of

[1] The same is true of other valuable borough records in the British
Museum ; for example, those of Dover, for which see *Journal of the
British Archæol. Assoc.*, xl. 131.

[2] *Hist. MSS. Com.*, xiii. pt. iv. 283. Two large boxes of early documents relating to Bury St. Edmund's were sold as waste paper not
many years ago : *Journal of British Archæol. Assoc.*, xl. 131.

[3] He seems to have obtained them some time during the first half
of the present century.

[4] *Hist. MSS. Com.*, v. 576. These records were still in Mr. Sherren's
possession in 1876, when Mr. Riley made his report for the MSS.
Commission. They seem to have been regained by the town through
purchase in 1879. See Moule, *Catalogue* (No. 2954), pp. viii., 222.

[5] Manship, *History of Yarmouth*, p. ii.

[6] *Hist. MSS. Com.*, ix. pt. i. 300.

[7] Worth, *Calendar* (No. 2589), p. ix. In 1601–2 a Totnes man went
to Plymouth, and burned a chest in the Council Chamber, " wherein

Hedon, which for centuries were in a room over the vestry of St. Augustine's Church :

"Charters, deeds, rent rolls, court rolls, inquisitions, writs of citations, records of the borough court, accounts of procurators of chantries . . . as well as lists of mayors and bailiffs of the olden time ; open to the winds of heaven, these documents, which lay in heaps, were, from apathy and neglect, allowed to moulder and rot. In addition to these devastating effects, large quantities were used for lighting the vestry fires, and others taken away by any persons whose inclination or curiosity induced them to fill their pockets ; what is yet left is a mass of dirty and useless rubbish." [1]

Such examples of a lack of vigilance in the care of town records might easily be multiplied.[2]   They make us inclined to wonder, not that so much has perished, but that so much has survived.   Despite the lamentable losses due to apathy and carelessness, an immense mass of documentary material, reaching far back into the Middle Ages, still exists in the local archives.   Owing largely to the efforts of the Historical MSS. Commission, much has been accomplished during the past twenty-five years for the arrangement and preservation of these muniments.   Custodians of local record-rooms are gradually becoming imbued

Surviving records.

were contayned divers evidences and writings concerning the towne : " *ibid.*, p. ix.

[1] Poulson, *History of Holderness* (1840–1), ii. 138 ; Boyle, *Hedon*, pp. vi.–viii. Among these records were court books of Edward III.'s time and the Order Book of the corporation, commencing in Edward IV.'s reign. Shortly after the period when Poulson wrote, Mr. Gillyat Sumner, "by methods which it is unnecessary to particularize," got most of the town records into his possession. After his death they were advertised for sale with the rest of his library, and were purchased by the corporation of Hedon, who, however, refused to pay the purchase money. See Boyle, *Hedon*, p. viii.

[2] *Hist. MSS. Com.*, viii. pt. i. 355; ix. pt. i. 177, 223; xi. pt. vii. 167 ; xiv. pt. viii. I. Cf. *Gentleman's Magazine*, 1830, ii. 402 ; Rogers, *Oxford City Documents*, 145.

with the sentiment of the ancient town clerk of Guildford, who, after transcribing the old Black Book for
the burgesses, pleaded that, in the future, they should
not cast it away, " appering old and ragged, but
rather to accompte of him the more in that he doth
proceed from your auncient predecessors, and afford
him that favour to let him have abode amongest
you, where he may rest safelie." [1]   There is, however,
still room for improvement.   In some boroughs the
ancient records are a filthy, disorderly mass of parchment and paper, placed in some garret or out-house,
where they are exposed to destruction from damp-
ness, fire, and theft.

Lack of archi-
vists.

It is also deplorable that there are in England so
few municipal archivists.[2]   The records are usually
in charge of the town clerk, who rarely has the requi-
site knowledge or training to appreciate their value,
to supervise their re-arrangement, or to assist the in-
vestigator in finding documents.   It should be added,
however, that most of these officials are willing to do
all they can to facilitate the work of investigators.

Accessibility
of town ar-
chives.

The latter seldom meet with any difficulty in securing
access to the archives, though in some cases it may
be necessary to obtain formal permission from the
Common Council.   In this respect there has been
great improvement during the last fifty years.   Formerly it was very difficult in England to obtain access
either to the public or to the local records.[3]   Before
1835, when " select bodies " had charge of the finances
of rotten boroughs and monopolized the municipal

[1] Gross, *Gild Merchant*, ii. 92.

[2] I know of only one, namely, the Records Clerk of the City of
London.

[3] Palgrave, *Proceedings of the Record Commission*, 1832–33, p. 430,
and *Parliamentary Writs*, vol. i., Preface ; Willmore, *Walsall*, p. ix.;
Hist. MSS. Com., ix. pt. i. 299; *Westminster Review*, x. 394–402;
Munic. Corp. Com. (No. 60), iv. 2302.

government, the archives in some of these towns were kept hermetically sealed; for the civic magistrates seemed to fear that a knowledge of the past, drawn from such a reliable source, might betray to the public their usurpations of power, and cause the overthrow of the aristocratic regime.[1] All this is now changed. Probably in no other country in the world are the national and town records more easily accessible than in England. Even in the City of London, where some of the old unreformed spirit still survives, and the civic muniments are jealously guarded, the Common Council seems to be quite willing to unroll the records of the City for any genuine student of history, for any one who is really investigating the past and not seeking to change the present.

During the past two decades there has also been much progress in the publication of town records,[2] though herein England is still surpassed by some of her continental neighbors and by Scotland.[3] The corporations of cities like Bristol, Canterbury, Chester, Exeter, Leicester, Newcastle-upon-Tyne, Norwich, Winchester, and York would confer a great boon ' upon students of history by publishing some of their rich stores of muniments, as Bath, Carlisle, Dublin, Gloucester, Liverpool, London, Manchester, Nottingham, Oxford, Reading, and some other boroughs have recently done.

Publication of town records.

---

[1] The close corporation system must have helped to preserve the records of many towns from careless borrowers, but it may also have tempted members of the governing body wantonly to destroy certain documents containing a record of their transactions.

[2] For a list of published town records, see *American Hist. Review*, ii. 191–200. All the titles in that list are included in this Bibliography.

[3] There is no collection in England comparable with the publications of the Scottish Burgh Records Society or with the Records of the Convention of Royal Burghs.

B

§ 3. Town Chronicles.

The town chronicles of England form an unexplored field of historical literature of considerable interest. In the latter part of the Middle Ages and far into modern times we find, in London, Bristol, and other boroughs, mayors' chronicles or calendars, which, like the Roman *fasti consulares*, were drawn up in the form of annals, containing the names of the chief civic officers, together with brief notices of the municipal and national events which occurred during each mayoralty. These chronicles vary in fullness, some, especially those of London, widening here and there into a narrative of national affairs, while others are little more than catalogues of mayors, with a few meagre memoranda of municipal transactions; on many pages nothing beyond the names of the principal town officers appears.

The London chronicles are of considerable value for the history, not merely of that city, but also of the kingdom. London was the " hub " of the realm, the focus of national life; much of the history of England could be viewed from the windows of the Gildhall. Owing to the important part which London played in the history of the kingdom, the civic annalists were not inclined to ignore national events. And for this reason London is the only English city which has produced town chronicles at all comparable with those of cities on the continent. Most of the English boroughs were, during the Middle Ages, politically insignificant, having, as an old writer expresses it, " gret frawnches [franchises] and smale liberte ";[1] despite their chartered privileges, they were subject to the control of a strong royal power. There were

---

[1] Furnivall, *Ballads from MSS.*, i. 99.

in England no independent city-republics or great leagues of towns, like those of Germany or Italy, that could cope with popes and kings. Each borough maintained a quiet, uneventful provincial life, absorbed mainly in its own local affairs, except when, at long intervals, its repose was disturbed by some great civil strife from which the burgesses could not keep aloof. Therefore we find fewer town chronicles of national importance in England than on the continent, — nothing comparable with the splendid series of " Chroniken der deutschen Städte." [1]

The oldest mayors' chronicles are those of London, namely, the Latin " Liber de Antiquis Legibus," compiled in 1274, and the French " Croniques," compiled about the middle of the fourteenth century. These were followed, in the fifteenth and sixteenth centuries, by several English chronicles of London.[2] Ricart's " Kalendar " of Bristol [3] ranks in age and importance next to those of London. Many such calendars, or chronicles, were compiled in other boroughs during the sixteenth and seventeenth centuries, and some of them were continued into the present century. They seem to have been particularly numerous in Chester and Bristol. Seyer, writing in 1821, says that most of those of Bristol were compiled within the last two hundred years, but that they were evidently derived from more ancient copies transcribed by various hands, having in general a great similarity but many differences in detail. " Several of the older," he continues, " are written on narrow rolls of vellum. . . .

Age and prevalence.

---

[1] Edited by K. Hegel, 25 vols., Leipzig, 1862–96. Most of the monastic chronicles of England have little value for the study of municipal history ; some of them, however, throw light on the relations of certain boroughs to their ecclesiastical lords. See Nos. 1193, 1198, 1481, 2485, 2712, and Gross, *Gild Merchant*, i. 91.

[2] Nos. 1982–1991a, 3089.

[3] No. 1150. Most of the text is in English.

Many have been destroyed, but probably forty or fifty still remain, chiefly in families of long continuance in Bristol, of which about twenty have passed under my inspection." [1] At least five of these Bristol chronicles are still in existence, namely, Ricart's " Kalendar " in the town archives, three calendars in the Bristol Museum, and one in the possession of Mr. F. F. Fox. [2]

Official compilations. Ricart's work is remarkable as being an official compilation ; in other words, it was drawn up by him for the town. The mayor, he says, " hath commaunded me, Robert Ricart . . . Toune Clerk of the saide worshipfull towne, for to devise, ordeigne, and make this present boke for a remembratif evir hereaftir, to be called and named the Maire of Bristow is Register, or ellis the Maire is Kalendar " (p. 3). [3] The " Liber de Antiquis Legibus " [4] seems likewise to have been an official compilation, and the Black Book of Plymouth contains a similar chronicle compiled by town clerks of the sixteenth and seventeenth centuries. [5] Rattenbury's " Journal," written in the

---

[1] Seyer, *Bristol*, vol. i., p. x. For the Chester chronicles, see below, p. xxi.

[2] Hudd, *Two Bristol Calendars* (No. 1182), 105–7. Mr. Fox's calendar extends from 1216 to 1814 ; the three in the Bristol Museum begin early in the thirteenth century, and end in 1608, 1740, and 1774 respectively. Mr. Hudd prints the first of these three and part of Mr. Fox's. The historical notices in all of them are few and meagre.

[3] Ricart's record of the mayoralties, which is found mainly in pt. iii. of his " Kalendar," was continued by his successors, to 1698, in the same MS.

[4] No. 1987. The MS. is in the Gildhall, London.

[5] Worth, *Calendar* (No. 2589), p. viii. The Black Book continued to be used as a record of mayoralties down to 1709. For extracts, from 1441 to 1709, see *ibid.*, 14–25, and *Hist. MSS. Com.*, ix. 277–8. The historical notices, which commence early in the sixteenth century and are in the handwriting of Mary Tudor's time, are valueless when they relate to national history, but are of some importance when they refer to local matters.

seventeenth century by the town clerks, John Rattenbury and Thomas Austin, and preserved in the archives of Okehampton, is a record of the mayoralties
of that borough.[1]   Bacon's "Annals of Ipswich"[2]
was also the official work of a town clerk of the seventeenth century, but its contents, though arranged
under the names of the municipal magistrates, consist mainly of abstracts of town records.[3]

Many mayors' calendars have never been published. List of town chronicles.
The following is an incomplete list of those that exist
in print and in manuscript : —[4]

BEVERLEY.   Lansdowne MS. 896, f. 8.

BRISTOL.   Ricart's "Kalendar" and four others : above
p. xx.

CAMBRIDGE.   Harley MS. 4116, ff. 8, 43, 617 (A. D. 1488–
1673) ; Additional MSS. 5813, f. 132 (A. D. 1488–
1781) ; 5833, f. 123 (A. D. 1263–1500).

CHESTER.   Harley MSS. 1948, ff. 93, 113 ; 2057, f. 12 (26
Henry III.–1658); 2105, f. 345 (A. D. 1348–1580) ;
2125, ff. 181, 197, 271 (A. D. 1257–1651–1705) ; 2133,
f. 487 (A. D. 1240–1635) ; Additional MSS. 29777 (A. D.
1326–1584) ; 29779 (to A. D. 1646).   Additional MS.
29777 was compiled toward the end of the sixteenth
century ; most of the others, in the seventeenth.

COVENTRY.   Dugdale, *Warwickshire*, i. 147–53 (A. D. 1348–
1723) ; Hearne's edition of Fordun's *Scotichronicon*, pp.
1438–74 (A. D. 1349–1675) ; a MS. list of mayors, from
1347 to 1590(?), in the library of the Marquis of Salisbury (*Hist. MSS. Com.*, v. 264).

---

[1] Bridges, *Okehampton*, new edition, p. ix.

[2] No. 1801.

[3] There is also an official roll of mayors, with historical notes, in
the archives of Leicester.   See No. 1875, and Jeaffreson, *Index* (No.
1870), 26.   For official town chronicles in Germany during the fourteenth and fifteenth centuries, see O. Lorenz, *Deutschlands Geschichts-
quellen* (3rd edition), i. 196, ii. 65–6, 165.

[4] Most of the MSS. mentioned in the list are in the British
Museum.

DUBLIN. "The Register of the Mayors of Dublin, from 1406 to 1622": Additional MS. 4791, art. 37.

GREAT GRIMSBY. Lansdowne MS. 207a, f. 523 (A. D. 1200–1669).

IPSWICH. Bacon's "Annals" (A. D. 1200–1648): below, No. 1801.

KENDAL. Wharton's "Chronological Table:" No. 1815.

LEICESTER. In 1874 Mr. Thompson had access to three lists or rolls of mayors, to which brief marginal notes of historical events were appended: one, extending from 1223 to 1721, in the Leicester archives; another, beginning in 1233, in private hands; and the third, beginning in 1266 and compiled in 1574, belonging to William Perry-Herrick, of Beau Manor Park. See No. 1875, and Jeaffreson, *Index* (No. 1870), 26.

LIMERICK. Additional MS. 31885, ff. 253–77 (A. D. 1169–1648); compiled in the seventeenth century. Cf. Lenihan, *Limerick*, 690–709, and Additional MS. 19865, f. 115.

LONDON. Above p. xix.; Additional MS. 5444 (A. D. 1195–1316); Arundel MS. xix. in the College of Arms (A. D. 1189–1451–1522); a chronicle compiled in the fifteenth century (6 Henry III.–1440, continued by a later hand to 7 Elizabeth), belonging to Matthew Wilson, of Eshton Hall, Yorkshire. See *Chronicle of Grey Friars* (No. 1982), p. vii., and *Hist. MSS. Com.*, iii. 299.

LUDLOW. Wright, *Ludlow* (No. 2291), 486–503 (A. D. 1462–1783); seemingly compiled in James I.'s reign and continued by various hands.

LYNN REGIS. Additional MS. 8937 (A. D. 1517–1623, continued by various hands to 1673).

NEWCASTLE-UPON-TYNE. Egerton MS. 2425, ff. 1–80 (A. D. 1432–1776); "A catheloge of all the maiores and sherifs . . . with sarton brefes of cronicles that hapned . . . sence anno Dom: 1432" (A. D. 1432–1634, compiled before 1640, and continued to 1802), printed from the Carr MS., in T. Tonge's *Heraldic Visitation* (Surtees Society, 1863), app. liv.–lxxvii.; a roll of municipal

officers, from 1251 to 1739 [1742], in the possession of
William Adamson, of Cullercoats.   See the histories of
Newcastle, by Welford, i. 416 ; Bourne, ch. iv. ; Brand,
i. pp. v.–vi. and ii. 393 sq.

NORTHAMPTON.   *History of Northampton*, 1817 (No. 2465).

NOTTINGHAM.   Thoroton, *Nottinghamshire* (No. 640), vol. ii.

OKEHAMPTON.   Rattenbury's "Journal," in Bridges, *Okehampton*, new edition, 78–107.   Rattenbury died in
1655.   Some additions were made by Thomas Austin,
and the work was continued by Richard Shebbeare to
10 William III.   See Bridges, p. ix.

PLYMOUTH.   The Black Book of Plymouth (A. D. 1441–
1709), above p. xx.

RIPON.   "The Account Book of William Wray" (A. D. 1400–
1617), in the *Antiquary*, xxxii. 119, 178, 212.   Wray
was wakeman of Ripon in 1584.

SHREWSBURY.   Additional MS. 21024, f. 57 (A. D. 1372–
1665) ; " Early Chronicles of Shrewsbury," A. D. 1372–
1606 (No. 2771).

SOUTHAMPTON.   Egerton MS. 868 (A. D. 1498–1671), partly
in French and partly in English.

STAMFORD.   Harrod, *Stamford*, i. 210 (A. D. 1461–1700) ;
Butcher, *Stamford*, ch. xiii. (A. D. 1461–1659).

WORCESTER.   A chronicle, beginning 9 Henry VI., compiled
by Thomas Vaulx in 1677 ; in the library of Charles
Isham, of Lamport Hall, Northamptonshire.   See *Hist.
MSS. Com.*, iii. 253.

YORK.   Harley MS. 6115 (Edward I.–1677) ; Hildyard's
" List of Mayors," to 1664 (No. 3071).   Similar lists
are printed in the works of Gent and Torr (Nos. 3056,
3060).

§ 4. General Histories of Boroughs.

The oldest general history of English boroughs is Brady.
Brady's *Treatise*.[1]   Brady was regius professor of
physic at Cambridge, keeper of the records in the

---

[1] No. 78.

Tower, the household physician of Charles II. and James II., and a member of Parliament in 1681 and 1685. His treatise on municipal history has had a greater influence than any other in moulding public opinion, and in diffusing erroneous views concerning the development of towns. To any one who probes beneath the surface of this book, it is plain that the author wrote in a partisan spirit to uphold the royal prerogative, especially to justify the recent measures of the crown against municipal corporations. Charles II. and James II. had nullified the charters of many towns, and had remodelled their constitution to suit the interests of the crown. The town councils, or select aristocratic bodies, were filled with non-resident royalists, who controlled the election of the parliamentary representatives of boroughs. Brady strives to show that municipalities originated in grants of the crown for the benefit of trade; that all their privileges and authority came from the bounty of English kings; that ever since their foundation boroughs had select bodies (with non-resident members), to which was committed exclusive control of municipal government. Hence the king, their creator, had the right to transform these civic governing bodies to suit his inclination and interests. Thus Brady's object was to influence public opinion on one of the most momentous questions of the day; and he succeeded. His specious arguments helped to give a legal title to the existence of select bodies. They now began to prevail more than ever before against the burgesses at large in controverted elections of members of Parliament.[1] There can be little doubt that Brady wilfully perverted the truth to countenance the pretensions of his royal patrons and to promote their cause.

[1] Merewether, *Sketch of History of Boroughs* (No. 429), 64.

Madox's *Firma Burgi*[1] is the work of a painstaking, Madox. truth-loving scholar.   In his Preface he makes a statement which is still pertinent at the present day. " Whoso desireth," he says, " to discourse in a proper manner concerning Corporated Towns and Communities, must take in a great variety of matter, and should be allowed a great deal of Time and Preparation.   The subject is extensive and difficult.   In England much hath been said by Writers to Puzzle and entangle, little to Clear it.   Insomuch that when I first entered upon discussing onely One part or branch of it, namely the Theme of this Essay, I found myself encompassed with Doubts."   Madox throws much light upon the nature of the fee-farm rents, payable by the boroughs to the king or other lord, and upon the obscure subject of municipal incorporation.   The solution of many other problems of town history is incidently aided by his copious extracts from the public records.   In fact, his book is a valuable storehouse of material illustrating this subject, rather than a comprehensive survey of the history of municipal institutions.   One can also learn from Madox the value of dry records, the love of historical truth, and abstinence from hypothesis or hasty generalization. He tells us that " writing of History is in some sort a Religious act.   It imports solemnity and sacredness ; and ought to be undertaken with purity and rectitude of mind."[2]

The work of Merewether and Stephens[3] is the most Merewether and Stephens. elaborate of all treatises on English municipal history, and is commonly regarded as the best authority on the subject.   The object of the authors in writing this book was eminently practical.   They wished to influ-

[1] No. 158.
[2] *History of the Exchequer* (1711), p. iii.
[3] No. 79.

ence public opinion in favor of municipal reform; they fervently desired to undermine that huge accretion of abuses to the growth of which Brady's pen had contributed.

Contents of
their work. The book begins with a long Introduction, in which the authors give an abstract of the results of their investigations; these results are embodied in eleven propositions, whose general drift is to show that the bad features of borough government were abnormal and modern, and that the only way to remedy these evils was to restore the ancient municipal system. The body of the book, consisting of about 2400 large octavo pages, is filled with extracts from the Statute Rolls, Parliament Rolls, town charters, and other sources relating to boroughs. The arrangement is mainly chronological, the material being grouped under the names of successive monarchs of England. The result is a huge mass of undigested material. There is no systematic or comprehensive treatment of the nature and growth of municipal institutions, nothing to connect the myriad of details save the frequent and wearisome reiteration of the eleven propositions enunciated in the Introduction. The investigations of Merewether and Stephens are, in fact, circumscribed by these propositions, which were framed for the special purpose of promoting municipal reform. For example, though scores of pages are devoted to Domesday Book, no attempt is made to solve the question of prime importance to the student of history, namely, What change in the general condition and constitution of boroughs was wrought by the Norman Conquest? Domesday is interpreted not from the standpoint of the true historian, but from the standpoint of the practical reformer who has certain preconceived propositions to demonstrate.

Its value. As regards the propositions themselves, most of

them are untenable. For example, the statement, so often repeated by the authors, that boroughs through-out Great Britain were essentially alike in the Middle Ages, is certainly erroneous. Any one who carefully studies the subject must perceive that there is a great divergence between Scotland and England in this respect. Municipal development in Scotland re-sembles that of the continent more than that of England in many important features, for example, in the federative union of Scotch towns, in their more autonomous position relative to the crown, and in the bitter struggle between their crafts and the merchant gild.[1] Even in England boroughs were not cast in one mould, as Merewether and Stephens would have us believe: on the contrary, there was great diversity in local institutions and customs. Therefore it is difficult and dangerous to generalize concerning the municipal constitution of England or Great Britain. Even more stress is laid in their book upon the proposition that municipal incorporation was not introduced until the reign of Henry VI. (A. D. 1440). Their object was to ascribe its origin to as recent a period as possible, because most of the evils of borough government were considered to be the outcome of the idea of incorporation; if this idea was modern, then the abuses must also be modern. In reality, Mere-wether and Stephens prove only that the *formula* of municipal incorporation, the words employed in the charters incorporating towns, underwent a change in Henry VI.'s time. The thing itself certainly existed as early as the reign of Edward I.[2] Merewether and Stephens, in discussing this and other important topics, expend all their energy upon concomitants. It is far more essential to ascertain how the technical

[1] Gross, *Gild Merchant*, vol. i., app. D.
[2] *Ibid.*, i. 93.

idea of incorporation originated, what potent affinities gradually drew the burgesses together into a single personality, and what municipal incorporation really signified after it came into existence, than to fix the date of the first charter of incorporation. In short, the materials in this book have not passed through the alembic of a thoroughly critical, historical mind, bent upon finding the truth in all its varied phases, but have been thrown together mechanically, to illumine only so much of the truth as is contained in eleven practical propositions, the most important of which are untenable. To uphold their views, Merewether and Stephens do not hesitate to resort to sophistry and forensic quibbles. In their book their real vocation is clearly reflected: they are practical lawyers pleading a cause. "Antiquarian research," they exclaim in their Introduction, "for the mere purpose of curiosity may have little claim to general attention; but some advantage will be derived from recalling past events, if the improvement of our present condition be the practical object of the inquiry." This is a most laudable sentiment, but it is liable to abuse; "antiquarian research for the mere purpose of curiosity" is better than research which to reform the present deforms the past.

Thompson. Thompson's *Essay on English Municipal History*[1] is an unpretentious little book, consisting mainly of brief sketches of the history of St. Albans, Leicester, Preston, Norwich, and Yarmouth. These are separate essays between which there is not much coherence. Of the very few broad generalizations which the author ventures to make, the most important relates to the gild merchant. Misled doubtless by the abnormal prominence of this institution at Leicester, Thompson ascribes to it a significance which it did

[1] No. 80.

not possess. He asserts that, anterior to the reign of Elizabeth, "the governing body in every leading mediæval borough was called the Guild"; and, "to think of a civic community without its Guild would, in truth, be to think of the human body without the vital principle sustaining its activity and progress." His views on this subject have been refuted in recent years.[1] The gild merchant looms up more prominently than any other municipal institution of the thirteenth and fourteenth centuries; but Thompson and Brady both exaggerate its influence upon the burghal constitution, while Merewether and Stephens, going to the other extreme, underestimate its importance.

Of the four works whose value we have briefly esti-Faults of all mated, two (Brady and Merewether-Stephens) are these writers. warped by partisan feeling; the other two (Madox and Thompson) are written in an impartial spirit, but are mere fragments of a general history of municipalities. The treatises of Brady and Thompson are now of little value; while those of Madox and Merewether-Stephens still contain much crude material that can be turned to account. All of these authors, except Thompson, have devoted their attention mainly to the relations between the boroughs and the crown, and have neglected the constitution or internal organization of boroughs. Not one of them made much use of the most important and most authentic source of local history, namely, the documents in the town archives. In short, not one of them gives a comprehensive account of the history of boroughs; such a treatise remains to be written. A book of this sort is much needed. Certain cardinal features of the medieval borough, such as the *firma burgi*, the judi-

---

[1] Gross, *Gild Merchant*, vol. i. ch. vi.; Hegel, *Städte und Gilden*, i. 57–72.

ciary, and the governing body, still need illumination;
the influence of the dissolution of gilds and monasteries upon the municipal constitution, the causes and
results of the *quo warranto* proceedings of the seventeenth century, and the political significance of the
rotten borough system in modern times, have not yet
been properly investigated; and many good historical
scholars have never even heard of the Convention
of Royal Burghs of Scotland. Whatever may be
said of the Middle Ages,[1] the modern period of
borough history is certainly not lacking in political
interest.[2]

§ 5. Histories of Particular Boroughs.

Their value
and contents.   The historian who, at the present day, undertakes
to deal with any general phase of English municipal
development, will at the outset have to lament the
absence of good histories of particular boroughs.[3]
The average town history in England is a farrago of
heterogeneous odds and ends thrown together at hap-
hazard, no scholarly work being displayed either in
the selection of the material or in its elaboration.
The bulk of the book comprises verbose antiquarian
disquisitions on such subjects as the age of the town,
the etymology of its name, and architectural remains,
gossip or anecdotes concerning local worthies,[4] long

---

[1] Above, p. xviii.

[2] Some estimate of the works of such writers as Hegel, Mrs. Green,
Gneist, Stubbs, Maitland, and Ashley is given in the text of this
Bibliography.

[3] " In England we do not possess one single complete and detailed
monograph on town life:" Stubbs, *Lectures on Mediæval and Modern
History* (1886), 64.

[4] Such gossip often forms the staple of the local history, especially
of its later chapters. For example, about three quarters of Wildridge's *Old and New Hull* (1889) is devoted to the careers of local
worthies.

accounts of royal visits to the town, genealogies that
are often inaccurate, a careful verbatim transcript of
epitaphs in the local churchyards, and, in some cases,
a chapter on the fauna or geology of the region.
Though many town histories rise far above this level
and contain much valuable material, it is difficult to
find any which can be called model works of their
kind.

The mania for copying sepulchral inscriptions is *Sepulchralia and genealogy.*
not so prevalent as it used to be.   But in a history of
Croydon, published as recently as 1883,[1] the author
attempts to cheer the reader by stating in his Preface,
that he has not, like other less scholarly local historians, contented himself with copying laudatory epitaphs of the " more influential inhabitants," but that
he has gone to the churchyard and copied *all* the inscriptions.   Accordingly this veracious historian devotes 196 pages of his book to sepulchralia, while 56
pages suffice for all remaining topics.   Again, some
local writers sacrifice everything to inordinate love of
genealogy.   In Abram's edition of the gild rolls of
Preston, published in 1884,[2] he gives in full all the
lists of members, but omits the laws made by the
gild, because the latter are of no interest to him, and,
as he states, of no use to genealogists.   To a real
student of history, this is the play of Hamlet with the
Prince of Denmark left out.

Town histories of England are also frequently marred *" The Roman dance."*
by an excessive antiquarian spirit, the fantastic play
of the imagination in connection with the remote
past (what Tacitus calls *licentia vetustatis*), inter-
mingled with intense local pride.   Often an energetic
attempt is made to trace the history of the borough

---

[1] *Croydon in the Past, Historical, Monumental, and Biographical.*
Printed and published by Jesse W. Ward, Croydon, 1883.

[2] No. 2647.

back to Roman times, to show that it is identical with Calleva, Mediolanum, or some other lost Roman city. A few Roman coins, urns, pots, fibulæ, or other vestiges of antiquity, turned up by the spade, often form sufficient data for a long disquisition on the borough's ancient greatness. Madox, in one of his manuscripts in the British Museum, calls this "the Roman dance." He says that one of the first to lead it was Camden.[1] In another part of this manuscript Madox observes that " when men would fain say some splendid thing of a burgh and can find nothing to say, then they will say that it is a very ancient burough." [2] This characteristic of local historians is visible as far back as the twelfth century, when Fitz-Stephen,[3] in describing London, assures us that, according to authentic chronicles, this city was much older than Rome. That " the Roman dance " is still in vogue is demonstrated by the long disquisitions on Roman times in such recent works as Jarman's *Bridgwater*, Tomlinson's *Doncaster*, and Hedges's *Wallingford*.[4]

Neglect of medieval history. The opening chapters of most town histories consist of vague conjectures concerning the antiquity of the borough, together with a heavy padding of generalities concerning the Celts, Romans, and Anglo-Saxons. Then the writers plunge abruptly into the fifteenth, sixteenth, or seventeenth century. The town history is thus, in reality, often left a complete blank down to the end of the Middle Ages. For example, Jarman's *Bridgwater*, which is somewhat better than the average local history, begins with

---

[1] Additional MS. 4529, ff. 141–4. Madox refers particularly to the mania for writing disquisitions on the Roman names of towns.

[2] *Ibid.*, f. 209.

[3] No. 2008.

[4] On this antiquarian mania in parish histories, see Rye, *Records and Record Searching* (1888), 21.

various vague remarks concerning the Celts, Roman coins, Cæsar's invasion, the Anglo-Saxons and Danes (including the story of Alfred and the cakes), an extract from Domesday concerning Bridgwater, an account of the lord's manor and castle, some allusions to the Black Death, and a few casual references to the burgesses; then the author launches into the history of the sixteenth and seventeenth centuries.

Antiquarian and genealogical studies, or even the exploration of graveyards and gossip concerning kings and local worthies, are good things in their proper place, but they should not constitute the essence of a town history. The growth of the civic constitution, the development of the municipal government, is usually either meagrely treated or wholly ignored. Too little use is made of the town records, the richest source of local history.[1] In the seventeenth and eighteenth centuries more attention was devoted to these records, as the works of writers like Bacon, Boys, Brand, Drake, Manship, Speed, and Swinden testify. When local writers learn to attach as much value to the muniments in the town-hall as to family genealogies, tombstones, and Roman urns, we shall have better town histories, works that will interest not merely the inhabitants of the town, but also students of general constitutional history, works that will furnish data for a good general treatise on the development of municipal government. Moreover,

Neglect of town records.

---

[1] " Grave est omnia ab archivis rimari, et incertum est quod non inde petitur:" Spelman, *Glossarium*, 344. Some local writers speak with scorn of the town records. Baker, in his history of Ludlow, p. vii., says that he has " met people who collected them, but never any one who read them." See also Nos. 978, 2421. On the other hand, several town histories have recently been published which show a thorough appreciation of the value of the records; for example, Nos. 1263, 1390, 1601, 1745, 1856, 2411, 2795, 2920.

every local history, properly written, will add to our knowledge of the making of the English nation, for every town is an important stone of that great edifice. The town government often anticipated and perhaps even guided the development of the national government.

BIBLIOGRAPHY

OF

BRITISH MUNICIPAL HISTORY.

Part I. — GENERAL AUTHORITIES.

§ 1. BIBLIOGRAPHIES AND CATALOGUES.

a. General, Nos. 1–16.
b. County Bibliographies, Nos. 17–43.

The main defect of most of the bibliographies mentioned below is that they do not indicate the historical value of books; they are compiled mainly for book-sellers and book-collectors, not for students of history.

Besides the bibliographies mentioned below, the following works are useful: R. Watt's *Bibliotheca Britannica* (1824), W. T. Lowndes's *Bibliographer's Manual of English Literature,* and the printed catalogues of the British Museum Library, the Bodleian Library, the Advocates' Library, the Signet Library, the Trinity College Library (Dublin), the libraries of the London Society of Antiquaries and the London Guildhall, and the free libraries of Birmingham, Liverpool, and Manchester. Special bibliographies of particular towns are mentioned below, in Part II., under the names of the towns.

a. **GENERAL.**

The most useful work is Anderson's. The sale catalogues included in the list all contain many town histories.

1. *ANDERSON, J. P. The book of British topography : a classified catalogue of the topographical works in the library of the British Museum relating to Great Britain and Ireland. London, 1881. 4°. and 8°.

Many of the older town histories have been acquired by the British Museum Library since this work was compiled. Even if these are added in a future edition of Mr. Anderson's bibliography, it will still exclude many books which are not in the British Museum. His lists of Scotch books are particularly defective.

2. BELL, THOMAS.   The Thomas Bell library.   The catalogue of 15,000 volumes of scarce and curious printed books, and unique manuscripts, comprised in the unrivalled library collected by the late Thomas Bell between the years 1797 and 1860, which will be sold by auction. . . . Newcastle-upon-Tyne, 1860.   4°.

Rich in works relating to towns, especially those of the northern counties.

2a. BROOKS, R. C.   A bibliography of municipal administration and city conditions.   *Municipal Affairs* [published quarterly by the Reform Club of New York], No. 1.   New York, 1897.   8°.

Deals mainly with the literature relating to the present administration of municipalities in the United States and Great Britain.

3. COMERFORD, JAMES.   Catalogue of the extensive and very valuable library of the late James Comerford. . . . [Sold by Sotheby, Wilkinson & Hodge, Nov. 16–30, 1881.]   London, 1881.   8°.

4. GOMME, G. L.   The literature of local institutions.   London, 1886.   8°.

Useful, but very incomplete.

5. [GOUGH, RICHARD.]   British topography : or an historical account of what has been done for illustrating the topographical antiquities of Great Britain and Ireland.   2 vols.   London, 1780.   4°.

This is a much enlarged edition of his " Anecdotes of British topography," 1768, 1 vol., 4°.

6. ——— A catalogue of the books relating to British topography, and Saxon and northern literature, bequeathed to the Bodleian library in the year 1799 by Richard Gough.   [Compiled by B. Bandinel.]   Oxford, 1814.   4°.

7. GRAY, HENRY.   Catalogue of British topography and local and other miscellanea [6,193 titles], offered for sale by Henry Gray. . . . Manchester, 1884.   4°.

8. ——— Reference catalogue of British topography and family history.   London, 1887.   8°.

9. HARTLEY, L. L.   Catalogue of the valuable library of the late Leonard Lawrie Hartley.   Part the first.   [Sold by Puttick & Simpson, June 1–June 12, 1885.]   London, 1885.   8°.

10. HOARE, R. C. A catalogue of books relating to the history and topography of England, Wales, Scotland, Ireland. By R. C. Hoare. Compiled from his library at Stourhead in Wiltshire. [Only twenty-five copies printed.] London, 1815. 8°.

11. —— Catalogue of the Hoare library at Stourhead, Co. Wilts. . . . [Compiled by J. B. Nichols.] London, 1840. 8°.

This includes the greater part of the Catalogue of 1815. For British topography, see pp. 93–542.

12. HOTTEN, J. C. A hand-book to the topography and family history of England and Wales : being a descriptive account of twenty thousand most curious and rare books, old tracts. . . . London, [1863.] 8°.

13. [RAWLINSON, RICHARD.] The English topographer : or an historical account . . . of all the pieces that have been written relating to the antiquities, natural history, or topographical description of any part of England. . . . By an impartial hand. London, 1720. 8°.

Wholly superseded by Gough and Upcott.

14. SMITH, J. R. A catalogue of ten thousand tracts and pamphlets, and fifty thousand prints and drawings, illustrating the topography and antiquities of England, Wales, Scotland, and Ireland, collected during the last thirty-five years by the late William Upcott and J. R. Smith. Now offered for sale. . . . London, 1878. 8°.

Contains many tracts relating to town history.

15. *UPCOTT, WILLIAM. A bibliographical account of the principal works relating to English topography. 3 vols. London, 1818. 4°.

This excellent work is still useful, though very incomplete even as regards books published before 1818.

16. WORRALL, JOHN. Bibliotheca topographica Anglicana : or a new and compleat catalogue of all books extant relating to the antiquity, description, and natural history of England. London, 1736. 12°.

A brief list, of little value.

b. COUNTY BIBLIOGRAPHIES.

Notes and Queries, 1896, ix. 361, mentions the following works, to which I have not had access:

Catalogue of books relating to Nottinghamshire, in the library of J. Ward. Nottingham, 1892. 8°.

Lincolnshire topography. Supplement to catalogue of Lincoln library, pp. 266–86. Lincoln, 1845. 8°.

Buckinghamshire.

17. Bibliotheca Buckinghamiensis. [By Henry Gough.] *Archit. and Archæol. Soc. for the County of Buckingham*, Records of Buckingham, vols. v.–vi. Aylesbury, 1885–90. 8°.

Cambridgeshire.

18. BOWES, ROBERT. A catalogue of books printed at or relating to the university, town, and county of Cambridge from 1521 to 1893, with bibliographical and biographical notes. Cambridge, 1894. 8°.

Cheshire.

See No. 32.

19. A list of books, etc., relating to Cheshire history. *The Cheshire and Lancashire Collector*, vols. i.–ii. London and Manchester, 1853–55. 8°.

Cornwall.

20. *BOASE, G. C., and COURTNEY, W. P. Bibliotheca Cornubiensis: a catalogue of the writings, both manuscript and printed, of Cornishmen, and of works relating to the county of Cornwall, with biographical memoranda and copious literary references. 3 vols. London, 1874–82. 8°.

Devonshire.

21. DAVIDSON, JAMES. Bibliotheca Devoniensis : a catalogue of the printed books relating to the county of Devon. Exeter, 1852. 4°.

Incomplete, but useful.

22. ROWE, J. B. Address [delivered before the Devonshire Association for the Advancement of Science, etc.]. Plymouth, 1882. 8°.

Reprinted from the Transactions of the Association, 1882, xiv. 33--116.

App. B contains a list of histories of towns, parishes, etc., in Devonshire, printed or in MS.

Dorset.

23. *MAYO, C. H. Bibliotheca Dorsetiensis : being a carefully compiled account of printed books and pamphlets relating to the history and topography of the county of Dorset. London, 1885. 4°.

Gloucestershire.

24. *HYETT, F. A., and BAZELEY, W. The bibliographer's manual of Gloucestershire literature. 3 vols. Gloucester, 1895–97. 8°.

Vol. iii. Works relating to Bristol.

25. PHELPS, J. D. Collectanea Glocestriensia : or a catalogue of books, tracts, coins, etc., relating to the county of Gloucester, in the possession of John Delafield Phelps, Esq., Chavenage House. London, 1842. 8°.

Hampshire.

26. COPE, W. H. A list of [701] books relating to Hampshire . . . in the library at Bramshall, collected by Sir William H. Cope, Bart. Wokingham, 1879. 8°.

27. GILBERT, H. M. Bibliotheca Hantoniensis : an attempt at a bibliography of Hampshire. Southampton, [1872.] 8°. pp. 43.

28. GILBERT, H. M., and GODWIN, G. N. Bibliotheca Hantoniensis : a list of books relating to Hampshire, including magazine references, etc. Southampton, [1891.] 8°.

The best bibliography of Hampshire.

Herefordshire.

29. ALLEN, JOHN. Bibliotheca Herefordiensis : or a descriptive catalogue of books, pamphlets, maps, prints, etc., relating to the county of Hereford. Hereford, 1821. 8°.

Kent.

30. SMITH, J. R. Bibliotheca Cantiana : a bibliographical account of what has been published on the history, topography, antiquities, customs, and family history of the county of Kent. London, 1837. 8°.

Valuable.

Lancashire.

31. *FISHWICK, HENRY.   The Lancashire library: a bibliographical account of books on topography, biography, history, science, and miscellaneous literature, relating to the county palatine. . . . London and Warrington, 1875.   4°.

One of the best county bibliographies.

32. SUTTON, ALBERT.   Bibliotheca Lancastriensis: a catalogue of books on the topography and genealogy of Lancashire.   Manchester, 1893.   8°.   pp. 39.

A sale catalogue, of little value.   There is a list of books relating to Cheshire on pp. 34–9.

Norfolk.

33. RYE, WALTER.   An index to Norfolk topography.   *Index Society*.   London, 1881.   8°.

Supplementary volume, Norwich, 1896.

34. WOODWARD, SAMUEL.   The Norfolk topographer's manual: being a catalogue of the books and engravings hitherto published in relation to the county: by the late Mr. Samuel Woodward.   The whole revised and augmented by W. C. Ewing. . . . London, etc., 1842.   8°.

Northamptonshire.

35. †TAYLOR, JOHN.   A bibliographical account of what has been written or printed relating to the history, topography, anti- quities, family history, customs, etc., of Northamptonshire. . . . [Northampton] n. d.   f°.

A recent work, the impression of which is limited to six copies.   It comprises about 25,000 references.

Shropshire.

36. WALCOTT, M. E. C.   An introduction to sources of Salopian topography.   Reprinted from the Transactions of the Shropshire Archæol. and Nat. Hist. Society.   Shrewsbury and Oswestry, [1879.] 8°.   pp. 20.

A brief list, of little value.

Staffordshire.

37. *Simms, Rupert. Bibliotheca Staffordiensis : or a biblio-graphical account of books and other printed matter relating to . . . any portion of the county of Stafford. . . . Lichfield, 1894. 4°.

Surrey.

38. Manning, Owen, and Bray, William. Catalogue of books relating to this county [Surrey], or particular parts of it. [Manning and Bray's History and antiquities of the county of Surrey, iii. 683–702. 3 vols. London, 1804–14. f°.]

Sussex.

39. Butler, G. S. Topographica Sussexiana : an attempt towards forming a list of the various publications relating to the county of Sussex. [Lewes, 1866.] 8°.

Reprinted from the Collections of the Sussex Archæological Society, vols. xv.–xviii., Lewes, 1863–66.

40. Sawyer, F. E. Recent Sussex bibliography (1864–1882). *Sussex Archæol. Soc.*, Collections, xxxii. 201–12 ; xxxiii. 207–12. Lewes, 1882–83. 8°.

Yorkshire.

41. *Boyne, William. The Yorkshire library : a bibliographical account of books on topography . . . and miscellaneous literature, relating to the county of York. With collations and notes on the books and authors. London, 1869. 4°.

42. Hailstone, Edward. Catalogue of a collection of historical and topographical works and civil war tracts relating to the county of York . . . in the library of Edward Hailstone. Printed for private distribution. [Bradford,] 1858. 8°. pp. 76.

Superseded by Boyne.

43. †Turner, J. H. Ten thousand Yorkshire books : a hand-book for buyers and sellers. Bradford, —.

Announced for publication. It will include the works mentioned in Boyne and Hailstone, and many other titles.

§ 2. GENERAL PUBLIC RECORDS, ETC.

a. Reports of Committees, Nos. 44–64.
b. Statutes, Nos. 65–77.

For public records relating mainly to particular topics and periods, see below, §§ 4–14.

a. REPORTS OF COMMITTEES.

44. Reports from committees of the House of Commons which have been printed by order of the House, and are not inserted in the Journals [1715–1802]. 15 vols. [London, 1773–1803.] f°.

See No. 47.
This collection has been continued in the numerous folio volumes which are commonly cited as "Parliamentary Papers." The volumes (about 5500 in all) are numbered continuously under each session. They contain reports of committees, bills, accounts, etc.

Indexes and Catalogues.

All the volumes mentioned below, except No. 56, are Parliamentary Papers. An Index to each session will usually be found in the last volume for the session.

45. Catalogue of papers printed by order of the House of Commons, 1731–1800. [London,] 1807. f°.

46. Catalogue of parliamentary reports, and a breviate of their contents : arranged under heads according to the subjects, 1696–1834. [London,] 1834. f°.

47. General index to the reports from committees of the House of Commons, 1715–1801 ; forming the series of fifteen volumes of reports. [London,] 1803. f°.

See No. 44.

48. [General] indexes to the subject matters of the reports of the House of Commons, 1801–34. [London,] 1834. f°.

49. General index to the sessional papers, 1801–37. [London,] 1840. f°.

50. General index to the bills, printed by order of the House of Commons, 1801–52. [London,] 1854. f°.

51. General index to the reports of the select committees, printed by order of the House of Commons, 1801–52. [London,] 1854. f°.

52. General index to the accounts and papers, reports of commissioners, estimates, etc., etc., printed by order of the House of Commons, or presented by command, 1801–52. [London,] 1854. f°.

53. General index to the bills, reports, accounts, and other papers, printed by order of the House of Commons, or presented by command, 1852–53 — 1861. [London,] 1862. f°.

54. General index to the bills, reports, estimates, accounts, and papers . . . 1852–53 — 1868–69. [London,] 1870. f°.

55. General index to the bills, reports, estimates, accounts, and papers . . . 1870 — 1878–79. [London,] 1880. f°.

56. Law reports (The). Index to the orders in council, proclamations, royal commissions of inquiry, orders, and notices of government departments ; and all other matter published in the London Gazette, from Jan. 1st, 1830, to Dec. 31st, 1883. . . . Together with references to statutes and parliamentary papers connected therewith. Compiled for the incorporated Council of Law Reporting for England and Wales by Alexander Pulling. London, 1885. 8°.

Particular Reports.

Only the more important reports are given below. Many others may be found with the help of the Indexes. A few of the reports relating to particular towns are included in Part II. of this Bibliography. See also Nos. 253, 294–5, 718–9, 768–72.

57. Reports (First and Second) from the select committee, appointed to inquire into the state of the public records of the kingdom, etc. [London, 1800.] f°.

Vol. xv. of the Reports from Committees, 1715–1802: see above, No. 44.

Many records relating to municipal corporations are referred to in table ii. pp. 565–667.

58. Report (General) to the king in council from the honourable board of commissioners on the public records. . . . *Record Com.* [London,] 1837. f°.

Pp. 428–512 contain reports upon the records of the following towns:

Altrincham
Andover
Ashburton
Axbridge
Banbury
Basingstoke
Beccles
*Beverley
Bishop's Castle
Bodmin
*Bradninch
Bridgnorth
Bridgwater
Bridport
Burford
Callington
Cardiff
Cardigan
Carlisle
Carnarvon
Chard
Chesterfield
Chippenham
Christchurch
Cirencester
Cockermouth
Colnbrook
Cowbridge
Cricklade
Dartmouth
Deal
Devizes
Dover
Dudley
Dunmow
*Dunwich
Durham
Falmouth
Farnham

*Folkestone
Garstang
Glastonbury
Godalming
Grampound
Grantham
Greenwich
Grinstead (East)
Guildford
Harwich
Hastings
Hemel Hempstead
Hereford
Holt
Honiton
Horsham
Huntingdon
* Hythe
Knaresborough
Lampeter
Langport
Laugharne
Leeds
Leominster
Lincoln
Liskeard
Llanidloes
*London
Looe (East)
Looe (West)
Loughor
Louth
Lydford
Lyme
Maidenhead
Maldon
Marazion
Monmouth
Morpeth

Newcastle-under-Lyme
Newport (Monmouthshire)
Newton (Lancashire)
Oswestry
Penryn
Plymouth
*Pontefract
Portsmouth
*Preston
Queenborough
Radnor
Reigate
Retford
Saffron Walden
St. Germains
Salisbury
*Sandwich
*Scarborough
*Southampton
*Southwold
*Tenterden
Thornbury (Gloucestershire)
Tiverton
Totnes
Tregony
Usk
*Wareham
*Warwick
Watchet
Wenlock
Weobly
Westbury
Weymouth
Wisbech
Wokingham
Woodstock
Worcester
Wycombe
Yarmouth (Isle of Wight)

Most of these reports are very brief; those for the towns marked with an asterisk are more detailed, some of them giving extracts from charters and other records. The report on Southampton is very full.

59. Reports from the select committee on municipal corporations; with the minutes of evidence taken before them. *Parl. Papers*, 1833, vol. xiii. [London,] 1833. f°.

This inquiry covers the following towns:

Bath	Denbigh	Hull	Saltash
Berwick	Dover	Monmouth	Usk
Bradninch	Dublin	Newport (Monmouthshire)	Wisbech
Brecon	Gloucester	Northampton	Yarmouth (Great)
Coventry	Grantham	Portsmouth	

60. * Report (First) of commissioners appointed to inquire into the municipal corporations in England and Wales [with appendix, pts. i.–v.]. *Parl. Papers*, 1835, vols. xxiii.–xxvi. 4 vols. [London,] 1835. f°.

This report deals with 284 towns.

Analytical index: *Parl. Papers*, 1839, vol. xviii.

Second Report . . . London and Southwark, London companies: *Parl. Papers*, 1837, vol. xxv.

Reports upon certain boroughs, drawn by T. J. Hogg: *Parl. Papers*, 1837–8, vol. xxxv.

Mr. Hogg reports on the following boroughs:

Bala	Llanfyllin	Machynlleth	Newtown	Welshpool
Conway	Llanidloes	Montgomery	Pwllheli	Wigan
Criccieth	Macclesfield	Nevin	Stockport	

For the reports on Ireland and Scotland, see below, Nos. 718, 772.

These various reports on the boroughs of Great Britain form one of the most important sources for the study of municipal history. They should not be ignored by the historians of particular towns.

61. Report of the commissioners appointed to inquire into municipal corporations not subject to the Municipal Corporations Act [of 1835] (other than the city of London); together with minutes of evidence, index, etc. *Parl. Papers*, 1880, vol. xxxi. [London,] 1880. f°.

This inquiry covers 110 corporations in England and Wales; the appendix contains special reports concerning 86 of them. On this Report was based the Municipal Corporations Act, 1883, 46 & 47 Vict. c. 18.

62. * Reports of the royal commission on historical manuscripts. [15 Reports, with appendices; about 60 vols.] London, 1870–97. f° and 8°.

Aberdeen, i. 121-3
Abingdon, i. 98-9, ii. 149-50
Axbridge, iii. 300-8
Barnstaple, ix. 203-16
Berwick-on-Tweed, iii. 308-10
Bishop's Castle, x. pt. iv. 399-407
Bridgnorth, x. pt. iv. 424-37
Bridgwater, i. 99, iii. 310-20
Bridport, vi. 475-99
Bury St. Edmunds, xiv. pt. viii. 121-58
Cambridge, i. 99-100
Canterbury, ix. pt. i. 129-77
Carlisle, ix. pt. i. 197-203
Chester, viii. 355-403
Cinque Ports, iv. 428
Cork, i. 128-9
Coventry, i. 100-102
Dartmouth, v. 597-606
Dublin, i. 129
Edinburgh, i. 126
Eye, x. pt. iv. 513-36
Faversham, vi. 500-11
Folkestone, v. 590-92
Fordwich, v. 606-8
Galway, x. pt. v. 380-520
Glasgow, i. 126
Glastonbury, i. 102
Great Grimsby, xiv. pt. viii. 237-91
Hastings, xiii. pt. iv. 354-64
Hereford, xiii. pt. iv. 283-353
Hertford, xiv. pt. viii. 158-64
Hythe, iv. 429-39
Ipswich, ix. pt. i. 222-62
Kendal, x. pt. iv. 299-318
Kilkenny, i. 129-30
Kingston-upon-Thames, iii. 331-3
Kirkcudbright, iv. 538-9

Launceston, vi. 524-6
Leicester, viii. 403-41
Limerick, i. 131
Lincoln, xiv. pt. viii. 1-120
Lydd, v. 516-33
Lynn, xi. pt. iii. 145-247
Montrose, ii. 205-6
Morpeth, vi. 526-38
New Romney, iv. 439-42, v. 533-54, vi. 540-45
Norwich, i. 102-4
Nottingham, i. 105-6
Perth, v. 655
Plymouth, ix. pt. i. 262-84, x. pt. iv. 536-60
Pontefract, viii. 269-76
Reading, xi. pt. vii. 167-227
Rochester, ix. pt. i. 286-9
Rye, v. 488-516, xiii. pt. iv. 1-246
St. Albans, v. 565-8
Salisbury, v. 568-71
Sandwich, v. 568-71
Southampton, xiii. pt. iii. 1-144
Stratford, ix. pt. i. 289-93
Tenterden, vi. 569-72
Totnes, iii. 341-50
Wallingford, vi. 572-95
Waterford, i. 131-2, x. pt. v. 265-339
Wells, i. 106-8, iii. 350
Wenlock, x. pt. iv. 420-24
Weymouth and Melcombe Regis, v. 575-90
Winchester, vi. 595-605
Wisbech, ix. pt. i. 293-9
Wycombe (High), v. 554-65
Yarmouth (Great), ix. 299-324
York, i. 108-10

An invaluable collection, containing many long extracts from the town archives. The First Report was reprinted in 1874.

63. Reports of the royal commission on market rights and tolls. . . . *Parl. Papers*, 1888, vols. liii.–lv.; 1889, vol. xxxviii.; 1890–91, vols. xxxvii.–xli.   9 [14] vols.   [London,] 1889–91.   f°.

Relates to England, Wales, Ireland, and Scotland.

64. Return of all boroughs and cities in the United Kingdom possessing common or other lands, in respect of which the freemen or other privileged inhabitants claim any exclusive right of property or use. . . . *Parl. Papers*, 1870, vol. lv. [London,] 1870. f°.

b. STATUTES.

For various other collections of statutes, besides those mentioned below, see vol. i. of the Record Commission edition (No. 65), Introd., ch. i. § i.; and Lowndes's *Bibliographer's Manual*, under "Statutes."

65. Statutes (The) of the realm. [Edited by A. Luders, T. E. Tomlins, J. France, W. E. Taunton, and J. Raithby.] *Record Com.* 9 vols. [London,] 1810–22. f°.

This is the most complete collection for the period which it covers; it extends to 1713.

For the index volumes, see Nos. 72, 73.

66. Statutes (The) at large from Magna Charta [to 1800] . . . . By Owen Ruffhead [and others.] 18 vols. London, 1763–1800. 4°.

67. Statutes (The) at large of the United Kingdom of Great Britain and Ireland [1801–69]. . . . By T. E. Tomlins [J. Raithby, N. Simons, and others.] 29 vols. London, 1804–69. 4°.

68. Statutes (The public general) [1830–87]. . . . [Published annually since 1830.] London, 1830–87. 8°.

69. —— The public general acts [1888–96]. . . . Published by authority [annually.] London, 1888–96. 8°.

70. Statutes (The) [1235–1878.] Revised edition. By authority. 18 vols. London, 1870–[1885.] 8°.

See No. 71.

71. —— The statutes [1235–1871.] Second revised edition. By authority. 12 vols. London, 1888–96. 8°.

These "revised editions" of the statutes include only those statutes which are unrepealed. They are published under the direction of the Statute Law Committee.

For the index, see No. 75.

Indexes and Digests.

72. Alphabetical index (The) to the statutes of the realm, from Magna Charta to the end of the reign of Queen Anne. [By J. Raithby.] *Record Com.* [London,] 1824. f°.

73. —— The chronological index to the statutes, from Magna Charta to the end of the reign of Queen Anne. [By J. Raithby. Edited by J. Caley and W. Elliott.] *Record Com.* [London,] 1828. f°.

In these two indexes see the titles " Cinque Ports," " London," " Towns," etc.

74. [CHITTY, JOSEPH.] Chitty's Collection of statutes. . . . Fourth edition down to 1880, by J. M. Lely. 6 vols. London, 1880. 8°.

Corporations, i. 1246-1434.

75. Chronological table and index of the statutes [1235-1895.] By authority. Thirteenth edition. 2 vols. London, 1896. 8°.

Published under the direction of the Statute Law Committee.
Vol. i. Chronological table of all the statutes.
Vol. ii. Index to the statutes in force.
For boroughs, see ii. 108-45.
Vol. i. of this valuable work gives all the old, repealed statutes, and shows how they were affected by later legislation.

76. Index (An) to the statutes, public and private [1801-59.] *Parl. Papers*, 1860, vols. lxxi.–lxxii. 2 vols. [London,] 1860. f°.

Pt. i. Public general acts.
Pt. ii. Local and personal acts.
See especially pt. ii. 301-50.

77. TYRWHITT, R. P., and TYNDALE, T. W. A digest of the public general statutes, from Magna Charta, A. D. 1224-5 to 1 & 2 Geo. IV. A. D. 1821 inclusive, with an analytical index. . . . 2 vols. London, 1822. 4°.

See the titles " Corporation," " Franchises," " Liberties," " London," " Parliament," " Scotland," " Wales."

§ 3.   GENERAL MUNICIPAL HISTORIES.

a. Principal Treatises, Nos. 78–80.
b. Short Accounts, Nos. 81–94.

a. PRINCIPAL TREATISES.

There is no good general history of English municipalities. Brady is biased and unreliable. The material in Merewether and Stephens is valuable, but many of their general conclusions are untenable. Thompson's little book is readable, but fragmentary. Mrs. Green's *Town Life* and Madox's *Firma Burgi* (Nos. 153, 158), though they do not cover the whole range of municipal history, are of considerable general interest.

78. BRADY, ROBERT. An historical treatise of cities and burghs or boroughs. Shewing their original, and whence and from whom they received their liberties, privileges, and immunities ; what they were, and what made and constituted a free burgh and free burgesses. As also shewing when they first sent their representatives to Parliament. With a concurrent discourse of most matters and things incident or relating thereto. Second edition. London, 1704. f°.

The body of the work is occupied mainly with extracts from Domesday Book, and with a long discussion of parliamentary writs and returns.

The appendix contains the following Latin charters : King John and Edw. III. to Great Yarmouth; King John to Dunwich (two charters) ; Hen. II. to Wallingford; Rich. I. to Portsmouth, Winchester, and Lincoln; King John to Andover, Bridgwater, Helston, Lynn, Hartlepool, London, York, and Norwich; Edw. IV. to London, inspecting charters of Hen. I., Hen. II., and Rich. I. ; James II. to Windsor. The appendix also gives documents relating to the disputes between Great Yarmouth and Gorleston (Hen. III. — Edw. I.), and several returns of writs.

Brady wrote in a partisan spirit, to justify the measures of Charles II. and James II. against municipal corporations.

1st edition, 1690, f°; new edition, 1777, 8°.

For a detailed account and criticism of this work, see Merewether and Stephens (No. 79), iii. 1900–1938. See also No. 168.

79. *MEREWETHER, H. A., and STEPHENS, A. J. The history of the boroughs and municipal corporations of the United Kingdom, from the earliest to the present time ; with an examination of records, charters, and other documents, illustrative of their constitution and powers. 3 vols. London, 1835. 8°.

c

The most elaborate history of boroughs. Besides an analysis of the Anglo-Saxon Laws, Domesday Book, the Year Books, the Statutes of the Realm, and other important general sources, it contains much valuable material illustrating the history of many particular towns.

80. THOMPSON, JAMES. An essay on English municipal history. London, 1867. 8°.

Ch. i. The Roman-British municipalities.	Chs. xiii.–xiv. On market towns.
Ch. ii. Saxon town institutions.	Ch. xv. Municipal insignia.
Ch. iii. The borough of St. Albans.	Ch. xvi. The French communes.
Chs. iv.–vii. The borough of Leicester.	Ch. xvii. Comparison between French
Ch. viii. The borough of Preston.	communes and English boroughs.
Ch. ix.–xi. The city of Norwich.	Ch. xviii. Practical conclusions.
Ch. xii. The borough of Yarmouth.	

b. SHORT ACCOUNTS.

The only works of importance under this head are those of Gneist, Hegel, and Stubbs. Gneist's views of municipal development are interesting, but he is inclined to follow Merewether and Stephens too closely. Hegel's work contains one of the most valuable recent contributions to English municipal history in the Middle Ages.

81. CONNELL, ARTHUR. A treatise on the election laws in Scotland ; to which is added [pp. 403–536] an historical enquiry concerning the municipal constitution of towns and boroughs. With an appendix. Edinburgh, 1827. 8°.

82. GLASSON, ERNEST. Histoire du droit et des institutions politiques, civiles et judiciaires de l'Angleterre. . . . 6 vols. Paris, 1882–83. 8°.

Boroughs, ii. 164-7, iii. 100–118, iv. 88–92, v. 84-7, vi. 64-84.

83. GNEIST, RUDOLPH. Das heutige englische Verfassungs- und Verwaltungsrecht. 3 pts. Berlin, 1857–63. 8°.

Pt. iii., the Ergänzungsband, bearing the title " Geschichte des Selfgovernment in England," contains Gneist's fullest account of municipal history. This account will also be found in his " Communalverfassung," 2nd edition, 1863, but not in the 3rd edition, 1871.

84. —— Selfgovernment, Communalverfassung und Verwaltungsgerichte in England. Dritte Auflage (in einem Bande). Berlin, 1871. 8°.

Ch. viii. Die Stadtverfassung. Deals mainly with the 19th century.

85. —— Englische Verfassungsgeschichte. Berlin, 1882. 8°.

Municipal history, 311–14, 437–43, 473–5, 673–4, 720–22.
This work has been translated by P. A. Ashworth : " The History of the English Constitution," 2 vols., London, 1886 ; 2nd edition, 1889.

86. —— Das englische Verwaltungsrecht. . . . Dritte Auflage.
2 vols. Berlin, 1883–84. 8°.

87. *Hegel, Karl. Städte und Gilden der germanischen Völker
im Mittelalter. 2 vols. Leipzig, 1891. 8°.

England, i. 13–120, 441–57.
He proves that the municipal constitution is not derived from the gilds.

88. Merewether, H. A. Report of the case of the borough
of West Looe . . . 18th April, 1822 ; with a preface, notes, and
cases, illustrative of the general history of boroughs, and of the law
relating to them. London, 1823. 8°.

See also No. 429.

89. Origin and progress of municipal corporations. *Westminster
Review*, xxii. 408–39. London, 1835. 8°.

90. Penny cyclopædia. 30 vols. London, 1833–58. 4°.

Vol. v. pp. 193–220 contains quite a good account of the boroughs of England
and Wales; viii. 48–53, boroughs of Ireland ; v. 220-2, burghs of Scotland.

91. Picton, J. A. Our municipal institutions in their past and
future. Liverpool, 1882. 8°.

A lecture, containing a brief sketch of the history of boroughs.

92. Pike, L. O. A history of crime in England. . . . 2 vols.
London, 1873–76. 8°.

See his index, under " Towns."

93. Stephens, A. J. The rise and progress of the English constitution : the treatise of J. L. de Lolme. With an historical and
legal introduction, and notes, by A. J. Stephens. 2 vols. London,
1838. 8°.

For the history of boroughs, see the introduction, i. 15–18, 26–7, 33–4, 57–65,
138–9, 149–50, 259–60, 274–81, 316–20, 427, 455–8, 479–83. This account is derived from Merewether and Stephens's *Municipal Corporations* (No. 79), giving
all their main facts and arguments without wearisome repetitions.

94. *STUBBS, WILLIAM.   The constitutional history of England in its origin and development.   3 vols.   Oxford, 1874–78.   8°.

Contains a good general sketch of municipal history to the end of the 15th century : see §§ 44, 131, 165, 211–14, 218, 219, 422, 484.

5th edition, Oxford, 1891–96, 8°.

§ 4.   THE ROMAN AND ANGLO–SAXON PERIODS.

The meagre sources for the history of Roman Britain deal mainly with roads and stations, or topographical and military matters ; they give very little information concerning municipal government.   The most elaborate plea in favor of the continuance of the Roman municipal régime in England after the Anglo-Saxon Conquest will be found in Coote's *Romans of Britain;* this theory is also maintained by Wright.   Their arguments are not convincing, and have been rejected by Freeman, Gomme, Green, Scrutton, and Stubbs (*Constitutional History*, § 44).   There are some modern works relating to particular towns in the Roman period, such as H. M. Scarth's *Aquæ Solis, or Notices of Roman Bath*, 1864 ; C. R. Smith's *Illustrations of Roman London*, 1859 ; C. Wellbeloved's *Eburacum, or York under the Romans*, 1842 ; Whitaker's *Manchester* (No. 2368) ; T. Wright's *Uriconium*, 1872 ; see also below, No. 2009.   These books deal mainly with topographical, military, and archæological matters.   For some account of the sources and modern literature relating to Roman Britain, see K. Elze, *Grundriss der Englischen Philologie*, Halle, 1887, pp. 101–108 ; T. Mommsen and J. Marquardt, *Manuel des Antiquités Romaines* edited by G. Humbert, Paris, 1892, ix. 153–4.

For the Anglo-Saxon period, also, our sources of information are meagre. The principal sources are the Anglo-Saxon laws (Nos. 95–96) and Domesday Book (No. 123): supplemented by a few stray passages in the Anglo-Saxon Chronicles ; Kemble's *Codex Diplomaticus*, 6 vols., 1839–46 ; Birch's *Cartularium*, 3 vols., 1885–93 ; and Thorpe's *Diplomatarium*, 1865.   Kemble, in his *Saxons in England*, gives a detailed account of the history of towns, but it is vague and based largely on continental analogies of a later period ; there is a good short account in Hegel's *Städte* (No. 87), and in Stubbs's *Constitutional History* (No. 94), § 44.   Maitland's essay (No. 110) is valuable and suggestive.

95.   Ancient laws and institutes of England. . . . [Edited by Benjamin Thorpe.]   *Record Com.*   [London,] 1840.   f°.

Also in 2 vols., 1840, 8°.
See No. 96.

96. —— Die Gesetze der Angelsachsen . . . herausgegeben von Reinhold Schmid. Zweite Auflage. Leipzig, 1858. 8°.

1st edition, 1832. The second edition should be used; it is better than Thorpe's. A new edition of the Anglo-Saxon laws is being prepared by Dr. F. Liebermann; it will doubtless supersede all others.

The principal passages relating to boroughs are indicated in Thorpe's index, under the words "Burh," "Gemot," "London," and "Port," and on pp. 541–2 of Schmid. For gilds, see Schmid, 588.

97. Coote, H. C.   A neglected fact in English history.   London, 1864.   8°.

98. —— The Romans of Britain.   London, 1878.   8°.

This is an expansion of No. 97.
Roman and Anglo-Saxon municipalities and gilds, 342–413.
A learned plea in favor of the continuance of Roman civilization in England; the author's arguments are ingenious and plausible, but he relies too much on general analogies. See Freeman's criticism of *A Neglected Fact*, in *Macmillan's Magazine*, July, 1870.

99. Eckerdt, Hermann.   De origine urbium Angliæ.   Königsberg, 1859.   8°.   pp. 32.

A thesis for the degree of Ph. D.

100. Fellows, G. E.   The Anglo-Saxon towns and their polity. . . .   Berne, 1890.   8°.

Unscholarly; of no value.

101. Freeman, E. A.   History of the Norman Conquest of England, its causes and its results.   6 vols.   Oxford, 1867–79.   8°.

Ch. xxiv. § 5.   English origin of English towns, etc.
2nd edition, 1870–79.

102. Gomme, G. L.   Primitive folk-moots : or open-air assemblies in Great Britain.   London, 1880.   8°.

Open-air courts in boroughs, 150–9.

103. —— On traces of the primitive village community in English municipal institutions.   *Soc. of Antiq. of London*, Archæologia, xlvi. 403–22.   London, 1881.   4°.

A valuable essay.

104. —— The old land-rights of municipal corporations.   *The Antiquary*, ix. 157–62, 203–6.   London, 1885.   4°.

105. GOMME, G. L.   The village community, with special reference to the origin and form of its survivals in Britain.   London, 1890.   8°.

In ch. iii. he combats the view that the Roman polity survived in England; and in chs. vii.–viii. he deals with the modern survivals of the village community in Chippenham, Elgin, Kells, Lauder, London, Malmesbury, Newton-upon-Ayr, etc.   The same general subject is dealt with in Nos. 103, 104.

106. GREEN, J. R.   The making of England.   London, 1881.   8°.

See especially ch. iv.

107. —— The conquest of England.   London, 1883.   8°.

See ch. ix.

108. KEMBLE, J. M.   The Saxons in England.   A history of the English commonwealth till the period of the Norman Conquest.   A new edition, revised by Walter de Gray Birch.   2 vols.   London, 1876.   8°.

See vol. ii. ch. vii. and app. C.
1st edition, 1849.

109. †KENRICK, JOHN.   On the probable origin of modern corporations from the municipia of the Romans, etc.   *Lit. and Philosoph. Soc. of Manchester*, Memoirs, vi. 33–77.   Manchester, 1842.   8°.

110. MAITLAND, F. W.   The origin of the boroughs.   *English Hist. Review*, xi. 13–19.   London, 1896.   8°.

He contends that the special royal peace conferred upon fortified places " is the original principle which serves to mark off the borough from the village." See also his *Domesday Book* (No. 160), 184–92.

111. PALGRAVE, FRANCIS.   The rise and progress of the English commonwealth.   Anglo-Saxon period. . . . 2 pts.   London, 1832.   4°.

See i. 195, 329–36, 349, 628–36, 644–5, etc.

112. PEARSON, C. H.   Historical maps of England. . . . Second edition.   London, 1870.   f°.

Roman Britain, 6–18.

113. POSTE, BEALE.   Britannia antiqua, or ancient Britain brought within the limits of authentic history.   London, 1857.   8°.

Ch. xi.   The Roman walled towns of Britain.

114. SCARTH, H. M. Early Britain. — Roman Britain. London, [1883.] 12°.

Chs. xv.-xvi. Roman cities.

115. SCRUTTON, T. E. The influence of the Roman law on the law of England. Being the Yorke prize essay of the University of Cambridge for the year 1884. Cambridge, 1885. 8°.

Pp. 53-57 contain a brief summary of the theories regarding the origin of towns and gilds.

116. WRIGHT, THOMAS. The Celt, the Roman, and the Saxon : a history of the early inhabitants of Britain, down to the conversion of the Anglo-Saxons to Christianity. . . . Fourth edition. London, 1885. 8°.

Chs. iv., xvi. Roman and Anglo-Saxon towns.
His arguments in favor of the survival of Roman municipalities are even less convincing than those of Coote.
Earlier editions, 1852, 1861, 1875.

117. —— On the existence of municipal privileges under the Anglo-Saxons. *Soc. of Antiq. of London*, Archæologia, xxxii. 298–311. London, 1847. 4°.

This paper is reprinted in No. 116, ch. xvi.

§ 5. THE LATER MIDDLE AGES: 1066–1500.

a. Public Records, etc., Nos. 118–148.
b. Modern Writers, Nos. 149–169.

The principal general sources for the study of this period are Domesday Book and the publications of the Record Commission. A good account of these public records will be found in S. R. Scargill-Bird's *Guide to the Documents in the Public Record Office* (2nd edition, 1896), and in C. P. Cooper's *Account of the most important Public Records* (2 vols., 1832). The archives of particular towns are also of great value ; some of the local records of the thirteenth century have been preserved, but in most towns the oldest muniments are of later date. The printed collections are mentioned in Part II. of this Bibliography, and many extracts are given in the Reports of the Historical MSS. Commission (No. 62). The best modern authorities besides Hegel and Stubbs (Nos. 87, 94) are Mrs. Green, and Pollock and Maitland (Nos. 153, 164).

a. PUBLIC RECORDS, ETC.

Domesday Book, Charters, etc.

See Nos. 173, 174, 603.

118. BOLDON BUKE, a survey of the possessions of the see of Durham, made by order of Bishop Hugh Pudsey, in the year 1182. With a translation, an appendix of original documents, and a glossary. By William Greenwell. *Surtees Society.* Durham, 1852. 8°.

Also printed in Domesday Book, vol. iv. (No. 123).
The appendix of Greenwell's edition contains charters granted by Bishop Hugh Pudsey to Gateshead and Wearmouth.

119. Calendarium rotulorum chartarum [1199–1483] et inquisitionum ad quod damnum. [Edited by John Caley.] *Record Com.* [London,] 1803. f°.

Refers to many town charters.

120. Calendarium rotulorum patentium in Turri Londinensi. [3 John — 23 Edw. IV. Edited by John Caley.] *Record Com.* [London,] 1802. f°.

121. —— Calendar of the patent rolls. . . [Edw. I.—Rich. II.] *Rolls Series.* 7 vols. London, 1891–95. 8°.

These calendars refer to many letters patent granted to towns.

122. Collections for a history of Staffordshire. Edited by the William Salt Archæological Society. Vols. i.–xvii. Birmingham, 1880 [1881]–96. 8°.

Contains copious extracts from the early Pipe Rolls, Pedes Finium, Plea Rolls, Hundred Rolls, and other public records.

123. * Domesday Book, seu liber censualis Wilhelmi primi. . . . [Edited by Abraham Farley.] 4 vols. [London, 1783]–1816. f°.

Vol. iii., Indices, and vol. iv., Additamenta, were edited by H. Ellis, Record Com., 1816. Vol. iii. also contains Ellis's *General Introduction to Domesday Book*, a new edition of which appeared in 1833, Record Com., 2 vols, 8° (cities and boroughs, i. 190–210, ii. 417–510).

W. de Gray Birch's *Domesday Book* (London, 1887), ch. x., contains a popular account of boroughs. For better accounts, see the works of Maitland and Round (Nos. 160, 166).

124. Fœdera, conventiones, literæ, et cujuscunque generis acta pub-
lica, inter reges Angliæ et alios quosvis imperatores, reges, pontifices,
principes, vel communitates . . . [1101–1654.]   Accurante Thoma
Rymer.   [Vols. xvi.–xx. by Robert Sanderson.]   20 vols.   Londini,
1704–35.   f°.

Vols. i.–xvii., published in 1704–17, are often called the first edition.   Second
edition, by George Holmes, 17 vols., London, 1727–29; another edition, 10 vols.,
The Hague, 1739–45; new edition [1066–1383], by Adam Clarke, F. Holbrooke,
and J. Caley, 4 vols. in 7 pts., Record Com., 1816–69 (vol. iv. printed in 1830, published in 1869).   All the editions are fully described in T. D. Hardy's *Syllabus of
Documents in Rymer's Fœdera* (Rolls Series, 3 vols., 1869–85), which also contains
a good subject index of the various editions.   The Record Commissioners' edition
is much more valuable than the other editions for the study of the internal affairs
of boroughs; it contains many municipal charters, the most important of which
were granted to the following towns :

> Beverley, Hen. I., Hen. II., i. 10, 40.
> Cambridge, 8 John, 10 Edw. III., i. 94, ii. 934 (bis).
> Cinque Ports, 6 Edw. I., 38 Edw. III., i. 558, iii. 743.
> Dublin, 3 Rich. I., 2, 17 John, 13 Edw. I., i. 55, 82, 135, 661.
> Kingston-upon-Thames, 10 John, i. 102.
> Lincoln, Hen. II., Rich. I., i. 40, 52.
> London, Hen. I., 1 John, 38 Edw. III., i. 11, 76, iii. 734.
> Malmesbury, 5 Rich. II. and Athelstan, iv. 135.
> Newcastle-upon-Tyne, 14 John, 18 Hen. III., i. 108, 213.
> Norwich, 5 Rich. I., i. 63.
> Nottingham, Hen. II., i. 41.
> Oxford, 39 Hen. III., 29 Edw. III., i. 323, iii. 311.
> Portsmouth, 5 Rich. I., i. 63.
> Rye, 2 Rich. I., i. 53.
> Salisbury, 1 Rich. II., iv. 41.
> Wallingford, 51 Hen. III. and Hen. II., i. 471.
> Winchelsea, 2 Rich. I., i. 53.
> Winchester, 1 Rich. I., i. 50.
> Yarmouth (Great), 9 John, i. 100.

There are also many other documents relating to the political and commercial
history of boroughs.   See Hardy's *Syllabus*, iii., Index.

125. JONES, EDWARD.   Index to records called the originalia and
memoranda on the lord treasurer's remembrancer's side of the exchequer . . . containing all the grants of abbey lands, and other
property, granted by the crown, from the beginning of the reign of
Henry VIII. to the end of Queen Anne.   Also inrollments of charters,
grants, and patents to several religious houses, and to cities, boroughs,

towns, companies, colleges, and other public institutions from the earliest period. . . . 2 vols. London, 1793–95. f°.

126. Liber Niger Scaccarii. Edited by Thomas Hearne. Editio altera. 2 vols. London, 1771. 8°.

The Liber Niger is of little value for municipal history, but in this edition Hearne prints the following documents :

Exeter, inspeximus, 28 Edw. I., 812–15.
Kingston-upon-Thames, charters of Edw. IV., Eliz., and Charles I., 397–401.
New Malton, privileges claimed by the burgesses (1596), 796–805.
Oxford, charters of John and Hen. III., 819–20.
Wallingford, charter of Hen. II., 816–19.

127. Materials for a history of the reign of Henry VII. From original documents preserved in the Public Record Office. Edited by Rev. William Campbell. *Rolls Series.* 2 vols. London, 1873–77. 8°.

The following references are to some of the more important documents relating to boroughs :

Corfe Castle, ii. 256	Pontefract, ii. 335, 419
Hereford, i. 312–13	Waterford, ii. 149–50, 306–7
Lancaster, i. 545–6	Yarmouth (Great), i. 326–7, 330
Leicester, ii. 244–5, 369–70, 456–7	York, i. 462, ii. 552–3

128. Nonarum inquisitiones in curia scaccarii, temp. Regis Edwardi III. [Edited by George Vanderzee.] *Record Com.* [London,] 1807. f°.

Contains lists of burgesses in various towns, with the amount of tax that each burgess paid.

129. [Pipe Rolls.] The great roll of the pipe for the fifth [–20th] year of the reign of King Henry the Second, A. D. 1158 [–1174]. *Pipe Roll Society.* 16 vols. London, 1884–96. 8°.

The following rolls were printed by the Record Commission :

Magnum rotulum scaccarii, 31 Hen. I., edited by J. Hunter, 1833.
The great roll of the pipe, 1 Rich. I., by J. Hunter, 1844.
The great rolls of the pipe, 2, 3, 4 Hen. II., by J. Hunter, 1844.
Rotulus cancellarii, vel antigraphum magni rotuli pipæ, 3 John, 1833.

There are also many extracts from the Pipe Rolls in Madox's works (Nos. 158, 159).

130. *Rotuli chartarum in Turri Londinensi asservati. Accurante T. D. Hardy. Vol. i. Pars i. 1199–1216. *Record Com.* [London,] 1837. f°.

Contains the following borough charters :

Alnwick, 2 John, 87
Andover, 2, 6, 7, 15 John, 93, 148, 152, 195
Appleby, 1 John, 41
Beverley, 1 John, 53
Boston, 5 John, 118
Bridgnorth, 16 John, 205
Bridgwater, 2 John, 73
Cambridge, 2 John, 83
Cardigan, 1 John, 63
Carmarthen, 2 John, 83
Cowbridge, 2 John, 87
Derby, 6 John, 138
Dover, 2, 7 John, 83, 153
Droitwich (Wick), 17 John, 216
Dublin, 2, 17 John, 78, 210
Dungarvan, 17 John, 211 (bis)
Dunwich, 1, 7, 17 John, 51, 159, 211
Exeter, 2 John, 70
Eye, 7 John, 153
Gloucester, 1 John, 56
Grimsby, 2, 9 John, 91, 168
Hartlepool, 2 John, 86
Hastings, 7 John, 153
Helston, 2 John, 93 (bis)
Hereford, 17 John, 212
Huntingdon, 7 John, 157
Ilchester, 5 John, 130
Ipswich, 2 John, 65

Kingston-upon-Thames, 1, 10 John, 52, 182
Lancaster, 1 John, 26
Leicester, 1 John, 32 (bis)
Limerick, 17 John, 211
Lincoln, 1 John, 5, 56
London, 16 John, 207
Lynn, 5, 6 John, 118, 138
Marlborough, 6 John, 135
Newcastle-upon-Tyne, 2, 14, 17 John, 87, 190, 219
Northampton, 1 John, 45
Norwich, 1 John, 20
Nottingham, 1 John, 39
Pembroke, 2 John, 95
Pickering, 1 John, 41
Portsmouth, 2 John, 77
Preston, 1 John, 26
Romney, 7 John, 154
Rye, 7 John, 153
Sandwich, 7 John, 153
Scarborough, 1, 2 John, 40, 85, 103
Shrewsbury, 1, 6 John, 46 (bis), 142
Whitby, 1, 2 John, 14, 84
Wilton, 5 John, 125
Winchelsea, 7 John, 173
Winchester, 17 John, 217
Yarmouth (Great), 9 John, 175
York, 1, 14 John, 49, 187

131. Rotuli hundredorum temp. Hen. III. et Edw. I. in Turr' Lond' et in curia receptæ scaccarii Westm. asservati. [Edited by W. Illingworth.] *Record Com.* 2 vols. [London,] 1812–18. f°.

Contains many valuable details relating to boroughs.

132. Rotuli litterarum clausarum in Turri Londinensi asservati. Accurante Thoma Duffus Hardy. [Vol. i. 1204–1224 ; vol. ii. 1224–1227.] *Record Com.* 2 vols. London, 1833–44. f°.

133. Rotuli litterarum patentium in Turri Londinensi asservati. Accurante Thoma Duffus Hardy. Vol. i. Pars i. 1201–1216. *Record Com.* [London,] 1835. f°.

The letters patent and close are less important than the charters for town history.

134. * Rotuli parliamentorum ; ut et petitiones et placita in parliamento [1278–1503]. . . . [Printed by order of the House of Lords, March 9, 1767 ; completed about 1783.] 6 vols. [London,] n. d. f°.

An elaborate " Index to the Rolls of Parliament " was edited, by order of a committee of the House of Lords, by John Strachey, John Pridden, and Edward Upham, 1832, f°.

The following are references to some of the more important documents :

> Berwick, 22 Edw. IV., vi. 224–5.
> Cambridge, 5 Rich. II., iii. 106–9.
> Canterbury, 1 Rich. III., vi. 258–9.
> Colchester, 24 Edw. I., i. 228–36, 243–65.
> Coventry, 3 Hen. V., iv. 75.
> Exeter, 22 Edw. IV., vi. 219–20.
> Harlech, 2 Edw. III., ii. 17–18.
> Leicester, 5 Hen. VII., vi. 432.
> Liverpool, 2 Hen. V., iv. 55.
> Newcastle-upon-Tyne, 18 Edw. I., i. 26–9.
> Northampton, 5 Hen. vii., vi. 431–2.
> Plymouth, 4 Edw. IV., v. 555–61.
> Salisbury, 33 Edw. I., i. 174–6.
> Shrewsbury, 11–23 Hen. VI., iv. 476–80, v. 121–7.
> Torrington, 42 Edw. III., ii. 459–60.
> York, 4–6 Rich. II., 49 Hen. VI., iii. 96–7, 135–6, v. 455–6.

See also the titles " Artificer," " Borough," " City," " Corporation," " Gild," " Town," and the names of the various boroughs, in the index volume.

135. Rotulorum originalium in curia scaccarii abbreviatio, temporibus regum Hen. III., Ed. I., Ed. II. et Ed. III. [Edited by Henry Playford.] *Record Com.* 2 vols. [London,] 1805–10. f°.

Refers to many borough charters, etc.

136. STUBBS, WILLIAM. Select charters and other illustrations of English constitutional history from the earliest times to the reign of Edward the First. Arranged and edited by William Stubbs. Eighth edition. Oxford, 1895. 8°.

Contains extracts from Anglo-Saxon laws, Domesday customs of Chester, Lincoln, and Oxford, and the following borough charters:

Beverley, grant of Archbishop Thurstan, temp. Hen. I.

Dunwich
Hartlepool
Helston (bis) } John.
Northampton
York

Lincoln, Hen. II., Rich. I., John.
London, Wm. I., Hen. I., John.
Nottingham, Hen. II., John.
Oxford, Hen. III.
Winchester, Hen. II., Rich. I.

Contains also the customs of Newcastle-upon Tyne, temp. Hen. I., and extracts from many other public records.

1st edition, 1870.

Plea Rolls.

See Nos. 122, 2446.

137. Bracton's Note Book. A collection of cases decided in the king's courts during the reign of Henry the Third, annotated . . . seemingly by Henry of Bratton. Edited by F. W. Maitland.   3 vols. London and Cambridge, 1887.   8°.

See his index, under "Municipal Bodies."

138. Placita de quo warranto temporibus Edw. I. II. et III. in curia receptæ scaccarii Westm. asservata.   [Edited by W. Illingworth.] *Record Com.*   [London,] 1818.   f°.

Some of these documents throw much light on the constitution of boroughs. See especially the proceedings relating to the following towns:

Aberystwyth, 817–18
Appleby, 792
Bedford, 17–18
Cardigan, 820–21
Carlisle, 118, 121
Chesterfield, 138–9
Derby, 158–61

Gloucester, 241
Helston, 108–9
Ilchester, 701
Lancaster, 384–5
Liverpool, 381
London, 445–74
Newcastle-upon-Tyne, 601

Nottingham, 618–23
Preston, 385
Retford, 629–31
Shrewsbury, 708
Wigan, 371–2
Wycombe, 85

139. Placitorum in domo capitulari Westmonasteriensi asservatorum abbreviatio . . . [Rich. I.—Edw. II. Edited by W. Illingworth.] *Record Com.*   [London,] 1811.   f°.

Contains many valuable notices relating to boroughs. See the index rerum, 517–85.

140. Select cases from the coroners' rolls, A. D. 1265–1413, with a brief account of the history of the office of coroner. Edited by Charles Gross. *Selden Society.* London, 1896. 4°.

| London, 127–30 | Oxford, 87–91 | Scarborough, 126–7 |
| Northampton, 79–87 | Salisbury, 106–8 | York, 112–13, 119–20 |

141. Select pleas of the crown, 1200–1225. Edited by F. W. Maitland. *Selden Society.* London, 1888. 4°.

For municipal bodies, see his index, p. 148.

142. [Year Books.] Les reports des cases argue et adjudge . . . [Edw. II.—27 Hen. VIII.] 11 pts. London, 1678–80. f°.

Several Year Books of the reigns of Edw. I. and Edw. III., edited and translated by A. J. Horwood and L. O. Pike, have been published in the Rolls Series, 12 vols., 1863–96.

Wales.

143. B[ANKS], R. W. On the early charters to towns in South Wales. *Cambrian Archæol. Assoc.*, Archæologia Cambrensis, Fourth Series, ix. 81–101. London, 1878. 8°.

See No. 145.

144. —— On the Welsh records in the time of the Black Prince. By R. W. B. *Cambrian Archæol. Assoc.*, Archæologia Cambrensis, Fourth Series, iv. 157–88. London, 1873. 8°.

Throws light upon the status of Welsh boroughs in the 14th century.

145. * Charters referred to in the paper of Mr. Banks on the early charters to towns in South Wales [No. 143]. *Cambrian Archæol. Assoc.*, Archæologia Cambrensis, Fourth Series, x., Supplement of Original Documents, pp. xxvi.–xlvi. London, 1879. 8°.

Contains a petition of Carmarthen to Parliament, 9 Edw. II., and the charters of the following towns:

> Aberystwyth, 6 Edw. I.
> Builth, 7 Rich. II.
> Carmarthen, 2 John — 10 Rich. II.
> Haverfordwest, 5 Edw. III., 9—10 Rich. II.
> Laugharne, undated charter of Guido de Brion.
> Montgomery, 11 Hen. III.
> St. Clears, 16 Rich. II.

146. Registrum vulgariter nuncupatum "The record of Caernarvon;" e codice MS^to Harleiano 696 descriptum. [Edited by Sir Henry Ellis.] *Record Com.* [London,] 1838. f°.

This valuable work contains quo warranto proceedings, temp. Edw. III., reciting town charters granted by Edw. I. and Edw. II. to the following boroughs:

Bala, 172–7

Beaumaris, 158–61, 238

Carnarvon, 184–7

Conway, 161–7

Crukyn, 195–8

Harlech, 191–5

Newborough, 177–81, 298

Consuetudines Herefordiæ, 22 Edw. III., 130.

147. TAYLOR, HENRY. The first Welsh municipal charters. *Cambrian Archæol. Assoc.*, Archæologia Cambrensis, Fifth Series, ix. 102–119. London, 1892. 8°.

Contains the royal charter granted to Flint, 12 Edw. I., with a translation.

148. Welsh records: calendar of recognizance rolls of the palatinate of Chester, 1139–1830. [Annual reports of the deputy keeper of the public records, 36th Report, app. ii.; 37th Report, app. ii.; 39th Report, app. i. *Parl. Papers*, 1875, vol. xli.; 1876, vol. xxxix.; 1878, vol. xlv. London, 1875–78. 8°.]

Contains references to charters, letters patent, deeds, etc., relating to boroughs of Wales and Cheshire.

b. MODERN WRITERS.

149. ASHLEY, W. J. An introduction to English economic history and theory. 2 vols. London and New York, 1888–93. 8°.

Bk. ii. ch. i. The supremacy of the towns from the 14th to the 16th centuries. Valuable.

3rd edition of vol. i., 1894.

150. BÉCHARD, FERDINAND. Droit municipal au moyen âge. 2 vols. Paris, 1861–62. 8°.

For England, see i. 392–411, etc.

His chief authorities are Blackstone and Hallam.

151. COLBY, CHARLES W. The growth of oligarchy in English towns. *English Hist. Review*, v. 633–53. London, 1890. 8°.

Contends that the drift of later medieval development was from a democratic to an aristocratic régime.

152. GREEN, J. R. History of the English people. 4 vols. London, 1877–80. 8°.

Medieval boroughs, i. 206-25, 355-8.

153. * GREEN, MRS. J. R. Town life in the fifteenth century. 2 vols. London and New York, 1894. 8°.

Deals also with medieval borough history since 1066. Her view that the burgesses were a ruling council before the 14th century, while the "communitas" formed a second corporate body, seems to be untenable.

154. GROSS, CHARLES. The affiliation of mediæval boroughs. Reprinted from The Antiquary [vol. xi.] London, [1885.] 4°.

A revised edition in his *Gild Merchant*, i. app. E. (No. 541.)

155. HALLAM, HENRY. View of the state of Europe during the Middle Ages. Tenth edition. 3 vols. London, 1853. 8°.

English towns, iii. 19-37, 219-31.

156. JESSOPP, AUGUSTUS. Studies by a recluse in cloister, town, and country. London, 1893. 8°.

Ch. iv. The origin and growth of English towns.

157. LAW, ALICE. The English nouveaux riches in the fourteenth century. *Royal Hist. Soc.*, Transactions, New Series, ix. 49–73. London, 1895. 8°.

158. * MADOX, THOMAS. Firma burgi, or an historical essay concerning the cities, towns, and buroughs of England, taken from records. London, 1726. f°.

Contains many extracts from the Pipe Rolls and other public records. The most important documents belong mainly to the 13th and 14th centuries and relate to the following towns :

Andover	Exeter	Lyme Regis	Plympton
Appleby	Gloucester	Maldon	Salisbury
Bala	Hull	Oswestry	Southampton
Bedford	Kingston-upon-Thames	Overton	Southwold
Colchester	London	Oxford	York
Dunwich			

See his index.

159. —— The history and antiquities of the exchequer of the kings of England . . . [from 1066 to 1327.] Second edition. With a full and compleat index. 2 vols. London, 1769. 4°.

Contains many valuable extracts from the public records, relating to boroughs. 1st edition, 1 vol., 1711, f°.

160. *MAITLAND, F. W. Domesday Book and beyond. Three essays in the early history of England. Cambridge, 1897. 8°.

The boroughs, 172–219.
The best account of the boroughs just after the Norman conquest.

161. MORGAN, J. F. England under the Norman occupation. London, etc., 1858. 8°.

Ch. vi. Boroughs and cities.

162. NEILSON, GEORGE. Trial by combat. London and Glasgow, 1890. 8°.

Ch. xx. deals with town charters.

163. NORGATE, KATE. England under the Angevin kings [to 1206.] 2 vols. London and New York, 1887. 8°.

Municipal history, ii. 468–86.

164. *POLLOCK, F., and MAITLAND, F. W. The history of English law before the time of Edward I. 2 vols. Cambridge, 1895. 8°.

The borough, i. 625–678.

165. ROGERS, J. E. T. Six centuries of work and wages. The history of English labour. 2 vols. London, 1884. 8°.

Town life, i. 102–127. See also ii. 310, 339.

166. ROUND, J. H. Danegeld and the finance of Domesday. [Pp. 77–142 of Domesday studies, being the papers read at the meetings of the Domesday Commemoration, 1886. . . . Edited by P. E. Dove. Vol. i. London, 1888. 4°.]

Boroughs in Domesday, 118–42.

167. SMITH, ADAM. An inquiry into the nature and causes of the wealth of nations. Edited by J. E. T. Rogers. 2 vols. Oxford, 1869. 8°.

Bk. iii. chs. iii.–iv. Cities and towns.

168. TYRRELL, JAMES. The general history of England. . . . 3 vols. London, 1697–1704. 4°.

Vol. iii. pt. ii. app. 139–200 contains a long answer to Brady's *Treatise* (No. 78).

169. WRIGHT, THOMAS. Remarks on the municipal privileges and legislation in the Middle Ages, as illustrated from the archives of Winchester and Southampton. *Brit. Archæol Assoc.*, Transactions at Winchester, 16–27. London, 1846. 8°.

§ 6. MODERN TIMES: 1500–1800.

a. General Authorities, Nos. 170–177.
b. Charles II. and James II.: Seizure of Charters, Nos. 178–187.
c. Law Reports, Nos. 188–201.

The principal sources for the study of this period are the Journals of the House of Commons (No. 287), the Law Reports (§ 6 *c*), the Reports of the Historical MSS. Commission and of the Municipal Corporations Commission (Nos. 60, 62), and the records of particular towns, mentioned below in Part II. There is no good general history of municipal development in this period. The best account is given by Merewether and Stephens (No. 79); they are more trustworthy here than in the earlier portions of their treatise.

See also Nos. 124–126, 148, 1271, and § 8 *e*, *f*.

a. GENERAL AUTHORITIES.

170. Calendar of state papers. Domestic Series [1547–71, 1689–90]. . . . *Rolls Series.* 59 vols. London, 1856–95. 8°.

The period Edw. VI.–James I. was edited by Robert Lemon and M. A. E. Green; the reign of Charles I., by J. Bruce and W. D. Hamilton; the Commonwealth and Charles II., by M. A. E. Green and F. H. B. Daniell; William & Mary, by W. J. Hardy.

171. HALLAM, HENRY. The constitutional history of England from the accession of Henry VII. to the death of George II. Eighth edition. 3 vols. London, 1855. 8°.

See i. 45–6, 264–8, ii. 453–5, iii. 36–47, 74–6.

172. Letters and papers, foreign and domestic, of the reign of Henry VIII. Preserved in the Public Record Office, the British Museum, and elsewhere in England. Arranged and catalogued by J. S. Brewer. [Vols. v.–xv., by James Gairdner.] *Rolls Series.* 15 vols. London, 1862–96. 8°.

173. Proceedings and ordinances of the Privy Council of England [1386–1542.] Edited by Harris Nicolas. *Record Com.* 7 vols. [London,] 1834–37. 8°.

174. —— Acts of the Privy Council of England. New Series. [1542–87.] Edited by J. R. Dasent. *Rolls Series.* 14 vols. London, 1890–97. 8°.

175. Reflections on the constitution of incorporated boroughs, and the powers vested in the officers or persons who manage their concerns. By Ereunetes. *Gentleman's Magazine,* lvii. 9–10, 105–7, 953–4. London, 1787. 8°.

176. ROBERTS, GEORGE. The social history of the people of the southern counties of England in past centuries; illustrated in regard to their habits, municipal bye-laws, civil progress. . . . London, 1856. 8°.

> The arming of towns, 100–123.
> Importance of the office of early mayors, 141–3.
> Orders regarding the gaol and the mainprize of Dorchester, 171–7.
> Extracts from town accounts of King's Lyme, 319–24.
> Payment of parliamentary representatives of Lyme, 468–80
> The decay of old mercantile coast towns, 540–59.
>
> This work deals mainly with the 16th and 17th centuries.

177. True friends (The) to corporations vindicated. In answer to a letter concerning the disabling clauses lately offer'd to the House of Commons for regulating corporations. Printed in the year 1690. [A Collection of State Tracts, published . . . during the reign of King William III., i. 705–12. 3 vols. London, 1705–7. 4°.]

b. **CHARLES II. AND JAMES II.: SEIZURE OF CHARTERS.**

See Nos. 189, 195, 1759, 2024–2059, 2462, 2513.

178. BURNET, GILBERT. History of his own time. . . . Second edition. 6 vols. Oxford, 1833. 8°.

> The surrender of town charters and the London quo warranto case, 1682, ii. 332–8.

179. COOKE, G. W. The history of party; from the rise of the Whig and Tory factions in the reign of Charles II., to the passing of the Reform Bill. 3 vols. London, 1836–37. 8°.

> Seizure of town charters, 1681–84, i. 223–35.

180. HUNT, THOMAS. A defence of the charter and municipal rights of the city of London and the rights of other municipalities and towns of England. London, [1682.] 4°. pp. 46.

See No. 2039.

181. NORTH, ROGER. Examen : or an enquiry into the credit and veracity of a pretended complete history ; shewing the perverse and wicked design of it. . . . All tending to vindicate the honour of the late king, Charles the Second, and his happy reign, from the intended aspersions of that foul pen. London, 1740. 4°.

The seizure of the charters of London and other corporations, 595–646; see also pp. 90–94 (London).

182. Power (The) of the kings of England to examine the charters of particular corporations and companies, exemplified by the statutes and laws of this realm. London, 1684. f°.

183. Proceedings at the court at Whitehall, with reference to charters, patents, or grants made to several cities, boroughs, and towns corporate. London, 1688. f°.

A single sheet.

184. † Proclamation for restoring corporations to their ancient charters, liberties, rights, and franchises, by King James II. London, 1688. f°.

For this proclamation, see also *London Gazette*, No. 2391, and "A Collection of State Tracts, published . . . during the reign of King William III." (3 vols., 1705-7), i. 49–50. See also No. 660.

185. [RALPH, JAMES.] The history of England during the reigns of K. William, Q. Anne, and K. George I. . . . 2 vols. London, 1744–46. f°.

Proceedings of Charles II. against London and other corporations, i. 682-99, 712-20.

186. † Right (The) of cities and towns to choose their own officers, temp. Jacobi. 4°.

187. Seasonable reflections on dissolving corporations, in the late two reigns, by surrendering of and giving judgments against charters, particularly against that of the city of London. . . . London, 1689. f°.

c. LAW REPORTS.

The following list includes only the most valuable cases in some of the more important reports. Many other cases are cited by Merewether and Stephens (No. 79). See also No. 910.

For Irish and Scotch reports, see No. 746 and § 13 *e.*

For election cases, see § 8 *e.*

188.   Abridgment (An) of the modern determinations in the courts of law and equity : being a supplement to Viner's Abridgment. . . . 6 vols.   London, 1799–1806.   8°.

Many interesting cases are cited under "Corporations," ii. 339–57.

189.   BROWN, JOSIAH.   Reports of cases, upon appeals and writs of error, determined in the high court of Parliament.   Second edition, by T. E. Tomlins.   8 vols.   London, 1803.   8°.

John Prowse *v.* Samuel Foot, 1725 (office of alderman of Truro), ii. 289–94.

Peter Pender *v.* Rex, 1725 (office of mayor of Penryn), ii. 294–8.

Hugh Powell *v.* Rex, 1728 (election of burgesses of Brecknock), ii. 298–303.

Richard Tucker *v.* Rex, 1742 (election of mayor of Weymouth), ii. 304–11.

Rex *v.* John Ponsonby and others, 1758 (non-resident burgesses of Newtown, Co. Down), ii. 311–21.

Henry Pippard *v.* the Mayor of Drogheda, 1759 (seizure of town charters by James II., etc.), ii. 321–8.

John Hoblyn and others *v.* Rex, 1772 (election of freemen of Helston), ii. 329–36.

Rex *v.* Thomas Amery, 1790 (charter of Chester), ii. 336–69.

190.   BURROW, JAMES.   Reports of cases argued and adjudged in the court of King's Bench [1756–72]. . . . Fourth edition.   5 vols. London, 1790.   8°.

Green *v.* the Mayor of Durham, 30 Geo. II. (admission into the city companies), i. 127–33.

Rex *v.* Richardson, 31 Geo. II. (election of portmen of Ipswich), i. 517–41.

Rex *v.* Cowle, 32 & 33 Geo. II. (abstract of charters of Berwick), ii. 834–64.

Rex *v.* Spencer, etc., 6–8 Geo. III. (select body of Maidstone), iii. 1827–40, iv. 2204–8.

Hesketh *v.* Braddock, 6 Geo. III. (freemen's monopoly of trade in Chester), iii. 1847–59.

Winchelsea causes, 7 Geo. III. (qualifications of a freeman, etc.), iv. 1962–5, 2022–5, 2120–5.

Rex *v.* Corporation of Wells, 7 Geo. III. (removal of a recorder), iv. 1999–2008.

Rex *v.* the Mayor, etc., of Cambridge, 7 Geo. III. (election of mayor), iv. 2008–11.

Mayor of Norwich *v.* Berry, 7 Geo. III. (refusal to accept office of sheriff), iv. 2109–16.

Rex *v.* Charles Malden, etc., 8 Geo. III. (election of bailiff and aldermen of Maldon), iv. 2130–2, 2241–3.

Rex *v.* the Mayor and the Town Clerk of Northampton, 9 Geo. III. (their authority to admit freemen), iv. 2260–7.

Rex *v.* Abraham Head and others, 10 Geo. III. (their qualifications as freemen of Helston), iv. 2515–25.

Rex *v.* Grimes, 10 Geo. III. (his election as chief burgess of Yarmouth, Isle of Wight), v. 2598–2602.

Rex *v.* May and others, 11 Geo. III. (election irregularities in Saltash), v. 2681–3.

191. COKE, EDWARD. The reports of Sir Edward Coke, in thirteen parts. New edition, by J. H. Thomas and J. F. Fraser. 6 vols. London, 1826. 8°.

The case of corporations, Mich. 40 & 41 Eliz., ii. 476–7.

The case of the Mayor and Burgesses of Lynn Regis, concerning misnomer of corporations, 10 Jac. I., v. 467–78.

The case of the tailors, etc., of Ipswich, 12 Jac. I. (their trade monopoly), vi. 101–4.

Ireland and free borough, 12 Jac. I. (election of burgesses in Dungannon), vi. 366–7.

192. DOUGLAS, SYLVESTER. Reports of cases . . . in the court of King's Bench [19–25 Geo. III.] . . . 4 vols. London, 1790–1831. 8°.

The King *v.* the Mayor, etc., of Lyme Regis, 19 Geo. III. (removal of capital burgesses), i. 79–85, 149–59, 177–82.

The King *v.* Tunwell, Mayor of Cambridge, 23 Geo. III. (election of mayor), iii. 207–9.

Vols. i.–ii. are 3rd edition, 1790.

193. DURNFORD, C., and EAST, E. H. Term reports in the court of King's Bench [26–40 Geo. III.] . . . New edition. 8 vols. London, 1794–1802. 8°.

Kirk *v.* Nowill and Butler, 1786 (monopoly of cutlers of Sheffield), i. 118–25.

The King *v.* Amery, 1788 (the charter of Chester), ii. 515–69.

Newling *v.* Francis, 1789 (election of mayor of Cambridge), iii. 189–99.

The King *v.* Pasmore, 1789 (office of mayor of Helston ; doctrine of incorporation), iii. 199–250.

The King *v.* Bellringer, 1792 (powers of the common council of Bodmin), iv. 810–24.

The King *v.* Miller, 1795 (election of mayor of Northampton), vi. 268–81.

The King *v.* the Coopers' Company of Newcastle-upon-Tyne, 1798 (apprentices). vii. 543–9.

194. HARGRAVE, FRANCIS. Juridical arguments and collections. 2 vols. London, 1797-99. 4°.

The Corporation of Liverpool *v.* the Corporation of London, 1796, i. 471-510.
King's Lynn *v.* the City of London, 1788, i. app. v.

Both cases relate to the claim of freemen of London to be exempt from toll throughout England.

195. HOWELL, T. B. and T. J. Complete collection of state trials. . . . 34 vols. London, 1809-28. 8°.

The King *v.* the City of London, 1681-83 (full account of the quo warranto proceedings), viii. 1039-1358; cf. ix. 187-298.

Trial of Wm. Sacheverell and others, 1684 (the surrender of the charter of Nottingham), x. 29-104.

Ashby *v.* White and others of Aylesbury, 1704-5 (right of voting for M. P.'s), xiv. 695-888.

The King *v.* Gibbon, 1734 (freemen of Romney; extracts from town records), xvii. 801-44.

Henry Moore *v.* the Port of Hastings, 1736 (throws light on the old town constitution), xvii. 845-924.

196. PETERSDORFF, CHARLES. A practical and elementary abridgment of the cases argued and determined in the courts of King's Bench, Common Pleas, Exchequer, and at nisi prius, and of the rules of court [1660 to 4 Geo. IV.] . . . 15 vols. London, 1825-30. 8°.

Under the title "Corporation" (vi. 601-783) there are many interesting cases relating to boroughs.

197. RAYMOND, ROBERT. Reports of cases . . . in the courts of King's Bench and Common Pleas [1694-1732]. . . . Fourth edition, by John Bayley. [Vol. iii. Entries of pleadings to the cases comprehended in the two former volumes. By George Wilson.] 3 vols. London, 1790. 8°.

Mayor of Winchester *v.* Wilks, 4 Anne (the gild merchant), ii. 1129-35.

John Stevenson, etc. *v.* Wm. Nevinson, 10 Geo. I. (election of common council of Appleby), ii. 1353-60.

The King *v.* the Mayor, etc. of Doncaster, 3 Geo. II. (the office of capital burgess), ii. 1564-6.

The case of Banbury, 13 Wm. III., iii. 1.

The case of Wells, 6 Wm. & Mary, iii. 166.

The case of Lincoln, 9 Wm. III., iii. 203.

198. RUMSEY, JOHN. A report of the case of the King *v.* Westwood, with a preliminary digest of the authorities on the points of corporation law therein discussed and referred to. London, 1830. 8°.

Valuable for the history of Wycombe.

199. SALKELD, WILLIAM. Reports of cases adjudged in the court of King's Bench [1 Wm. & Mary — 10 Anne]. . . . Sixth edition, by W. D. Evans. 3 vols. London, 1795. 8°.

Butler *v.* Palmer, 11 Wm. III. (election of mayor of Dartmouth), i. 190.

200. STRANGE, JOHN. Reports of adjudged cases in the courts of Chancery, King's Bench, Common Pleas, and Exchequer [2 Geo. I. — 21 Geo. II.] . . . Third edition, by M. Nolan. 2 vols. London, 1795. 8°.

Rex *v.* Philips, 6 Geo. I. (the mayoralty of Bodmin), i. 394–9.

201. TREMAINE, JOHN. Placita coronæ : or pleas of the crown in matters criminal and civil . . . digested and revised by the late Mr. John Rice. London, 1723. f°.

Bath, 541–4	Norwich, 517–23	Saltash, 228–30, 454–5
Bristol, 230–3	Nottingham, 465–6	Torrington, 628–30
Carlisle, 523–35	Oxford, 456–61	Wincanton, 217–8
Chester, 516–7	Reading, 544–55	Winchelsea, 556–8
London, passim	Rye, 453–4	

All these cases were tried during Charles II.'s reign.

§ 7. NINETEENTH CENTURY: MUNICIPAL REFORM.

a. General, Nos. 201a–232.
b. Municipal Reform, 1835, Nos. 233–259.
c. The Act of 1882, Nos. 260–266.
d. The Act of 1888 : County Councils, Nos. 267–284a.

The most valuable parliamentary papers for the study of this period are the various Reports on Municipal Corporations (Nos. 59–61). The important legislative changes of 1835, 1882, and 1888 are recorded in the Public General Statutes (Nos. 68–69). The First Schedule of the Act of 1882 (45 & 46 Vict. c. 50) enumerates all the older acts relating to municipal corporations ; see also *Index of Statutes* (No. 75), under "Boroughs." The discussions in Parliament concerning these legislative changes will be found in Hansard's *Debates*, and more briefly in the *Annual Register*.

There is no good general history of municipal development during this century. May and Walpole (Nos. 246, 258) give a good short account of the reform of 1835. Vine (No. 228) gives a detailed but dry survey of municipal affairs for the years 1835–79. Some of the works mentioned in § 8 *f* also throw much light on the government of boroughs in the first decades of this century. One of the best accounts of the present condition of municipal institutions is furnished by Shaw (No. 225). The French and Italian books mentioned in § 7 *a* contain some interesting comparisons between English and continental municipalities.

Many works dealing with the details of municipal administration are mentioned in No. 2a.

a. GENERAL.

201a. ARMINJON, PIERRE. L'administration locale de l'Angleterre. Paris, 1895. 8°.

Ch. v. Les bourgs.
Ch. viii. La police des bourgs.
Ch. xiv. La métropole.

202. BERNARDO, DOMENICO DI. L'amministrazione locale in Inghilterra, Scozia ed Irlanda. Palermo, 1877. 8°.

203. CAREY, P. S. Borough court rules, made, allowed, and confirmed, in pursuance of the municipal corporation acts, and of the act for regulating the proceedings of the borough courts of England and Wales, 2 & 3 Vict. c. 27. With an appendix of statutes and statutory rules. London, 1841. 8°.

204. CHALMERS, M. D. [E. S.] Local government. [English Citizen Series.] London, 1883. 8°.

Ch. v. contains a good short account of the existing machinery of borough government.

205. COLAJANNI, NAPOLEONE. Le istituzioni municipali. Cenni ed asservazioni. Piazza Armerina, 1883. 8°.

England in the 19th century, 45–75.

206. † Defects in the law for municipalities and a plea for amendment. . . . London, 1854. 8°.

207. DILKE, C. W. [Speeches in the House of Commons on unreformed municipal corporations, 1875–76.] *Hansard's Debates*, ccxxiv. 1009–31 ; ccxxvii. 1126–59. London, 1875–76. 8°.

208. DOLMAN, FRED. Municipalities at work. The municipal policy of six great towns and its influence on their social welfare.

[Social Questions of To-day. Edited by H. de B. Gibbins.] London, 1895. 12°.

Deals with Birmingham, Bradford, Glasgow, Leeds, Liverpool, Manchester.

208a. †DONALD, ROBERT. The municipal year book of the United Kingdom. London, 1897. 8°.

209. ESCOTT, T. H. S. England : its people, polity, and pursuits. New and revised edition. London, 1885. 8°.

Ch. v. Municipal government.
A good account.
1st edition, 2 vols., [1879.]

210. FERRON, HENRI DE. Institutions municipales et provinciales comparées. Organisation locale en France et dans les autres pays de l'Europe ; comparaison ; influence des institutions locales sur les qualités politiques d'un peuple et sur le gouvernement parlementaire ; réformes. Paris, 1884. 8°.

Pt. ii. contains a short account of English municipal institutions and a comparison of the municipalities of England with those of France.

211. FISCO, É., et VAN DER STRAETEN, J. Institutions et taxes locales du Royaume-Uni de la Grande-Bretagne et d'Irlande. Deuxième édition. Paris, Bruxelles, et Leipzig, 1863. 8°.

A detailed account of municipal government, especially of the fiscal organization of towns.

212. FLETCHER, JOSEPH. Statistics of the municipal institutions of the English towns. *Statistical Society of London*, Journal, v. 97–168. London, 1842. 8°.

Also separately printed. A valuable essay.

213. HEREFORD, EDWARD. On the principles and practice of municipal institutions in England. *Manchester Statistical Society*, Transactions, 1865, pp. 41–58. Manchester, 1865. 8°.

Points out certain evils of the municipal system.

214. HOLDSWORTH, W. A. The municipal corporations directory, 1866. . . . London, 1866. 8°.

Ch. i. of the preliminary essay on municipal laws (pp. 1–80) is a brief historical sketch of municipal corporations, based on Merewether and Stephens (No. 79). The remaining chapters are devoted to municipal legislation in the present century.

215. JENKS, EDWARD. An outline of English local government. London, 1894. 8°.

Chs. xii.–xiii. The borough.

216. LEROY–BEAULIEU, PAUL. L'administration locale en France et en Angleterre. Ouvrage couronné par l'Académie des Sciences Morales et Politiques. Paris, [1872.] 8°.

Du régime municipal en France et en Angleterre, 73–124.

217. Local government and taxation. Edited by J. W. Probyn. *Cobden Club Essays.* London, etc., 1875. 8°.

Local government in England, by G. C. Brodrick, 1–96.
Local government and taxation in Scotland, by A. McNeel-Caird, 97–172.
Local government and taxation in Ireland, by W. N. Hancock, 173–232.

218. Local government and taxation in the United Kingdom. A series of essays published under the sanction of the Cobden Club. Edited by J. W. Probyn. *Cobden Club Essays.* London, 1882. 8°.

The essays of interest to us are : —
Local government in England, by G. C. Brodrick, 5–88.
London government, and how to reform it, by J. F. B. Firth, 147–270.
Municipal boroughs and urban districts, by J. T. Bunce, 271–318.
Local government and taxation in Ireland, by R. O'Shaughnessy, 319–84.
Local government and taxation in Scotland, by W. Macdonald, 385–464.

219. MANFRIN, PIETRO. Il sistéma municipale inglese e la legge comunale italiana. Studi comparativi. 2 vols. Firenze,1869–71. 8°.

Vol. i.　La costituzione municipale inglese.
Vol. ii.　La legge comunale italiana.

220. PICTON, J. A. Self-government in towns. *Contemporary Review*, xxxiv. 678–99. London, 1879. 8°.

Considers the condition of boroughs since 1835.

221. RATHBONE, WILLIAM. Local government and taxation. A few suggestions for organization and improvement. Liverpool and London, [1875.] 8°. pp. 36.

See also his articles on the same subject in the *Nineteenth Century*, 1883, xiii. 297–313, 509–28.

222. †ROBERTON, JOHN. Suggestions for the improvement of municipal government in . . . towns. *Manchester Statistical Society*, Transactions. Manchester, 1854. 8°.

223. SEAGER, J. R.   The Municipal Elections Act, 1884.   With introduction and full index.   London, [1884.]   8°.

224. SHAW, ALBERT.   Municipal government in Great Britain. *Political Science Quarterly*, iv. 197–229.   New York, 1889.   8°.

225. —— Municipal government in Great Britain.   New York, 1895.   8°.

A good account of the present working of municipal institutions, especially in Birmingham, Glasgow, London, and Manchester.

226. VALFRAMBERT, CHARLES.   La commune en Angleterre.   Régime municipal et institutions locales de l'Angleterre, de l'Écosse, et de l'Irlande.   Paris, 1873.   8°.

New edition, 1882.

227. VAUTHIER, MAURICE.   Le gouvernement local de l'Angleterre. Paris, 1895.   8°.

Ch. iv.   Le bourg.
Ch. x.   La métropole.

228. VINE, J. R. SOMERS.   English municipal institutions ; their growth and development from 1835 to 1879, statistically illustrated. London, 1879.   8°.

229. —— The municipal corporations' companion, diary, directory, and year book of statistics. . . . London, [1877.]   8°.

Issued annually.   Since 1890 combined with " The county companion."   Present title, "The county councils, municipal corporations, urban district, rural district, and parish councils companion . . . for 1896."   London, [1896.]   8°.
Gives a brief sketch of the municipal history of each corporation, lists of officers for the current year, etc.

230. †WRIGHT, R. S.   Local government : Memorandum, No. 1, General view ; Memorandum, No. 2, Law, with references.   Privately printed.   2 pts.   [London,] 1877.   f°.

Memoranda containing a review of the existing organization of local government prepared by R. S. Wright under the supervision of William Rathbone and Samuel Whitbread.   See the *Contemporary Review*, xxxiv. 694.

231. WRIGHT, R. S., and HOBHOUSE, HENRY.   An outline of local government and local taxation in England and Wales (excluding the metropolis), together with some considerations for amendment. . . . London, 1884. 8°.

"Based on two memoranda on local government, written by Mr. Wright in the year 1877, which were privately circulated among members of Parliament and others interested in the subject.   These memoranda have now been revised, amalgamated, brought down to date, and to some extent, rearranged, by Mr. Hobhouse."
Supplement, 1888.
Second edition, by H. Hobhouse and E. L. Fanshawe, 1894.

232. WTOROFF, NICHOLAS.   A comparative sketch of the municipal institutions in France, Belgium, Italy, Prussia, and Austria, with the addition of an outline of local self-government in England.   St. Petersburg, 1864. 8°.

This is a translation of the Russian title.

b. MUNICIPAL REFORM, 1835.

The Muncipal Corporations Act (England and Wales), 5 & 6 Wm. IV. c. 76.
For the report on which this act was based, see No. 60.

233. Acts of Parliament respecting the regulation of municipal corporations in England and Wales from 5 & 6 Will. IV. (1835) to 11 & 12 Vict. (1848) inclusive.   [London, 1851.]   8°.

234. ARCHBOLD, J. F.   The Municipal Corporations Act (5 & 6 Wm. IV. c. 76), compared with and corrected by the roll.   With a practical introduction, notes. . . . London, 1836.   12°.

235. Black Book (The) ; or corruption unmasked.   Being an account of places, pensions, and sinecures . . . the whole forming a complete exposition of the cost, influence, patronage, and corruption of the borough government.   [By John Wade.]   2 vols.   London, 1820–23.   8°.

Vol. ii. " Supplement to the Black Book; or corruption unmasked !! " London, 1823.
New edition : "The Black Book : an exposition of abuses in church and state . . . municipal corporations," etc.   London, 1835.
Other editions appeared in 1831 and 1832 under the title, " The Extraordinary Black Book " : see No. 395.

236. † BURRIDGE, J. D. A concise and impartial essay on the British constitution . . . with remarks on the close borough system. . . . London, 1819. 8°.

237. CHAPMAN, H. S. The act for the regulation of municipal corporations in England and Wales, 6 William IV. cap. lxxvi. With a complete index and notes. . . . London, 1835. 12°.

238. COCKBURN, A. J. E. The corporations of England and Wales : containing a succinct account of the constitution, privileges, powers, revenues, and expenditures of each corporation ; together with details shewing the practical working of the corporate system in each borough or city, and any defects or abuses which may have been found to exist. The whole collected and abridged from the reports of the commissioners for inquiring into municipal corporations. Vol. i. London, 1835. 8°.

See No. 60.

239. COOPER, CHARLES. The act for the regulation of municipal corporations in England and Wales (5 & 6 Wm. IV. c. 76). With an introduction and notes. London, 1835. 12°.

240. CRUDEN, R. P. Observations upon the municipal bodies in cities and towns, incorporated by royal charters, within England and Wales. London, 1826. 8°. pp. 72.

Deals especially with trade regulations and the qualifications for admission to the freedom of boroughs. A plea for reform.

241. ELWORTHY, J. E. Lex Angliæ non patitur absurdum. A letter to the right hon. George Canning, on usurpations in boroughs. London, 1825. 8°.

242. GLOVER, WILLIAM. A practical treatise on the law of municipal corporations, adapted to the recent reforms in the corporate bodies of England, Wales, and Scotland ; with the statutes relating to municipal corporations, mandamus, and quo warranto. To which is prefixed an historical summary of the corporate system of Great Britain and Ireland. London, 1836. 8°.

Historical summary, pp. vii.–lxx.

243. GUPPY, ROBERT. A familiar abridgment of the Municipal Corporation Act, 5 & 6 Will. IV. c. 76 ; intended as a guide to citi-

zens and burgesses; with a table of periods, notes, and a copious
index. London, 1835. 12°.

244. McCarthy, Justin. The epoch of reform, 1830–50. [Epochs
of Modern History.] London, 1882. 8°.

Ch. ix. Poor law and municipal reform. See also pp. 25–30.

245. Martineau, Harriet. The history of England during the
thirty years' peace, 1816–1846. 2 vols. London, 1849–50. 8°.

Municipal reform, ii. 234–45.

246. May, T. E. The constitutional history of England since the
accession of George the Third, 1760–1860. Seventh edition. 3
vols. London, 1882. 8°.

Ch. xv. Municipal reform, 1835-40.
1st edition, 2 vols., 1861.

247. Molesworth, W. N. The history of England from the year
1830. New edition. 3 vols. London, 1874. 8°.

Vol. i. ch. vi. Municipal reform.
1st edition, 1871–73.

248. On the abuses of civil incorporations; in a letter to Hudson
Gurney, Esq., M. P. London, 1830. 8°.

249. Palgrave, Francis. Observations on the principles to be
adopted in the establishment of new municipal corporations, together
with the heads of a bill for their future regulation and government.
London, 1832. 8°.

250. —— Corporate reform. Observations on the principles to
be adopted in the establishment of new municipalities, the reform of
ancient corporations, and the cheap administration of justice; addressed to H. Hallam. . . . London, 1833. 8°.

This is a new edition of No. 249.

251. R., J. A. Municipal corporation reform. *Westminster Review*, xxx. 48–76. London, 1835. 8°.

252. Rawlinson, Christopher. The Municipal Corporation Act,
5 & 6 Will. IV. c. 76, and the acts since passed for amending the
same; with notes and references to the cases thereon; also an appendix containing the principal statutes. . . . London, 1842. 12°.

See No. 264.

253. Report from select committee on freemen of cities and boroughs; with the minutes of evidence, appendix, and index. *Parl. Papers*, 1840, vol. xi. [London,] 1840. f °.

This committee was appointed to inquire into the operation of the Act of 1835 on the privileges and property of freemen in England and Wales.

254. SEWELL, R. C. The Municipal Corporation Act, 5 & 6 Will. IV. c. 76. With legal and explanatory notes. . . . London, 1835. 12°.

The Introduction (pp. ix.–xxviii.) is "a sketch of the original constitution of municipal corporations," based mainly upon Merewether and Stephens (No. 79).

255. † STEPHENS, A. J. A letter, addressed to his grace the Duke of Richmond upon corporate reform, with observations upon the constitutional rights of the permanent and responsible inhabitants of cities and boroughs to exercise the municipal and parliamentary franchises. London, 1835. 8°.

256. ——— A treatise on the Corporation Act, 5 & 6 Will. iv. c. 76; with practical directions to town clerks and overseers. . . . London, 1835. 12°.

257. STEPHENSON, H. F. A letter to the right hon. James Abercrombie, M. P., chairman of the committee on corporations. London, 1833. 8°. pp. 79.

A general discussion of municipal corporations, past and present. Deals particularly with the trade restrictions imposed upon non-freemen, especially in London. A plea for reform.

258. WALPOLE, SPENCER. A history of England from the conclusion of the great war in 1815. 5 vols. London, 1878–86. 8°.

Chs. xiv.–xv. Municipal reform.

258a. WETHERELL, CHARLES. Speech of Sir Charles Wetherell, at the bar of the House of Lords, against the Municipal Corporation Bill, on Thursday, 30th, and Friday, 31st July, 1835. Fifth edition. London, 1835. 8°.

259. What should the lords do with the Corporation Reform Bill? With tables, showing the extent of its proposed constituency in comparison with the parliamentary franchise. London, 1835. 8°.

c. THE ACT OF 1882.

The Municipal Corporations Act, 45 & 46 Vict. c. 50. An Act for consolidating, with amendments, enactments relating to Municipal Corporations in England and Wales. See No. 282.

See also 46 & 47 Vict. c. 18 : An Act to make provision respecting certain Municipal Corporations and other local authorities not subject to the Municipal Corporation Act [of 1835]. On these " unreformed corporations," see Nos. 61, 207.

260. BAZALGETTE, C. N., and HUMPHREYS, G. The law relating to local and municipal government. London, 1885. 8°.

An elaborate work; it contains 140 statutes, including the Act of 1882, with a full commentary.

261. CHAMBERS, G. F. A digest of the law relating to municipal corporations, with the statutes in full; various precedents; various official documents ; brief notes of leading cases : forming a complete guide to the new act of 1882. London, 1882. 8°.

261a. †DEHAYE, ALEXANDRE. Les municipalités anglaises. Loi organique du 18 août, notice, traduction et notes. Paris, 1883. 8°.

262. LELY, J. M. The law of municipal corporations : containing the Municipal Corporations Act, 1882, and the enactments incorporated therewith . . . with notes. London, 1882. 8°.

263. OWEN, HUGH. The Municipal Corporations Act, 1882, and provisions of the Ballot Act and Corrupt Practices Prevention Acts applicable to municipal elections, and other statutes. With notes. London, 1883. 8°.

264. RAWLINSON, CHRISTOPHER. The Municipal Corporations Act, 45 & 46 Vict. c. 50 ; and the general rules made in pursuance thereof, and acts since passed for amending the same, and otherwise in relation to municipal corporations. With notes and references to the cases thereon; and an appendix containing the principal statutes referred to. . . . Eighth edition, by Thomas Greary. London, etc., 1883. 8°.

This is the 8th edition of No. 252.

265. †SAUNDERS, T. W. The Municipal Corporations Act, with part of the Ballot Act. London, 1882. 8°.

D

266. WILLIAMS, J. W. H., and VINE, J. R. S.   The English municipal code : being the Municipal Corporations Act, 1882. . . .
London, 1882.   8°.

3rd edition, by J. R. S. Vine, 1888.

d. **THE ACT OF 1888 : COUNTY COUNCILS.**

The Local Government Act (England and Wales), 51 Vict. c. 41.

267. BAKER, C. E.   Local Government Act, 1888.   With notes
and index.   London, 1888.   8°.

268. BAZALGETTE, C. N.   The law relating to county councils :
being the Local Government Act, 1888, County Electors Act, 1888,
etc.   Third edition, by George Humphreys.   London, 1889.   8°.

1st and 2nd editions, 1888.

269. CHAMBERS, GEORGE F.   A popular summary of the law relating
to local government : forming a complete guide to the new act of 1888.
Second edition.   London, 1888.   4°.

270. GLEN, ALEX.   The law relating to county government under
the Local Government Act, 1888, and other statutes affecting county
councils.   London, 1890.   8°.

271. GLEN, ALEX. and R. C.   Handbook to the Local Government Act, 1888.   London, 1888.   8°.

272. GOODNOW, F. J.   The English Local Government Bill.
Political Science Quarterly, iii. 311–33.   New York, 1888.   8°.

273. HERBERT, N., and JENKIN, A. F.   The councillors' handbook :
a practical guide to the election and business of a county council. . . .
London, 1888.   8°.

Another edition, 1889.

274. HOBHOUSE, H., and FANSHAWE, E. L.   The county councillors'
guide : being a handbook to the Local Government Act, 1888. . . .
London, 1888.   8°.

275. HOLDSWORTH, W. A.   The Local Government Act. . . .
Third edition.   London, 1888.   8°.

276. Local Government [Bill of 1888.] *London Quarterly Review,* lxxi. 123–41. London, 1888. 8°.

277. Local Government Bill (The). *Quarterly Review,* clxvii. 249–72. London, 1888. 8°.

278. MACMORRAN, ALEX. The Local Government Act, 1888. . . . Second edition, revised and enlarged. London, 1888. 8°.

279. PARKER, F. R. The election of county councils under the Local Government Act, 1888. Second edition. London, 1892. 8°. 1st edition, 1888.

280. —— The duties of county councils under the Local Government Act, 1894; with the act and the regulations made thereunder. London, 1894. 8°.

281. PULLING, ALEX. A handbook for county authorities. London, 1889. 8°.

282. RYDE, W. C., and THOMAS, E. L. The Local Government Act, the County Electors Act, 1888, the Municipal Corporations Act, 1882. . . . London, 1888. 8°.

283. STEPHEN, H., and MILLER, H. E. The county council compendium or digest of the Municipal Corporations Act, 1882, the County Electors Act, 1888, and the Local Government Act, 1888. London, 1888. 8°.

284. THRING, Lord. Local Government [Bill of 1888.] *Nineteenth Century,* xxiii. 423–40, 641–60. London, 1888. 8°.

284a. † URLIN, R. D. The county council guide. London, 1891. 8°.

§ 8. PARLIAMENTARY HISTORY.

a. Records, and Reports of Committees, Nos. 285–295.
b. General Histories, etc., Nos. 296–315a.
c. Particular Counties, Nos. 316–328.
d. History and Law of Elections, Nos. 329–344.
e. Election Cases, Nos. 345–357.
f. Parliamentary Reform, Nos. 358–527.

Though the following list contains all the most important works relating to general parliamentary history, it is to be regarded as a bibliography of only one phase of the subject, namely, the representative history of boroughs. Many of the works enumerated are valuable for the study of the internal municipal development, with which indeed the representative history is closely connected. This is notably true of the cases of controverted elections discussed in the Journals of the House of Commons (No. 287) and in the collections of reports (§ 8 e).

For minor additions to the lists given below, see the old printed catalogue of the British Museum Library, vol. v. (London, 1817), under the word "Parliament"; Lowndes, *Bibliographer's Manual* (1861), 1781-86; R. Sims, *Manual for the Genealogist, Topographer*, etc. (1856), 148–58; Parry, *Parliaments and Councils* (No. 306), Preface, 8–29; R. Watt, *Bibliotheca Britannica* (1824), under the words "Parliament" and "Reform."

For Ireland and Scotland, see §§ 12, 13.

a. RECORDS, AND REPORTS OF COMMITTEES.

The chief sources for the study of the medieval representation of boroughs are the Parliamentary Writs (Nos. 292, 293), the Rolls of Parliament (No. 134), and the Peers' Reports (No. 295). For modern times the principal sources are the Journals of the House of Commons (No. 287), the Statutes (§ 2 b), and Hansard's *Debates*.

285. * HANSARD, T. C. Parliamentary debates, from the year 1803 to the present time : forming a continuation of the work entitled " The parliamentary history of England from the earliest period to the year 1803," [by William Cobbett. See No. 297.]   41 vols. London, 1812–20. 8°.

New series. 25 vols. London, 1820–30. 8°.

Third series.   356 vols.   London, 1831–91.   8°.
Fourth series.   40 vols.   London, 1892–96.   8°.

A General Index to the 1st and 2nd series, edited by John Philippart, appeared in 1834. Since 1830 there is an index for each session.

A briefer account of the debates will be found in the *Annual Register*, published since 1758.

For earlier collections of debates, see Lowndes, *Bibliographer's Manual* (1861), 1781.

286. Indexes to reports of commissioners, 1832–1854. (Parliamentary representation.) *Parl. Papers*, 1854, vol. lxiv. [London,] 1854. f°.

287. * Journals of the House of Commons [1547–1895.] 150 vols. [London, n. d.—1895.] f°.

A reprint of the old Journals was begun in 1803.

The following General Indexes have been printed:

       1547–1714, vols. i.–xvii., by T. Vardon and T. E. May, 1852.
       1714–1774, vols. xviii. –xxxiv., by E. Moore, 1778.
       1774–1790, vols. xxxv.–xlv., by S. Dunn, 1796.
       1790–1801, vols. xlvi.–lv., by S. Dunn, 1803.
       1801–1820, vols. lvi.–lxxv., by M. C. Burney, 1825.
       1820–1837, vols. lxxv.–xcii., by T. Vardon, 1839.
       1837–1852, vols. xciii.–cvii., by T. Vardon, 1857.

The early volumes of the Journals throw much light upon general municipal history; they contain valuable material concerning most of the boroughs of England.

288. Journals of the House of Lords [1509–1895.] 127 vols. [London, n. d.—1895.] f°.

Calendar of the Journals, 1509–1826, 2 vols., [1810.]
Indexes to vols. i.–lxiv., 1509–1833, 5 vols., 1817-55.

289. Members of Parliament. [Return of the name of every member of the lower house of the Parliaments of England, Scotland, and Ireland, with name of constituency represented, and date of return, from 1213 to 1874.] *Parl. Papers*, 1878, vol. lxii., pts. i.–iii. 3 vols. [London,] 1878. f°.

Valuable.

290. —— Return containing . . . the index to the names of members of Parliament from 1705 to 1885, in continuation of the

Return of members of Parliament . . . of session 1878. *Parl. Papers*, 1890–91, vol. lxii. [London,] 1891. f°.

Contains a list of M. P.'s for 1880–85, and an index of names from 1705 to 1885.

291. —— BEAN, W. W. The parliamentary returns of members of the House of Commons, from 1213 to 1874. . . . Notices of various errors and omissions found in the above-named work, in several Parliaments from 1603 to 1830. London, [1883.] 8°.

292. * Parliamentary writs (The) and writs of military summons . . . relating to the suit and service due and performed to the king's high court of Parliament and the councils of the realm, or affording evidence of attendance given at Parliaments and councils. Collected and edited by Francis Palgrave. *Record Com.* 2 vols. [Vol. ii. in three divisions.] London, 1827–34. f°.

The most elaborate source for the study of parliamentary history in the reigns of Edw. I. and Edw. II.

293. * PRYNNE, WILLIAM. A brief register, kalendar, and survey of the several kinds [or] forms of all parliamentary writs [to 1483]. . . . 4 vols. London, 1659–64. 4°.

The third part has the separate title, " Brevia Parliamentaria Rediviva," London, 1662.

Vols. iii.–iv. contain many writs of expenses of burgesses, returns of boroughs (Edw. I.—Edw. IV.), etc.

294. Report from the select committee on parliamentary and municipal elections. *Parl. Papers*, 1868–69, vol. viii. ; 1870, vol. vi. ; 1876, vol. xii. [London,] 1869–76. f°.

295. * Reports from the lords' committees appointed to search the Journals of the House, rolls of Parliament, and other records and documents, for all matters touching the dignity of a peer of the realm. . . . 4 vols. London, 1820–25. f°.

Vol. i. First Report: The general history of legislative assemblies in England, etc.

Vols. ii.–iii. Appendix: " Summonitiones temp. Johannis — Edw. IV."

Vol. iv. Second, Third, and Fourth Reports.

Reprinted in Parl. Papers, 1826, vols. vi.–ix.

The First Report and the Summonses will also be found in Journals of the House of Lords, 5 Geo. IV., 470–1104.

One of the most valuable sources of parliamentary history.

b. GENERAL HISTORIES, ETC.

Gneist's *English Parliament* (No. 299) and the Peers' Reports (No. 295) contain the best general accounts of parliamentary history. Smith's work (No. 309) is fuller than Gneist's, but much of his material is borrowed from Gneist, Stubbs, and other writers. The most useful books for the study of the medieval period are the Peers' Reports, Stubbs's *Constitutional History* (No. 94), and Riess's *Wahlrecht* (No. 341). The treatise of Merewether and Stephens (No. 79) contains much material, especially for the modern period. The works of Oldfield and Willis (Nos. 304, 315, 315a) are in large part antiquated.

296. BEATSON, ROBERT. A chronological register of both houses of the British Parliament, from the union in 1708 to the third Parliament of the United Kingdom of Great Britain and Ireland, in 1807. 3 vols. London, 1807. 8°.

This is now superseded by No. 289.

297. [COBBETT, WILLIAM.] The parliamentary history of England, from the earliest period [1066] to the year 1803, from which last-mentioned epoch it is continued downwards in the work entitled "The parliamentary debates." 36 vols. London, 1806–20. 8°.

See Nos. 285, 305.

298. FRANQUEVILLE, Le Comte de [A. C. E. Franquet.] Le gouvernement et le parlement britanniques. 3 vols. Paris, 1887. 8°.

The representation of towns, ii. 251–66, 288–95.

299. GNEIST, RUDOLPH. Das englische Parlament in tausendjährigen Wandelungen vom 9. bis zum Ende des 19. Jahrhunderts. Berlin, 1886. 8°.

The representation of towns, 168–73, 197, 388, etc.
2nd edition, 1886.
There are two translations of this work :
"The English Parliament in its transformations through a thousand years," by R. J. Shee, London, 1886. "The student's history of the English Parliament," by A. H. Keane, London, 1887 ; 3rd edition, 1889.

300. HARE, THOMAS. The machinery of representation. Second edition. London, 1857. 8°. pp. 55.

1st edition, 1857.

300a. HARE, THOMAS. A treatise on the election of representatives, parliamentary and municipal. London, 1859. 8°.

Valuable.

Other editions, 1861, 1865, 1873.

301. History of the English legislature. *Edinburgh Review*, xxxv. 1–43. Edinburgh, 1821. 8°.

See also ibid., 1827, xlvi. 479–89.

302. LEWIS, SAMUEL. View of the representative history of England, with engraved plans shewing the . . . boundaries of the cities and boroughs. London, 1840. 4°. pp. 83 (116 plates).

303. LUDERS, ALEXANDER. A treatise on the constitution of Parliament in the reign of Edward the First. Bath, 1818. 8°.

For Parliament in the time of Henry III., see his *Tracts*, ii. 239–326.

304. OLDFIELD, T. H. B. The representative history of Great Britain and Ireland : being a history of the House of Commons, and of the counties, cities, and boroughs of the United Kingdom, from the earliest period. 6 vols. London, 1816. 8°.

His first work on this subject was published anonymously under the title, " An entire and complete history of the boroughs of Great Britain," 3 vols., 1792 ; 2nd edition [abridged], 2 vols., 1794. His " History of the original constitution of Parliaments," 1797, is a sort of abridgment of the preceding treatise. Both works were reprinted under the title, " A complete history of the boroughs of Great Britain," 3 vols., 1805. " The representative history " of 1816 is an enlarged edition of the work published in 1792. Vols. i.–ii. contain a general history of the House of Commons ; vols. iii.–vi. give a brief sketch of the municipal and representative history of each borough ; the appendix of vol. vi. contains a table of parliamentary patronage, etc.

305. Parliamentary or constitutional history (The) of England : being a faithful account of all the most remarkable transactions in Parliament, from the earliest times . . . [to Dec. 29, 1660.] Collected . . . by several hands. 24 vols. London, 1751–61. 8°.

2nd edition, 24 vols., London, 1761–63. 8°.

This was superseded by Cobbett's work (No. 297).

306. [PARRY, C. H.] The Parliaments and councils of England, chronologically arranged, from the reign of William I. to the revolution in 1688. . . . London, 1839. 8°.

307. RANKIN, M. H.   Present state of representation in England and Wales : being an alphabetical arrangement of all the counties, cities, and boroughs sending members to Parliament ; with an appendix, containing a summary of the representation in England and Wales, the Reform and Boundary Acts, and a copious index.   London, 1832.   12°.

308. SKOTTOWE, B. C.   A short history of Parliament.   London, 1886.   8°.

Another edition, 1892.

309. SMITH, G. B.   History of the English Parliament, together with an account of the Parliaments of Scotland and Ireland.   2 vols. London, 1892.   8°.

A useful compilation.

310. SMITH, H. S.   The Parliaments of England, from 1st George I. to the present time.   3 vols.   London, 1844–50.   8°.

A list of the M. P.'s of all the counties and boroughs.
Superseded in large part by No. 289.

311.   [STOCKDALE, JOHN.]   Stockdale's Parliamentary guide ; or members' and electors' complete companion : being an historical account of the several cities, counties, and boroughs in Great Britain ; their right of election ; when they were first represented in Parliament, and the number of voters at each place ; with references to the Journals of the House of Commons, for every proceeding to be found in them relating to matters of election. . . . London, 1784. 8°.

Useful on account of the references to the Journals, etc.   Gives only a meagre sketch of the history of each borough.

312. SYME, DAVID.   Representative government in England, its faults and failures.   Second edition.   London, 1882.   8°.

Ch. i.   Early representative Parliaments.
1st edition, 1881.

313.   [WHITELOCKE, BULSTRODE.]   Whitelocke's notes upon the king's writt for choosing members of Parlement, xiii. Car. II ; being disquisitions on the government of England by king, lords, and commons.   Published by Charles Morton, M.D.   2 vols.   London, 1766.   4°.

Boroughs, i. 489–518, ii. 92–180.

314. WHITWORTH, CHARLES. The succession of Parliaments: being exact lists of the members chosen at each general election, from the Restoration to the last general election, 1761, with other useful matters. London, 1764. 12°.

This is now superseded by No. 289.

315. WILLIS, BROWNE. Notitia parliamentaria: or an history of the counties, cities, and boroughs in England and Wales. Shewing what boroughs were anciently parliamentary, but now disus'd. What do at this day return to Parliament. Their antiquities, charters, privileges, lords, churches, monasteries, government, number of electors, etc. To which are subjoin'd lists of all the knights, citizens, and burgesses (as far as can be collected from records) from the first summons to Parliament to this time. . . . 2 vols. London, 1715–16. 8°.

See No. 315a.

315a. —— Notitia parliamentaria: containing an account of the first returns and incorporations of the cities, towns, and boroughs in England and Wales that send members to Parliament. . . . Also an account of the disused boroughs, and . . . a series of lists of the representatives in the several Parliaments held from the Reformation, 1541, to the Restoration, 1660. . . . [Generally called vol. iii. of No. 315.] London, 1750. 8°.

The account of the history of each borough in these three volumes is brief; in some cases extracts from the town charters are given.

2nd edition of vol. i., 1730.

c. PARTICULAR COUNTIES.

See Nos. 621, 657, 669.

316. BEAN, W. W. The parliamentary representation of the six northern counties of England . . . and their cities and boroughs, from 1603 to the general election of 1886. With lists of members and biographical notices. Hull, 1890. 8°.

The material is mainly biographical.

317. BREESE, EDWARD. Kalendars of Gwynedd: or chronological lists of lords-lieutenants, custodes rotulorum, sheriffs, and knights of the shire, for the counties of Anglesey, Caernarvon, and Merioneth, and of the members for the boroughs of Caernarvon and Beaumaris. . . . Compiled by Edward Breese. With notes by W. W. E. Wynne. London, 1873. 4°.

318. † Chronological tables of the high sheriffs of the county of Lincoln, and of the knights of the shire, citizens and burgesses in Parliament within the same, from the earliest accounts to the present time. London, 1779. 4°. pp. 59.

319. Cooper, W. D. The parliamentary history of the county of Sussex and of the several boroughs and Cinque Ports therein. Lewes, 1834. 4°.

Arundel, 7–10	Hastings, 38–41	Rye, 41–64
Bramber, 11–13	Horsham, 20–23	Seaford, 46–49
Brighton, 13–14	Lewes, 24–27	Steyning, 34–36
Chichester, 14–17	Midhurst, 28–30	Winchelsea, 50–53
East Grinstead, 18–20	New Shoreham, 30–34	
See No. 657.		

320. Courtney, W. P. The parliamentary representation of Cornwall to 1832 [especially since 1547.] London, 1889. 8°.

321. * Ferguson, R. S. Cumberland and Westmorland M. P.'s from the Restoration to the Reform Bill of 1867 (1660–1867). London and Carlisle, 1871. 8°.

" The Author's intention is to furnish a complete Political History of the two Counties of Cumberland and Westmorland and their Boroughs of Carlisle, Cockermouth, Whitehaven, Appleby, and Kendal, from 1666 to 1867."

322. O'Byrne, R. H. The representative history of Great Britain and Ireland, comprising biographical and genealogical notices of the members of Parliament from 1 Edward VI., 1547, to 10 Victoria, 1847. [Part i. Bedfordshire. Part ii. Berkshire.] London, 1848. 8°.

Abingdon, ii. 82–6	Reading, ii. 86–91	Windsor, ii. 96–100
Bedford, i. 6–14	Wallingford, ii. 92–5	

323. Park, G. R. The parliamentary representation of Yorkshire, from the earliest authentically recorded elections to the present time [Edw. I. to 1886.] Hull, 1886. 8°.

324. PINK, W. D., and BEAVEN, A. B.   Parliamentary representation of Lancashire, county and borough, 1258–1885.   London, 1889.   8°.

325. SMITH, H. S.   The parliamentary representation of Yorkshire. London, 1854.   8°.

A list of M. P.'s for the county and boroughs.
Superseded by No. 289.

326. STENNING, A. H.   A return . . . of the members of Parliament for the county and boroughs of Sussex [to 1754]. . . . *Sussex Archæol. Soc.*, Collections, vols. xxx.–xxxv.   Lewes, 1880–87.   8°.

Compiled from the Returns of 1878 (No. 289).

327. WILLIAMS, W. R.   The parliamentary history of the county of Hereford, including the city of Hereford, and the boroughs of Leominster, Weobly, Bromyard, Ledbury, and Ross, from the earliest times to the present day, 1213–1896. . . . Brecknock, 1896.   8°.

328. —— The parliamentary history of the principality of Wales, from the earliest times to the present day, 1541–1895. . . . Brecknock, 1895.   4°.

Contains a list of the M. P.'s for the boroughs, with biographical notes.

d. HISTORY AND LAW OF ELECTIONS.
See Nos. 294, 486, and § 8 *e.*

329. Considerations offered to all the corporations of England, well worth their observation, containing seasonable advice to them in their future elections of burgesses to serve in Parliament, merely in relation to, and so far forth only, as such elections affect trade, and are, as will appear hereby, the main cause of its present great decay. London, 1681.   f°.

330. CORBETT, UVEDALE.   An inquiry into the elective franchise of the freeholders of, and the rights of election for, the corporate counties in England and Wales; also a report of the proceedings of the Warwickshire election committee, in 1821.   London, 1826.   8°.

Valuable for the municipal history of the following boroughs:

Bristol	Coventry	Hull	Newcastle	Southampton
Canterbury	Exeter	Lichfield	Norwich	Worcester
Carmarthen	Gloucester	Lincoln	Nottingham	York
Chester	Haverfordwest	London	Poole	

331. Cox, HOMERSHAM.   Antient parliamentary elections.   A history showing how Parliaments were constituted and representatives of the people elected in antient times.   London, 1868.   8°.

The representatives of boroughs, 133–93.

332. CULLEN, C. S.   A review of the law and judicature of elections, and of the change introduced by the late Irish Disfranchisement Bill. London, 1829.   8°.

333. DISNEY, JOHN.   A collection of acts of Parliament relative to county and borough elections, with references to several reported cases, containing the determinations of the House of Commons.   In two parts. . . . Chronologically arranged, with a copious index. London, 1811.   8°.

334. GREGO, JOSEPH.   A history of parliamentary elections and electioneering in the old days, showing the state of political parties and party warfare at the hustings and in the House of Commons from the Stuarts to Queen Victoria.   London, 1886.   8°.

New edition, 1892.

335. HEYWOOD, SAMUEL.   A digest of so much of the law respecting borough elections as concerns cities and boroughs in general, their representatives, and returning officers. . . . London, 1797.   8°.

336. † Laws concerning the election of members of Parliament, with the determinations of the House of Commons thereon, and all their incidents; also an appendix of precedents.   By a gentleman of the Inner Temple.   Sixth edition.   London, 1780.   8°.

1st edition, 1768.

337. LELY, J. M., and FOULKES, W. D. I.   The parliamentary election acts for England and Wales . . . being a treatise on the law of the election of members in England and Wales to the House of Commons of the United Kingdom.   London, 1885.   8°.

Ch. iii. shows how the reforms of 1832, 1867, and 1885 influenced the parliamentary representation of boroughs.

338. MALE, ARTHUR.   A treatise on the law and practice of elections.   Second edition.   London, 1820.   8°.

Introduction: "The rise and progress of parliamentary representation; the history of the writ, and of the disfranchisement of boroughs which formerly sent members to parliament."
Appendix, xlix.: "Present state of representation, comprising all the counties,

cities, and boroughs which send members to parliament, alphabetically arranged,
describing their municipal government, returning officers, and right of election as
by last decision."

1st edition, 1818.

339. Orders and resolutions of the honourable House of Commons on controverted elections and returns, determining the qualifications of candidates and voters ; the rights of election for the several
cities and boroughs. . . . Third edition. London, 1741. 12°.

Other editions, 1734, 1736. "Additions" were printed in 1747.

340. ORME, ROBERT. A practical digest of the [parliamentary]
election laws. London, 1796. 8°.

Elections for cities, towns, boroughs, and Cinque Ports, 61–97.
Electors in cities, towns, boroughs, and Cinque Ports, 205–54.

341. *RIESS, LUDWIG. Geschichte des Wahlrechts zum englischen Parlament im Mittelalter. Leipzig, 1885. 8°.

Borough representation, 17–35, 59–66, 103–5.

342. ROE, W. T. A practical treatise on the law of elections
relating to England, Scotland, and Ireland. London, 1812. 8°.

343. —— An appendix to a treatise on the law of elections :
containing acts relating to controverted elections, etc., etc., the Scots
and Irish statutes, and form and precedents, etc. London, 1812. 8°.

344. ROGERS, F. N. The law and practice of elections and election committees ; with an appendix, containing the acts of Parliament
for England, Scotland, and Ireland, brought down to the end of the
session 1837. Fifth edition, with very considerable additions. London, 1837. 12°.

The chapter on " Voters for cities and boroughs " cites many cases.
1st edition, 1820; 16th edition, 1892.

e. **ELECTION CASES.**

The collections of cases are of considerable value for the study, not
merely of parliamentary representation, but of municipal history in general.
The most useful are those of Carew, Douglas, Fraser, Glanville, Luders,
and Peckwell. After the reforms of 1832 and 1835, the collections are
of less value, and therefore most of them have been omitted. The tables
of contents appended to the titles given below include only the more
important cases.

The Parliamentary Papers contain many reports of committees appointed to consider cases of controverted elections: e. g. 1806–7, vol. iv. ; 1819, vol. iv. ; 1826–27, vol. iv.   For many other cases, especially in the years 1801–34, see *Catalogue of Parl. Papers*, 1696–1834 (No. 46), pp. 34–7.   Some of the most valuable of these cases are mentioned below, in Part II., under the names of particular towns.

See § 8 *d*.

345. BOHUN, WILLIAM.   A collection of debates, reports, orders, and resolutions of the House of Commons, touching the right of electing members to serve in Parliament, for the several counties, cities, boroughs, and towns corporate in England and Wales ; together with several ancient charters, and extracts out of Domesday-Book, and other records relating to the said right.   London, [1702.]   f°.

Most of the cases reported fall within the years 1674–1700.

Abingdon	Calne	Ilchester	Southampton
Aldborough (Suff.)	Carlisle	Kingston-upon-Hull	Southwark
Aldborough (York)	Chester	Lincoln	Stockbridge
Amersham	Chippenham	Liverpool	Tavistock
Andover	Cirencester	London	Thetford
Arundel	Clitheroe	Ludgershall	Totnes
Aylesbury	Colchester	Ludlow	Tregony
Banbury	Corfe Castle	Lymington	Truro
Bath	Cricklade	Maldon	Wallingford
Bedford	Dartmouth	Marlow	Wells
Beeralston	Devizes	Mitchell	Weobly
Berwick	Dorchester	Morpeth	Westminster
Bewdley	Dover	Newark	Wigan
Bishop's Castle	Droitwich	Newport (Cornwall)	Winchester
Bletchingley	Dunwich	Plymouth	Windsor
Boston	Fowey	Plympton	Wootton-Bassett
Bramber	Gatton	Portsmouth	Worcester
Brecon	Grantham	Radnor (New)	Yarmouth (Great)
Bridgwater	Grinstead (East)	St. Ives	Yarmouth (Hants)
Bridport	Haslemere	Saltash	York
Bristol	Hastings	Sandwich	
Buckingham	Helston	Shaftesbury	

346. [CAREW, THOMAS.]   An historical account of the rights of elections of the several counties, cities, and boroughs of Great Britain ; collected from public records and the Journals of Parliament, to the year one thousand seven hundred and fifty-four.   By a late member of Parliament.   2 pts.   London, 1755.   f°.

For the period covered (circa 1600–1754), this is the most exhaustive parliamentary history of boroughs. The history of the following towns is considered:

Abingdon	Corfe Castle	Ludgershall	St. Maws
Aldborough (Suff.)	Coventry	Ludlow	St. Michael
Aldborough (York)	Cricklade	Lyme Regis	Salisbury
Amersham	Dartmouth	Lymington	Sandwich
Andover	Denbigh	Lynn Regis	Sarum (Old)
Appleby	Derby	Maidstone	Scarborough
Arundel	Devizes	Maldon	Seaford
Ashburton	Dorchester	Malmesbury	Shaftesbury
Aylesbury	Dover	Malton	Shoreham
Banbury	Downton	Marlborough	Shrewsbury
Bath	Droitwich	Marlow	Southampton
Beaumaris	Dunwich	Midhurst	Southwark
Bedford	Durham	Milborne Port	Stafford
Bedwin (Great)	Evesham	Minehead	Steyning
Beeralston	Exeter	Monmouth	Stockbridge
Berwick	Flint	Montgomery	Sudbury
Bewdley	Fowey	Morpeth	Tamworth
Bishop's Castle	Gatton	Newark	Taunton
Bletchingley	Gloucester	Newcastle-under-Lyme	Tavistock
Bodmin	Grantham	Newport (Cornwall)	Tewkesbury
Boroughbridge	Grimsby (Great)	Newport (Hants)	Thetford
Bossiney	Grinstead (East)	Northampton	Totnes
Boston	Guildford	Norwich	Tregony
Brackley	Harwich	Nottingham	Truro
Bramber	Haslemere	Okehampton	Wallingford
Brecon	Hastings	Orford	Wareham
Bridgnorth	Haverfordwest	Pembroke	Warwick
Bridgwater	Helston	Penryn	Wells
Bridport	Hereford	Peterborough	Wendover
Bristol	Hertford	Petersfield	Weobly
Buckingham	Higham Ferrers	Plymouth	Westbury
Callington	Hindon	Plympton	Westminster
Calne	Honiton	Pontefract	Weymouth
Cambridge	Horsham	Poole	Whitchurch
Camelford	Hull	Portsmouth	Wigan
Canterbury	Huntingdon	Preston	Wilton
Cardiff	Hythe	Queenborough	Winchelsea
Cardigan	Ilchester	Radnor (New)	Winchester
Carlisle	Ipswich	Reading	Windsor
Castle Rising	Knaresborough	Reigate	Wootton-Bassett
Chester	Launceston	Retford	Worcester
Chichester	Leicester	Richmond	Wycombe
Chippenham	Leominster	Ripon	Yarmouth (Great)
Christchurch	Lichfield	Rochester	Yarmouth (Hants)
Cirencester	Lincoln	Rye	York
Clitheroe	Liverpool	St. Albans	
Cockermouth	London	St. Edmund's Bury	
Colchester	Lostwithiel	St. Ives	

347. COCKBURN, A. E., and ROWE, W. C.　Cases of controverted elections determined in the eleventh Parliament of the United Kingdom, being the first session after the passing of the reform acts. Vol. i.　London, 1833.　8°.

Bath, 1–15	Ennis, 224–7	Oxford, 139–73
Bedford, 37–99	Galway, 390–437	Petersfield, 16–36
Bristol, 529–34	Hertford, 184–223	Portarlington, 257–9
Carnarvon, 127–38, 550–60	Limerick, 535–49	Ripon, 291–303
Clonmel, 452–61	Lincoln, 372–89	Salisbury, 304–30
Coleraine, 489–528	Londonderry, 248–56	Southampton, 100–126
Coventry, 260–90	Montgomery, 331–51	
Dover, 477–88	Newry, 174–83	

348. CORBETT, UVEDALE, and DANIELL, E. R.　Reports of cases of controverted elections, in the sixth Parliament of the United Kingdom [1819.]　London, 1821.　8°.

Barnstaple, 192–4	Inverkeithing, 177–91	Reading, 114–24
Bristol, 73–88	Lancaster, 195–6	Rochester, 229–38
Camelford, 239–57	Leominster, 1–25	Shaftesbury (1813), 265–7
Chester, 68–72	Limerick, 89–92	Truro, 175–6
Drogheda, 93–114	Milborne Port, 204–28	Worcester, 172–4
Evesham, 26–54	Nottingham, 197–203	
Fowey, 125–71, 258–63	Penryn, 55–68	

349. CUNNINGHAM, TIMOTHY.　An historical account of the rights of election of the several counties, cities, and boroughs of Great Britain : containing the time when each of them was first represented in Parliament, and by what authority ; together with abstracts of the proceedings relative to controverted elections, under every place. . . . 2 pts.　London, 1783.　8°.

350. DOUGLAS, SYLVESTER.　The history of the cases of controverted elections which were tried and determined during the first (and second) sessions of the fourteenth Parliament of Great Britain, xv. (and xvi.) Geo. III.　4 vols.　London, 1775–77.　8°.

Abingdon, i. 417–58	Haddington, Jedburgh, etc., ii. 421–74
Bedford, ii. 67–128	Haslemere, ii. 317–42
Bristol, i. 241–90	Helston, ii. 1–66
Cardigan, etc., iii. 171–236	Hindon, i. 171–204, iv. 271–328
Cricklade, i. 291–314, iv. 1–84	Ilchester, iii. 149–70, iv. 165–76
Derby, iii. 285–371	Milborne Port, i. 95–144
Dorchester, i. 345–64	Morpeth, i. 145–56
Downton, i. 205–40	Peterborough, iii. 61–148

Petersfield, iii. 1-18
Pontefract, i. 377-416
Poole, ii. 223-300
Radnor (New), i. 315-44
St. Ives, ii. 389-98
Seaford, iii. 19-60
Shaftesbury, ii. 301-316

Shrewsbury, i. 459-71, iv. 329-74
Southampton, iv. 85-164
Sudbury, ii. 129-78
Taunton, i. 365-76
Westminster, i. 157-70
Wigtown, etc., ii. 179-222
Worcester, iii. 237-84

Many of these cases are important; the editor's notes are valuable.

351. FRASER, SIMON. Reports of the proceedings before select committees of the House of Commons, in the following cases of controverted elections; viz. [vol. i.] Hellston, Oakhampton, Pontefract, Dorchester, Newark, Orkney and Zetland [vol. ii. Horsham, Sutherland, Honiton, Steyning, Roxburgh, Cirencester]; heard and determined during the first (and second) sessions of the seventeenth Parliament of Great Britain. 2 vols. London, 1791-93. 8°.

The appendices contain town charters and other documents: e. g., the charters granted to Pontefract by Roger de Lacy, Henry de Lacy, Richard II., Richard III., and James I. (vol. i. app.).

352. GLANVILLE, JOHN. Reports of certain cases, determined and adjudged by the commons in Parliament, in the twenty-first and twenty-second years of the reign of King James the First. Collected by John Glanville, Esq., sergeant-at-law, then chairman of the committee of privileges and elections. To which is prefixed an historical account of the ancient right of determining cases upon controverted elections. [Edited by J. Topham.] London, 1775. 8°.

Amersham
Arundel, 71-5
Bletchingley, 29-46
Chippenham, 47-62
Cirencester, 104-111
Dover, 63-70

Haverfordwest, 112-4
Hertford, 87-96
Marlow, 87-96
Monmouth, 120-123
Newcastle-under-Lyme, 76-9
Pontefract, 133-43

Retford (East), 128-32
Southwark, 7-11
Stafford, 25-8
Stockbridge, 97-8
Wendover, 87-96
Winchelsea, 12-24

353. KNAPP, J. W., and OMBLER, E. Cases of controverted elections in the twelfth Parliament of the United Kingdom, being the second Parliament since the passing of the acts for the amendment of the representation of the people. London, 1837. 8°.

The cases of the following towns are considered:

Canterbury
Cork
Drogheda
Droitwich
Dungarvan

Ennis
Falmouth
Horsham
Hull

Ipswich
Monaghan
Monmouth
Penryn

Rochester
Windsor
Worcester
Youghal

354. LUDERS, ALEXANDER. Reports of the proceedings in committees of the House of Commons, upon controverted elections, heard and determined during the present Parliament [1784–86.] 3 vols. London, 1785–90. 8°.

Carlisle, ch. xxv.
Colchester, ch. vi.
Cricklade, ch. xi.
Downton, chs. iv., xviii.
Honiton, ch. xvii.
Ilchester, ch. vii.

Ipswich, ch. ii.
Kirkwall, ch. xx.
Lyme Regis, ch. viii.
Mitchell, ch. iii.
Newport (Hants), ch. x.
Norwich, ch. xxiv.

Pontefract, ch. i.
Preston, ch. xix.
Saltash, ch. ix.
Seaford, chs. xiv.-xvi.

A valuable collection ; well edited.

355. PECKWELL, R. H. Cases of controverted elections in the second Parliament of the United Kingdom, begun and holden Aug. 31, 1802. 2 vols. London, 1805 [1804]–1806. 8°.

Aylesbury, ii. 258–67
Barnstaple, i. 90–92
Berwick-upon-Tweed, i. 401–5
Boston, i. 434–5
Bridgwater, i. 101–9
Chippenham, i. 262–85
Cirencester, i. 466–8
Colchester (1789), i. 503–11
Coventry, i. 93–100
Dunfermline, etc., i. 1–18
Durham, ii. 170–86
Evesham, i. 471–4
Fowey (1791), i. 512–25
Glasgow, i. 351–8
Grimsby, i. 59–76
Grinstead (East), i. 307–39
Harwich, i. 381–400

Ilchester, i. 302–6, ii. 235–55
Knaresborough, ii. 382–7
Leominster (1796), ii. 391–6
Liskeard, i. 110–45, ii. 275–337
London, ii. 268–73
Malmesbury (1796–97), ii. 397–421
Newcastle-under-Lyme, i. 489–93
Nottingham, i. 77–89
Okehampton, i. 359–78
Retford (East), i. 475–88
Southwark, ii. 149–69
Taunton, i. 406–33
Tewkesbury (1797), i. 146–83
Waterford, i. 217–50
Weymouth and Melcombe, ii. 195–234
Windsor, ii. 187–94

356. PERRY, H. J., and KNAPP, J. W. Cases of controverted elections in the eleventh Parliament of the United Kingdom, being the first Parliament since the passing of acts for the amendment of the representation of the people. London, 1833. 8°.

Bath, 21–31
Bedford, 112–48
Bristol, 574–82
Carnarvon, 106–11, 435–61
Carrickfergus, 529–34
Clonmel, 425–34
Coleraine, 472–510
Coventry, 335–54
Dover, 412–24

Ennis, 528
Galway, 302–34
Hertford, 541–63
Limerick, 355–74
Lincoln, 375–92
Londonderry, 272–9
Mallow, 266–8
Montgomery, 162–73, 462–71
Newry, 149–61

Norwich, 564–73
Oxford, 58–105
Petersfield, 31–57
Portarlington, 238–41
Ripon, 202–12
Salisbury, 242–65
Southampton, 213–37
Tiverton, 269–71
Warwick, 535–40

357. PHILIPPS, JOHN. Election cases; determined during the first session of the fifteenth Parliament of Great Britain, by committees of the House of Commons, appointed by virtue of Stat. 10 Geo. III. London, 1782. 8°.

Lyme Regis, 317–400.
Milborne Port, 217–316.
Sudbury, 131–216.

f. PARLIAMENTARY REFORM.

The question of parliamentary reform was first raised in practical shape by Mr. Pitt, who in 1782 introduced resolutions in favor of reform; but no definite action was taken until 1832. In each of the years 1852, 1854, 1859, 1860, 1864, 1865, and 1866 reform bills were introduced, but were ultimately withdrawn or defeated. The important acts of 1832, 1867, and 1884–5 will be found in the Statutes (No. 68); the discussions in Parliament, in Hansard's *Debates*, and more briefly in the *Annual Register* (especially for the years 1831–2, 1866–7, 1884–5). The best general histories of the various reforms are those of Heaton and Murdoch. For a list of all the acts relating to parliamentary representation, see the *Index of Statutes* (No. 75), under " House of Commons."

No attempt is made to give an exhaustive list of all the books and pamphlets dealing with parliamentary reform; only those works are named which throw light on the parliamentary representation of boroughs.

For Ireland and Scotland, see below, §§ 12–13. For the periodical literature, see Poole's *Index* (1882), 973, and his First Supplement (1888), 330, 370.

General.

358. BAGEHOT, WILLIAM. Essays on parliamentary reform. London, 1883. 8°.

Parliamentary reform (1859), 1–106.
The history of the unreformed Parliament (1860), 107–82.
The Reform Act of 1867 (1872), 183–248.

359. COURTNEY, HERBERT. The House of Commons, in the past, present, and future; showing our representative assembly as it was, as it is, and as it should be. Revised edition. London, 1887. 8°. pp. 38.

360. DICKINSON, G. L. The development of Parliament during the nineteenth century. London, 1895. 8°.

360a. GREY, H. G. (3rd Earl). Parliamentary government considered with reference to a reform of Parliament: an essay. New edition. London, 1864. 8°.

Deals with the reform of 1832, and the reform bills of 1859–60, and presents a project of reform.
1st edition, 1858.

361. HEATON, WILLIAM. The three reforms of Parliament. A history, 1830–1885. London, 1885. 8°.

A compact and lucid epitome of parliamentary history since 1830.

362. MARTIN, J. B. Electoral statistics: a review of the working of our representative system from 1832 to 1881, in view of prospective changes therein. *Statistical Society*, Journal, xlvii. 75–124. London, 1884. 8°.

363. MOLESWORTH, W. N. The history of England from the year 1830. New edition. 3 vols. London, 1874. 8°.

For the reforms of 1832 and 1867, see vol. i. chs. i.–iv., and vol. iii. ch. v.
1st edition, 1871–73.

364. MURDOCH, JAMES. A history of constitutional reform in Great Britain and Ireland; with a full account of the three great measures of 1832, 1867, and 1884. Glasgow, etc., 1885. 8°.

A detailed but dry epitome of parliamentary history.

365. NEWMARCH, WILLIAM. On the electoral statistics of the counties and boroughs in England and Wales during the twenty-five years from the Reform Act of 1832 to the present time. *Statistical Society*, Journal, xx. 169–232, 314–40; xxii. 101–168, 297–305. London, 1857–59. 8°.

Valuable.

366. PAUL, ALEXANDER. The history of reform. A record of the struggle for the representation of the people in Parliament. Fifth edition, with addenda for 1884–1885. . . . London, 1885. 8°.

1st edition, 1884.

367. RAVEN, JOHN. The parliamentary history of England, from the passing of the Reform Bill of 1832. London, 1885. 8°.

A concise account; incomplete and inaccurate.

The Reform of 1832.

2 Wm. IV. c. 45 : An Act to amend the Representation of the People of England and Wales.

The long agitation preceding the first great reform produced a vast number of pamphlets. For many additions to the list given below, see Watt's *Bibliotheca Britannica*, under the word " Reform "; and the bound volumes of pamphlets in the British Museum bearing the press-marks, T. 1321, T. 1328, T. 1329, T. 1378, T. 1379, T. 1380, T. 1402, and 8142. c. These volumes of tracts contain about one hundred and twenty-five pamphlets dealing with the reform of 1832 or with the agitation preceding it. Many of the pamphlets mentioned below will be found in these volumes. There is also a good collection in the Boston Public Library (*6517. 1-7), comprising seven volumes of tracts which formerly belonged to the Duke of Sussex.

Heaton (No. 361), May, and Walpole give good accounts of the whole movement; Molesworth and Roebuck are the fullest authorities for the history of the Reform Bill of 1832.

368. Address (An) to the members of the legislature on reform. London, 1831. 8°.

369. ALLEN, JOHN. A short history of the House of Commons with reference to reform. London, 1831. 8°. pp. 30.

370. Answer (An) to a pamphlet entitled A reply to the speech of the right honourable Lord Brougham, lord high chancellor of England ; with some remarks on reform. London, 1832. 8°.

371. Appeal (An) from clamour to common sense : or some enquiry into the details and operation of the reform proposed for England and Wales. London, 1831. 8°.

372. ARNOT, HUGO. A letter to the freeholders of the county of Fife, on the subject of reform. London, etc., 1812. 8°.

373. Barrister (A). Notes on the Reform Bill. By a barrister. Third edition, with a preface and other additions. London, 1831. 8°.

1st and 2nd editions, 1831.

374. BEAUMONT, G. Full particulars of the Reform Bill, with observations. London, 1831. 8°.

375. BEAUMONT, J. T. B. Thoughts on the causes and cure of the present distresses; with a plan of parliamentary reform. Second edition. London, 1831. 8°.

1st edition, 1830.

376. BENTHAM, JEREMY. Plan of parliamentary reform, in the form of a catechism, with reasons for each article; with an introduction, shewing the necessity of radical and the inadequacy of moderate reform. London, 1817. 8°.

377. Bill for parliamentary reform, as proposed by the Marquess of Blandford in the House of Commons, Feb. 18, 1830, with the declaration of the Birmingham political council thereon. London, 1831. 8°.

378. BROUGHAM, HENRY. The speech of Lord Brougham, lord high chancellor of England, delivered in the House of Lords, Oct. 7, 1831, on the second reading of the Reform Bill. . . . London, [1831.] 8°.

Also printed in " Speeches of Henry Lord Brougham " (Edinburgh, 1838), ii. 533–630.
See No. 463.

379. BULLER, CHARLES. On the necessity of a radical reform. London, 1831. 8°.

380. CARR, GEORGE. Rational reform on constitutional principles; addressed to the good sense of the English nation. London, 1818. 8°.

381. COCKBURN, A. E. The Act 2 Will. IV. c. xlv. to amend the representation of the people in England and Wales. With notes and copious index. London, 1832. 12°.

382. COMTE, CHARLES. De la réforme parlementaire en Angleterre. *Revue Encyclopédique,* l. 217–41. Paris, 1831. 8°.

383. CONDY, GEORGE. An essay on the elective right and the rejected bill. London, 1831. 8°.

384. Constitutional principles (The) of parliamentary reform. By a freeholder and landowner of Scotland. Edinburgh, 1831. 8°.

385. Corrected report of the speech of the right honourable the lord advocate of Scotland [F. Jeffrey], upon the motion of Lord John Russell, in the House of Commons, on the first of March, 1831, for reform of Parliament. London, 1831. 8°.

386. CORY, WILLIAM. A guide to modern English history [1815–35.] 2 vols. New York, 1880–82. 8°.

The Reform Bill, ii. 76–245.

387. CRABB, GEORGE. The reformer's guide : or a comprehensive analysis of the Reform Act. . . . London, 1832. 8°.

388. Crisis (The) : or a warning voice to the lords. London, 1831. 8°.

389. CROKER, J. W. The speech of the right honourable John Wilson Croker on the reform question, on Friday, March 4, 1831. London, 1831. 8°.

390. Debates in the House of Commons on the sixth and seventh of May, 1793, upon the motion of Charles Grey, Esq., for parliamentary reform. . . . Edinburgh, 1793. 8°. pp. 106.

391. DURHAM, Lord. The speech of Lord Durham in the House of Lords, Monday, March 28, 1831, on the Reform Bill. London, 1831. 8°.

392. Essay (An) on Parliament, and the causes of unequal representation. Also, a specimen of some regulations, with a prospect of general reform. London, 1793. 8°. pp. 52.

393. EVANS, R. H. A letter on the expediency of a reform in Parliament, addressed to the right hon. Lord Erskine. London, 1817. 8°.

394. [EVERETT, EDWARD.] The prospect of reform in England. London, 1831. 8°.

2nd and 3rd editions, 1831.
From the *North American Review*, July, 1831.

395. [――――] The progress of reform in England. . . . From the North American Review for January, 1832. London, 1832. 8°.

396. Extraordinary Black Book (The) : an exposition of the united church of England and Ireland . . . representation and prospects of reform under the new ministry. [By John Wade.] New edition. London, 1832. 8°.

Boroughs, 452-78, 610-22.
Earlier edition, 1831. See No. 235.

397. FLINTOFF, OWEN. The rise and progress of the laws of England and Wales. . . . London, 1840. 8°.

The Reform Bill and a sketch of the representative history of boroughs, 213-32.

398. Friendly advice to the ministers. Being a summary of the arguments against the bill for the amendment of the representation. London, 1831. 8°.

399. [GORE, MONTAGUE.] An address to the members of the legislature on reform. London, 1831. 8°.

400. —— Further observations on the Reform Bill; or what are the advantages of close boroughs? London, 1831. 8°.

2nd edition, 1831.

401. [——] What will be the practical effects of the Reform Bill? London, 1831. 8°.

The author of these three tracts favors reform.

402. GORTON, JOHN. Analysis of the English, Scotch, and Irish acts of Parliament, for amending the representation of the United Kingdom; with alphabetical summaries of the counties and boroughs represented. . . . London, 1833. 8°.

403. Great Britain in 1841, or the results of the Reform Bill. London, 1831. 12°.

404. Great charter reform (The) of 1832; comprised in the three reform bills. [London, 1832.] f°.

Without title-page.
Preceded by an " Introductory history of the progress of constitutional reform . . . as published in the Double Atlas Newspaper of August 19th, 1832, and the following number."

405. GREY, CHARLES (2nd Earl). Earl Grey's speech on moving the second reading of the Reform Bill, in the House of Lords, Oct. 3, 1831 ; with his lordship's reply on the morning of October 8th. London, 1831. 8°.

406. GRIFFITH, EDWARD.   Parliamentary reform attainable without the bill.   An essay on the elective franchise, as exercised by select prescriptive corporations.   London, 1832.   8°.

407. GROTE, GEORGE.   Essentials of parliamentary reform.   London, 1831.   8°.

408. HARROWBY, Earl of.   Substance of the speech of the right honourable the Earl of Harrowby [Dudley Ryder], in the House of Lords, October 4th, 1831, on the motion, that the Reform Bill be read a second time.   London, 1831.   8°.

409. HAWKINS, J. H.   A speech delivered in the House of Commons, in the debate of Tuesday, April 19, 1831, previous to the House resolving itself into a committee on Lord John Russell's bill for amending the representation of the people of England and Wales.   London, 1831.   8°.

410. HILL, M. D.   The speech of M. D. Hill, Esq. [in favor of the Reform Bill], at a public dinner given to him by the electors of Newark, on Thursday, March 10, 1831.   London, 1831.   8°.

411. History (The) of Parliament with a view to constitutional reform.   Edinburgh, 1831.   8°.   pp. 39.

412. JONES, WILLIAM.   Biographical sketches of the reform ministers; with a history of the passing of the reform bills. . . . London, 1832.   8°.

History of the reform bills, 738–817.

413. Jubilee (The) of the first reform act.   *Westminster Review,* New Series, lxii. 425–72.   London, 1882.   8°.

A sketch of the reform movement.

415. LECKY, W. E. H.   A history of England in the eighteenth century.   8 vols.   London, 1878–90.   8°.

For parliamentary reform, see especially ch. xi.

416. Letter (A) from a freeholder of Middlesex to his brother freeholders.   London, 1831.   8°.

417. Letter (A) to field-marshal his grace the Duke of Wellington upon the ministerial plan of reform.   London, 1831.   8°.

418. Letter (A) to Henry Brougham, Esq., M. P. for the county of York, on the present state of the English representation [especially that of the boroughs.]   London, 1830.   8°.

419. Letter to a noble lord who voted for the second reading of the Reform Bill, on the amendments which it may be expedient to make in the committee.   London, 1832.   8°.

Devoted wholly to the consideration of boroughs.

420. Letter (A) to the people of Lancashire, concerning the future representation of the commercial interest, by the return of members for its new boroughs to the reformed Parliament.   London, 1831.   8°.

421. Letters to Lord John Russell, upon his notice of a motion for a reform in Parliament.   London, 1826.   8°.

422. LYNDHURST, Lord.   The speech of the right honourable Lord Lyndhurst, in the House of Peers, on the Reform Bill, Oct. 7, 1831.   London, 1831.   8°.

423. MACAULAY, T. B.   Speeches, parliamentary and miscellaneous.   2 vols.   London, 1853.   8°.

Parliamentary reform, i. 11-52, 64-78, 81-102.

424. McCARTHY, JUSTIN.   The epoch of reform, 1830-1850.   [Epochs of Modern History.]   London, 1882.   8°.

425. MARTINEAU, HARRIET.   The history of England during the thirty years' peace, 1816-1846.   2 vols.   London, 1849-50.   8°.

Parliamentary reform, i. 46, 507, ii. 24-71.

426. MAY, T. E.   The constitutional history of England since the accession of George the Third, 1760-1860.   Seventh edition.   3 vols.   London, 1882.   8°.

For an excellent account of parliamentary reform and the causes leading to it, see i. 327-459 and iii. 425-42.

1st edition, 2 vols., 1861.

427. MEADLEY, G. W.   A sketch of the various proposals for a constitutional reform in the representation of the people, introduced into the Parliament of Great Britain from 1770 to 1812.   *The Pamphleteer*, ii. 297-312.   London, 1813.   8°.

428. MEREWETHER, H. A.   An address to the king, the lords, and commons, on the representative constitution of England.   London, 1830.   8°.

Discusses the abuses of municipal corporations.

429. —— A sketch of the history of boroughs and of their corporate rights of election, in a letter to Lord J. Russell on practical parliamentary reform.   London, 1822.   8°.   pp. 108.

Early history of elective franchise in boroughs, 3–23.
Some suggestions for reform, 81–108.

430. MOLESWORTH, W. N.   The history of the Reform Bill of 1832.   London and Manchester, 1865.   8°.

431. Necessity (The) of a speedy and effectual reform in Parliament.   [By George Philips.]   Manchester, [1792.]   8°.

432. New constitution (The).   "The Bill, the whole Bill, and nothing but the Bill."   London, [1831.]   12°.

433. Objections to the Reform (England) Bill.   Resolutions and protests.   London, 1832.   12°.

434. O'CONNELL, DANIEL.   Letters on the Reform Bill.   Dublin, 1832.   8°.   pp. 42.

435. —— Letters to the reformers of England on the Reform Bill.   London, 1832.   8°.   pp. 71.

436. On the French Revolution and parliamentary reform.   *Blackwood's Edinburgh Magazine*, xxix. 429–46, 745–62, 919–35.   Edinburgh, 1831.   8°.

437. On parliamentary reform.   From the American Quarterly Review, published at Philadelphia, September, 1831.   London, 1831.   8°.

438. PALGRAVE, FRANCIS.   Conciliatory reform.   A letter addressed to the right hon. Thomas Spring Rice, M. P., on the means of reconciling parliamentary reform to the interests and opinions of the different orders of the community, together with the draft of a bill, founded on the ministerial bill, but adapted more closely to the principles and precedents of the constitution.   London, [1831.]   8°.   pp. 48.

439. Palgrave, Francis. On the legal right of the dormant parliamentary boroughs, namely Newby, Ely . . . Tickhill, to the revival of their ancient franchise. A letter addressed to the rt. hon. Charles W. Williams Wynn, M. P. London, 1830. 8°.

46 boroughs are enumerated in the title of this pamphlet.

440. Pamphleteer (The) ; dedicated to both houses of Parliament. 29 vols. London, 1813–28. 8°.

Contains several papers on reform.

441. [Papers] relating to parliamentary representation. *Parl. Papers*, 1831–32, vols. xxxvi. –xxxvii. [London,] 1831–32. f°.

442. Parliamentary reform. *Edinburgh Review*, xvii. 253–90 ; xxxiv. 461–501. Edinburgh, 1811–20. 8°.

443. Parliamentary reform. *Quarterly Review*, xvi. 225–78. London, 1817. 8°.

444. Pauli, Reinhold. Geschichte Englands seit den Friedensschlüssen von 1814 und 1815. 3 vols. Leipzig, 1864–75. 8°.

Vol. ii. chs. i.–iii. Reform bills, 1830–33.

445. Plain reading for plain people ! Being an account of the English constitution and the king's Reform Bill. London, 1831. 8°.

446. Playfair, William. Inevitable consequences of a reform in Parliament. London, 1792. 8°.

447. Pocket boroughs. *Cornhill Magazine*, xviii. 299–310. London, 1868. 8°.

448. Political correspondence : or letters to a country gentleman retired from Parliament, on the subject of some of the leading characters and events of the present day. London, 1793. 8°.

The fifth letter deals with parliamentary reform.

449. Political disquisitions : or an enquiry into public errors, defects, and abuses. Illustrated by and established upon facts and remarks extracted from various authors, ancient and modern. . . . 3 vols. London, 1774–75. 8°.

Parliamentary representation of boroughs, and corruption in boroughs, i. 39–82, 278–344.

450. Pros and cons of Lord John Russell's Bill. By no party man. London, 1831. 8°.

451. PUSEY, PHILIP. The new constitution: remarks by Philip Pusey. London, 1831. 8°.

452. Question (The) of reform considered; with hints for a plan. London, 1831. 8°. pp. 142.

A detailed discussion of the subject.
2nd edition, 1831.

453. Reform. *Blackwood's Edinburgh Magazine*, xxix. 235–54. Edinburgh, 1831. 8°.

454. Reform. A letter to Lord John Russell on reform in Parliament. London, 1831. 8°.

455. Reform in Parliament. *Quarterly Review*, xlv. 252–339. London, 1831. 8°.

456. Reform not a new constitution. London, 1831. 8°.

457. Reform versus corruption: or a word to the people of England on the present crisis of the struggle against the borough-mongers. London, 1831. 8°.

458. Reform, with or without the consent of the lords. London, 1831. 8°.

A general sketch of the parliamentary history of boroughs.

459. Reform without innovation: or cursory thoughts on the only practicable reform of Parliament, consistent with the existing laws and the spirit of the constitution. London, 1810. 8°.

460. Reform Bill (The) considered. London, 1831. 8°.

461. Reform Bill (The) for England and Wales examined. London, 1831. 8°.

462. †Reformers versus borough-mongers and constitution-mongers. London, 1831. 8°.

463. Reply to a pamphlet, entitled Speech of the right hon. Lord Brougham, lord high chancellor of England, delivered in the House of Lords, on Friday, Oct. 7, 1831. London, 1831. 8°.

See No. 378.

464. ROEBUCK, J. A. History of the Whig ministry of 1830, to the passing of the Reform Bill. 2 vols. London, 1852. 8°.

465. ROWE, W. C. The act for the amendment of the representation of the people in England and Wales, 2 William IV. cap. xlv. With notes. . . . London, 1832. 12°.

Among other publications of the Reform Act, may be mentioned those edited by James Whishaw, F. N. Rogers, William Finelly, and Samuel Miller, all 1832, 12°. See also Nos. 381, 470, 486.

466. RUSSELL, JOHN. Recollections and suggestions, 1813–1873. Second edition. London, 1875. 8°

For parliamentary reform, see ch. i.

467. —— Speech of Lord John Russell in the House of Commons, on December 14th, 1819, on moving resolutions relative to corrupt boroughs. With extracts from the evidence on the Grampound bribery indictments. London, 1820. 8°.

468. —— Substance of the speeches of Lord John Russell on moving resolutions on reform of Parliament, on May 9, 1821, and April 25, 1822. London, 1822. 8°.

469. —— Lord John Russell's speech on reform, delivered in the House of Commons, March 1, 1831. London, 1831. 8°.

470. RUSSELL, WILLIAM. A treatise on the Reform Act, 2 William IV. chap. 45. . . . London, 1832. 12°.

471. SCARLETT, JAMES. Substance of the speech of Sir James Scarlett, on the motion for the second reading of the bill for reform, in the House of Commons; with a letter to Lord Viscount Milton. London, 1831. 12°.

472. SEWELL, R. C. Collectanea parliamentaria: or an historical inquiry into the constitution of the British Parliament, as connected with the proposed reform. London, 1831. 8°.

473. SINCLAIR, JOHN. Thoughts on parliamentary reform, with tables exhibiting the original amount and progressive increase of the number of national representatives; together with some observations on the representation of Scotland, and the improvements to which it is susceptible. Edinburgh, 1831. 8°. pp. 35.

474. Six speeches delivered in the House of Commons at the close of the debate upon the Reform Bill [by Sir J. Scarlett, Thomas Pemberton, Alexander Baring, J. W. Croker, Sir C. Wetherell, Sir R. Peel.] London, 1831. 12°.

475. State (The) of the representation of England and Wales, delivered to the Society, the Friends of the People, associated for the purpose of obtaining a parliamentary reform, on Saturday the 9th of Feb., 1793. London, [1793.] 4°. pp. 43.

476. STEWART, MATTHEW. Some remarks on the present state of affairs; respectfully addressed to the Marquis of Lansdowne. Second edition. London, 1831. 8°.

477. TANCRED, H. W. A legal review of the origin of the system of representation in England, and of its present state. With observations on the reform necessary. London, 1831. 8°.

478. Thoughts on moderate reform in the House of Commons. London, 1830. 8°.

479. Thoughts on parliamentary reform, and on reform in general; in which the nature of the British constitution, its component parts and establishments, etc., etc., etc., are freely but briefly considered. By an ex-member of the present Parliament. London, 1801. 8°.

480. TWISS, HORACE. Conservative reform, being outlines of a counterplan enclosed in a letter to Lord Lyndhurst. London, 1832. 8°.

481. Two [three] letters to the right honourable Lord John Russell, on the classification of boroughs. London, 1832. 8°.

The third letter has a separate title-page, but the pagination of the three is continuous.

482. VINDEX. A letter to the House of Peers on the present crisis. By Vindex. London, 1831. 8°.

483. WALL, C. B. A few words to the electors of Guildford, on reform. London, 1831. 8°.

484. WALPOLE, SPENCER. A history of England from the conclusion of the great war in 1815. 5 vols. London, 1878–86. 8°.

For parliamentary reform, see chs. ii., viii., xi.

485. WILLIAMS, JOSEPH.   Parliamentary reformation, examined under the following articles: extending the right of election; abolition of boroughs; qualification of members; abridging the duration of Parliament. . . . London, 1782.   4°.

486. WORDSWORTH, C. F. F.   The law and practice of elections (for England and Wales) as altered by the Reform Act, etc., including the practice of election petitions.   With a copious appendix, containing all the acts on elections; with the reform, and the division of counties and boundary of borough acts; new forms to be used in elections; lists of boroughs, etc., etc.   London, [1832.]   8°.

487. † WYVILL, CHRISTOPHER.   Political and historical arguments proving the necessity of parliamentary reform.   2 vols.   York, 1811.   8°.

488. —— Political papers, chiefly respecting the attempt of the county of York and other considerable districts, commenced in 1779 and continued during several subsequent years, to effect a reformation of the Parliament of Great Britain.   6 vols.   York, [1794–1802.]   8°.

Many of these papers discuss borough representation.

489. —— A summary explanation of the principles of Mr. Pitt's intended bill for amending the representation of the people in Parliament.   London, 1785.   8°.

The Reform of 1867.

30 & 31 Vict. c. 102: an Act further to amend the laws relating to the Representation of the People in England and Wales.
The fullest account is that of Cox (No. 496).

490. ANSTEY, T. C.   Notes upon "The Representation of the People Act" 1867 (30 & 31 Vict. c. 102).   With appendices concerning the antient rights, the rights conferred by the [Act] 2 & 3 Will. IV. c. 45. . . . London, 1867.   8°.

491. —— Plea of the unrepresented commons for restitution of franchise.   An historic inquiry.   London, 1866.   8°.

A good general sketch of the history of borough suffrage.

E

492. AUSTIN, JOHN. A plea for the constitution [against reform.] Third edition. London, 1859. 8°. pp. 42.

493. BRIGHT, JOHN. Speeches on parliamentary reform, etc.; delivered during the autumn of 1866. . . . Manchester and London, [1867.] 8°.

494. BROUGHAM, HENRY. Lord Brougham's speech on parliamentary reform, in the House of Lords, August 3rd, 1857. London, 1857. 8°.

495. COLE, H. W. The middle classes and the borough franchise. London, 1866. 8°.

496. COX, HOMERSHAM. A history of the Reform Bills of 1866 and 1867. London, 1868. 8°.

497. DISRAELI, BENJAMIN. Constitutional Reform: five speeches by the right hon. Benjamin Disraeli (1859–1865). Edited (by permission), with an introduction, by John F. Bulley. To which is added an appendix. London, 1866. 8°.

498. —— Parliamentary reform. A series of speeches on that subject delivered in the House of Commons by the right hon. B. Disraeli (1848–1866). . . . Edited by Montagu Corry. London, 1867. 8°.

499. Essays on reform. London, 1867. 8°.

Essays by G. C. Brodrick, A. H. Hutton, Lord Houghton, A. V. Dicey, Leslie Stephen, J. B. Kinnear, B. Cracroft, C. H. Pearson, Goldwin Smith, James Bryce, A. O. Rutson, G. Young.

500. Few facts (A) and fallacies about parliamentary reform. London, 1859. 8°.

501. GLADSTONE, W. E. Speeches on parliamentary reform in 1866. With an appendix. London, 1866. 8°.

2nd and 3rd editions, 1866.

502. GLEN, W. C., and LOVESY, C. W. The Representation of the People Act, 1867, the Boundary Act, 1868, and the Parliamentary Electors Registration Act, 1868. With introduction, notes, and index. Third edition. London, 1868. 12°.

1st edition, 1867.

503. Hickson, W. E. Tracts for inquirers. No. i. Reform. No. ii. Reform illusions. 2 pts. London, 1867. 8°.

504. Lowe, Robert. Speeches and letters on reform; with a preface. London, 1867. 8°.

505. McCarthy, Justin. A history of our own times from the accession of Queen Victoria to the general election of 1880. A new edition. 4 vols. London, 1882. 8°.

Chs. li.-lii. The reform of 1867.

506. Marmion, Anthony. A letter addressed to the people of Great Britain and Ireland on parliamentary reform, past, present, and to come. Dublin, 1859. 8°.

507. Mill, J. S. Thoughts on parliamentary reform. Second edition, with additions. London, 1859. 8°.

1st edition, 1859.
Reprinted in Mill's *Dissertations and Discussions* (4 vols., London, 1859-75), iii. 1-46. Cf. also his essay, " Recent Writers on Reform," ibid., iii. 47-96.

508. Parliamentary reform. London, 1867. 8°.

509. Parliamentary reform, considered under the views suggested by evidence given before the election committees of 1853. London, 1854. 8°.

510. Parliamentary reform. A letter to Richard Freedom, Esq., on the re-distribution, extension, and purification of the elective franchise. By a revising barrister. London, 1853. 8°.

511. † Wilkinson, Robert. The Representation of the People Act, 1867. . . . London, 1868. 12°.

The Reforms of 1884-1885.

48 Vict. c. 3 : An Act to amend the law relating to the Representation of the People of the United Kingdom.

48 & 49 Vict. c. 23 : An Act for the Redistribution of Seats at Parliamentary Elections, and for other purposes.

The best accounts are those of Heaton, Murdoch, and McCarthy (Nos. 361, 364, 520). For the periodical literature, see No. 523.

512. † Amerdroz, H. F. The reform measure of 1885 and subsequent general election, with its bearings on proportional representation. London, 1886. 8°.

513. BERNARD, H. F.   Redistribution by proportional representation considered with special reference to : 1. Population ; 2. Voting power.   London, 1884.   8°.

514. CURTIS, G. B.   Some facts about redistribution.   *National Review,* ii. 632–42.   London, 1884.   8°.

515. DILKE, C. W.   Parliamentary reform.   [Political Library for the People, No. 2.]   London and Belfast, 1879.   8°.   pp. 43.

516. GLEN, W. C.   The Representation of the People Act, 1884. With introduction, notes, and index.   London, 1885.   8°.

2nd edition, 1885.

517. HARE, THOMAS.   The distribution of seats in Parliament. . . . A paper read at the Manchester Congress of the Social Science Association, 1879.   London, [1880.]   8°.   pp. 11.

518. HARRISON, O. B. C.   The Representation of the People Act, 1884 (48 Vict. cap. 3), with introduction, notes, and tables, explanatory of its operation in England.   London, 1885.   8°.   pp. 86.

519. HOLDSWORTH, W. A.   The new Reform Act : comprising the Representation of the People Act, 1884 (or Franchise Act), the Redistribution of the Seats Act, 1885, and the Elections (Hours of Poll) Act, 1885 ; together with an introduction containing a complete description of the various franchises.   With notes and index. London, [1885.]   8°.

520. McCARTHY, J. H.   England under Gladstone, 1880–1884. Second edition, revised and enlarged.   London, 1885.   8°.

Ch. x.   Parliamentary reform.
Ch. xvi.   The Reform Bill.
1st edition, 1884.

521. MATTINSON, M. W.   The franchise acts, 1884–1885 : being the Representation of the People Act, 1884 ; Registration Act, 1885 ; and Parliamentary Elections (Redistribution) Act, 1885.   With introduction and notes.   London, 1885.   8°.

522. MAYNE, J. D.   The coming reform.   London, 1884.   8°. pp. 68.

2nd edition, 1884.

523. [Periodical literature.]

Essays dealing with the reforms of 1884–85 will be found in:

Contemporary Review, xliv. 905 (F. Seebohm).

Edinburgh Review, clix. 560; clxi. 272, 570.

Fortnightly Review, xli. 175 (A. Arnold); xliii. 1, 26, 202 (T. Hare).

Macmillan's Magazine, l. 241; li. 190.

National Review, i. 240 (H. C. Raikes); ii. 807 (P. Greg); iii. 373 (T. H. Hall); v. 94 (F. H. B. Daniell).

Nineteenth Century, xv. 293 (R. B. Hayward); xv. 703 (J. Lubbock).

Quarterly Review, clix. 220.

524. PIMBLETT, W. M.   English political history, 1880–1885. London, 1885. 8°.

For the Reform Bill of 1884, see chs. xiv.–xv.

525. SEAGER, J. R.   The Representation of the People Act, 1884. With introduction and index.   London, 1885.   12°.

2nd edition, 1885.

526. SWIRE, WILLIAM.   A project of electoral reform, containing a complete scheme for the redistribution of seats in England, Wales, Scotland, and Ireland. . . . London, [1884.] 8°. pp. 28.

527. WHITEWAY, A. R.   The three R's, representation, reform, redistribution, as taught in the national liberal school.   London, 1884. 8°. pp. 32.

§ 9. GILDS.

Many documents relating to religious and merchant gilds are printed by Smith (No. 537) and by Gross (No. 541).   A general collection of the ordinances of craft gilds is needed; abundant material for such a work is accessible in the Public Record Office and in the town archives.   Many ordinances of the crafts are printed in the histories of particular towns. (See below, Index, under " Gilds.")

No good comprehensive history of gilds has as yet been written. Brentano's sketch is brilliant, but unreliable.   Ashley, Cunningham, and Seligman give good short accounts.   The most detailed account of the gild merchant has been written by Gross; and the best account of the craft gilds, by Ashley.   Hegel's work is valuable, especially for the relations of the gilds to the origin of municipal government; Von Ochenkowski throws much light upon the relations of the crafts to the town authorities.

For a brief criticism of the principal authorities, see Gross, *Gild Merchant*, vol. i. app. A.

528. * ASHLEY, W. J.   An introduction to economic history and theory.· 2 vols.   London and New York, 1888–93.   8°.

Vol. i. ch. ii.   Merchant and craft gilds.
Vol. ii. ch. ii.   The crafts.
Valuable, especially for the history of the craft gilds.
3rd edition of vol. i., 1894.

529.   BECK, S. W.   Gloves, their annals and associations : a chapter of trade and social history.   London, 1883.   8°.

Companies of glovers, 135–61.

530.   BRENTANO, LUJO.   On the history and development of gilds, and the origin of trade-unions. . . . [A reprint of the introductory essay to Smith's English Gilds.]   London, [1870.]   8°.

See Nos. 531, 537.

531. —— Die Arbeitergilden der Gegenwart.   Erster Band.   Zur Geschichte der englischen Gewerkvereine.   Leipzig, 1871.   8°.

Some of Brentano's general conclusions are untenable.
The introduction and ch. i. of the German work contain the English essay (No. 530) with revisions.

532.   CUNNINGHAM, WILLIAM.   The formation and decay of craft gilds.   *Royal Hist. Soc.*, Transactions, New Series, iii. 371–92.   London, 1886.   8°.

Also separately printed, 1887.

533. —— The growth of English industry and commerce. . . . [Second edition.]   2 vols.   Cambridge, 1890–92.   8°.

A good account of the history of gilds will be found in §§ 67, 103–5, 127, 144–8, 177–9, 215; see also vol. i. app. E. of the 3rd edition.
1st and 3rd editions of vol. i., 1882, 1896.

534.   Diplomatarium Anglicum aevi Saxonici. . . . With a translation of the Anglo-Saxon.   By Benjamin Thorpe.   London, 1865.   8°.

Statutes of Anglo-Saxon gilds, 605–17.

535.   DOREN, ALFRED.   Untersuchungen zur Geschichte der Kaufmannsgilden des Mittelalters. . . . Leipzig, 1893.   8°.

§ 13.   Die Gilden in England.
A good short account.

536. DRIOUX, JOSEPH. Étude économique et juridique sur les associations. Paris, 1884. 8°.

General discussion of medieval gilds, 101–264.

537. *English gilds. The original ordinances of more than one hundred early English gilds : together with the olde usages of the cite of Wynchestre ; the ordinances of Worcester . . . with notes, by J. T. Smith, with an introduction and glossary . . . by his daughter, L. T. Smith. And a preliminary essay . . . by Lujo Brentano [No. 530.] *Early English Text Society.* London and Oxford, 1870. 8°.

The principal source for the study of social-religious gilds.

Exeter: ordinances, etc., of the gilds of tailors, cordwainers, and bakers, Edw. IV.—Hen. VIII., 299–337.

Winchester : old usages of the city, 14th century, 347–69.

Worcester: ordinances of the city (1467), 370–412.

538. FORTUYN, C. J. Specimen historico politicum inaugurale de gildarum historia, forma et auctoritate politica, medio imprimis aevo. . . . Amstelodami, 1834. 8°.

De gildis in Britannia, 87–103.

539. GIERKE, OTTO. Das deutsche Genossenschaftsrecht. 3 vols. Berlin, 1868–81. 8°.

Anglo-Saxon gilds, i. 221–37.

540. GROSS, CHARLES. Gilda mercatoria : ein Beitrag zur englischen Verfassungsgeschichte. Göttingen, 1883. 8°.

541. —— The gild merchant: a contribution to British municipal history. 2 vols. Oxford, 1890. 8°.

This is an expansion of No. 540.

Vol. i. app. D. The Scotch gild merchant.

Vol. ii. contains many documents concerning municipal history. The most important relate to the following towns :

Andover	Cirencester	Ipswich	Shrewsbury
Beverley	Coventry	Leicester	Southampton
Boston	Devizes	Lincoln	Totnes
Bristol	Dorchester	Lynn Regis	Wilton
Builth	Dublin	Newcastle-under-Lyme	Winchester
Burford	Exeter	Newcastle-upon-Tyne	Windsor
Bury St. Edmund's	Guildford	Newton (S. Wales)	York
Cardiff	Hope	Reading	Youghal
Chester	Hull		

The same writer gives a sketch of the general history of gilds in R. H. I. Palgrave's *Dictionary of Political Economy* (London, 1896), ii. 209–13.

542. HARTWIG, O[TTO]. Untersuchungen über die ersten Anfänge des Gildewesens. *Forschungen zur deutschen Geschichte,* i. 133–63. Göttingen, 1862. 8°.

543. HASBACH, WILHELM. Das englische Arbeiterversicherungswesen. . . . Leipzig, 1883. 8°.

Ch. i. Relations of medieval gilds to modern friendly societies.

544. *HEGEL, KARL. Städte und Gilden der germanischen Völker im Mittelalter. 2 vols. Leipzig, 1891. 8°.

See No. 87.

545. HELD, ADOLF. Zwei Bücher zur socialen Geschichte Englands. Leipzig, 1881. 8°.

Contains a good account of the craft gilds in the 18th century, 479–92.

546. HIBBERT, F. A. The influence and development of English gilds: as illustrated by the history of the craft gilds of Shrewsbury. [Cambridge Historical Essays, No. 5.] Cambridge, 1891. 8°.

547. HOWELL, GEORGE. The conflicts of capital and labour historically and economically considered : being a history and review of the trade-unions of Great Britain. . . . Second edition. London, 1890. 8°.

Ch. i., which deals with the history of gilds, is a résumé of Brentano's essay. 1st edition, 1878.

548. KROPTOKIN, P. Mutual aid in the mediæval city. *Nineteenth Century,* xxxvi. 183–202, 397–418. London, 1894. 8°.

549. LAMBERT, J. M. Two thousand years of gild life : or an outline of the history and development of the gild system from early times. . . . Hull and London, 1891. 8°.

The greater and more valuable part of the book deals with the gilds of Kingston-upon-Hull. General history of gilds, 1–110.

550. —— Some old Lincolnshire gilds. [William Andrews's Bygone Lincolnshire, 160–80. Hull, 1891. 8°.]

551. LIEBERMANN, FELIX. Die englische Gilde im achten Jahrhundert. *Archiv für das Studium der neueren Sprachen und Litteraturen,* xcvi. 333–40. Braunschweig, 1896. 8°.

Deals with the religious gilds mentioned in two letters of Alcuin.

552. LUDLOW, J. M.   Gilds and friendly societies.   *Contemporary Review*, xxi. 553–72, 737–62.   London, 1873.   8°.

553. —— Old guilds and new friendly and trade societies.   *Fortnightly Review*, New Series, vi. 390–406.   London, 1869.   8°.

554. OCHENKOWSKI, W. VON.   Englands wirthschaftliche Entwickelung im Ausgange des Mittelalters.   Jena, 1879.   8°.

Crafts, 49–150.
Valuable.

555. PAPPENHEIM, MAX.   Die altdänischen Schutzgilden. . . . Breslau, 1885.   8°.

Deals with the question of the origin of gilds in general.

556. PRING, J. H.   On the origin of gilds, with a notice of the ancient gild-hall of Taunton.   [Reprinted from the Proceedings of the Somerset Archæol. and Nat. Hist. Society, Dec. 18, 1882.]   Taunton, 1883.   8°.

557. ROCK, DANIEL.   The church of our fathers, as seen in St. Osmund's rite for the cathedral of Salisbury, with dissertations on the belief and ritual in England before and after the coming of the Normans.   3 vols., 4 pts.   London, 1849–53.   8°.

Gilds, ii. 395–453.
Deals especially with their religious observances.

558. ROGERS, J. E. T.   The economic interpretation of history. Lectures delivered in Worcester College Hall, Oxford, 1887–88. London and New York, 1888.   8°.

The gild and apprentice system, 295–317.

559. SALVIONI, G. B.   Le gilde inglesi.   Studio storico.   Firenze, 1883.   8°.

He adopts most of Brentano's general conclusions.   On pp. 34–69 he gives a careful analysis of the statutes in Smith's *English Gilds* (No. 537).

560. SELIGMAN, E. R. A.   Two chapters on the mediæval guilds of England.   *American Economic Assoc.*, Publications, vol. ii. No. 5. [Baltimore,] 1887.   8°.

Ch. i.   The guilds-merchant.   Ch. ii.   The craft guilds.

561. SMITH, [LUCY] TOULMIN.   Old English gilds.   A paper read before the Rotherham Literary and Scientific Society, December 2nd,

1878. (First read at Highgate, London, February 5, 1878.) Rotherham, 1879. 8°.

562. SULLIVAN, W. K. On the manners and customs of the ancient Irish. A series of lectures, delivered by the late Eugene O'Curry. . . . Edited with an introduction, appendixes, etc., by W. K. Sullivan. 3 vols. London, etc., 1873. 8°.

Pp. cxc.–ccxx. of the introduction treat of Anglo-Saxon and Irish gilds.

563. WALFORD, CORNELIUS. Gilds : their origin, constitution, objects, and later history. London, 1888. 8°.

This is the expansion of a paper on gilds, in the *Insurance Cyclopædia*, 1878, vol. v. (separately printed, 1880), and in the *Antiquarian Magazine and Bibliographer*, vols. i.–ix. (1881–86).
Reproduces the views of Brentano and other writers ; exhibits no research.

564. WEBB, SIDNEY and BEATRICE. The history of trade unionism. London and New York, 1894. 8°.

Ch. i. contains a good account of the various views concerning the supposed connection between trade unionism and the craft gilds.

565. WILDA, W. E. Das Gildenwesen im Mittelalter. Halle, [1831.] 8°.

English gilds, 43, 51–3, 65–6, 244–55, 376–86.
Valuable for the general history of European gilds, but not reliable for the study of English gilds.

566. WINZER, J. Die deutschen Bruderschaften des Mittelalters, insbesondere der Bund der deutschen Steinmetzen und dessen Umwandlung zum Freimaurerbund. Giessen, 1859. 8°.

Ch. iv. Englische Schutzgilden in den ersten Zeiten. (Based on Wilda.)
Ch. v. Die Bauhandwerker in England.

567. YEATS, JOHN. Guilds and their functions. *Society of Arts*, Journal, xxi. 178–89. London, 1873. 8°.

§ 10. COUNTY HISTORIES.

a. General, Nos. 568–570.
b. Particular Counties, Nos. 571–676.

Few of the county histories deal satisfactorily with the boroughs; but in some cases they contain the only account of the history of a town that has been written, and in other cases documentary material not printed elsewhere. The tables of contents given below under the various titles include only those boroughs the municipal history of which is considered in the county histories.

The older general topographical works, like Leland's *Itinerary* and *Collectanea*, Camden's *Britannia*, and Nichols's *Bibliotheca Topographica*, devote little attention to municipal history. Such portions of these works as fall within the scope of this Bibliography are included in Part II. under the names of particular towns.

Some of the publications of the county societies are of considerable value, and much use has been made of them below in Part II.

For works relating to the parliamentary history of counties, see § 8 *c.* For county histories of Ireland and Scotland, see §§ 12–13. For county bibliographies, see § 1.

a. GENERAL.

568. Beauties (The) of England and Wales: or original delineations, topographical, historical, and descriptive, of each county. Embellished with engravings. By E. W. Brayley and J. Britton [and others.] 19 vols. London, 1801–18. 8°.

569. [Cox, Thomas.] Magna Britannia et Hibernia, antiqua et nova: or a new survey of Great Britain, wherein to the topographical account given by Mr. Cambden, and the late editors of the Britannia, is added a more large history, not only of the cities, boroughs, towns, and parishes mentioned by them, but also of many other places of note. . . . Collected and composed by an impartial hand. 6 vols. London, 1720–31. 4°.

Only the English counties were published. Though each borough is very briefly considered, the municipal history receives more attention than in most of the older general topographical works.

570. LYSONS, DANIEL and SAMUEL. Magna Britannia : being a concise topographical account of the several counties of Great Britain. 6 vols., 8 pts. London, 1806–22. 4°.

Comprehends only the counties of Bedfordshire, Berks, Bucks, Cambridge, Cheshire, Cornwall, Cumberland, Derby, and Devon. The municipal history of the boroughs is briefly considered.

Vol. i. was re-issued in 1813.

b. PARTICULAR COUNTIES.

Brecknockshire.

571. JONES, THEOPHILUS. A history of the county of Brecknock. 2 vols., 3 pts. Brecknock, 1805–9. 4°.

Borough of Brecknock, ii. 7–26, 786–812.

571a. POOLE, EDWIN. The illustrated history and biography of Brecknockshire, from the earliest times to the present day. . . . Brecknock, 1886. 4°.

Borough of Brecknock, 26–33, 398–422 ; app. iv. (extracts from the town records, 1667–1730).

Buckinghamshire.

572. GIBBS, ROBERT. Buckinghamshire. A record of local occurrences and general events, chronologically arranged [A. D. 1400–1880.] 4 vols. Aylesbury, 1878–82. 8°.

Contains many brief notices of Amersham, Aylesbury, Buckingham, Marlow, Wendover, and Wycombe.

573. LANGLEY, THOMAS. The history and antiquities of the hundred of Desborough and deanery of Wycombe, in Buckinghamshire ; including the borough towns of Wycombe and Marlow, and sixteen parishes. London, 1797. 4°.

Of little value for municipal history.

574. LIPSCOMB, GEORGE. The history and antiquities of the county of Buckingham. 4 vols. London, 1847. 4°.

Amersham, iii. 146–80   Buckingham, ii. 546–87   Wendover, ii. 466–91
Aylesbury, ii. 1–71   Great Marlow, iii. 594–605 Wycombe, iii. 639–52

Brief accounts of municipal history.

Cambridgeshire.

575. BLOMEFIELD, FRANCIS. Collectanea Cantabrigiensia : or collections relating to Cambridge, university, town, and county, containing . . . a list of the mayors, the most ancient charters of the town, and other historical memoirs of several colleges, etc. Norwich, 1750. 4°.

Town of Cambridge (two Latin charters of Henry I. and two of John, etc.), 220–28.

Cardiganshire.

576. MEYRICK, S. R. The history and antiquities of the county of Cardigan. Collected from the few remaining documents which have escaped the destructive ravages of time, as well as from actual observation. London, 1810. 4°.

Aberystwyth, 411–29, 488–96, 503-7   Cardigan, 81–112, 486-8, 497–503

Contains the charters granted by Hen. VII. to these towns, with a translation. Apart from these charters, the work is of little value for municipal history.

Cheshire.

See No. 621.

577. EARWAKER, J. P. East Cheshire, past and present: or a history of the hundred of Macclesfield in the county palatine of Chester. From original records. 2 vols. London, 1877–80. 4°.

Borough of Macclesfield (town ordinances of 1602, etc.; the best history of Macclesfield), ii. 459–525.
Stockport (a brief account), i. 344–53.

578. HANSHALL, J. H. The history of the county palatine of Chester. Chester, 1817. 4°.

The dedication is dated 1823.
City of Chester (quite a detailed account of the history of the civic government), i. 130–304.

579. KING, DANIEL. The vale-royall of England, or the county-palatine of Chester . . . performed by W. Smith and W. Webb. Published by Daniel King. To which is annexed an exact chronology of all its rulers and governors. . . . 4 pts. London, 1656. f°.

Reprinted in Ormerod's history (No. 581), vol. i. Abridged by T. Hughes, London, 1852.

580. LEYCESTER, PETER. Historical antiquities, in two books. The first treating in general of Great Brettain and Ireland. The

second containing particular remarks concerning Cheshire. . . .
London, 1673. f°.

> Charter of Hamon de Massy granted to Altrincham, circa 1290, p. 203.
> Charter of William de Tabley to Knutsford, circa 1292, p. 295.
> Reprinted in Ormerod's history (No. 581), vol. i.

581. ORMEROD, GEORGE. The history of the county palatine and
city of Chester. . . . Second edition, revised and enlarged, by
Thomas Helsby. 3 vols. London, [1875–] 1882. f°.

Altrincham, i. 536–8	Knutsford, i. 488–93	Over, ii. 181–5
Chester, i. 181–395	Macclesfield, iii. 739–57	Stalybridge, iii. 86
Congleton, iii. 35–9	Middlewich, iii. 173–86	Stockport, iii. 788–806
Frodsham, ii. 46–59	Nantwich, iii. 421–50	

> Contains various early town charters.
> The best history of Cheshire.
> 1st edition, 1819.

Cornwall.

582. Complete parochial history (A) of the county of Cornwall,
compiled from the best authorities, and corrected and improved from
actual survey. Illustrated. 4 vols. Truro and London, 1867–
72. 8°.

Bodmin, i. 81–109	Helston, ii. 169–83	St. Germains, ii. 36–64
Camelford, i. 191–3	Launceston, iii. 64–92	St. Ives, ii. 252–72
Falmouth, i. 387–412	Liskeard, iii. 133–59	Saltash, iv. 134–7
Fowey, ii. 13–32	Looe (East and West), iii. 159–68	Truro, iv. 250–62
Grampound, ii. 112–14	Lostwithiel, iii. 169–79	

> Of little value for municipal history.

583. * MACLEAN, JOHN. The parochial and family history of the
deanery of Trigg Minor. 3 vols. London and Bodmin, 1873–
79. 4°.

> Bodmin, i. 101–346   Tintagel, iii. 185–276

584. WORTH, R. N. The ancient boroughs of Cornwall, with notes
on their arms and devises. *British Archæol. Assoc.*, Journal, xxxiii.
179–90. London, 1877. 8°.

Cumberland.

See Nos. 660, 662.

585. FERGUSON, R. S. A history of Cumberland. [Popular
County Histories.] London, 1890. 8°.

> Ch. xiii. The city of Carlisle.

586. HUTCHINSON, WILLIAM. The history of the county of Cumberland and some places adjacent. . . . 2 vols. Carlisle, 1794. 4°.

Carlisle (a brief account), ii. 585–681.
Egremont (charter of Richard de Lucy, temp. John), ii. 17–28.

587. JEFFERSON, SAMUEL. History and antiquities of Cumberland. . . . 2 vols. Carlisle, etc., 1840–42. 8°.

Egremont (charter of Richard de Lucy, temp. John, etc.), ii. 21–50.

Derbyshire.

588. BAGSHAW, SAMUEL. History, gazetteer, and directory of Derbyshire. . . . Sheffield, 1846. 8°.

Borough of Derby, 41–104.

589. GLOVER, STEPHEN. The history and gazetteer of the county of Derby. . . . Edited by Thomas Noble. 2 vols. Derby, 1831–33. 4°.

Chesterfield, ii. 293–330.
Derby (translation of charter of Charles II., etc.), i. app., 89–99, ii. 399–623.
Another edition, 1829.

590. PILKINGTON, JAMES. A view of the present state of Derbyshire; with an account of its most remarkable antiquities; illustrated by an accurate map and plates. 2 vols. Derby, 1789. 8°.

Borough of Derby (a brief account), ii. 134–96.

591. YEATMAN, J. P. The feudal history of the county of Derby, chiefly during the 11th, 12th, and 13th centuries. 2 vols., 4 pts. London, etc., [1886–] 1890. 8°.

Vol. ii. § iii. chs. viii.–ix. Chesterfield.
Contains valuable material.

Devonshire.

592. WORTHY, CHARLES. Devonshire parishes: or the antiquities, heraldry, and family history of twenty-eight parishes in the archdeaconry of Totnes. 2 vols. Exeter and London, 1887–89. 8°.

Dartmouth, i. 326–76, ii. 1–30.

Dorset.

593. HALLIWELL, J. O. On the municipal archives of Dorset. *British Archæol. Assoc.*, Journal, xxviii. 28–31. London, 1872. 8°.

The archives of Blandford, Bridport, Dorchester, Lyme Regis, Wareham, and Weymouth are briefly described.

594. *HUTCHINS, JOHN. The history and antiquities of the county of Dorset. . . . Third edition, corrected, augmented, and improved, by William Shipp and J. W. Hodson. 4 vols. Westminster, 1861–70. f°.

Blandford Forum, i. 214–47
Bridport, ii. 1–36
Corfe Castle, i. 469–549
Dorchester (by-laws, 1414, etc.), ii. 335–409
Lyme Regis, ii. 37–80

Poole, i. 1–76
Shaftesbury (extracts from court rolls 1449–88, etc.), iii. 1–112
Wareham (constitutions, 1664, etc.), i. 77–134
Weymouth and Melcombe Regis, ii. 418–78

The municipal history of these places is considered in detail. The work contains a translation of many borough charters.

1st edition, 2 vols., 1774 ; 2nd edition, 4 vols., 1796–1815.

Durham.

See Nos. 118, 657. The best histories are those of Hutchinson and Surtees.

595. FORDYCE, WILLIAM. The history and antiquities of the county palatine of Durham. . . . 2 vols. Newcastle, [1857.] 4°.

Durham, i. 194–386
Hartlepool, ii. 246–82
A brief account.

Stockton, ii. 149–200
Sunderland, ii. 391–423

596. HUTCHINSON, WILLIAM. The history and antiquities of the county palatine of Durham. 3 vols. Newcastle, 1785–94. 4°.

Barnard Castle, iii. 229–52
Durham (town charters in full), ii. 1–60
Gateshead, ii. 453–69
Hartlepool (translation of charter of 1593), iii. 16–38

Northallerton, iii. 421–41
Stockton, iii. 120–36
Sunderland, ii. 516–34

597. MACKENZIE, E., and ROSS, M. An historical, topographical, and descriptive view of the county palatine of Durham. . . . 2 vols. Newcastle-upon-Tyne, 1834. 4°.

Barnard Castle, ii. 222–48
Darlington, ii. 122–56
Durham, ii. 341–440
Gateshead, i. 79–107

Hartlepool, i. 458–90
Stockton, ii. 11–50
Sunderland, i. 257–338

598. RAINE, JAMES. The history and antiquities of North Durham. . . . London, 1852. f°.

Berwick (royal charter of 1604), app., 145–54.   Norham, 256–320.

599. SURTEES, ROBERT. The history and antiquities of the county palatine of Durham, compiled from original records. . . . 4 vols. London, 1816–40. f°.

Barnard Castle, iv. 50–126	Hartlepool, iii. 99–120, 386–8
Darlington, iii. 350–77	Stockton, iii. 168–96
Durham, i. pp. cxlvii.–cli., and iv. 1–168	Sunderland, i. 253–68, 297–8
Gateshead, ii. 105–35	

The early town charters are printed in full.

600. SYKES, JOHN. Local records : or historical register of remarkable events which have occurred exclusively in the counties of Durham and Northumberland, town and county of Newcastle-upon-Tyne, and Berwick-upon-Tweed. . . . New edition. 2 vols. Newcastle, 1833. 8°.

Contains notes on the municipal history of Berwick, Durham, Gateshead, Hartlepool, Morpeth, Newcastle, North Shields, South Shields, Stockton, Sunderland.

1st edition, 1 vol., 1824. Continuation (1832–57) by John Latimer, Newcastle, 1857.

Essex.

601. MORANT, PHILIP. The history and antiquities of the county of Essex, compiled from the best and most ancient historians. . . . 2 vols. London, 1768. f°.

Colchester, i. 1–195, and app.	Harwich, i. 499–502	Maldon, i. 331–8

Reprinted, Chelmsford, 1816.

602. WRIGHT, THOMAS. The history and topography of the county of Essex. . . . 2 vols. London, 1831–35. 4°.

Colchester, i. 266–361	Maldon, ii. 638–57	Harwich, ii. 813–20

Another edition, 1836.

Glamorganshire.

603. Cartae et alia munimenta quae ad dominium de Glamorgan pertinent. Curante Geo. T. Clark. 4 vols. Dowlais and Cardiff, 1885–93. 4°.

Contains charters granted to the following boroughs :

Avene, i. 208	Neath (1359, 1423, 1468), ii. 55, 100, 194
Cardiff (1453, 1465, 1477, 1600), ii. 170, 182, 216, 370	Swansea (1153–84), iii. 95
Kenfig (1423), ii. 101	Tewkesbury (12th century), iii. 78

Gloucestershire.

604. ATKYNS, ROBERT. The ancient and present state of Glocestershire. Second edition. London, 1768. f°.

Chipping Campden, 161–8   Gloucester, 44–101
Chipping Sodbury, 347–54   Tewkesbury, 375–400

Contains a translation of the charters granted to these towns in the 17th
century.

1st edition, 1712.

605. [RUDDER, SAMUEL.] A new history of Gloucestershire. . . .
Also the ecclesiastical, civil, and military history of Gloucester, from
its first foundation to the present time. . . . Cirencester, 1779. f°.

Chipping Campden, 319–25; app., xxxix.–xlii. Tewkesbury, 733–49; app., xxxi.–
Chipping Sodbury, 671–6   xxxix.
Cirencester, 343–68   Wotton-under-Edge, 846–54
Gloucester, 81–207; app., iv.–xii.

A brief account.

The appendix contains a translation of the charters of Charles II. to Gloucester, Wm. III. to Tewkesbury, James I. to Chipping Campden.

Hampshire.

The best history is Woodward's.

606. ADAMS, W. H. D. The history, topography, and antiquities
of the Isle of Wight. London and Ryde, 1856. 4°.

Newport, 114–22   Yarmouth, 174–8

A brief account, of little value.

New edition, 1884, 8°.

607. MOODY, HENRY. Notes and essays, archæological, historical,
and topographical, relating to the counties of Hants and Wilts.
Winchester, 1851. 8°.

Salisbury (a brief account), 232–47.

Southampton and Winchester (extracts from municipal records), 147–69.

608. SHORE, T. W. Early boroughs in Hampshire. *Archæol.
Review*, iv. 286–91. London, 1889. 8°.

609. WARNER, RICHARD. The history of the Isle of Wight. . . .
Southampton, 1795. 8°.

Newport, Newtown, Yarmouth, 129–46.

610. WARNER, RICHARD. Topographical remarks, relating to the south-western parts of Hampshire. . . . 2 vols. London, 1793. 8°.

Christchurch, ii. 37–88, and app.   Lymington, i. 1–44

611. WOODWARD, B. B., WILKS, T. C., and LOCKHART, C. A general history of Hampshire, or the county of Southampton, including the Isle of Wight. 3 vols. London, [1861–69.] 4°.

Andover, iii. 160–89   Petersfield, iii. 317–22
Basingstoke, iii. 208–68   Portsmouth, iii. 332–49
Christchurch, iii. 102–136   Southampton, ii. 131–374
Lymington, iii. 47–57   Winchester, i. 9–317

The best history of this county.

612. [WORSLEY, RICHARD.] The history of the Isle of Wight. London, 1781. 4°.

Newport, 147–55; app., Nos. 21, 41,   Newtown, 155–8; app., Nos. 41, 45
   45, 46   Yarmouth, 158–62; app., Nos. 41, 45

Herefordshire.

613. DUNCUMB, JOHN. Collections towards the history and antiquities of the county of Hereford. [Vol. iii. by W. H. Cooke.] 3 vols. Hereford and London, 1804–82. 4°.

City of Hereford, i. 219–604.
Contains a translation of the medieval customs or privileges of Hereford.

Hertfordshire.

614. CHAUNCY, HENRY. The historical antiquities of Hertford-shire ; with the original of counties, hundreds or wapentakes, boroughs, corporations, towns. . . . [A reprint of the first edition, one folio vol., 1700.] 2 vols. London, 1826. 8°.

Berkhamstead, ii. 515–50   Hertford, i. 452–524
Bishop Stortford, i. 323–35   St. Albans, ii. 240–336

Contains quite a full account of the history of Hertford and St. Albans.

615. CLUTTERBUCK, ROBERT. The history and antiquities of the county of Hertford. . . . 3 vols. London, 1815–27. f°.

Berkhamstead, i. 291–317; app., 41–6   Hertford, ii. 138–97 ; app., 1–5
Hemel Hempstead, i. 416–26; app., 48   St. Albans, i. 5–125; app., 1–41

For municipal history, the most important parts of the work are the appendices of vols. i.–ii., which contain the charters of Edw. VI. to St. Albans, James I. to Berkhamstead, Hen. VIII. to Hemel Hempstead, Mary to Hertford; and a survey of Hertford, temp. Edw. III.

616. CUSSANS, J. E. History of Hertfordshire. . . . 3 vols. London and Hertford, 1870–81. f°.

Berkhamstead, iii. (hundred of Dacorum) 48–85.
Hertford (survey in 1621, etc.), ii. (hundred of Hertford) 47–101, 261–6.

617. SALMON, NATHANIEL. The history of Hertfordshire; describing the county and its antient monuments. . . . London, 1728. f°.

Berkhamstead, 119–26   Hertford, 29–44   St. Albans, 67–93
Contains one of the best accounts of the municipal history of Hertford.

Kent.

618. FURLEY, ROBERT. A history of the weald of Kent, with an outline of the early history of the county. . . . 2 vols., 3 pts. Ashford and London, 1871–74. 8°.

Cinque Ports, i. 242–51, 309–14, ii. 73–5, 97–9.
Ancient corporate cities and towns (a brief account), i. 289–314.

619. HASTED, EDWARD. The history and topographical survey of the county of Kent. . . . Second edition, improved, corrected, and continued to the present time. 12 vols. Canterbury, 1797–1801. 8°.

Canterbury, vols. xi.-xii.   Fordwich, ix. 56–67   Queenborough, vi. 233–45
Deal, x. 1–23   Hythe, viii. 231–53   Rochester, iv. 45–191
Dover, ix. 475–548   Lydd, viii. 420–39   Romney (New), viii. 439–64
Faversham, vi. 318–71   Maidstone, iv. 260–324 Sandwich, x. 152–216
Folkestone, viii. 152–88

Much attention is given to the municipal history of Canterbury.
1st edition, 4 vols., 1778–99, f°. New edition by H. H. Drake, pt. i., 1886, f°.

Lancashire.

620. BAINES, EDWARD. The history of the county palatine and duchy of Lancaster. A new, revised, and enlarged edition . . . by James Croston. 5 vols. Manchester and London, 1888–93. 4°.

Ashton-under-Lyne, ii. 299–329   Kirkham, v. 356–79   Preston, v. 297–355
Blackburn, iv. 1–73   Lancaster, v. 442–90   Rochdale, iii. 1–92
Bolton, iii. 164–233   Liverpool, v. 114–207   Stalybridge, ii. 329–32
Bury, iii. 93–123   Manchester, ii. 3–299   Warrington, iv. 394–440
Clitheroe, iii. 336–54   Newton, iv. 381–93   Wigan, iv. 251–311
Garstang, v. 416–32   Oldham, ii. 372–87

Representative history of county and boroughs, i. 118–38, 370–75
The best history of this county.
1st edition, "History, directory, etc., of Lancaster," 2 vols., 1824, 8°; another edition, 4 vols., 1836, 4°; revised edition by John Harland [and B. Herford], 2 vols., 1868–70, 4°.

621. BAINES, THOMAS. Lancashire and Cheshire, past and present : a history and description of the palatine counties of Lancaster and Chester. . . . By T. Baines. With an account of the rise and progress of manufactures and commerce . . . by William Fairbairn. 2 vols. London, [1868–69.] 4°.

Chester (old customal, etc.), i. 551–4,   Liverpool, i. 701–11, ii. 147–58, 457–9
   637–56   Manchester, i. 686–701, ii. 130–7, 440–6
Lancaster, i. 665–79, ii. 190–5, 451–2   Preston, i. 679–85, ii. 453
   Progress of parliamentary and municipal boroughs, i. 635–7, ii. 440–60
   A good short account of municipal history.

622. CORRY, J[OHN]. The history of Lancashire. 2 vols. London, 1825. 4°.

Ashton-under-Lyne, ii. 497–522   Manchester, ii. 381–480
Lancaster, i. 552–616   Preston, ii. 49–241
Liverpool, ii. 683–706
   A brief account.

623. HARLAND, JOHN. Mamecestre, edited by John Harland. *Chetham Society.* 3 pts. [Manchester,] 1861–62. 4°.

Lancashire town charters, iii. 178–207 : translation of charters of Chester, Clitheroe, Lancaster, Liverpool, Preston, Salford, most of them of the 13th century.

Leicestershire.

624. NICHOLS, JOHN. The history and antiquities of the county of Leicester. . . . Including also Mr. Burton's description of the county, published in 1622, and the later collections of Mr. Stavely, Mr. Carte, Mr. Peck, and Sir T. Cave. 4 vols. London, 1795–1815. f°.

Hinckley, iv. 669–711   Leicester, vol. i., and app.
   The best history of this county.

625. THROSBY, JOHN. The memoirs of the town and county of Leicester. . . . 6 vols. Leicester, 1777. 12°.

The corporation of Leicester, ii. 6–27.
   A brief account.

Lincolnshire.

626. [ALLEN, THOMAS.] The history of the county of Lincoln, from the earliest period to the present time. By the author of the

histories of London, Yorkshire. . . . 2 vols. London and Lincoln,
1834. 4°.

Boston, i. 211–66   Great Grimsby, ii. 239–50   Louth, ii. 186–93
Gainsborough, ii. 1–30   Lincoln, i. 100–210   Stamford, ii. 318–40
Grantham, ii. 300–317

627. MARRAT, WILLIAM. The history of Lincolnshire, topographical, historical, and descriptive. 3 vols. Boston, 1814–16. 12°.

Boston, i. 1–80   Stamford, ii. 217–380
   A brief account.

Norfolk.

628. BLOMEFIELD, FRANCIS. An essay towards a topographical
history of the county of Norfolk. . . . Second edition. 11 vols.
London, 1805–10. 8° and 4°.

Castle Rising, ix. 42–59   Thetford, ii. 1–147
Lynn, viii. 476–533   Yarmouth (Great), xi. 255–399
Norwich, iii. 1–671, iv. 1–503
   Contains the best general history of Norwich.
   1st edition, 5 vols., 1739–75, f°, continued from p. 678 of vol. iii., by C. Parkin.
   Index nominum of 2nd edition, by J. N. Chadwick, King's Lynn, 1862.

629. LE STRANGE, HAMON. Norfolk official lists, from the earliest
period to the present day. Norwich, 1890. 8°.

   Lists of town officers and members of Parliament of Castle Rising, Lynn,
Norwich, Thetford, and Yarmouth. Similar lists were issued anonymously by
W. C. Ewing in 1837, but some of them begin at the Reformation.

630. RYE, WALTER. A history of Norfolk. [Popular County
Histories.] London, 1885. 8°.

Ch. x. The town life.   Ch. xii. The towns.

Northamptonshire.

See No. 2574.

631. BAKER, GEORGE. The history and antiquities of the county
of Northampton. [Not completed.] 2 vols. London, 1822–
41. f°.

   Brackley (abstract of charters of 1686 and 1688, etc.), i. 560–86.
   Daventry (translation of charters of 1576 and 1674, etc.), i. 304–47.
   The best history of this county.

632. BRIDGES, JOHN. The history and antiquities of Northampton-shire. Compiled from the manuscript collections of the late learned antiquary, John Bridges. By the Rev. Peter Whalley. 2 vols. Oxford, 1791. f°.

Brackley, i. 143–53   Higham Ferrers, ii. 169–79   Peterborough, ii. 537–77
Daventry, i. 41–9   Northampton, i. 420–58
A brief account.

Northumberland.

See No. 600.

633. * BATESON, EDWARD, and HINDS, A. B. A history of North-umberland. Vols. i.–iii. Newcastle-upon-Tyne and London, 1893–96. 4°.

Alnmouth, ii. 465–89   Hexham, iii. 236–308
Bamburgh Township, i. 112–74   Warenmouth, i. 193–7

634. HODGSON, JOHN. A history of Northumberland, in three parts. [Pt. iii. vol. i., 1820; pt. i. by J. H. Hinde, 1858.] 2 pts., 6 vols. Newcastle-upon-Tyne, 1820–58. 4°.

Morpeth, pt. ii., vol. ii. 369–534. (Valuable.)
Other boroughs are not considered in detail, though many documents refer to them.

635. HUTCHINSON, WILLIAM. A view of Northumberland, with an excursion to the abbey of Mailross in Scotland. 2 vols. Newcastle, 1778. 4°.

Berwick, ii. 41–105   Newcastle, ii. 366–430
A brief account.

636. MACKENZIE, E. An historical, topographical, and descriptive view of the county of Northumberland, and of those parts of the county of Durham situated north of the river Tyne, with Berwick-upon-Tweed. . . . Second edition, carefully corrected. 2 vols. Newcastle, 1825. 4°.

Alnwick, i. 433–84   Berwick, i. 265–302.   Morpeth, ii. 177–202
1st edition, " A historical and descriptive view," etc., 1811, 8°. (Anon.)

637. RICHARDSON, M. A. The local historian's table book of re-markable occurrences, historical facts, traditions, legendary and descriptive ballads, etc., etc., connected with the counties of New-

castle-upon-Tyne, Northumberland, and Durham. [Historical division, 5 vols. Legendary division, 3 vols.] 8 vols. London and
Newcastle, 1841–46. 8°.

Contains notes on the municipal history of Alnwick, Berwick, Durham, Gateshead, Hartlepool, Morpeth, Newcastle, North Shields, South Shields, Stockton,
Sunderland. See his indexes.

638. WALLIS, JOHN. The natural history and antiquities of
Northumberland; and of so much of the county of Durham as
lies between the rivers Tyne and Tweed, commonly called North
Bishoprick. 2 vols. London, 1769. 4°.

Berwick, ii. 431–45.
Morpeth (charter of Roger de Merlay, etc.), ii. 285–304.
Newcastle, ii. 177–249.

Nottinghamshire.

639. BAILEY, THOMAS. Annals of Nottinghamshire. History of
the county of Nottingham, including the borough. 4 vols. London
and Nottingham, [1852–55.] 8°.

See the indexes in vol. iv., under "East Retford," "Newark," and "Nottingham."

640. THOROTON, ROBERT. Thoroton's History of Nottinghamshire;
republished, with large additions, by John Throsby. . . . 3 vols.
London, 1797. 4°.

Newark, i. 388–406   Nottingham, ii. 1–171
   1st edition, "Antiquities of Nottinghamshire," 1 vol., 1677, f°; new edition,
with additions, by John Throsby, 3 vols., 1790, 4°.

Oxfordshire.

641. History, gazetteer, and directory of the county of Oxford:
comprising a general survey of the county; and embracing separate
historical descriptions of the university and city of Oxford, the
boroughs of Banbury and Woodstock. . . . Peterborough, 1852.
8°.

Banbury, 393–447   Chipping Norton, 509–21   Oxford, 264–336
Burford, 497–508   Henley-upon-Thames, 531–51   Woodstock, 447–73
   A brief account, of little value.

Radnorshire.

642. WILLIAMS, JONATHAN. History of Radnorshire. *Cambrian Archæol. Assoc.*, Archæologia Cambrensis, Third Series, vols. i.–iv. London, 1855–58. 8°.

Knighton, iv. 479–93   Rhayader (town customs, 1637), iv. 555–68
New Radnor, iv. 187–95, 233–4

Shropshire.

643. ANDERSON, J. C. Shropshire : its early history and antiquities. . . . London, 1864. 8°.

Bridgnorth, 11–35   Newport, 122–3   Wenlock, 239–45
Montgomery, 456–61   Shrewsbury, 166–94

A brief account, based mainly on Eyton's *Shropshire.*

644. EYTON, R. W. Antiquities of Shropshire. 12 vols. London, 1854–60. 8°.

Bridgnorth, i. 241–384   Ludlow, v. 233–301   Oswestry, x. 316–59
Burford, iv. 301–46   Montgomery, xi. 117–72 Wenlock, iii. 223–95
Clun, xi. 225–45   Newport, ix. 129–43

Contains valuable material for the medieval history of some of these boroughs, especially Bridgnorth.

The best history of this county.

645. LLOYD, EDWARD. Antiquities of Shropshire, from an old manuscript of Edward Lloyd ; revised and enlarged from private and other manuscripts, with illustrations, by Thomas Farmer Dukes. Shrewsbury, 1844. 4°.

Bishop's Castle, 97–8   Ludlow, 53–65   Shrewsbury, 1–42
Bridgnorth, 44–51   Oswestry, 301–6   Wenlock, 66–94

A brief account.

Somerset.

646. COLLINSON, JOHN. The history and antiquities of the county of Somerset, collected from authentick records and an actual survey made by the late Mr. Edmund Rack. . . . 3 vols. Bath, 1791. 4°.

Bath, i. pt. ii. 1–84   Wells, iii. 375–411
Taunton, iii. 226–40   Yeovil, iii. 203–12

A brief account.

647. PHELPS, WILLIAM.   The history and antiquities of Somersetshire. . . . 2 vols.   London, 1836–39.   4°.

Glastonbury, i. 485–565   Wells, ii. 1–169
   A brief account.
   Vol. i. re-issued in 1839.

648. RUTTER, JOHN.   Delineations of the north-western division of the county of Somerset. . . . London, 1829.   4°.

Axbridge, 170–81.

Staffordshire.

See No. 122.

649. PITT, WILLIAM.   A topographical history of Staffordshire. . . . Newcastle-under-Lyme, 1817.   8°.

Lichfield, 89–127   Stafford, 283–303
Newcastle-under-Lyme, 351–82   Tamworth, 138–45
   A brief account.

650. SHAW, STEBBING.   The history and antiquities of Staffordshire . . . including Erdeswick's Survey of the county and the approved parts of Dr. Plot's Natural History. . . . Vol. i., and vol. ii. pt. i. London, 1798–1801.   f°.

Lichfield, i. 231–375   Tutbury, i. 37–59
Tamworth, i. 415–34   Walsall, ii. 70–82
   A brief account.

651. Staffordshire and Warwickshire, past and present, by John Alfred Langford, C. S. Mackintosh, and J. C. Tildesley, assisted by eminent authorities in both counties.   With numerous illustrations from original drawings by H. Warren.   2 vols., 4 pts.   London, [1884.]   4°.

Birmingham, ii. 139–213   Stafford, i. 277–83   Uttoxeter, i. 319–28
Coventry, ii. 353–7   Sutton Coldfield, ii. 216–25 Walsall, i. 167–73
Newcastle-under-Lyme, i. 274–6 Tamworth, ii. 250–4   Warwick, ii. 286–319
   The notices of municipal history are brief.

Suffolk.

652. SUCKLING, ALFRED.   The history and antiquities of the county of Suffolk, with genealogical and architectural notes of its several towns and villages.   2 vols.   London, 1846–48.   4°.

Beccles, i. 1–24   Dunwich, ii. 229–307
   The account of Beccles is brief; that of Dunwich is fuller, and is taken from Gardiner's *Dunwich* (No. 1483).

Surrey.

653. ALLEN, THOMAS. The history of the counties of Surrey and Sussex. . . . 2 vols. London, 1829–30. 8°.

Arundel, ii. 520–4
Bletchingley, ii. 80–2
Bramber, ii. 534–5
Brighton, ii. 561–90
Chichester, ii. 491–511
Farnham, ii. 225–34
Grinstead (East), ii. 593–5
Guildford, ii. 105–42

Haslemere, ii. 68–70
Hastings, ii. 606–15
Horsham, ii. 528–30
Kingston, ii. 342–80
Lewes, ii. 543–61
Midhurst, ii. 511–13
Pevensey, ii. 601–3

Reigate, ii. 263–9
Rye, ii. 621–5
Seaford, ii. 597–601
Shoreham (New), ii. 531–4
Southwark, i. 199–319
Steyning, ii. 535–7
Winchelsea, ii. 625–31

A brief account.

654. BRAYLEY, E. W. A topographical history of Surrey. New edition. Revised and edited by Edward Walford. With numerous illustrations. 4 vols. London, [1878–81.] 4°.

Bletchingley, iii. 324–35
Farnham, iv. 316–35
Gatton, iv. 88–93
Guildford, i. 94–206

Haslemere, iv. 309–10
Kingston, ii. 190–238
Reigate, iv. 28–46
Southwark, iv. 354–88

Earlier editions, 5 vols., 1841–48 and 1850.

655. MANNING, OWEN. The history and antiquities of the county of Surrey. . . . Continued to the present time by William Bray. 3 vols. London, 1804–14. f°.

Bletchingley, ii. 290–316
Farnham, iii. 130–66
Gatton, ii. 227–40

Guildford, i. 7–111
Kingston, i. 329–406

Reigate, i. 271–328
Southwark, iii. 545–654

Sussex.

See No. 653.

656. DALLAWAY, JAMES. A history of the western division of the county of Sussex. Including the rapes of Chichester, Arundel, and Bramber, with the city and diocese of Chichester. 2 vols., 3 pts. London, 1815–30. 4°.

Arundel, ii. pt. i. 89–186
Bramber, ii. pt. ii. 172–213
Chichester, i. 1–215
Horsham, ii. pt. ii. 334–60

Midhurst, i. 281–94
New Shoreham, ii. pt. ii. 50–61
Steyning, ii. pt. ii. 157–71

Pt. ii. of vol. ii. by Edmund Cartwright; 2nd edition of this part, 1832.

657. HORSFIELD, T. W. The history, antiquities, and topography of the county of Sussex. 2 vols. Lewes and London, 1835. 4°.

Arundel, ii. 122–32; app., 29–32
Bramber, ii. 226–7; app., 33–5
Brighton, i. 104–56; app., 35–6
Chichester, ii. 4–32; app., 36–9
Cinque Ports, app., 58–9
East Grinstead, i. 385–91; app., 40–42
Hastings, i. 441–63; app., 60–63
Horsham, ii. 262–6; app., 42–5

Lewes, i. 201–18; app., 46–9
Midhurst, ii. 92–4; app., 50–52
Pevensey, i. 303–16
Rye, i. 487–501; app., 63–8
Seaford, i. 275–81; app., 68–71
Shoreham (New), ii. 208–14; app., 52–6
Steyning, ii. 227–9; app., 56–8
Winchelsea, i. 477–87; app., 72–5

Parliamentary history (by W. D. Cooper), app., 23–75.

658. PARRY, J. D. An historical and descriptive account of the coast of Sussex. . . . Brighton and London, 1833. 8°.

Brighton, 1–175
Cinque Ports, 300–308
Hastings, 219–40

Lewes, 325–36
Pevensey, 254–69
Rye, 285–99

Seaford, 189–94
Winchelsea, 270–84

A brief account.

Warwickshire.

See No. 651.

659. DUGDALE, WILLIAM. The antiquities of Warwickshire illustrated. . . . Second edition . . . revised, augmented, and continued down to this present time by William Thomas. 2 vols. London, 1730. f°.

Coventry, i. 134–200
Stratford-upon-Avon, ii. 680–97

Sutton Coldfield, ii. 909–19
Warwick, i. 371–467

1st edition, 1 vol., 1656, f°; reprinted, Coventry, 1765.

Westmoreland.

660. NICOLSON, JOSEPH, and BURN, RICHARD. The history and antiquities of the counties of Westmoreland and Cumberland. 2 vols. London, 1777. 4°.

Appleby, i. 308–55, ii. 563–6.
Carlisle (charters of Hen. III., and Edw. III., etc.), ii. 228–310, 538–46, 580–83
Egremont (charter of Richard de Lucy, etc.), ii. 31–5, 526–8.
Kendal, i. 65–86.
Proclamation by James II. for restoring to corporations their ancient charters, ii. 584–7.

661. SAYER, [W.] Sayer's History of Westmorland, containing the substance of all the remarkable events recorded by Burn and Nicolson, together with a variety of interesting and useful information from ancient MSS. . . . Vol. i. Kendal and London, 1847. 8°.

Appleby, i. 457–80   Kendal, i. 105–48

662. WHELLAN, WILLIAM. The history and topography of the counties of Cumberland and Westmoreland, comprising their ancient and modern history. . . . Pontefract, etc., 1860. 4°.

Appleby, 713–20   Cockermouth, 299–312   Kendal, 838–57
Carlisle, 83–141   Egremont, 378–89   Whitehaven, 440–58

Wiltshire.

See No. 607.

663. HOARE, R. C. The modern history of South Wiltshire. 6 vols. London, 1822–43. f°.

The hundreds of Everley, Heytesbury, and Mere, by R. C. Hoare; Branch and Dole, by R. C. Hoare and John Offer; Westbury, by R. C. Hoare and Richard Harris; Downton, by George Matcham; Old and New Sarum, by Robert Benson and Henry Hatcher.

Downton, iii. (Downton) 13–72   Old and New Sarum, vi. 1–855
Heytesbury, i. (Heytesbury) 82–154 Westbury, iii. (Westbury) 1–65
Hindon, i. (Mere) 194–5   Wilton, ii. (Branch and Dole) 55–158, 214–26
Ludgershall, ii. (Everley, etc.) 83–8

The volume on Salisbury is particularly valuable.

Worcestershire.

664. [NASH, T. R.] Collections for the history of Worcestershire. 2 vols. London, 1781–82. f°.

Bewdley, vol. i. p. xxxi., ii. 274–94   Kidderminster, ii. 34–62
Bromsgrove, i. 150–78   Worcester, vol. i. p. xxix.; ii. app.,
Droitwich, vol. i. pp. xxxii., 295–357   xcvi.-clxviii.
Evesham, vol. i. pp. xxx., 396–438

Contains a brief account of municipal history; the charter of King John and a translation of the charter of James I. to Droitwich; a translation of James I.'s charters to Bewdley and Evesham.

The second edition, 1799, is a reprint of the first. Index by John Amphlett, 2 vols., Oxford, 1894–95, f°.

665. [Noake, John.] Noake's Guide to Worcestershire. London and Worcester, 1868. 8°.

Bewdley, 33–45   Evesham, 150–60   Worcester, 359–81
Droitwich, 113–27   Kidderminster, 213–28
A brief account.

Yorkshire.

See Nos. 1386, 2658.

666. Allen, Thomas. A new and complete history of the county of York. . . . 3 vols. London, 1828–31. 4°.

Beverley, ii. 111–204   Malton, iii. 464–7   Scarborough, iii. 446–57
Doncaster, iii. 175–99   Pontefract, iii. 200–222 Sheffield, iii. 1–72
Hull, ii. 1–110   Richmond, iii. 508–12   York, i. 225–465
Leeds, ii. 469–598
Also published in six vols., 1829–31, 8°.

667. Baines, Thomas. Yorkshire, past and present: a history and description of the three ridings of the great county of York, from the earliest ages to the year 1870. . . . 2 vols. London, etc., [1871–77.] 4°.

Bradford, ii. 242–352   Hull, ii. 509–46   Sheffield, ii. 470–508
Dewsbury, ii. 445–56   Leeds, ii. 91–241   Wakefield, ii. 457–69
Halifax, ii. 353–418   Middlesborough, ii. 570–80 York, ii. 1–90
Huddersfield, ii. 419–44 Scarborough, ii. 547–64
Early charters of Yorkshire boroughs, i. 506–7

668. Boyle, J. R. The lost towns of the Humber. . . . Hull and London, 1889. 8°.

Ravenser, 1–65.

669. Cartwright, J. J. Chapters in the history of Yorkshire : being a collection of original letters, papers, and public documents, illustrating the state of that county in the reigns of Elizabeth, James I., and Charles I. Wakefield, 1872. 8°.

Ch. iv. Yorkshire representatives and their contemporaries, 1603-1628.
Ch. v. Towns and their trades (Doncaster, Halifax, Hull, Leeds, Scarborough, Wakefield, York).

670. Mayhall, John. The annals of York, Leeds, Bradford, Halifax, Doncaster, Barnsley, Wakefield, Dewsbury, Huddersfield,

Keighley, and other places in the county of York, from the earliest period to the present time.　Leeds, 1860.　12°.

A brief account, of little value.

Other editions : " The annals of Yorkshire," 2 vols., [1866]; 3 vols., [1878] and [1885.]

671.　PARSONS, EDWARD.　The civil, ecclesiastical, literary,. commercial, and miscellaneous history of Leeds, Halifax, Huddersfield, Bradford, Wakefield, Dewsbury, Otley, and the manufacturing district of Yorkshire.　2 vols.　Leeds, 1834.　8°.

A brief account.

672.　POULSON, GEORGE.　The history and antiquities of the seigniory of Holderness, in the east riding of the county of York. . . . 2 vols.　Hull, 1840–41.　4°.

Hedon, ii. 104–80　　　　　　　　Ravenser, ii. 527–40

Contains the charter of Edw. III. to Hedon, and brief extracts from the town records of Hedon, from the 13th to the 18th century.

673.　SHEAHAN, J. J., and WHELLAN, T.　History and topography of the city of York ; the Ainsty wapentake ; and the east riding of Yorkshire : embracing a general review of the early history of Great Britain, and a general history and description of the county of York. [Vol. iii. History of the wapentake of Claro.]　3 vols.　Beverley, 1855–56–71.　8°.

Beverley, ii. 166–302　　Knaresborough, iii. 78–136.　　York, i. 289–694
Hull, ii. 1–165　　　　　Ripon, iii. 1–78

A brief account.

674.　SMITH, WILLIAM.　Old Yorkshire.　Edited by William Smith. 5 vols.　London, 1881–84.　8° and 4°.

Halifax parliamentary representation, etc., by J. W. Davis, ii. 205–10, v. 17–25, 286–90.

Leeds parliamentary representation, etc., by J. D. Shaw and others, ii. 186–205, iii. 200–203.

Seals, plate, and insignia of Yorkshire corporations, i. 226–36, ii. 194–8.

The new series, 3 vols., 1889–91, is of little value for municipal history.

675.　WAINWRIGHT, JOHN.　Yorkshire.　An historical and topographical view of the wapentake of Strafford and Tickhill. . . . Vol. i. Sheffield, 1826.　4°.

Doncaster, i. 1–151.

676. WHITAKER, T. D. A history of Richmondshire, in the north riding of the county of York. . . . 2 vols. London, 1823. f°.

The borough of Richmond, i. 55, 60, 94–103. (A brief account.)

§ 11. THE CINQUE PORTS.

a. Records, Nos. 677–685.
b. General Histories, etc., Nos. 686–705.

Most of the records belonging to the Cinque Ports are kept in an iron chest at New Romney; some of them are in Dover Castle. The records at New Romney are: reports of the bailiffs who looked after the interests of the Cinque Ports at the Yarmouth fair, 1582–1630; the White Book, containing acts and decrees of the courts of brotherhood, 10 Hen. VI.— 9 Eliz.; the Black Book or Register Book, containing acts of the courts of brotherhood, 14 Eliz. — 1865. See No. 62.

There is no good detailed history of the Cinque Ports. Burrows (No. 689) gives the best general account. Much documentary material will be found in Jeake's *Charters* and Lyon's *Dover* (Nos. 680, 682). The works of Boys and Holloway (Nos. 687, 693) are also valuable.

a. RECORDS.

677. †Collection (A) of the statutes relating to the Cinque Ports. London, 1726. 8°.

678. Great and ancient charter (The) of the Cinque Ports of our lord the king, and of the members of the same [Dec. 23, 1668.] Printed for the mayor and jurats of Hastings. London, 1682. 12°.

Translation only.

679. Great and ancient charter (The) of the Cinque Ports, and its members. From the first granted by King Ed. the 1st to the last charter granted by King Charles the 2d. Printed from an ancient copy dated 1668. By C. Mate. Dover, [1807.] 8°.

Translation only.

680. *JEAKE, SAMUEL. Charters of the Cinque Ports, two ancient towns, and their members; translated into English, with annotations historical and critical thereupon. Wherein divers old words are ex-plain'd, and some of their ancient customs and privileges observ'd. London, 1728. f°.

Latin, with English translation.

681. LARKING, L. B. The Domesday Book of Kent. . . . London, 1869. f°.

App. v. contains a brief account of the lost "Ports Domesday Book."

682. *LYON, JOHN. The history of the town and port of Dover, and of Dover Castle; with a short account of the Cinque Ports. 2 vols. Dover, 1813–14. 4°.

Vol. i. pp. 246–366 deals mainly with the institutions of the Cinque Ports.
Vol. ii. contains an English version of the medieval customals of Dover, Romney, Rye, Sandwich, and Winchelsea.

683. Magna et antiqua charta Quinque Portuum domini regis et membrorum eorundem. [Printed for the mayor and jurats of Hastings.] Cantabrigiæ, 1675. 8°.

Latin charter of Charles II., 1668, inspecting charters of Edw. I., Edw. IV., and Elizabeth.

684. ROSS, THOMAS. Recorde of Thomas Lake, bailiff to Yarmouth from Hastings, and Henry Lennarde, bailiff to Yarmouth from Dover, in 1588. *Sussex Archæol. Soc.*, Collections, xii. 159–95. London, 1860. 8°.

685. SWINDEN, HENRY. The history and antiquities of the ancient burgh of Great Yarmouth. . . . Norwich, 1772. 4°.

Section viii. contains documents relating to the Cinque Ports.

b. GENERAL HISTORIES, ETC.

686. BLAAUW, W. H. The vessels of the Cinque Ports, and their employment. *Sussex Archæol. Soc.*, Collections, iv. 101–26. London, 1851. 8°.

687. BOYS, WILLIAM. Collections for an history of Sandwich in Kent, with notices of the other Cinque Ports and members, and of Richborough. Canterbury, 1792. 4°.

Deal (charter of Wm. III., 1699, with a translation, etc.), 615-50, 823-31.
Dover, 791-8.
Folkestone, 816-21.
Hythe, 811-13.
New Romney (compotus ville, 4–5 Rich. II., and other documents), 798-811.
Sandwich (see No. 2740).
Extracts from the registers of the Cinque Ports, Hen. VI. — Car. II., 773-82.
A valuable book.

F

688. BURROWS, MONTAGU. The antiquity of the Cinque Ports charters. *Archæol. Review*, iv. 439–44. London, 1890. 8°.

689. —— Cinque Ports. [Historic Towns. Edited by E. A. Freeman and W. Hunt.] London, 1888. 8°.

A good short account.

690. Cinque Ports (The) : their history and institutions. *St. James Magazine*, ii. 387–98. London, 1861. 8°.

691. Court of Shepway (1866). Statement of the right of precedence of Hastings [in that court.] [Hastings, 1866.] 4°.

692. HALE, MATTHEW (Chief Justice). Concerning the Five Ports; their names, privileges, and charges. [Francis Hargrave's Collection of tracts relative to the law of England . . . i. 106–13. Dublin, 1787. 8°.]

693. HOLLOWAY, WILLIAM. The history and antiquities of the town and port of Rye, in the county of Sussex. With incidental notices of the Cinque Ports. Compiled from manuscripts and original authorities. London, 1847. 8°.

The origin and services required of the Cinque Ports, 51–136. Valuable.

694. KNOCKER, EDWARD. An account of the Grand Court of Shepway, holden on the Bredenstone Hill, at Dover . . . August 28, 1861. London, 1862. 4°.

695. LOWER, M. A. Observations on the seals of the Sussex Cinque Ports. *Sussex Archæol. Soc.*, Collections, i. 14–25. London, 1848. 8°.

696. MANTELL, T[HOMAS]. An account of Cinque Ports meetings, called brotherhoods and guestlings. Dover, 1811. 4°. pp. 18.

697. —— Cinque Ports brotherhoods and guestlings. An account of the antiquity thereof, with the proceedings at the brotherhood and guestling in 1771. A new edition. Dover, 1828. 4°. pp. 36.

698. —— Coronation ceremonies and customs, relative to barons of the Cinque Ports, as supporters of the canopy. Dover, 1820. 4°. pp. 55.

699. MANTELL, THOMAS. Sir Thomas Mantell's new editions of tracts, relative to Cinque Ports and coronations, from 1771 to 1828. . . . To which is added a full report of the proceedings at the last coronation; and also a complete account of the brotherhood and guestling, last holden in 1828. Dover, 1828. 4°.

700. MARTIN, K. B. Oral traditions of the Cinque Ports and their localities, compared with antiquarian researches, natural causes, and their effects. London, 1832. 8°.

Of little value.

701. MOSS, W. G. The history and antiquities of the town and port of Hastings. . . . London, 1824. 8°.

The Cinque Ports, 6–38.

702. ROSS, THOMAS. Coronation services of the barons of the Cinque Ports. *Sussex Archæol. Soc.*, Collections, xv. 178–210. Lewes, 1863. 8°.

703. ROUND, J. H. Feudal England: historical studies on the 11th and 12th centuries. London, 1895. 8°.

Communal house demolition in the Cinque Ports, 552–62.
The Cinque Ports charters, 563–71.
Mr. Round seems to be right in rejecting Professor Burrows's view, that the Ports were chartered as a confederation by Edward the Confessor.

704. †RUSSELL, JAMES. The ancient liberties and privileges of the Cinque Ports and ancient towns; to which is prefixed an original sketch of constitutional rights, and the principles of our ancient representation, traced from the most authentic records, and supported by undeniable testimonials from the most respectable legal, political, and historical authorities. By James Russell, [of] Rye. London, 1809. 12°.

705. †Services (The) of the Cinque Ports. London, 1641. 4°.

" Rare and probably unique ": J. R. Smith, *Bibliotheca Cantiana*, 159.

§ 12.   IRELAND.

a. Bibliographies, Nos. 706, 707.
b. Records, and Reports of Committees, Nos. 708–721.
c. General Histories, etc., Nos. 722–724.
d. County Histories, Nos. 725–733.
e. Parliamentary History, Nos. 734–745.
f. Miscellaneous: Municipal Reform, etc., Nos. 746–754.

The most valuable sources for the study of the medieval history of Irish boroughs are the *Chartæ* and *Historic Documents* (Nos. 714, 715). The Report of the Corporations Commission, Gale's *Inquiry*, and Lynch's *Law of Election* (Nos. 718, 722, 723) throw much light on the general history of the subject.

a. BIBLIOGRAPHIES.

706. † Catalogue of the library of James Weale, Esq., containing an extraordinary collection of rare books relating to Ireland.   1840. 8°.

707. Catalogue of the library of Lough Fea, in illustration of the history and antiquities of Ireland.   [By E. P. Shirley.]   London, 1872.   8°.

b. RECORDS, AND REPORTS OF COMMITTEES.

See No. 722.

708. Calendar of documents relating to Ireland, preserved in her majesty's Public Record Office, London [1171–1307.]   Edited by H. S. Sweetman.   [Vol. v. by G. F. Handcock.]   *Rolls Series.* 5 vols.   London, 1875–86.   8°.

709. Calendar of the patent and close rolls of chancery in Ireland, of the reigns of Henry VIII., Edward VI., Mary, and Elizabeth.   Edited by James Morrin.   *Rolls Series.*   2 vols.   Dublin and London, 1861–62.   8°.

710. —— Calendar of the patent and close rolls of chancery in Ireland, of the reign of Charles the First, first to eighth year, inclusive.   By James Morrin.   *Rolls Series.*   Dublin and London, 1863.   8°.

711. —— A repertory of the inrolments on the patent rolls of chancery in Ireland, commencing with the reign of King James I. By J. C. Erck. Vol. i. pt. i. Dublin, 1846. 8°.

712. —— Rotulorum patentium et clausorum cancellariæ Hiberniæ calendarium. Vol. i. pars i. Hen. II.—Hen. VII. [Edited by Edward Tresham.] *Irish Record Com.* [Dublin,] 1828. f°.

The following publications of the Irish Record Commission were left unfinished and have no title-pages :
Calendar of patent rolls of Ireland, 5–35 Hen. VIII., f°.
Calendar of patent rolls of Ireland, 1–16 James I., f°. (Completed in 1886 by adding 17–22 James I., and the whole then published.)

713. Calendar of state papers relating to Ireland . . . [1509–99, 1603–25.] Edited by H. C. Hamilton [E. G. Atkinson, C. W. Russell, and J. P. Pendergast.] *Rolls Series.* 12 vols. London, 1860–95. 8°.

714. * Chartæ, privilegia et immunitates : being transcripts of charters and privileges to cities, towns, abbeys, and other bodies corporate, 18 Henry II. to 18 Richard II. (1171–1395). Printed by the Irish Record Commission, 1829–30. London, 1889. f°.

One of the most valuable sources for the study of the municipal history of Ireland. The principal documents (mainly town charters) relate to the following boroughs :

Carlow, Edw. I., 37.
Cashel, Hen. III.—Rich. II., 21, 52, 75.
Clonmel, Edw. I.—Edw. III., 38, 59, 64, 66, 71.
Cork, Hen. III.—Rich. II., 24, 36, 41, 48, 49, 54, 73, 79, 87.
Drogheda, Hen. III.—Rich. II., 20, 25, 28, 41, 46, 49–55, 62, 69, 78, 82, 83, 89, 90.
Dublin, Hen. II.—Rich. II., 1, 6, 11, 12, 19–21, 32, 47, 48, 50, 53, 56, 61, 76.
Galway, Edw. III., 69, 73.
Kells, Rich. I.—Rich. II., 10, 16, 17, 83.
Kilkenny, Hen. III.—Rich. II., 33, 34, 53, 69, 78–80, 89.
Kinsale, Rich. II., 79, 84.
Leighlin, Edw. II., 43.
Limerick, Edw. I.—Rich. II., 36, 40, 44, 45, 52, 71, 74, 88.
Rathcoole, Hen. III., 24, 33.
Roscommon, Edw. II., 43.
Ross, Edw. I.—Rich. II., 39, 47, 67, 73, 74, 84–6, 91.
Swords, Rich. I., 9.
Thomastown, Edw. III., 58, 68.
Trim, Rich. I.—Rich. II., 10, 36, 89.
Waterford, John—Rich. II., 13, 21, 22, 31–4, 42, 44, 60, 63, 65, 66, 70, 77, 79, 82, 83.
Wexford, Edw. II., 47.
Youghal, Edw. III., 67, 70.

715. * Historic and municipal documents of Ireland, A. D. 1172–1320, from the archives of the city of Dublin, etc. Edited by J. T. Gilbert. *Rolls Series.* London, 1870. 8°.

Contains many important documents relating to Dublin (town charters, Hen. II.—Edw. I., rolls of the gild merchant, town ordinances, etc.) ; the charters of Hen. III. to Drogheda towards Uriel and Meath, Nos. 26, 37, and 44 ; a compact between Drogheda and Dublin in 1252, No. 43 ; murage charter of Edw. II. to Drogheda in 1318, No. 91 ; compact of mutual support between Cork, Drogheda, Dublin, Limerick, and Waterford, No. 55, etc.

716. Journals (The) of the House of Commons of the kingdom of Ireland, from the eleventh year of King James I., anno 1613, to Aug. 2, 1800. [With appendix and index.]   21 vols.   Dublin, 1796–1802.   f°.

717. Liber munerum publicorum Hiberniæ, ab an. 1152 usque ad 1827 : or the establishments of Ireland. . . . Being the report of Rowley Lascelles. . . . Ordered to be printed, 1824.   7 pts., 2 vols. [London, 1852.]   f°.

Pt. i., " The parliamentary register of the Commons," contains a list of the M. P.'s of all Irish towns since the time of Elizabeth, and an abstract of the charters of the following boroughs :

Armagh, 3	Cork, 6	Ennis, 6	Londonderry, 26
Bandon, 8	Downpatrick, 11	Enniskillen, 16	Mallow, 8
Belfast, 1	Drogheda, 13	Galway, 17	Newry, 12
Carlow, 4	Dublin, 14	Kilkenny, 20	Sligo, 35
Carrickfergus, 2	Dundalk, 30	Kinsale, 7	Tralee, 19
Cashel, 36	Dungannon, 37	Limerick, 24	Waterford, 39
Coleraine, 28	Dungarvan, 40	Lisburn, 2	Youghal, 8

Pt. vi.   An abstract of the statutes of Ireland (1310–1829).

Pt. vii. pp. 162–72.   A further contribution to the parliamentary history of Irish boroughs (Jac. I.–Geo. III.).

This work was printed between 1812 and 1830, under the direction of the Irish Record Commission; it was issued from the Rolls House of England in 1852.

Index to the Liber Munerum, in 9th Report of Deputy Keeper of the Public Records of Ireland : Parl. Papers, 1877, vol. xlvi., app. iii.

718. * Report (First) of the commissioners appointed to inquire into the municipal corporations in Ireland.   [Report and appendix.]

Parl. Papers, 1835, vols. xxvii.–xxviii.; 1836, vol. xxiv. 3 vols. [London,] 1835–36. f°.

The appendix is in three parts, comprising six circuits and dealing with 116 boroughs. A separate appendix, in two parts, deals with Dublin.

One of the most valuable works relating to Irish municipal history.

719. Reports from the commissioners appointed by his majesty to execute the measures recommended in an address of the House of Commons, respecting the public records of Ireland; with supplements and appendixes. 1810–1815. *Irish Record Com.* [London, 1813–15.] f°.

Brief memoranda concerning the contents of the archives of the following boroughs:

Armagh, 209	Drogheda, 226	Limerick, 246	Tralee, 244
Athlone, 233	Dublin, 196–8	Londonderry, 214	Trim, 230
Belfast, 208	Enniskillen, 213	Maryborough, 232	Waterford, 249–51
Carrickfergus, 208	Irishtown, 222	Ross, 235	Wexford, 234
Cashel, 248	Kilkenny, 220–22	Sligo, 260	Wicklow, 237
Clonmel, 247	Kinsale, 241	Strabane, 217	Youghal, 241–3
Cork, 239–40			

720. Rules, orders, and directions by the lord lieutenant [Arthur Capel, Earl of Essex] and council, for the regulating of all cities, walled towns, and corporations in this kingdom of Ireland. Dublin, 1701. 8°.

For each of the boroughs of Drogheda, Dublin, Galway, and Limerick there are special Rules; other Rules apply collectively to Athlone, Carrickfergus, Cashel, Charlemont, Clonmel, Coleraine, Cork, Dundalk, Kilkenny, Kinsale, Londonderry, Ross, Strabane, Trim, Waterford, Wexford, and Youghal; and there are Rules for all cities, towns, and corporations in Ireland not mentioned above.

Other editions, 1672, 1742.

721. Statutes at large passed in the Parliaments held in Ireland from 1310 to 1800. 22 vols. Dublin, 1786–1801. f°.

c. GENERAL HISTORIES, ETC.

722. * GALE, PETER. An inquiry into the ancient corporate system of Ireland, and suggestions for its immediate restoration and extension. With an appendix, containing numerous original documents. London and Dublin, 1834. 8°.

A general sketch of Irish municipal history. The appendix contains many charters and other valuable documents, some of which throw light upon the general history of Irish boroughs, especially in the time of James I.:

Drogheda (translation of charter, 37 Hen. III.), No. 2.
Dublin (translation of charter of 1192), No. 1.
Dundalk (inquisition concerning the corporation, 6 Edw. II.), No. 27.
Dungannon (translation of charter of James I.), No. 20.
Inistioge (charter of the Prior, 1209), No. 5.
Kilkenny (charter of William Marshal, temp. Hen. III.), No. 7.
Rathcoole (two charters of Lucas, Archbishop of Dublin, temp. Hen. III.), Nos. 3, 26.
Rathmore (charter of Maurice Fitzgerald, temp. Hen. III.), No. 6.
Ross (translation of charter of James I.), No. 16.
Waterford (articles of agreement, 1818), No. 34.
Wexford (charters of Earl of Pembroke, 1317–18, and of James I.), Nos. 5, 17.
Letter and report of the Earl of Essex on Irish corporations, 1674, No. 23.

723. LYNCH, WILLIAM. The law of election in the ancient cities and towns of Ireland traced from original records. With fac-simile engravings and an appendix of documents. London, 1831. 8°.

A valuable contribution to Irish municipal history.

724. MARMION, ANTHONY. The ancient and modern history of the maritime ports of Ireland. Fourth edition. London, 1860. 8°.

Municipal history is only incidentally considered.
1st edition, 1855.

d. COUNTY HISTORIES.

See No. 1819a.

Carlow.

725. RYAN, JOHN. The history and antiquities of the county of Carlow. Dublin, 1833. 8°.

Borough of Carlow (charters, etc.), 60–63, 134–9, 209–18, 222–31, etc.
Old Leighlin (charter of Edw. II., etc.), 59, 73, 75, etc.

Cork.

726. BENNETT, GEORGE. The history of Bandon and the principal towns in the west riding of county Cork. Enlarged edition. Cork, 1869. 8°.

Chs. iii. xiii., xxv., etc. Bandon.
Ch. xviii. Clonakilty.

727. GIBSON, C. B. The history of the county and city of Cork. 2 vols. London, 1861. 8°.

Vol. ii. ch. viii. The city and the corporation of Cork.
Vol. ii. ch. x. Disfranchisement of county boroughs, etc.
Vol. ii. ch. xvi. Government of Cork, mayors, etc.

728. SMITH, CHARLES. The ancient and present state of the county and city of Cork. . . . Second edition, with additions. 2 vols. Dublin, 1774. 8°.

Bandon, i. 236–40   Cork, i. 361–429   Kinsale, i. 215–31   Youghal, i. 104-124
Reprinted by the Cork Hist. and Archæol. Society, edited by R. Day and W. A. Copinger, Cork, 1893–94. Issued with the Journal of the Society.
1st edition, 1750.

Limerick.

729. FITZGERALD, P., and MCGREGOR, J. J. The history, topography, and antiquities of the county and city of Limerick; with a preliminary view of the history and antiquities of Ireland. 2 vols. Dublin, 1826–27. 8°.

Vol. ii. contains an abstract of the charters of the city of Limerick.

Waterford.

730. † EGAN, P. M. History, guide, and directory of the county and city of Waterford. 2 pts. Kilkenny, 1893. 8°.

731. HANSARD, JOSEPH. The history, topography, and antiquities . . . of the county and city of Waterford; including the towns, parishes, villages, manors, and seats. Dungarvan, 1870. 8°.

Compiled mainly from the works of Ryland and Smith (Nos. 732, 733).

732. RYLAND, R. H. The history, topography, and antiquities of the county and city of Waterford; with an account of the present state of the peasantry of that part of the south of Ireland. London, 1824. 8°.

733. SMITH, CHARLES. The ancient and present state of the county and city of Waterford. Containing a natural, civil, ecclesiastical, historical, and topographical description thereof. Second edition, with additions. Dublin, 1774. 8°.

Dungarvan, 60–70   Tallow, 39–40   Waterford, 96–205
The accounts of Dungarvan and Tallow are meagre.
1st edition, 1746.

e. PARLIAMENTARY HISTORY.

For the reform acts of 1832, 1868, 1884, and 1885, see Statutes 2 & 3 Wm. IV. c. 88; 31 & 32 Vict. c. 49; 48 Vict. c. 3; 48 & 49 Vict. c. 23; and Hansard's *Debates.* See also § 8 (Nos. 332, 342–344, 402, 512–527, etc.).

734. BELMORE, Earl of. Parliamentary memoirs of Fermanagh and Tyrone, from 1613 to 1885. By the Earl of Belmore [S. R. L. Corry]. Dublin, 1887. 8°.

Deals with Augher or Agher, Clogher City, Dungannon, Enniskillen, and Strabane.
See No. 1595.

735. Collection (A) of the letters which have been addressed to the volunteers of Ireland, on the subject of a parliamentary reform. . . . London, 1783. 8°. pp. 122.

736. FALKLAND. Parliamentary representation : being a political and critical review of the counties, cities, and boroughs of the kingdom of Ireland, with regard to the state of their representation. By Falkland [J. R. Scott]. Dublin, 1790. 8°.

737. GRATTAN, HENRY. Memoirs of the life and times of the right hon. Henry Grattan. 5 vols. London, 1839–46. 8°.

Vol. iii. app. ii. State of the borough representation of Ireland, 1783.

738. †History (The) of the proceedings and debates of the volunteer delegates of Ireland on the subject of a parliamentary reform. . . . Dublin, 1784. 8°. pp. 155.

739. †HOUSTON, ARTHUR. The Irish Reform Act, and Registration Act, 1868. . . . Second edition. Dublin, 1869. 12°.

740. HUDSON, W. E. Treatise on the elective franchise and the registration of electors in Ireland under the Reform Act; with an appendix, containing all the acts in force and unrepealed relative to electors and elective rights in Ireland. Dublin, 1832. 12°.

Introd. ch. ii. Of the elective franchise as originally constituted.
App. ii., No. 2. The case of the town of Wexford, 1830.

741. LYNCH, WILLIAM. A view of the legal institutions, honorary hereditary offices, and feudal baronies, established in Ireland during the reign of Henry the Second. Deduced from court rolls, inquisitions, and other original records. London, 1830. 8°.

Ch. xi. contains many parliamentary writs issued to boroughs in the middle ages.
See No. 723.

742. MALCOMSON, ROBERT. The Carlow parliamentary roll, comprising lists of the knights of the shire, and members of the borough of Carlow [1613–1868] . . . and of the representatives for Old Leighlin to the period of the Union [1634–1798.] Dublin, 1872. 8°.

743. NEWPORT, JOHN. The state of borough representation in Ireland in 1783 and 1800. London, 1832. 8°. pp. 36.

744. TENISON, C. M. Cork M. P.'s, 1559–1800. *Cork Hist. and Archæol. Soc.*, Journal, Second Series, vols. i.–ii. Cork, 1895–96. 8°.

Contains biographical details regarding the M. P.'s for the city and county of Cork, and for the boroughs of the county.

745. WAKEFIELD, EDWARD. An account of Ireland, statistical and political. 2 vols. London, 1812. 4°.

Ch. xx. Representation.
A brief account of the parliamentary representation of each borough in 1812.

f. MISCELLANEOUS: MUNICIPAL REFORM, ETC.

For the Municipal Reform Act of 1840, see Statutes, 3 & 4 Vict. c. 108, and Hansard's *Debates*.
See Nos. 217, 218, 718.

746. BATTY, ESPINI. Reports of cases argued and determined in the court of King's Bench in Ireland . . . [1825–26.] Dublin, 1828. 8°.

Rex *v.* the Corporation of Dublin, 7 Geo. IV. (qualifications of freemen), 628–39.

747. CAPEL, ARTHUR. Letters written by his excellency Arthur Capel, earl of Essex, lord lieutenant of Ireland, in the year 1675. . . . Second edition. Dublin, 1773. 8°.

Concerning the renewal of the charters of corporations, 23–6, 149–52.
For other matters relating to towns, see 37–41, 94–6, etc.
1st edition, London, 1770, 4°.
See No. 722.

748. Cox, Richard. Hibernia Anglicana : or the history of
Ireland from the conquest thereof by the English to this present time.
With an introductory discourse touching the ancient state of that king-
dom. 2 pts. London, 1689–90. f°.

Municipal corporations in James I.'s reign, ii. 16–29.

749. Desiderata curiosa Hibernica : or a select collection of state
papers, consisting of royal instructions, directions, dispatches, and
letters ; to which are added some historical tracts. The whole
illustrating and opening the political systems of the chief governors
and government of Ireland, during the reigns of Queen Elizabeth,
James the First, and Charles the First. [Edited by John Lodge.]
2 vols. Dublin, 1772. 8°.

Municipal corporations, i. 221–6, 344–59, 510–13, etc.

750. Epitome (An) of the case of Irish corporations, intended for
the perusal of Protestants generally, and especially submitted to the
dispassionate judgment of the members of the imperial legislature.
Dublin, 1839. 8°.

Speeches, resolutions, addresses, and petitions concerning Irish municipal reform.

751. G., J. Irish municipal government. *Westminster Review,*
xlviii. 82–109. London, 1848. 8°.

752. †Haig, Charles. The municipal corporation acts of Ireland,
with a commentary. Second edition. Dublin, 1845. 12°.

1st edition, London, 1841.

753. Lewis, Samuel. A topographical dictionary of Ireland, comprising the several counties, cities, boroughs, corporate, market and
post towns, parishes, and villages, with historical and statistical
descriptions ; embellished with engravings of the arms of the cities,
bishoprics, corporate towns, and boroughs ; and of the seals of the
several municipal corporations. Second edition. 2 vols. London,
1842. 4°.

1st edition, 1837.

754. Rate-Payer (A). The Irish Municipal Corporations Bill. A
few words in time, on the subject of reformed corporations, and of their
powers of taxation. Addressed to all who are liable to the payment
of poor-rates in Ireland. By a rate-payer. London, 1839. 8°.

§ **13.** SCOTLAND.

a. Records, and Reports of Committees, Nos. 755–776.
b. General Histories, Nos. 777–784.
c. County Histories, Nos. 785–818.
d. Municipal and Parliamentary Reform, Nos. 819–860.
e. Law of Elections and Law Reports, Nos. 861–874.
f. Miscellaneous : Convention of Burghs, etc., Nos. 875–893.

" The ordinary bibliographical dictionaries are woefully deficient in respect to Scottish books, and are frequently very inaccurate. Information on Scottish bibliography has to be sought in many devious ways, and the searcher has not seldom to go away disappointed by failure, or but moderately satisfied with scanty and doubtful information." — T. MASON, *Public and Private Libraries of Glasgow* (Glasgow, 1885), 24.

Though much material is accessible in the various collections of records and parliamentary reports, and in the works relating to particular towns, a good detailed history of Scotch burghs is still needed.

For the history of Scotch gilds, see Nos. 541, 1649, 1658.

a. **RECORDS, AND REPORTS OF COMMITTEES.**

See Nos. 828, 1063.

755. Accounts (The) of the great chamberlains of Scotland, and some other officers of the crown, rendered at the exchequer, 1326–1453. [Edited by Thomas Thomson.] *Bannatyne Club*. 3 vols. Edinburgh, 1817[–45.] 4°.

756. —— Accounts of the chamberlain of Scotland, in the years 1329, 1330, and 1331. From the originals in the exchequer. With some other concise papers. [By John Davidson.] Edinburgh, 1771. 4°.

Reprinted in Sir David Dalrymple's *Annals of Scotland*, 1797, iii. 340–75.

757. *Acts (The) of the Parliaments of Scotland, 1124–1707. [Edited by Thomas Thomson and Cosmo Innes.] *Record Com.* 12 vols. [London,] 1814–75. f°.

Vol. i., published in 1844, contains the following documents, which are valuable for the study of municipal history :

Charter of Bishop Robert to the burgh of St. Andrews, 85.
Charters of Wm. I. to Aberdeen, Inverness, Perth, and Rutherglen, 86–9.
Charter of Alex. II. to Aberdeen, 87.
Assise Regis David I., 317–25.
Leges burgorum Scocie, 327–56.
Assise Regis Willelmi, 367–84.
Statuta gilde, 429–38.
Acta Parl. David II., 491–542.
Articuli inquirendi in burgo in itinere camerarii, 680–82.
Juramenta officiariorum, 683.
Modus procedendi in itinere camerarii, 693–702.
Curia quatuor burgorum, 703–4.
Fragmenta collecta, 717–54.

The following are some of the more important acts relating to burghs: 1424, c. 17; 1427, cc. 3–4; 1455, c. 9; 1469, c. 5; 1474, cc. 11–12; 1487, cc. 12–15; 1493, c. 14; 1503, cc. 28, 34–47; 1535, cc. 35–6; 1567, cc. 56–70; 1579, cc. 52, 57; 1581, cc. 47, 58–9; 1584, c. 25; 1587, cc. 109–18, 126–31; 1592, cc. 74–87; 1593, vol. iv. pp. 30–31, 45–6; 1606, cc. 31–7; 1633, cc. 24, 78–92; 1661, c. 157; 1672, cc. 5, 15, 37–8; 1673, vol. viii. app. 28; 1681, c. 148, and vol. xii. pp. 44–5; 1689, cc. 22, 32, 48, 50, 90; 1698, cc. 38–9; 1699–1701, vol. x. app. 107–148.

For many important documents relating to particular towns, see the names of the towns in the excellent index of the acts; see also under the words " Burgh," " Convention of Burghs," " Craft " " Guild," etc.

For legislation since 1707, see above, § 2 b.

758. Analecta Scotica: collections illustrative of the . . . history of Scotland. 2 vols. Edinburgh, 1834–37. 8°.

Extracts from the account book of the treasurer of Linlithgow, 1659, i. 204–9.
Disputes between magistrates of Dysart and Lord Sinclair, 1504–10, etc., i. 368, ii. 188–93.
Municipal statutes regulating sports, pageants, and processions in Aberdeen, 1440–1565 (relating mainly to the crafts), ii. 289–328.

759. *Ancient laws and customs of the burghs of Scotland. Vol. i. A. D. 1124–1424. [Edited by Cosmo Innes, with a glossary by J. D. Marwick.] *Scottish Burgh Records Society.* Edinburgh, 1868. 4°.

Contains: Leges quatuor burgorum; extracts from Assise Regis Willelmi; Statuta gilde; extracts from Regiam Maiestatem; extracts from Quoniam attachiamenta; Constitutiones noue pro burgensibus; Assisa de tolloneis; Custuma portuum; Iter camerarii; Juramenta officiariorum; Curia quatuor burgorum; Fragmenta collecta; Acta Parl. David II.; obligation of burgesses anent the ransom of David II.

760. Calendar of documents relating to Scotland preserved in her majesty's Public Record Office, London [1108–1509.]   Edited by Joseph Bain.   4 vols.   H. M. Register House, Edinburgh, 1881–88.   8°.

Contains only a few brief notices of boroughs.

761. Constitution of the royal burghs of Scotland; from their charters as exhibited in the report of the committee of the House of Commons, ordered to be printed 17th June, 1793 [below, No. 768]. To which is now added a translation of the election clauses, and acts of Parliament, relating to the government of said burghs.   Glasgow, 1818.   8°.

"In consequence of the universal interest excited at present by the subject of Burgh Reform, we judged it might be acceptable to the Public to reprint the following Report . . . as containing the most authentic and complete Burgh History, compiled from original documents."

Ancient constitution of the royal burghs (particularly Aberdeen), 6–36.
Present mode of election of magistrates and common councils, 37–46.

App. A.   Schedule of the royal burghs in Scotland, and clauses of election in some of their charters, 79–125.

App. B.   Extracts from the records of Aberdeen (1399–1580), 125–64.

App. C.   Abstract of the setts of the royal burghs, 165–218, etc.

762. HoÜARD [DAVID].   Traités sur les coutumes anglo-normandes, publiés en Angleterre, depuis le onzième jusqu'au quatorzième siècle. . . . 4 vols.   Rouen, 1776.   4°.

Leges et consuetudines burgorum, ii. 361–460.
Curia quatuor burgorum, ii. 461–4.
Statuta gilde, ii. 465–88.
Assisa Regis David, ii. 489–92.
Iter camerarii, ii. 493–528.
Statuta Willelmi Regis, ii. 533–62.
Assisa et statuta David II., ii. 653–88.

This collection has been superseded by No. 757.

763. *Miscellany of the Scottish Burgh Records Society.   [Edited by J. D. Marwick.]   Containing : i. Report by Thomas Tucker upon the settlement of the revenues of excise and customs in Scotland, A. D. 1656.   ii. Register containing the state and condition of every burgh within the kingdom of Scotland, in the year 1692. iii. Setts of the royal burghs of Scotland.   *Scottish Burgh Records Society.*   Edinburgh, 1881.   4°.

The preface throws much light on the general history of burghs.   Pp. 158–295 contain the setts of 65 royal burghs.

764. *Records of the Convention of Royal Burghs of Scotland, with extracts from the records relating to the affairs of the burghs of Scotland. [1295–1738. Edited by J. D. Marwick.] Published for the Convention of Royal Burghs. 6 vols. Edinburgh, 1866–90. 4°.

Contains much information concerning the burghal life of Scotland. The material relates to almost every royal burgh, and is particularly abundant concerning the following towns :

Aberdeen	Dumfries	Inverurie	Pittenweem
Anstruther Easter	Dunbar	Irvine	Renfrew
Anstruther Wester	Dundee	Jedburgh	Rothesay
Arbroath	Dunfermline	Kinghorn	Rutherglen
Ayr	Dysart	Kirkcaldy	St. Andrews
Banff	Edinburgh	Kirkcudbright	Sanquhar
Berwick (North)	Elgin	Kirkwall	Selkirk
Brechin	Forfar	Lanark	Stirling
Burntisland	Forres	Linlithgow	Stranraer
Crail	Fortrose	Lochmaben	Tain
Cullen	Glasgow	Montrose	Whithorn
Culross	Haddington	Nairn	Wick
Cupar	Inverkeithing	Peebles	Wigtown
Dumbarton	Inverness	Perth	

There is also much material concerning the gildry and craftsmen.

The appendixes are valuable, containing :

Extracts from Edinburgh records (1484–1614), ii. 484–562.

Extracts from records of Aberdeen, Ayr, Dundee, and Haddington (1563–1614), ii. 581–600.

Register containing the state and condition of every burgh in 1692, iv. app. iii.

765. Register (The) of the Privy Council of Scotland. Edited and arranged by John Hill Burton, 1545–1625. [Vols. iii.–xiii. by David Masson.] 13 vols. H. M. Register House, Edinburgh, 1877–96. 8°.

Each volume has a separate index, in which see the word " Burghs."

766. Registrum magni sigilli regum Scotorum in archivis publicis asservatum, 1306–1424. [Edited by T. Thomson.] *Record Com.* [London,] 1814. f°.

767. —— Registrum magni sigilli regum Scotorum. The register of the great seal of Scotland [1424–1651.] Edited by J. B. Paul and J. M. Thomson. 8 vols. H. M. Register House, Edinburgh, 1882–97. 8°.

Contains abstracts of many burgh charters.

768. Report from the committee to whom the several petitions presented to the House of Commons from the royal burghs of Scotland, together with the several accounts and papers relating to the internal government of the said royal burghs, were referred. Ordered, by the House of Commons, to be printed, 17 June, 1793, and to be reprinted, 23 April, 1819. *Parl. Papers*, 1819, vol. vi. [London,] 1819. f°.

A valuable collection of materials. For the principal contents, see No. 761.

This report was also published in Parl. Papers, 1793, vol. xiv., and in *The Scotsman*, Sept. 25 and Oct. 2, 1819.

769. —— Report from the select committee to whom the several petitions from the royal burghs of Scotland were referred. *Parl. Papers*, 1819, vol. vi. [London,] 1819. f°.

Deals in detail with the internal government of Aberdeen, Dundee, Dunfermline, and Edinburgh.

Valuable.

770. —— Report from the select committee to whom the several petitions from the royal burghs of Scotland, in the years 1818, 1819, and 1820, were referred. *Parl. Papers*, 1820, vol. iii. [London,] 1820. f°.

The minutes of evidence deal mainly with Cupar.

The appendix contains a valuable abstract of the setts of the various burghs.

771. —— Report from the select committee to whom the several petitions from the royal burghs of Scotland, during the years 1818, 1819, 1820, and 1821 were referred; together with the minutes of evidence taken before the committee. *Parl. Papers*, 1821. vol. viii. [London,] 1821. f°.

772. * Reports of commissioners on municipal corporations. General report of commissioners appointed to inquire into the state of municipal corporations in Scotland. [With appendix and local reports.] *Parl. Papers*, 1835, vol. xxix.; 1836, vol. xxiii. 2 vols. [London,] 1835–36. f°.

One of the most important sources for the study of Scotch burghal history.

The General Report gives an account of the general history of Scotch towns. The Local Reports, pts. i.–ii., deal with 84 parliamentary and royal burghs; and pt. iii. (vol. ii.), with 44 burghs of barony and regality, etc. The appendix to the General Report (vol. ii.) contains: early royal charters granted to Aberdeen, Ayr, Inverkeithing, and Rutherglen; documents concerning the Convention of Burghs,

A. D. 1700–1834; report of the state of royal burghs made to the Convention in
1691 [1692]. The appendix to the Local Reports (vol. ii.) contains charters, etc.,
relating to :

Abernethy	Eyemouth	Lerwick	Prestwick
Airdrie	Fraserburgh	Maybole	St. Andrews
Bathgate	Kelso	Melrose	Spynie
Castle Douglas	Laurencekirk	Paisley	Stornoway
Culross			

773. ROBERTSON, WILLIAM.   An index, drawn up about the year
1629, of many records of charters, granted by the different sovereigns
of Scotland between the years 1309 and 1413, most of which records
have been long missing. . . . Edinburgh, 1798.   f °.

Refers to many burgh charters. Some of them are printed in full or in the
form of abstracts, for example :

David [I.] to Wigtown, p. li.
David II. to Dunbar, 89.
Robert II. to Irvine, 95.

774. Rotuli scaccarii regum Scotorum.   The exchequer rolls of
Scotland [1264–1536.]   Edited by George Burnett [and others.]
16 vols.   H. M. Register House, Edinburgh, 1878–97.   8°.

Contains the accounts of the provosts and custumars of burghs from 1327
onward, etc.

775. * Sets (The) or constitutions of the royal boroughs of
Scotland, as recorded in the books of the Convention [A. D. 1708.]
Edinburgh, 1787.   4°.

Aberdeen, 12	Dumbarton, 45	Inverness, 14–21
Annan, 75	Dumfries, 75–7	Inverurie, 52
Anstruther Easter, 68–9	Dunbar, 66	Irvine, 71–2
Anstruther Wester, 69–70	Dundee, 14	Jedburgh, 65
Arbroath, 51–2	Dunfermline, 24–36	Kilrenny, 67
Ayr, 71	Dysart, 59–60	Kinghorn, 62–4
Banff, 54–5	Edinburgh, 1–6	Kintore, 52
Berwick (North), 64	Elgin, 52–4	Kirkcaldy, 60–1
Brechin, 50–1	Forfar, 41	Kirkcudbright, 77–9
Burntisland, 61–2	Forres, 48–9	Kirkwall, 55–6
Campbeltown, 72	Fortrose, 49	Lanark, 47–8
Crail, 68	Galloway (New), 73	Lauder, 67
Cullen, 64	Glasgow, 6–12	Linlithgow, 46–7
Culross, 38	Haddington, 65–6	Lochmaben, 75
Cupar, 42	Inverbervie, 52	Montrose, 50
Dingwall, 57	Inverkeithing, 36–7	Nairn, 79

Peebles, 46	Rutherglen, 43–5	Stranraer, 70
Perth, 13–14	St. Andrews, 40–1	Tain, 58–9
Pittenweem, 74	Sanquhar, 74	Whithorn, 72–3
Queensferry, 38–9	Selkirk, 45–6	Wick, 56–7
Renfrew, 42–3	Stirling, 21–4	Wigtown, 73–4
Rothesay, 71		

See Nos. 761, 763, 770, 833, 872, 873.

776. STIRLING, Earl of. The Earl of Stirling's register of royal letters relating to the affairs of Scotland, 1615–35. 2 vols. Edinburgh, 1885. 4°.

b. GENERAL HISTORIES.

See No. 862 and § 13 *f.*

777. ARGYLE, Duke of. Scotland as it was and as it is. By the Duke of Argyle [G. D. Campbell]. 2 vols. Edinburgh, 1887. 8°.

A short account of burgh history, i. 85–94, ii. 229–43.

778. BURTON, J. H. The history of Scotland. . . . Second edition. 8 vols and index. Edinburgh and London, 1873. 8°.

Municipal corporations, A. D. 1000–1290, ii. 82–97.

779. CHALMERS, GEORGE. Caledonia : or a historical and topographical account of North Britain. . . . New edition. 7 vols. Paisley, 1887–94. 4°.

Bk. iv. ch. vi. contains a brief account of the early history of towns.
1st edition, 3 vols., 1807–24.

780. Chambers's encyclopædia. . . . New edition. 10 vols. London and Edinburgh, 1892. 8°.

The article on "Burghs" seems to have been written by Joseph Robertson. See also the articles on "Convention of Burghs," "Municipality," "Town Council."

781. IRVING, JOSEPH. On the origin and influence of burghs in Scotland. *Glasgow Archæol. Soc.,* Transactions, i. 333–53. Glasgow, 1866. 8°.

782. MACKINTOSH, JOHN. The history of civilisation in Scotland. New edition. 4 vols. Paisley and London, 1892–96. 8°.

Chs. iv., x., xix., xxx., contain a good brief account of municipal history.
1st edition, 1878–88.

783. ROBERTSON, E. W. Scotland under her early kings. A history of the kingdom to the close of the thirteenth century. 2 vols. Edinburgh, 1862. 8°.

A brief account of municipal history, i. 292–311.

784. ROGERS, CHARLES. Social life in Scotland from early to recent times. 3 vols. Edinburgh, 1884–86. 8°.

Chs. viii., x., contain a brief account of parliamentary and municipal history. Laws of the chapmen of Stirling, 1726, iii. 371–6.

c. COUNTY HISTORIES.

General.

785. Statistical account (The) of Scotland. Drawn up from the communications of the ministers of the different parishes. By Sir John Sinclair, Bart. 21 vols. Edinburgh, 1791–99. 8°.

Devotes little attention to municipal history.

786. Statistical account (The New) of Scotland. By the ministers of the respective parishes, under the superintendence of a committee of the Society for the Benefit of the Sons and Daughters of the Clergy. 15 vols. Edinburgh and London, 1845. 8°.

The accounts of the history of the separate burghs vary in length; most of them are brief.

Aberdeenshire, etc.

787. ROBERTSON, A. W. Hand-list of bibliography of the shires of Aberdeen, Banff, and Kincardine. *New Spalding Club*. Aberdeen, 1893. 8°.

This rough list forms the basis of a more elaborate bibliography, which Mr. Robertson is preparing for the press.

788. TURREFF, GAVIN. Antiquarian gleanings from Aberdeenshire records. Second edition, revised and enlarged. Aberdeen, 1871. 8°.

Contains many extracts from the Council Register of the burgh of Aberdeen. 1st edition, 1859.

Ayr and Wigton.

789. PATERSON, JAMES. History of the county of Ayr; with a genealogical account of the families of Ayrshire. Vols. i.–ii. Ayr, 1847–52. 8°.

Ayr, i. 157–201
Irvine, ii. 82–100

Kilmarnock, ii. 147–71
Newton-upon-Ayr, i. 213–21

790. PATERSON, JAMES. History of the counties of Ayr and Wigton. 3 vols., 5 pts. Edinburgh, 1863–66. 8°.

Ayr, i. 1–155	Kilmarnock, iii. 371–474	Maybole, ii. 364–449
Irvine, iii. 249–80	Kilmaurs, iii. 448–77	Newton-upon-Ayr, i. 156–79

A brief account.

791. ROBERTSON, GEORGE. Topographical description of Ayrshire; more particularly of Cunninghame; together with a genealogical account of the principal families in that bailiwick. Irvine, etc., 1820. 4°.

Irvine, 401–22　　　　　　Kilmarnock, 371–84

A brief account.

Bute.

792. [BLAIN, JOHN.] Blain's History of Bute. Edited by the Rev. William Ross. Rothesay, 1880. 8°.

Ch. xiv. contains brief extracts from the town council records of Rothesay, 1654–1707, etc.

793. HEWISON, J. K. The Isle of Bute in the olden time. 2 vols. Edinburgh and London, 1893–95. 8°.

Vol. ii. ch. vi. The burgh of Rothesay: translation of charters of Robert III., 1401, and James VI., 1584; extracts from the burgh records, 1660–1798, etc.
A good account of municipal history.

794. REID, JOHN E. History of the county of Bute, and families connected therewith. Glasgow, etc., 1864. 4°.

Ch. ix. Brief extracts from the council records of Rothesay, 1660–1862.
App. i.–ii. Rothesay charters, 1400 (Latin), 1584 (Latin and English).

Caithness.

795. CALDER, J. T. Sketch of the civil and traditional history of Caithness, from the tenth century. Glasgow, etc., 1861. 8°.

Charter granted by John, Earl of Caithness, to Thurso, 1680, pp. 278–83.

Dumbartonshire.

796. IRVING, JOSEPH. The book of Dumbartonshire: a history of the county, burghs, parishes, and lands, memoirs of families, and notices of industries carried on in the Lennox district. 3 vols. Edinburgh and London, 1879. 4°.

Contains a detailed history of the burgh of Dumbarton, with copious extracts from the municipal records, 1627–56, i. 58–64, 128–34, ii. 1–145.
This is a new edition of "The history of Dumbartonshire," 1 vol., Dumbarton, 1857; 2nd edition, 1860.

Fife.

797. CONOLLY, M. F. Fifiana : or memorials of the east of Fife. Glasgow, 1869. 4°.

Anstruther Easter and Anstruther Wester, 179–201.
Crail (inventory of old charters, 1369–1755, etc.), 105–78.
Pittenweem, 202–21.

798. MILLAR, A. H. Fife : its people, burghs, castles, and mansions. 2 vols. Cupar-Fife, etc., 1895. 4°.

Forfarshire.

799. JERVISE, ANDREW. Memorials of Angus and the Mearns : being an account . . . of the castles and towns visited by Edward I. . . . Rewritten and corrected by James Gammack. 2 vols. Edinburgh, 1885. 8°.

Aberdeen crafts, app. vi.	Brechin, pt. ii. ch. v.	Forfar, pt. ii, ch. i.
Arbroath, pt. ii. ch. vi.	Dundee, pt. ii. ch. vii.	Montrose, pt. ii. ch. iii.

1st edition, 1 vol., 1861.

800. WARDEN, A. J. Angus or Forfarshire, the land and people, descriptive and historical. 5 vols. Dundee, 1880–85. 4°.

Parliamentary representation, ii. 194–224: (1) Members for Forfarshire. (2) Members for Inverbervie, Aberdeen, Montrose, Arbroath, Brechin District of Burghs. (3) Members for Forfar, Perth, Dundee, St. Andrews, Cupar District of Burghs. (4) Burgh of Dundee.
Burghs, v. 273–84.

Of little value for municipal history.

Galloway.

801. MACKENZIE, WILLIAM. The history of Galloway, from the earliest period to the present time. . . . 2 vols. Kirkcudbright, 1841. 12°.

Charter of Charles I. to New Galloway, ii. app., 9–11.
Charter of James IV. to Kirkcudbright, ii. app., 11–13.

Lanarkshire.

802. HAMILTON, WILLIAM. Descriptions of the sheriffdoms of Lanark and Renfrew, compiled about 1710. By William Hamilton

of Wishaw.　With illustrative notes and appendices.　*Maitland Club.*
Glasgow, 1831.　4°.

> Dumbarton, 187–8, 282–4.
> Glasgow (early town charters, etc.), 4–5, 155–201.
> Lanark (charters of Robert I. and Alexander), 256–7.
> Renfrew (charter of Robert III.; disputes with Dumbarton, 1424–29, etc.), 273–84.
> Rutherglen (charter of Robert I., 1324, etc.), 26–7, 221–30.
>
> Reprinted in New Club Series, Paisley, 1878.

803.　IRVING, G. V., and MURRAY, A.　The upper ward of Lanark-shire described and delineated.　The archæological and historical section by G. V. Irving.　The statistical and topographical section by Alexander Murray.　3 vols.　Glasgow, 1864.　4°.

> Burgh of Lanark, ii. 336–61.

Moray.

804.　DUNBAR, E. D.　Documents relating to the province of Moray.　Edited by E. D. Dunbar.　Edinburgh, 1895.　8°.

> Ch. i.　Elgin affairs, 1547–1810.

805.　—— Social life in former days, chiefly in the province of Moray.　Illustrated by letters and family papers.　Edinburgh, 1865.　8°. — Second Series.　Edinburgh, 1866.　8°.

> First Series, ch. xxiii.　Elgin town council.
> First Series, ch. xxiv.　Incorporated trades of Elgin.
> Second Series, ch. xxii.　Elgin burgh politics.

806.　SHAW, LACHLAN.　The history of the province of Moray. . . . Enlarged and brought down to the present time by J. F. S. Gordon. 3 vols.　Glasgow and London, 1882.　8°.

> Elgin, i. 346–408, ii. 1–38, iii. 60–70　　Inverness, ii. 322–34, iii. 57–9
> Forres, ii. 163–76, iii. 72–5　　　　　　 Nairn, ii. 262–9, iii. 71–2
>
> A brief account.
> Earlier editions, 1 vol., 1775, 1827, 4°.

Peeblesshire.

807.　CHAMBERS, WILLIAM.　A history of Peeblesshire.　Edinburgh and London, 1864.　8°.

> Peebles, 78–80, 256–315, 531–48.
> Contains the charter granted by James VI. in 1621, etc.

Perthshire.

808. FITTIS, R. S.   Historical and traditional gleanings concerning Perthshire.   Perth, 1876.   8°.

Jottings from the civic records of Perth, 327–36.

809. —— Illustrations of the history and antiquities of Perthshire. Perth, 1874.   8°.

Simon Glover and his craftsmen of Perth, 299–371.
Valuable for the history of the glovers.

810. —— The Perthshire antiquarian miscellany.   Perth, 1875. 8°.

Feuds of the town of Perth, 72–81.
Rivalry betwixt Dundee and Perth, 355–73.
Old Council-House of Perth, 374–9.
Merchant princes of Perth, 523–56.

811. —— Recreations of an antiquary in Perthshire history and genealogy.   Perth, 1881.   8°.

Incidents of citizen life in old Perth, 43–109.

812. —— Sketches of the olden times in Perthshire.   Perth, 1878.   8°.

Culross, 473–508.
Municipal elections in Perth, 509–20.
Extracts from minute books of Perth (1529–1770), 521–31.

Renfrewshire.

See No. 802.

813. CRAWFORD, G., and ROBERTSON, G.   A general description of the shire of Renfrew, including an account of the noble and ancient families. . . . Published in 1710 by George Crawford, and continued to the present period by George Robertson.   Paisley, 1818.   4°.

Paisley (brief extracts from town records, 1594–1664), 331–41, 500–508.
Renfrew, 341–8, 505–6.

814. HECTOR, WILLIAM.   Selections from the judicial records of Renfrewshire. . . . Second Series.   Paisley, 1878.   8°.

Section vi.   Paisley: names of feuars, 1490–1545; tenure by booking, etc.

Roxburghshire.

815. JEFFREY, ALEXANDER. The history and antiquities of Roxburghshire and adjacent districts, from the most remote period to the present time. 4 vols. London and Edinburgh, 1857–64. 8°.

Hawick, iv. 271–92   Kelso, iii. 6–86, 355–9
Jedburgh, ii. 97–221   Roxburgh, ii. 54–96

An earlier work of the same writer : " An historical and descriptive account of Roxburghshire," Edinburgh, 1836.

816. OLIVER, J. R. Upper Teviotdale and the Scotts of Buccleuch : a local and family history. Hawick, 1887. 4°.

Ch. xiii. Hawick : municipal enactments of the first half of the seventeenth century.

App. ii. A translation of Queen Mary's confirmation (1545) of the charter granted by James Douglas to the town of Hawick, 1537.

Selkirkshire.

817. BROWN, T. CRAIG. The history of Selkirkshire, or chronicles of Ettrick Forest. 2 vols. Edinburgh, 1886. 4°.

Galashiels, i. 478–559.
Selkirk (extracts from burgh records since 1514), ii. 1–380.

Stirlingshire.

818. NIMMO, WILLIAM. A general history of Stirlingshire. . . . Third edition, revised, enlarged, and brought down to the present time [by B. Gillespie.] 2 vols. London and Glasgow, 1880. 8°.

Falkirk, i. 260–82.   Stirling, i. 355–74.

Of little value for municipal history.
Earlier editions, 1 vol., 1777 ; 2 vols., 1817.

d. MUNICIPAL AND PARLIAMENTARY REFORM.

For the municipal reform acts of 1833 and 1889, see Statutes, 3 & 4 Wm. IV. cc. 76–7 ; 52 & 53 Vict. c. 50 ; and Hansard's *Debates.* For the parliamentary reforms of 1832, 1868, 1884, and 1885, see Statutes, 2 & 3 Wm. IV. c. 65 ; 31 & 32 Vict. c. 48 ; 48 Vict. c. 3 ; 48 & 49 Vict. c. 23 ; and Hansard. The act of 1846, abolishing exclusive trade privileges (9 & 10 Vict. c. 17) and the Municipal Elections Act of 1868 (31 & 32 Vict. c. 108) are also important.

See also § 8 (Nos. 402, 512–527, etc.) and Nos. 768–772, 962, 964, and 1537.

819. Abstract of facts, etc., respecting the revenues of the royal boroughs of Scotland. London, 1788. 4°.

An answer to the arguments of the burgh reformers.

820. Bill (A) proposed to be submitted to the consideration of Parliament, for correcting the abuses and supplying the defects in the internal government of the royal boroughs, and in the manner of accounting for the property, annual revenues, and expenditures of the same, in that part of Great Britain called Scotland. Prepared by the committee of delegates. [Edinburgh, 1787.] 4°.

See No. 834.

821. † Bill (A) for the better regulating the mode of accounting for the common good and revenues of the royal burghs of Scotland, and for controulling and preventing the undue expenditure thereof. [Edinburgh,] 1818. 8°.

822. BLACK, WILLIAM G. The law relating to Scottish county councils : being the Local Government (Scotland) Act, 1889. . . Edinburgh, 1889. 8°.

2nd edition, 1890.

823. BROUGHAM, HENRY. Speech of the lord chancellor upon the Scotch Burgh Reform Bill. Delivered in the House of Lords, Tuesday, August 13, 1833. [Speeches of Henry Lord Brougham. . . . iii. 359–86. 4 vols. Edinburgh, 1838. 8°.]

824. Burgh reform. *Edinburgh Review*, xxx. 503–24. Edinburgh, 1818. 8°.

825. CAY, JOHN. An analysis of the Scottish Reform Act, with the decisions of the Court of Appeal. 2 pts. Edinburgh, 1837–40. 8°.

826. Constitutional principles (The) of parliamentary reform. By a freeholder and landholder of Scotland [Mr. Colquhoun]. Edinburgh, etc., 1831. 8°.

Deals with Scotland and England.

827. CORY, WILLIAM. A guide to modern English history [1815–35.] 2 vols. New York, 1880–82. 8°.

Reform Bill of 1833, ii. 357–64.

828. Documents connected with the question of reform in the royal burghs of Scotland. Second edition. Edinburgh, 1819. 8°.

Short historical deduction of the government of boroughs, 1–6.
Resolutions of the committee on reform in 1788, 10–27.
Sett, etc. of Edinburgh, 28–74, 126–9.
Sett, etc. of Montrose and Aberdeen, 78–106.
Resolutions of various burghs in favor of reform, 115–29.
Report of merchant company of Edinburgh (1818) on the Reform Bill, 130–36.
On the government of royal burghs, by Lord Kames (see No. 882), 141–4.
1st edition, 1817.

829. DUNLOP, ALEXANDER. Letter to the freeholders of the county of Dumbarton on parliamentary reform. Edinburgh and London, 1830. 8°. pp. 45.

830. †Essay (An) on parliamentary representation and the magistracies of our royal burghs; shewing that the abuses at present complained of respecting both are late deviations from our constitution, as well as from common sense, and the necessity of a speedy reform. Edinburgh, 1785. 8°.

831. FLETCHER, ARCHIBALD. A memoir concerning the origin and progress of the reform proposed in the internal government of the royal burghs of Scotland, which was first brought under public discussion in 1782. To which is added the bill for reforming the internal government of the burghs. . . . By Archibald Fletcher. To which are farther added the substance of the reports of specific grievances . . . and several other papers on the subject of burgh reform, particularly the correspondence with Mr. Dempster and Mr. Pitt, etc. Edinburgh, 1819. 8°.

832. [GOUDY, H., and SMITH, W. C.] Local government [in Scotland.] Edinburgh and London, 1880. f°.

" This memorandum has been prepared with the view of assisting discussion on the reform of local government in the United Kingdom."
The burgh, 25–37.

833. GRAHAM, ROBERT. A letter to the right honorable William Pitt, chancellor of the exchequer, on the reform of the internal government of the royal boroughs of Scotland. London, 1788. 8°.

App. i. Resolutions of the committee for the reform of the royal burghs, containing a detailed account of municipal abuses.
App. ii. Observations on the setts of the royal burghs.

834. Illustration (An) of the principles of the bill, proposed to be submitted to the consideration of Parliament, for correcting the abuses and supplying the defects in the internal government of the royal burghs. . . . By the committee of the delegates.   Edinburgh, 1787.   4°.

General observations on the government of burghs, the object of reform, etc., 1–10.

Short historical deduction of the government of burghs, 11–17.

Jurisdiction claimed by the Convention of Royal Burghs to call magistrates to an account, app., 4–20, etc.

See No. 820.

835. IRONS, J. C.   The Burgh Police (Scotland) Act, 1892. With notes thereon. . . . Edinburgh, 1893.   8°.

836. Letter (A) from a member of the general convention of delegates of the royal boroughs to the citizens of the royal boroughs which have not yet acceded to the plan of reform.   Edinburgh 1784.   4°.

837. Letter to the freeholders and electors in the counties and burghs of Scotland, on parliamentary reform ; with a plan of reform, congenial to the law of Scotland, and not materially affecting private rights.   By the author of Letter to the landowners on the Hypothec Bill [Walter Ferrier].   Edinburgh, etc., 1831.   8°.

838. Letter to the lord advocate on the Scottish Reform Bill. [Signed "A conservative."]   Edinburgh and London, 1832.   8°.

839. Loyal Reformers' Gazette (The).   Vol. i.   Glasgow, 1831. 8°.

Thirty numbers were published between May 7 and Nov. 26, 1831, strongly advocating burgh reform.   This periodical continued to appear at intervals ; the last issue seems to be No. 232, Jan. 30, 1841.

840. Memorial for the burgesses and inhabitants of the royal burghs of Scotland, associated for the purpose of correcting the abuses and supplying the defects in the internal government of these boroughs.   Humbly submitted to the members of the legislature. [Edinburgh, 1789 ?.]   4°.

Without title-page.

841. Memorial . . . to both houses of Parliament against the new Municipal Corporation Bill for Scotland.   Edinburgh, 1837.   8°.

842. MUIRHEAD, JAMES. The Burgh Police (Scotland) Act, 1892. *Scottish Law Review*, viii. 317–26.   Glasgow, 1892.   8°.

843. —— Burghs of barony and regality under the Burgh Police Act of 1892. *Ibid.*, ix. 234–43.   Glasgow, 1893.   8°.

844. Municipal and corporate revolution [in Scotland.] *Blackwood's Edinburgh Magazine*, xxxvii. 964–77.   Edinburgh, 1835.   8°.

Deals with the Report of the Municipal Commission (No. 772).

845. Municipal corporations in Scotland. *Westminster Review*, xxiv. 156–86.   London, 1836.   8°.

846. NICOLSON, J. B., and MURE, W. J. The county council guide for Scotland. A handbook to the Local Government (Scotland) Act, 1889. . . . Edinburgh, 1889.   8°.

847. Observations by the delegates for conducting the application to Parliament for a reform in the internal government of the royal boroughs of Scotland, on the case of the town councils . . . and on a paper entitled, "A state of facts, upon which objections . . . are made against the bill offered to Parliament for a pretended reform." [London, 1788.]   8°.

848. Parliamentary representation of Scotland. *Edinburgh Review*, lii. 208–27.   Edinburgh, 1830.   8°.

849. Political letters by Lucius Verus.   London, 1831.   8°.

On burgh reform in Scotland, especially in Glasgow.

850. Progress (The) of freedom : or downfall of burgh corruption. [By a citizen.]   Montrose, 1817.   12°.   pp. 12.

851. Report of the standing committee of the incorporation of the guildry of Edinburgh, upon the bill now pending in Parliament " For the better regulating the mode of accounting for the common good and revenues of the royal burghs of Scotland, and for controlling and preventing the undue expenditure thereof."   Humbly submitted to the general meeting of the guildry, held within Freemasons' Hall, Edinburgh, this 27th day of April, 1818.   [Edinburgh, 1818.]   f°.

Without title-page.

852. Report on the bill for better regulating municipal corporations in Scotland. By a committee of the merchants' house of Glasgow : approved and ordered to be printed by the house, 23d June, 1836. [Glasgow, 1836.] 8°.

853. Report by the law committee of the town council of Edinburgh on "A bill to provide for the better regulation of municipal corporations in royal burghs of Scotland." Edinburgh, 1840. 8°. pp. 9.

854. [SCOTT, FRANCIS.] Dissection of the Scottish Reform Bill, having the bill annexed. By a member of the hon. Society of the Middle Temple. London, 1831. 8°. pp. 70.

855. —— Further dissection of the new Reform Bill for Scotland, in a letter addressed to the Earl of Mansfield. London and Edinburgh, 1831. 8°.

In 1831 he also wrote a tract entitled " View of the Representation of Scotland in 1831."

856. SHAW, C. G. Local government in Scotland. *Scottish Review*, xiii. 1–28. Paisley and London, 1889. 8°.

857. † Short account (A) of the representation of Scotland in the Parliament of Great Britain ; with outlines of a plan for its reformation. Edinburgh, 1813. 8°.

858. SINCLAIR, JOHN. Thoughts on parliamentary reform . . . together with some observations on the present state of the representation of Scotland, and the improvements of which it is susceptible. Edinburgh, 1831. 8 . pp. 35.

859. Substance of the reports transmitted by the committees of burgesses of different boroughs (Feb. 14, 1789), in answer to the general instructions transmitted by the committee of convention at Edinburgh, etc. [Edinburgh, 1789.] 4°.

Without title-page.

A brief account of the abuses of municipal government in the various Scotch burghs.

860. WORDSWORTH, C. F. F. The law and practice of elections (for Scotland), as altered by the Reform Act. . . . With an appendix, containing . . . the Reform and Boundary Act for Scotland, together with the schedules and tables thereto annexed. London, 1832. 8°.

e. LAW OF ELECTIONS AND LAW REPORTS.

See Nos. 342–344, 761, 860, 961.

861. BROWN, M. P. General synopsis of the decisions of the Court of Session from its institution until November, 1827. 4 vols. Edinburgh, 1829. 4°.

Setts, elections, services, privileges, magistrates, etc. of burghs, i. 292–318.
Many cases relating to gilds are referred to.

862. CONNELL, ARTHUR. A treatise on the election laws in Scotland, to which is added an historical enquiry concerning the municipal constitution of towns and boroughs. With an appendix. Edinburgh, 1827. 8°.

Pt. iii. On the election of the representatives of the royal burghs of Scotland.
Ch. iii. of the appended Historical Inquiry deals with the burghs of Scotland.

863. Decisions (The) of the Court of Session, from its institution till the year 1764, with several decisions since that period, arranged under proper titles in the form of a dictionary. [By Henry Home, Lord Kames.] 5 vols. London, 1774. 12°.

Burgh royal, i. 95–106.

864. FERGUSSON, JAMES, of Kilkerran. Decisions of the Court of Session, from the year 1738 to the year 1752. . . . Edinburgh, 1775. f°.

The gildry of Dunfermline *v.* Buntein and Flockhart, 1743 (the trade of vintner not confined to the gildry), 100.
Corporations of St. Mary's Chapel *v.* Kellie, 1747 (the right of corporations to debar unfreemen), 102–4.
Coutts, etc. *v.* Doig and others, 1747 (election of magistrates of Montrose), 104–7.
Mason, etc. *v.* magistrates of St. Andrews, 1747 (election of magistrates), 107–10.
Burgesses of Wick *v.* magistrates of Wick, 1748–49 (election of magistrates), 110–12.
Coopers of Perth *v.* Davidson and others, 1752 (rights of the coopers), 112–3.
Burgh of Perth *v.* Clunie and others, 1752 (privileges of brewers), 113–5.

865. MARWICK, J. D. Acts of Parliament relating to municipal elections in the parliamentary burghs of Scotland. London, 1873. 8°.

866. Marwick, J. D. Acts of Parliament relating to municipal elections in the police burghs of Scotland. Edinburgh, 1873. 8°.

867. ——— Acts of Parliament relating to municipal elections in the royal burghs of Scotland. London, 1873. 8°.

868. ——— Observations on the law and practice in regard to municipal elections and the conduct of the business of town councils and commissioners of police in Scotland. Edinburgh and London, 1879. 8°.

869. *Morrison, W. M. The decisions of the Court of Session from its first institution to the present time. . . . [Supplemental volume, 1815; index volume, 1823.] 23 vols. Edinburgh, 1801–23. 4°.

Aberdeen, 1678, 1711, 1715, 1793, iii. 1866–70, 1919–24, 1979.
Burntisland, 1679, iii. 1836–7.
Dingwall, 1759, iii. 1877–82.
Dunfermline, 1743, iii. 1926–8.
Edinburgh, 1747, 1772–90, iii. 1861–6, 1885–6, 1931–4, 1967–9.
Forres, 1757, iii. 1855–7.
Glasgow, 1676, 1756–57, 1762, 1765, 1793, iii. 1908–16, 1948–52, 1959–62, 2010–14.
Inverness, 1724, iii. 1839–40.
Irvine, 1757, iii. 1857–60.
Linlithgow, 1755, 1775, iii. 1875–7, 1883–5.
Perth, 1752, 1756, iii. 1936–40, 1947.
St. Andrews, 1747, iii. 1871–5.
Stirling, 1681, iii. 1838–9.
Wick, 1749, iii. 1842–54.

Many other cases relating to the gildry, crafts, burgh magistrates, etc. are given in iii. 1835–2018.

870. Nicolson, J. B. Analysis of recent statutes affecting parliamentary elections in Scotland. Edinburgh, 1885. 8°.

871. Remarkable decisions of the Court of Session, from the year 1730 to the year 1752. Edinburgh, 1766. f°.

John Lang and others v. magistrates of Selkirk, 1748 (burgh revenues), 181–8.
James Anderson and others v. magistrates of Wick, 1749 (election of town council), 192–8.

872. View (A) of the political state of Scotland at the late general election : containing an introductory treatise on the election laws, lists of the peers . . . an abstract of the sets of the royal boroughs,

and the names of their delegates. . . . [By Alexander Mackenzie.]
Edinburgh, 1790. 8°.

The abstract of the setts is meagre.

873. View of the political state of Scotland, at Michaelmas, 1811 :
comprehending the rolls of the freeholders, an abstract of the setts or
constitutions of the royal boroughs, and a state of the votes of the
last elections. . . . [By James Bridges.] Edinburgh, 1812. 8°.

Abstract of setts, 159-294.

874. WIGHT, ALEXANDER. An inquiry into the rise and progress of
Parliament, chiefly in Scotland ; and a complete system of the law
concerning the elections of the representatives from Scotland to the
Parliament of Great Britain. To which is added an appendix, containing several curious papers and instruments, and full copies of the
election statutes. Edinburgh, 1784. 4°.

Constitution of royal burghs, 330-60.
Manner of electing representatives of burghs ; qualification of electors, 361-404.
Charter of James III. to Inverness, 408-14.
Warrant for election in Anstruther Wester, etc. (1690, 1767), 415-16, 486-8.
List of royal burghs in order of precedence, 453-4.
Charter of William the Lion to Ayr, 475-6.
Judgment of Privy Council respecting Stirling, 478-85.

Other editions : " A treatise on the laws concerning the election of representatives," etc., 1 vol., 1773 ; " An enquiry into the rise," etc., 2 vols., 1806.

f. MISCELLANEOUS : CONVENTION OF BURGHS, ETC.

See Nos. 217, 218 ; and for the Convention of Royal Burghs, Nos. 764,
772, 834.

875. B[LACK], W[ILLIAM]. The privileges of the royal burrows.
With an appendix, containing the privileges and jurisdictions of the
cities of Edinburgh and Aberdeen. Edinburgh, 1707. 8°.

876. † Caledoniad (The) : or Donald's letters to his country-
folk on borough politics, political economy, etc. Nos. 1-3. Aberdeen, 1818. 8°.

877. CHAMBERS, WILLIAM. The book of Scotland. Edinburgh,
1830. 8°.

Municipal institutions in 1830, pp. 46-96. (A good account.)

G

878. Early Scottish burghs. *Scottish Review*, ii. 45–70. Paisley and London, 1883. 8°.

879. FLETCHER, ARCHIBALD. An examination of the grounds on which the Convention of Royal Burghs, at their late extraordinary meeting, claimed to themselves the right of altering and amending the setts or constitutions of the individual burghs ; and a refutation of that claim. Edinburgh, 1825. 8°.

See No. 834.

880. FOSTER, JOSEPH. Members of Parliament, Scotland, including the minor barons, the commissioners for shires, and the commissioners for the burghs, 1357–1882. . . . Privately printed. London, etc., 1882. 4°.

2nd edition, 1882.

881. GRANT, JAMES. History of the burgh schools of Scotland. Vol. i. London and Glasgow, 1876. 8°.

882. HOME, HENRY, Lord KAMES. Sketches of the history of man. New edition. 3 vols. Edinburgh, 1813. 8°.

Government of royal burghs, iii. 464–71.
1st edition, 4 vols., Dublin, 1774–75.
See No. 828.

883. GROOME, F. H. Ordnance gazetteer of Scotland : a survey of Scottish topography, statistical, biographical, and historical. Edited by F. H. Groome. 6 vols. Edinburgh, 1885. 8°.

Contains a concise account of the municipal history of each burgh.

884. INNES, COSMO. Lectures on Scotch legal antiquities. . . . Edinburgh, 1872. 8°.

Early parliamentary history of burghs, 113–53.

885. —— Scotland in the Middle Ages. Sketches of early Scotch history and social progress. Edinburgh, 1860. 8°.

Burghs, 148–74, 231–4.

886. IRONS, J. C. Manual of the law and practice of the dean of guild court. . . . Edinburgh, 1895. 8°.

887. MACKAY, JOHN. The Convention of the Royal Burghs of Scotland, from its origin down to . . . 1707. Edinburgh, 1884. 8°. pp. 88.

888. † MARWICK, J. D.　List of markets and fairs now and formerly held in Scotland; with notes as to charters, acts of parliament, etc.　n. p.　1890.　f°.

889. McDOUALL, ANDREW [Lord BANKTON].　An institute of the laws of Scotland in civil rights; with observations upon the agreement or diversity between them and the laws of England, etc. 3 vols.　Edinburgh, 1751–53.　f°.

A good brief account of the constitution of burghs, i. 56–7, 561–4, ii. 577–85.

889a. † MUIRHEAD, J.　Byelaws and standing orders for burghs in Scotland.　Glasgow, 1895.　8°.

890. Origines parochiales Scotiæ.　The antiquities ecclesiastical and territorial of the parishes of Scotland.　[Edited by Cosmo Innes and J. B. Brichan.]　*Bannatyne Club.*　2 vols., 3 pts.　Edinburgh, 1850–55.　4°.

Contains some brief but useful notes on burghal history.

891. PHILOPOLITEIOUS [ALEXANDER SKENE].　Memorialls for the government of the royall-burghs in Scotland. . . . Aberdeen, 1685. 8°.

See No. 963.

892. Staple contract (The) betwixt the royal burrows of Scotland and the city Campvere in Zealand.　With the several amplifications, prolongations, and ratifications thereof.　Published by order of the general Convention of Royal Burrows, in July, 1749.　To which is prefixed an historical account of the staple, by a private gentleman. Edinburgh, 1749.　8°.

893. STUART, GILBERT.　Observations concerning the public law and the constitutional history of Scotland; with occasional remarks concerning English antiquity.　Edinburgh and London, 1779.　8°.

The history of burghs, 121–31, 306–44.

§ 14. MISCELLANEOUS (ENGLAND AND WALES).

894. ANDREWS, WILLIAM. Old-time punishments. Hull and London, 1890. 8°.

A new edition of " Punishments in the olden time," etc. [1881.]

895. COKE, EDWARD. First part of the institutes of the laws of England : or a commentary upon Littleton. . . . Eighteenth edition. 2 vols. London, 1823. 8°.

Bk. ii. ch. x. Tenure in burgage.

896. ELTON, C. J. The tenures of Kent. London, 1867. 8°.

Ch. vii. Tenure in burgage.

897. FOX-DAVIES, A. C., and CROOKES, M. E. B. The book of public arms. A cyclopædia of the armorial bearings, heraldic devices, and seals . . . of the counties, cities, towns, and universities of the United Kingdom. . . . Edinburgh, 1894. 4°.

Elaborately illustrated.

898. FREEMAN, E. A. City and borough. *Macmillan's Magazine,* lx. 29–37. London, 1889. 8°.

Considers the past and present application of these two terms.

899. —— English towns and districts. A series of addresses and sketches. London, 1883. 8°.

Contains essays on Carlisle, Exeter, Kidwelly, Lincoln, etc. Treats only casually of municipal affairs.

900. —— Historical essays. Fourth series. London and New York, 1892. 8°.

Ch. ii. French and English towns (reprinted from *Longman's Magazine,* May, 1884, and *Saturday Review,* Nov. 14, 1868).
Ch. xvii. Decayed boroughs.

901. GOMME, G. L. Curious corporation customs. *The Antiquary,* vi. 201–5. London, 1882. 4°.

902. —— Index of municipal offices ; compiled from the appendixes to the first report of the commissioners appointed to inquire into the municipal corporations in England and Wales, 1835. With an historical introduction. *Index Society.* London, 1879. 4°.

See No. 60.

903. GROSS, CHARLES. A plea for reform in the study of English municipal history. *American Hist. Assoc.*, Papers, vol. v. No. 4. New York and London, 1891. 8°.

904. †HIGSON, FRED. The corporator's manual. A concise treatise on municipal corporations. . . . Manchester, 1839. 12°.

905. HOPE, W. H. ST. JOHN. English municipal heraldry. Reprinted from the Archæological Journal [lii. 173–97], June, 1895. [London, 1895.] 8°.

See also his paper in Proceedings of the Society of Antiquaries of London, May 16, 1895.

906. —— Maces and swords of state belonging to mayors and corporations. *Soc. of Antiq. of London,* Proceedings, Second Series, xii. 176–200. London, [1888.] 8°.

907. JEWITT, LLEWELLYN. The burghmote horns and the office of horn-blower. *The Antiquary,* i. 252–6. London, 1880. 4°.

908. —— The corporation plate and insignia of office of the cities and towns of England and Wales. . . . Edited by W. H. St. John Hope. 2 vols. London, 1895. 4°.

An excellent work, well illustrated.

909. KELLY, WILLIAM. Corporate emblems and insignia in England and Wales. *Royal Hist. Soc.,* Transactions, New Series, iii. 337–45. London, 1874. 8°.

910. KYD, STEWART. A treatise on the law of corporations. 2 vols. London, 1793–94. 8°.

Many municipal by-laws are incidentally discussed. Many law cases are cited.

911. Law (The) of corporations : containing the laws and customs of all the corporations and inferior courts of record in England . . . together with the stiles and titles of most corporations in England. London, 1702. 8°.

Contains many customs and by-laws of municipal corporations.

912. Laws concerning trade and tradesmen. In two parts. The first treats of the doctrine of by-laws, made by corporations and companies concerning trade, etc. . . . The second part is a collection of the statute-law that concerns merchants, tradesmen, and artificers. . . . London, 1712.   12°.

913. LEWIS, SAMUEL. A topographical dictionary of England, comprising the several counties, cities, boroughs, corporate and market towns, parishes, and townships . . . embellished with engravings of the arms of the cities, boroughs, bishoprics, universities, and colleges; and of the seals of the various municipal corporations. Seventh edition.   4 vols.   London, 1849.   4°.

1st edition, 1831.

914. —— A topographical dictionary of Wales . . . embellished with engravings of the arms of the bishoprics, and of the arms and seals of the various cities and municipal corporations.   Fourth edition.   2 vols.   London, 1849.   4°.

Earlier editions, 1833, 1840, and 1843.

915. [NICHOLS, JOHN.] Illustrations of manners and expences of antient times in England, in the fifteenth, sixteenth, and seventeenth centuries. . . . London, 1797.   4°.

Contains extracts from churchwardens' accounts:
St. Margaret's, Westminster (1460–1692), 1–76.
St. Mary Hill, London (1427–1557), 85–129.
St. Helen's, Abingdon (1555–91), 140–47.
St. Michael, Spurrier-gate, York (16th century), 307–16.

916. PAYNE, WILLIAM. A treatise on municipal rights; commencing with a summary account of the origin and progress of society and government, and comprising a concise view of the state thereof, from the earliest period of British history to the institution of corporations in general, and that of the city of London in particular. . . . London, 1813.   8°.

Ch. vi.   Rise and progress of cities and towns.
Ch. vii.   Commencement and utility of corporations.
Brief and of little value.

917. SMITH, J. TOULMIN. Government by commission illegal and pernicious. The nature and effects of all commissions of inquiry . . .

and the rights, duties, and importance of local self-government. London, 1849. 8°.

918. —— Local self-government and centralization . . . Including comprehensive outlines of the English constitution. With copious index. London, 1851. 8°.

919. WALFORD, CORNELIUS. Fairs, past and present: a chapter in the history of commerce. London, 1883. 8°.

Much space is devoted to the history of Bartholomew Fair, London, and to the ordinances of the Cambridge corporation regarding Sturbridge Fair (1376–1855).

𝔓art II. — PARTICULAR TOWNS.

ABERDEEN.

    a. Town Records, Nos. 920–933.
    b. General Histories, Nos. 934–939.
    c. Gilds, Nos. 940–955.
    d. Miscellaneous, Nos. 956–967.

The archives of Aberdeen are very extensive, and are not excelled by those of any other Scotch burgh. The collections of records in print are valuable, and most of them are well edited.

The best histories of Aberdeen are those of Kennedy, Robbie, and Thom (Nos. 936–938). Kennedy's work is the most valuable. Robbie's is the best recent history. Bain (No. 940) gives the best account of the gilds.

a. Town Records.

See No. 788.

920. † Charters, etc., etc. Burgh of Aberdeen. [Aberdeen,] 1804. 4°.

A collection of charters, including that of King Robert in favor of Aberdeen, 1319, and ending with a royal charter in favor of the Aberdeen salmon fishing, 1804.

921. *Charters and other writs illustrating the history of the royal burgh of Aberdeen, 1171–1804. Edited with translations by P. J. Anderson. Aberdeen, 1890. 4°.

922. Extracts from Aberdeen burgh records, 1715–16, 1745–46. [Historical Papers, edited by James Allardyce, i. 39–54, 195–278. *New Spalding Club.* Aberdeen, 1895. 4°.]

923. Extracts from the accounts of the burgh of Aberdeen [1398–1645.] *Spalding Club,* Miscellany, v. 39–182. Aberdeen, 1852. 4°.

924. Extracts from the [council] registers of the burgh of Aberdeen [1317–1508.] *Spalding Club,* Miscellany, v. 1–38. Aberdeen, 1852. 4°.

925. —— * Extracts from the council register of the burgh of Aberdeen, 1398–1625. [Edited by John Stuart.]   2 vols.   *Spalding Club.*   Aberdeen, 1844–48.   4°.

926. —— * Extracts from the council register of the burgh of Aberdeen, 1625–1747.   [Edited by John Stuart.]   *Scottish Burgh Records Society.*   2 vols.   Edinburgh, 1871–72.   4°.

927. FORBES, Bailie [JAMES].   Paper on the social condition of Scotland during the 15th and 16th centuries, illustrated by extracts from the burgh records of the city of Aberdeen.   Read by Bailie Forbes, at a meeting of the Social Science Association, on 10th February, 1863.   Second edition.   Aberdeen, 1863.   8°.

928. GORDON, JAMES.   Abredoniæ vtrivsque descriptio.   A description of both towns of Aberdeen [compiled in 1661]. . . . With a selection of the charters of the burgh.   [Edited by Cosmo Innes.] *Spalding Club.*   Edinburgh, 1842.   4°.

Charters of Aberdeen, 29–95.

929. Inventories of records illustrating the history of the burgh of Aberdeen.   Aberdeen, 1890.   4°.   pp. 62.

930. † [Orders of Constables.]   Aberdeen the 24 of January, 1698.   Orders and inst[r]uctions for the constables of the burgh of Aberdeen, made and appointed by the magistrates, justices of peace of the said burgh, to be observed and gone about by the said constables. . . . Extracted forth of the justice court books of Aberdeen, by Master Alexander Thomson, town clerk of the said burgh. Aberdeen, 1698.   f°.

931. † —— Orders and instructions for the constables . . . to be observed and gone about by the said constables.   Aberdeen, the 4th of November, 1706.   [Aberdeen, 1706.]   f°.

932. Register of burgesses of guild and trade of the burgh of Aberdeen, 1399–1631.   *New Spalding Club,* Miscellany, i. 1–162, 359–91.   Aberdeen, 1890.   4°.

933. † Taken from the Aberdeen records.   [Extracts relating to the election of provosts and magistrates in 1398, the destruction of deer, etc., 1393–1507.]   The rents of the Bishop of Aberdeen, 1576.

Note of the prices of grain, etc., at different times [1435–1637.] [Aberdeen, circa 1730.] f°.

b. General Histories.

934. Book (The) of bon-accord : or a guide to the city of Aberdeen. [By Joseph Robertson.] Aberdeen, 1839. 12°.

Does not deal in detail with municipal institutions.

935. † CADENHEAD, GEORGE. Sketch of the territorial history of the burgh of Aberdeen. Enlarged from a paper read before the Aberdeen Philosophical Society, on 11th January, 1878. Aberdeen, 1878. 8°. pp. 43.

936. * KENNEDY, WILLIAM. Annals of Aberdeen, from the reign of King William the Lion to the end of 1818 ; with an account of the city, cathedral, and university of old Aberdeen. 2 vols. London, etc., 1818. 4°.

937. ROBBIE, WILLIAM. Aberdeen, its traditions and history. Aberdeen, 1893. 8°.

938. THOM, WALTER. The history of Aberdeen : containing an account of the rise, progress, and extension of the city, from a remote period to the present day. . . . 2 vols. Aberdeen, 1811. 12°.

939. WILSON, ROBERT. An historical account and delineation of Aberdeen. . . . Aberdeen, 1822. 12°.

The historical account is brief.

c. Gilds.

See Nos. 758, 958.

940. * BAIN, EBENEZER. Merchant and craft guilds. A history of the Aberdeen incorporated trades. Aberdeen, 1887. 8°.

Contains many extracts from the records of the gilds.

941. BANNERMAN, THOMAS. An inquiry into the rights of the guildry of Aberdeen. Aberdeen, 1834. 8°.

Deals especially with its financial affairs.

942. —— Notes on Mr. Bannerman's "Inquiry into the rights of the guildry of Aberdeen." By a burgess. Aberdeen, 1834. 8°. pp. 34.

Attributed to George Moir.

943. BULLOCH, JOHN. The pynours. Historical notes on an ancient Aberdeen craft. Aberdeen, 1887. 8°.

944. CLARK, LESLIE. Letter to the burgesses of guild of the city of Aberdeen, regarding the state of their affairs; with suggestions as to the course to be pursued by them. By Leslie Clark, dean of guild. Aberdeen, 1839. 8°. pp. 28.

945. † Constitution, rules, and regulations of the merchant society of old Aberdeen, 1794. [Aberdeen,] 1794. 12°. pp. 16.

946. † Follows the burgess oath to be sworn by all burgesses of gild and craftsmen of the burgh of Aberdeen at the time of their admission. . . . [Aberdeen, circa 1706.] f°.

947. † HUNTER, W. A. The guildry and the guildry funds. A lecture. . . . Aberdeen, 1877. 8°.

948. JERVISE, ANDREW. Inscriptions from the shields or panels of the incorporated trades, in the Trinity Hall, Aberdeen. Aberdeen, 1863. 8°.

1st edition, 1851, published anonymously.

949. † Letter (A) to the guildry on the present state of their affairs, and on the late extraordinary conduct of the lord provost, magistrates, and council. By a guild brother [Alexander Bannerman?]. Aberdeen, 1835. 8°.

950. † Letter (A) to the lord provost, magistrates, and town council of Aberdeen on the present condition of city matters, 1874. [By Alexander Walker.] Aberdeen, 1874. 8°.

951. List of the deans of guild of Aberdeen from 1436 to 1875, with contemporaneous matters added, meant to form a local leaflet in the history of Scotland. By one of them [Alexander Walker]. Printed for private circulation. Aberdeen, 1875. 8°.

952. † Regulations of the guildry company of Aberdeen, instituted 1826. Aberdeen, [1826.] f°. pp. 10.

953. Report on the affairs of the guildry of Aberdeen, ordered by a head court of the brethren, 5th October, 1835. By a committee of the assessors. Aberdeen, 1836. 8°.

Deals especially with financial affairs; contains extracts from the gildry accounts, 1616–1833.

954. Report of the committee of the dean of guild's assessors, appointed to inquire into the state of the funds appertaining to the guild brethren, to the dean of guild and assessors. March, 1834. Aberdeen, 1834. 8°. pp. 12.

955. † WOOD, JOSEPH. The guildry of the royal burgh of Aberdeen : who are they? what are they? and what will they be? A reply to Professor W. A. Hunter, of London, delivered in the Music Hall buildings on Thursday, 5th April, 1877 ; with a summary of the argument, and a sketch of the future of the guildry funds. Aberdeen, 1877. 12°. pp. 36.

See No. 947.

d. Miscellaneous.

956. † Aberdeen fifty years ago. . . . [By James Rettie.] Aberdeen, 1868. 8°.

957. B[LACK], W[ILLIAM]. The privileges of the royal burrows. . . . With an appendix containing the privileges and jurisdictions of the cities of Edinburgh and Aberdeen. Edinburgh, 1707. 8°.

958. BULLOCH, JOHN. Aberdeen three hundred years ago. Aberdeen, 1884. 8°.

A brief account of the craft gilds, etc.

959. † MUNRO, A. M. The common good of the city of Aberdeen, 1319–1887. A historical sketch. Aberdeen, 1888. 8°.

960. —— Notes on the members of Parliament for the burgh of Aberdeen, 1357–1886. [Aberdeen,] 1889. 8°.

A brief account.

961. † Notes as to the rights of the burgesses of Scotland, on a lapse of the burgh magistracy, suggested by the crown's refusal of the usual warrant for a poll election in the late case of Aberdeen. With an appendix of relative documents. Edinburgh, 1819. 8°.

962. Observations, by Civis of Aberdeen, on a letter under the signature of a cobler, in which the [Reform] Bill, prepared by the convention of the delegates of the burgesses of Scotland, has been attacked. To which is prefixed the letter of the cobler. Published by the committee of burgesses at Aberdeen. Aberdeen, 1786. 8°.

Relates mainly to Aberdeen.

963. PHILOPOLITEIOUS [ALEXANDER SKENE]. Memorialls for the government of the royall-burghs in Scotland. . . . As also a survey of the city of Aberdeen, with the epigrams of Arthur Johnstown, doctor of medicin, upon some of our chief burghs, translated into English by J. B. [John Barclay]. Aberdeen, 1685. 8°.

Reprinted, Edinburgh, 1867; "A succinct survey of the famous city of Aberdeen," etc., Aberdeen, 1833, a reprint of pp. 199–285 of the "Memorialls."

964. Proceedings of the burgesses of Aberdeen, in examining the public accounts, in the annual head court, September 21, 1784; and in an examination of the public records. . . . With an appendix including the letter of Dion Cassius, and its answer, on the subject of a reform in the elections of the burghs, addressed to the burgesses of Scotland. To which are prefixed preliminary observations. Published by the committee of burgesses at Aberdeen. [Aberdeen,] 1785. 8°.

965. —— Farther proceedings of the burgesses of Aberdeen, in the years 1785, 1786, and 1787, in an attempt to restrain an extra-assessment for the land tax of the borough. . . . To which is prefixed a preface, containing observations, by the committee of burgesses. Aberdeen, 1787. 8°.

966. ROSS, JAMES A. Record of municipal affairs in Aberdeen since the passing of the Burgh Reform Act in 1833. Aberdeen, 1889. 8°.

967. † WILSON, JAMES H. The bon-accord repository of local institutions, municipal, educational, ecclesiastical, and commercial. Aberdeen, etc., 1842. 12°.

ABERDOUR.

968. ROSS, WILLIAM. Aberdour and Inchcolme : being historical notices of the parish and monastery. In twelve lectures. Edinburgh. 1885. 8°.

ABERAVON.

969. [Translation of the] charter of Aberavon, Glamorganshire, 1351. *Cambrian Archæol. Assoc.*, Archæologia Cambrensis, Third Series, vi. 19–21. London, 1860. 8°.

ABINGDON.

970. † SHARP, THOMAS. Municipal government in the borough of Abingdon, from 1835 to the year 1859. [Abingdon,] 1859. 4°.

971. † Statesmen (The) of Abingdon : a full answer to the true letter written by the body politick of that corporation on the occasion of their late election of Mr. Harcourt, etc. London, 1702. 8°.

ALDBOROUGH.

972. HELE, N. F. Notes or jottings about Aldeburgh, Suffolk, relating to matters historical, antiquarian, ornithological, and entomological. London, 1870. 8°.

Ch. vi. contains extracts from the town records, 1500–1744.

ALLOA.

973. LOTHIAN, JAMES. Alloa and its environs. A descriptive and historical guide. Third and enlarged edition. Alloa, 1871. 12°.

The account of municipal history is meagre.
1st edition, 1861.

ALNWICK.

974. Appeal (An) to the public on the present existing grievances of the burgesses or freemen of the borough of Alnwick. Published by the committee, in order to raise public contributions to assist the freemen in carrying on their suit [against the common council] now pending in the high court of Chancery. Alnwick, 1819. 12°. pp. 27.

975. Descriptive and historical view (A) of Alnwick, the county town of Northumberland, and of Alnwick Castle. . . . [By W. Davison.] Second edition. Alnwick, 1822. 8°.

976. History (The) of Alnwick, the county town of Northumberland. Alnwick, 1813. 12°.

A brief account.

977. TATE, GEORGE.   The history of the borough, castle, and barony of Alnwick.   2 vols.   Alnwick, 1866–69.   8°.

Contains many extracts from records.   The appendix contains the charters granted to the burgesses by the De Vescys, Edw. III., and Hen. VI.
A useful book ; the best history of Alnwick.

ALTRINCHAM.

978. INGHAM, ALFRED.   A history of Altrincham and Bowdon, with an account of the barony and house of Dunham.   Altrincham, 1879.   4°.

" There are no footnotes or other aids to bewilderment and confusion ": Preface, p. vii.

AMERSHAM.

979. KELKE, W. H. H.   Amersham.   *Archit. and Archæol. Soc. for the County of Buckingham,* Records of Buckinghamshire, ii. 333–53.   Aylesbury, 1863.   8°.

A meagre account.

ANDERSTON.

980. TAYLOR, J. M.   Excerpts from the ancient records of the weavers' society of Anderston, instituted 3rd November, 1738.   Glasgow, 1879.   8°.

ANDOVER.

981. Archives (The) of Andover.   By C. Collier and R. H. Clutterbuck.   Pt. i. Churchwardens' accounts [1470.]   Pt. ii. Charters and grants.   2 pts.   Andover.   n. d.   8°.

982. [CLUTTERBUCK, R. H.]   Andover from old records.   *Andover Advertiser,* June — Oct., 1884.

983. —— The story of the quit-rent of Andover.   *Brit. Archæol. Assoc.,* Journal, l. 257–66.   London, 1894.   8°.

984. COLLIER, C.   Andover and its neighbourhood.   *Wilts. Archæol. and Nat. Hist. Soc.,* Magazine, xxi. 293–314.   Devizes, 1884.   8°.

985. [——] Archives of Andover.   *Andover Advertiser,* 1881.   Second Series.   *Andover Advertiser,* Dec., 1884 — Feb., 1885.

ANNAN.

986. LITTLE, JAMES. Annan, ancient and modern : a lecture, delivered in the hall of the Mechanics' Institution at Annan, on Feb. 9, 1853. Annan, 1853. 8°.

APPLEBY.

See No. 321.

987. HEWITSON, W. The Appleby charters. *Cumberl. and Westm. Antiq. and Archæol. Soc.*, Transactions, xi. 279–85. Kendal, 1891. 8°.

ARBROATH.

988. HAY, GEORGE. History of Arbroath to the present time, with notices of the civil and ecclesiastical affairs of the neighbouring district. Arbroath, 1876. 4°.

Contains extracts from the burgh records.
Valuable ; the best history of Arbroath.

989. McBAIN, J. M. Arbroath, past and present : being reminiscences chiefly relating to the last half century. Arbroath, 1887. 8°.

990. —— Bibliography of Arbroath periodical literature and political broadsides. Arbroath, 1889. 4°.

Pt. ii. contains an account of broadsides relating to parliamentary and municipal reform.

991. MILLER, DAVID. Arbroath and its abbey : or the early history of the town and abbey of Aberbrothock. Edinburgh, 1860. 8°.

App. iii. contains a selection from the burgh records, 1563–1649.

ARMAGH.

992. STUART, JAMES. Historical memoirs of the city of Armagh, for a period of 1373 years . . . and an appendix on the learning, antiquities, and religion of the Irish nation. Newry, etc., 1819. 8°.

ARUNDEL.

993. BLAAUW, W. H. The taxpayers of the borough of Arundel, with extracts from the subsidy roll of 1296 and other MSS. *Sussex Archæol. Soc.*, Collections, vii. 159–67. London, 1854. 8°.

994. TIERNEY, M. A.   The history and antiquities of the castle and town of Arundel, including the biography of its earls, from the Conquest to the present time.   London, 1834.   4°.

ASHBURTON.

995. Parish (The) of Ashburton in the 15th and 16th centuries; as it appears from extracts from the churchwardens' accounts, A. D. 1479–1580.   With notes and comments.   [By J. H. Butcher.]   London, 1870.   8°.

996. † PEARSON, J. H.   The representation of the borough of Ashburton.   *Devon. Assoc. for Advancement of Science,* Transactions, 1896.

997. WORTHY, CHARLES.   Ashburton and its neighbourhood: or the antiquities and history of the borough of Ashburton in the county of Devon. . . . Ashburton, 1875.   4°.

AXBRIDGE.

998. HUNT, WILLIAM.   On the charters and municipal government of Axbridge.   *Somerset. Archæol. and Nat. Hist. Soc.,* Proceedings, xv. [pt. ii.] 6–20.   Taunton, 1870.   8°.

999. JONES, W. A.   Early historical document among the muniments of the town of Axbridge.   *Somerset. Archæol. and Nat. Hist. Soc.,* Proceedings, xv. [pt. ii.] 21–6.   Taunton, 1870.   8°.

This document was published from another MS. by Smirke (No. 1000).

1000. SMIRKE, EDWARD.   Early historical document among the muniments of the town of Axbridge.   *Archæol. Journal,* xxiii. 224–30.   London, 1866.   8°.

This document gives a brief account of King Edmund's visit to Axbridge, and briefly describes the government of the town at that time.   It should be used with caution.

AYLESBURY.

1001. † Case of the Aylesbury men.   1704.   f°.

Ashby *v.* White: an action brought against the mayor, etc. of Aylesbury in 1704, for rejecting Ashby's vote at an election of M. P.'s for the borough.   See No. 195.

Another edition, 1721, 12°.

1002. * GIBBS, ROBERT. Buckinghamshire. A history of Ayles-bury with its borough and hundreds, the hamlet of Walton, and the electoral division. Aylesbury, 1885. 4°.

An excellent book. Particular attention is devoted to the parliamentary history of Aylesbury since the time of Queen Mary.

1003. PARKER, JOHN. The manor of Aylesbury. *Soc. of Antiq. of London*, Archæologia, l. 81–103. London, 1887. 4°.

The court roll of Aylesbury, 15 Hen. VII., is printed in full.

AYR.

1004. * Charters of the royal burgh of Ayr. Printed for the Ayrshire and Wigtonshire Archæological Association. Edinburgh, 1883. 4°.

Contains charters, "decreets," and other documents, extending from 1380 to 1715.

1005. DICKSON, THOMAS. Proceedings of the gild court of Ayr [1428–31], from the Ayr manuscript. *Ayrshire and Wigtonshire Archæol. Assoc.*, Collections, i. 223–30. Edinburgh, 1878. 4°.

1006. HOWIE, JAMES. An historical account of the town of Ayr for the last fifty years, with notable occurrences during that time from personal recollection. Illustrated by numerous local anecdotes. Kilmarnock, 1861. 8°.

1007. LYON, D. M. Ayr in the olden times. From unpublished notes by D. Murray Lyon. *Ayr Advertiser*, Aug.—Oct., 1875.

Contains many extracts from the burgh records.

1008. Munimenta fratrum predicatorum de Are. Charters of the friars preachers of Ayr. Printed for the Ayrshire and Wigtonshire Archæological Association. Edinburgh, 1881. 4°.

Contains some documents relating to the burgh of Ayr.

1009. † Reminiscences of auld Ayr. Edinburgh, 1864. 8°.

BALLYSHANNON.

1010. ALLINGHAM, HUGH. Ballyshannon: its history and antiquities; with some account of the surrounding neighbourhood. Londonderry and Ballyshannon, 1879. 8°.

Ch. viii. Ballyshannon as a corporate town.

BANBURY.

1011. BEESLEY, ALFRED.   The history of Banbury; including copious historical and antiquarian notes of the neighbourhood. London, [1841.]   8°.

BANDON.

1012. BENNETT, GEORGE.   The history of Bandon, and the principal towns in the west riding of County Cork.   Enlarged edition. Cork, 1869.   8°.

BANFF.

1013. † CRAMOND, WILLIAM.   Inventory of the charters, burgh court books, books of sasines, etc., belonging to the burgh of Banff, deposited within the council chamber of the burgh.   1887.   Banff, [1887.] 8°.   pp. 8.

1014. * —— The annals of Banff. *New Spalding Club.*   2 vols. Aberdeen, 1891–93.   4°.

Contains copious extracts from the burgh records.
The best history of Banff.

1015. IMLACH, JAMES.   History of Banff and familiar account of its inhabitants and belongings; to which are added chronicles of the old churchyard of Banff.   Banff, 1868.   8°.

A brief account.

1016. †Proceedings of the burgesses of Banff who have declared for reform in applying to the magistrates for an inspection of the town's books and accounts.   [Banff,] 1784.   12°.

BARNARD CASTLE.

1017. †Charters granted to the burgesses of Barnard Castle, in the county palatine of Durham.   G. Allan's Darlington Press.   n. d. 4°.

1018. WALBRAN, J. R.   The antiquities of Gainford in the county of Durham : comprising the baronial and ecclesiastical history of that place and of Barnardcastle ; with descriptive notices of Raby Castle, Staindrop Church, Denton, and many other objects of antiquity in their vicinity.   Part i.   Ripon, 1846.   8°.

No more published.
Barnard Castle, 125-54.

BARNSTAPLE.

1019. CHANTER, J. R.   The Barnstaple records. *North Devon Journal*, Jan. 9, 1879—May 5, 1881 ; *North Devon Herald*, Jan. 9, 1879—April 21, 1881.

A valuable descriptive catalogue of all the records in the town archives, with copies or translations of the most important documents, and extracts from others. There are in all 101 articles, some of which are by Thomas Wainright ; Nos. 51 and 101 are indexes.

1020. † —— Sketches of the literary history of Barnstaple . . . to which is appended the diary of Philip Wyot, town clerk of Barnstaple . . . 1586–1608.   Barnstaple, 1866.   8°.

1021. —— Vestiges of an early guild of St. Nicholas at Barnstaple. *Devon. Assoc. for Advancement of Science*, Transactions, xi. 191–212.   Plymouth, 1879.   8°.

Contains valuable extracts from the rolls of the gild merchant, temp. Edw. III.

1022. GRIBBLE, J. B.   Memorials of Barnstaple : being an attempt to supply the want of a history of that ancient borough.   Barnstaple, 1830.   8°.

Contains a translation of the town charters ; the by-laws made in 1689 ; and many other extracts from the town records.

The best history of Barnstaple.

1023. Journals of the House of Lords, 5 Geo. IV., 1824, vol. lvi. [London, 1824.]   f°.

Important documents, 18 Edw. III., relating to the liberties of Barnstaple, 1105–8. Also printed in Parl. Papers, 1826, ix. 11–16.

1024. WILLS, CHARLES.   A short historical sketch of the town of Barnstaple . . . with much interesting and valuable information relating to this ancient borough.   Barnstaple, 1855.   8°.

The "information relating to the ancient borough" is meagre.

BASINGSTOKE.

1025. *BAIGENT, F. J., and MILLARD, J. E.   A history of the ancient town and manor of Basingstoke in the county of Southampton ; with a brief account of the siege of Basing House, A. D. 1643–1645. Basingstoke and London, 1889.   8°.

Contains selections from the court rolls, 1390–1588 (pp. 247–356) ; also many extracts from other records.

1026. Book (The) of accounts of the wardens of the fraternity of the Holy Ghost in Basingstoke, A. D. 1557–1654. [Edited by J. E. Millard. Southampton, 1882.] 4°.

1027. History (The) of the brotherhood or guild of the Holy Ghost near Basingstoke in Hampshire. . . . With an account of another religious house founded at the same place by King Henry III. [By Samuel Loggon.] Reading, 1742. 8°. pp. 43.

BATH.

Though the literature relating to Bath is quite extensive, a good history of the town is still a desideratum. The best history is Warner's (No. 1040).

1028. EARLE, JOHN. A guide to the knowledge of Bath, ancient and modern. London and Bath, 1864. 8°.

1029. FALCONER, R. W. List of charters, etc., connected with the city of Bath. [Bath, 1858.] 8°.

A brief abstract of the charters.

1030. HUNT, WILLIAM. The early royal charters of Bath. *Somerset. Archæol. and Nat. Hist. Soc.,* Proceedings, xxii. 73–86. Taunton, 1877. 8°.

1031. KING, A. J. The municipal records of Bath. *Somerset. Archæol. and Nat. Hist. Soc.,* Proceedings, xli. 47–52. Taunton, 1895. 8°.

1032. KING, A. J., and WATTS, B. H. The municipal records of Bath, 1189 to 1604. Published with the approval of the town council and at the special request of the Bath Literary Society. London, [1885.] 4°.

Contains an account of the charters granted to Bath; a list of royal grants, writs, and commissions; extracts from the chamberlains' accounts, 1569–1602.

1033. MAINWAIRING, ROWLAND. Annals of Bath from the year 1800 to the passing of the new Municipal Act. . . . Bath, 1838. 8°.

A good detailed account of the history of Bath from 1801 to 1834.

1034. MURCH, JEROM. Biographical sketches of Bath celebrities, ancient and modern, with some fragments of local history. London and Bath, 1893. 8°.

Ch. v. Early mayors of Bath. (A brief account.)

1035. PAYNTER, Vice-Admiral. Ancient Bath charters. *Somerset. Archæol. and Nat. Hist. Soc.*, Proceedings, xxii. pt. ii. 1–9. Taunton, 1877. 8°.

1036. PEACH, R. E. M. Bath, old and new. A handy guide and a history; with map and illustrations. London, 1888. 8°.

A brief account.

1037. PEARSON, C. B. Some account of ancient churchwarden accounts of St. Michael's, Bath [1349–1575.] *Royal Hist. Soc.*, Transactions, vii. 309–29. London, 1878. 8°.

1038. —— The churchwardens' accounts of the parish of S. Michael, Bath, 1349–1575. Edited by C. B. Pearson. *Somerset. Archæol. and Nat. Hist. Soc.* Taunton, 1878–81. 8°.

Published with the proceedings of the Society, vols. xxiv.–xxvi.

1039. View (A) of Bath, historical, political, and chronological: representing facts, real, interesting, and instructive, from the earliest period to the present time. [By C. Hibbert.] Bath, 1813. 8°.

A defence of the right of the freemen to use Bath common.

1040. WARNER, RICHARD. The history of Bath. Bath and London, 1801. 4°.

The best general history of Bath.

1041. WOOD, JOHN. An essay towards a description of Bath. In four parts. Wherein the antiquity of the city . . . its divisions, subdivisions, laws, government, customs, trade, and amusements [are] severally pointed out. . . . 2 vols. London, 1749. 8°.

BEAUMARIS.

1042. Petition of the burgesses of Carnarvon, Conwy, and Beaumaris to Cardinal Wolsey. *Cambrian Archæol. Assoc.*, Archæologia Cambrensis, Fourth Series, xiii. 309–11. London, 1882. 8°.

BECCLES.

1043. Guild of the Holy Ghost, Beccles. *East Anglian Notes and Queries*, iii. 52–4, 91–2, 116–21. Lowestoft, 1867. 8°.

Contains extracts from the accounts of the gild, A. D. 1636–46.

BEDFORD.

1044. BLYTH, T. A. The history of Bedford and visitor's guide; with illustrations. Compiled by Thomas Allen Blyth; with contributions by several other gentlemen. London and Bedford, [1873.] 8°.

The account of municipal history is meagre.

1045. ELWES, D. G. C. Bedford and its neighbourhood. . . . Bedford, 1881. 8°.

A brief account.

1046. HURST, GEORGE. The corporation of Bedford. An historical sketch. *Royal Hist. Soc.*, Transactions, viii. 64–9. London, 1880. 8°.

1047. MATTHIASON, J. H. Bedford and its environs : or an historical and topographical sketch of the town of Bedford and places adjacent. . . . Bedford, 1831. 8°.

A brief account, of little value.

1048. Schedule (A) of the records and other documents of the corporation of Bedford. Printed by order of the corporation. Bedford, 1883. 4°.

1049. Short statement (A) of facts addressed to the electors of the borough of Bedford, in answer to some late speeches, pamphlets, and letters. London, 1831. 8°.

1050. WYATT, JAMES. Bedford after the Saxon period. A paper read at the Bedfordshire Architectural and Archæological Society's meeting, Dec. 15th, 1868. *Associated Architectural Societies*, Reports and Papers, ix. 255–82. Lincoln, [1868.] 8°.

1051. —— Memoirs of the corporation of Bedford. A paper read at the annual general meeting of the Bedfordshire Architectural and Archæological Society, held at Bedford, October 20th, 1852.

Architectural Societies of Northampton, York, Lincoln, Worcester, and Bedford, Reports and Papers, iii. 160–75. London, [1854.] 8°

BELFAST.

1052. BENN, GEORGE. A history of the town of Belfast from the earliest times to the close of the eighteenth century. [Vol. ii., from 1799 to 1810.] 2 vols. London and Belfast, 1877–80. 8°.

Ch. xi. of vol. i. contains extracts from the old Town Book, 17th century. The best history of Belfast. See No. 1054.

1053. Historical collections relative to the town of Belfast, from the earliest period to the union with Great Britain. Belfast, 1817. 8°.

Contains contributions to the parliamentary history of Belfast.

1054. History (The) of the town of Belfast, with an accurate account of its former and present state ; to which are added a statistical survey of the parish of Belfast, and a description of some remarkable antiquities in its neighbourhood. [By George Benn.] Belfast, 1823. 8°.

1055. YOUNG, R. M. Historical notices of old Belfast and its vicinity. . . . Edited with notes by R. M. Young. Belfast, etc., 1896. 8°.

Does not devote much attention to municipal history.

1056. * —— The Town Book of the corporation of Belfast . . . 1613–1816. Edited . . . by R. M. Young. Belfast, 1892. 8°.

BERE.

1057. W., W. W. E. Castell y Bere. *Cambrian Archæol. Assoc.*, Archæologia Cambrensis, iv. 214–17. London, 1849. 8°.

Contains a Latin charter granted to Bere in 1284, etc.

BERKELEY.

1058. FISHER, JOHN. A history of the town of Berkeley, its church, castle, etc., etc. Second edition, corrected and enlarged. London and Leicester, 1864. 8°.

A brief account.

1st edition, 1856.

BERKHAMSTEAD.

1059. COBB, J. W.   Two lectures on the history and antiquities of Berkhamstead.   Second edition.   London, 1883.   8°.

1st edition, [1855.]

BERWICK-UPON-TWEED.

The best histories are those of Fuller and Scott (Nos. 1060, 1064).
See No. 600.

1060. FULLER, JOHN.   The history of Berwick-upon-Tweed, including a short account of the villages of Tweedmouth and Spittal, etc.
Edinburgh, 1799.   8°.

The best of the older histories of Berwick.

1061. JOHNSTONE, THOMAS.   The history of Berwick-upon-Tweed and its vicinity; to which is added a correct copy of the charter granted to that borough [in 1604.]   Berwick, 1817.   12°.

The account of municipal history is meagre.

1062. † Roll (A) of the burgesses of Berwick-upon-Tweed, with the dates of their admission, etc.   Berwick, 1806.   4°.

Another edition, 1821.

1063. Rotuli Scotiæ in Turri Londinensi et in Domo Capitulari Westmonasteriensi asservati [Edw. I.—Hen. VIII.]   *Record Com.*
2 vols.   [London,] 1814–19.   f°.

Contains many documents relating to Berwick.

1064. SCOTT, JOHN.   Berwick-upon-Tweed.   The history of the town and guild.   London, 1888.   4°.

Contains an abstract of the court leet roll of 1616; a translation of the town charter of 1604; town statutes of 1560; a survey of Berwick in 1562; the Statuta Gildæ, etc.
Valuable; the best recent work on Berwick.

1065. SHELDON, FREDERICK.   History of Berwick-upon-Tweed: being a concise description of that ancient borough, from its origin down to the present time. . . . Edinburgh, 1849.   8°.

Does not devote much attention to municipal history.

1066. [Statuta gildæ : various enactments made by the gild merchant from 1249 to 1294.]

These statutes of the Berwick gild were regarded as a model by other Scotch towns. They are printed in Acts of the Parliament of Scotland, i. 431–8 ; Ancient Laws of the Burghs of Scotland, 64–96; Gross's *Gild Merchant,* i. 227–40: see Nos. 541, 757, 759, 1521. English translations will be found in Smith's *English Gilds,* 338–46, and Scott's *Berwick,* 465–9: see Nos. 537, 1064.

BEVERLEY.

1067. OLIVER, GEORGE. The history and antiquities of the town and minster of Beverley. . . . Beverley, 1829. 4°.

1068. POULSON, GEORGE. Beverlac : or the antiquities and history of the town of Beverley in the county of York, and of the provostry and collegiate establishment of St. John's. . . . Compiled from authentic records, charters, and unpublished manuscripts, with numerous embellishments. 2 vols. London, 1829. 4°.

Contains many extracts from the town records.
Valuable ; the best history of Beverley.

BEWDLEY.

1069. BURTON, J. R. A history of Bewdley ; with concise accounts of some neighbouring parishes. London, 1883. 8°.

1070. Speech (A) made in the House of Commons, upon the late ministry's forcing a new charter upon the town of Bewdly, in the county of Worcester, without a surrender of the old. 1710. [Lord Somers's Collection of scarce and valuable tracts, xii. 670–72. Second edition. 13 vols. London, 1809–15. 4°.]

1071. State (A) of the Bewdley case [relating to the magistracy of that place.] London, 1711. f°.

BIDEFORD.

1072. WATKINS, JOHN. An essay towards a history of Bideford, in the county of Devon. Exeter, 1792. 8°.

Reprinted, Bideford, 1883, 12°.

1073. WORTHY, CHARLES. Notes : genealogical and historical. Being a second " Essay towards a history of Bideford." . . . London, [1884.] 8°. pp. 35.

Reprinted from the Transactions of the Devon. Assoc. for the Advancement of Science, etc., xvi. 670–702. Plymouth, 1884.

BIGGAR.

1074. HUNTER, WILLIAM. Biggar and the house of Fleming. An account of the Biggar district, archæological, historical, and biographical. Second edition. Biggar and Edinburgh, 1867. 8°.

The municipal history of Biggar is briefly considered in ch. xv.
1st edition, 1862.

BIRKENHEAD.

1075. BENNETT, RICHARD. A record of elections, parliamentary and municipal, for Liverpool, Birkenhead, Bootle, south and south-west Lancashire, from the passing of the Reform Acts, 1832 and 1835, to January, 1878. Liverpool, 1878. 8°.

BIRMINGHAM.

    a. Town Records, Nos. 1076–1078.
    b. General Histories, Nos. 1079–1084.
    c. Miscellaneous, Nos. 1085–1095.

The best history of municipal affairs is that of Bunce (No. 1079).

a. Town Records.

1076. Birmingham (The) Corporation (Consolidation) Act, 1883; together with introduction, table of contents, notes of reference, appendices of incorporated statutes, and general index. By E. O. Smith and C. A. Carter. Published for the corporation. Birmingham, 1883. 8°.

1077. †Charter of incorporation of the borough of Birmingham, bearing date October 31, 1838. Birmingham, 1838. 12°.

This charter is also printed in Bunce's work (No. 1079), vol. i. app.

1078. Survey of the borough and manor of Birmingham, made in 1553. Translated by W. B. Bickley. With notes and introduction by Joseph Hill. Birmingham, [1891.] 4°.

b. General Histories.

1079. BUNCE, J. T. History of the corporation of Birmingham; with a sketch of the earlier government of the town. Published for the corporation. 2 vols. Birmingham, 1878–85. 8°.

The best account of the municipal history of Birmingham.

1080. DENT, R. K.   Old and new Birmingham.   A history of the town and its people.   3 pts.   Birmingham, 1879–80.   4°.

Contains a good account of the political history of Birmingham in the 19th century.

1081. —— The making of Birmingham : being a history of the rise and growth of the midland metropolis.   Birmingham and London, 1894.   4°.

1082. HUTTON, WILLIAM.   The history of Birmingham.   Sixth edition, with considerable additions.   Birmingham, 1835.   8°.

The best of the older works.

1st edition, 1781 ; other editions, 1783, 1795, 1806, 1819, 1835, 1840.

1083. LANGFORD, J. A.   A century of Birmingham life : or a chronicle of local events, from 1741 to 1841.   2 vols.   Birmingham and London, 1868.   8°.

1084. —— Modern Birmingham and its institutions : a chronicle of local events, from 1841 to 1871.   2 vols.   Birmingham and London, [1873–77.]   8°.

c. Miscellaneous.

1085. †BETOCCHI, C.   Birmingham.   Il comune modello.   Naples, 1893.   8°.   pp. 47.

1086. CHAMBERLAIN, J [OSEPH].   Municipal institutions in America and England.   *The Forum*, xiv. 267–81.   New York, 1892.   8°.

Deals mainly with Birmingham.

1087. MACDONALD, JOHN.   Birmingham : a study from the life.   *Nineteenth Century*, xx. 234–54.   London, 1886.   8°.

1088. MULLINS, J. D.   Catalogue of Birmingham books in the reference department of the Free Library.   Birmingham, 1874.   8°.

1089. —— Books about, printed in, or illustrative of the history of Birmingham, forming part of the reference department of the Birmingham Free Library.   Catalogued by J. D. Mullins.   Birmingham, 1885.   4°.

1090. RALPH, JULIAN.   The best governed city in the world.   *Harper's New Monthly Magazine*, lxxxi. 99–111.   New York, 1890.   8°.

1091. SEXAGENARIAN. Great towns and their public influence. i. Birmingham. *Gentleman's Magazine,* xiii. 43–54. London, 1874. 8°.

1092. SMITH, [J.] T. Memorials of old Birmingham. Traditions of the old Crown House in Der-Yat-End, in the lordship of Birmingham. With some notice of English gilds. Birmingham, 1863. 8°.

1093. SMITH, L. T. The gild of Holy Cross, Birmingham. Hull and London, 1894. 8°.

Reprinted from Andrews's *Bye-gone Warwickshire,* 1893.

1094. †Ten objections to the corporation of Birmingham. By a burgess. Birmingham, 1840. 12°.

1095. TENNYSON, CHARLES. A letter to the high-bailiff of Birmingham on the representation of that town and parliamentary reform. London, 1830. 8°.

BLACKBURN.

1096. ABRAM, W. A. Parish of Blackburn, county of Lancashire. A history of Blackburn, town and parish. Blackburn, 1877. 4°.

1097. †WHITTLE, P. A. Blackburn as it is : a topographical, statistical, and historical account . . . including a correct copy of the charter granted in the reign of Queen Victoria. . . . Preston and Blackburn, 1852. 8°.

BLETCHINGLEY.

1098. GOWER, G. L. Bletchingley manor and church. London, 1871. 8°.

Deals also with the borough.

BODMIN.

1099. Bodmin register (The) : containing collections relative to the past and present state of the parish of Bodmin. . . . [By John Wallis.] Bodmin, 1827–36. 8°.

Twenty numbers.
No. 8, Dec. 1833. Charters of Bodmin.
No. 13, March 12, 1835. The corporation.
Other numbers also touch upon municipal history.

1100. MACLEAN, JOHN. Parochial and family history of the parish and borough of Bodmin, in the county of Cornwall. London, 1870. 4°.

Vol. i. pp. 101–346 of Maclean's *Trigg Minor* (No. 583), with distinct pagination, index, etc.

BOLTON.

1101. Bolton corporation. Report of Captain Jebb, in respect of the Bolton charter. *Parl. Papers*, 1841, vol. xx. [London,] 1841. f°.

1102. †BRIMELOWE, W. Political and parliamentary history of Bolton. Vol. i. Bolton, 1882. 8°.

1103. †Bye-laws and local enactments relating to Bolton Corporation Acts. Bolton, 1872.

1104. CLEGG, JAMES. A chronological history of Bolton, from the earliest known records to 1879, compiled for the Bolton Chronicle. With parliamentary and municipal representation. Bolton, 1879. 8°.

Brief historical notes, a list of mayors, etc.
Other editions, 1870, 1875, 1877, and 1878.

1105. —— Annals of Bolton. . . . Bolton, 1888. 8°.

1106. †Copy of the charter of incorporation of the borough of Bolton. Bolton, 1838.

Bolton was incorporated in 1838.

1107. †Facts for burgesses on borough finance. Bolton, 1876.

1108. SCHOLES, JAMES C. Bolton bibliography, and jottings of book-lore ; with notes on local authors and printers. Manchester, 1886. 8°.

1109. WHITTLE, P. A. Bolton-le-Moors, and the townships in the parish : an historical . . . account of the corporate and parliamentary borough of Bolton. . . . Bolton, 1855. 8°.

Ch. ix. Corporation annals.

BOSTON.

1110. †Abstract (An) of the charter granted to Boston . . . also the bye-laws of that corporation. . . . Boston, 1813. 8°.

1111. Charters granted to the mayor and burgesses of the borough of Boston [1546–1605] . . . and the ordinances, by-laws, and constitutions founded thereon . . . in 1677. Stamford, 1825. 4°.

Contains also town ordinances made in 1708.
Only English versions of the charters are printed.

1112. †CLARKE, H. Observations addressed to the inhabitants of Boston on . . . the borough county rate. Stamford, 1825. 4°.

Contains the charters of Boston.

1113. Report (The) of the commissioners appointed to enquire into the municipal corporations in England and Wales, on the borough of Boston. Boston, 1835. 8°.

See No. 60.

1114. THOMPSON, PISHEY. Collections for a topographical and historical account of Boston and the hundred of Skirbeck in the county of Lincoln, with engravings. London and Boston, 1820. 4°.

1115. —— The history and antiquities of Boston and the villages of Skirbeck, Fishtoft. . . . Illustrated with one hundred engravings. Boston and London, 1856. 8°.

The best history of Boston.

BRADFORD.

The best histories are those of Cudworth and James (Nos. 1120, 1124).

1116. Bibliography of Bradford. *The Antiquary, the Journal of the Bradford Hist. and Antiq. Soc.*, pts. i.–v. Bradford, 1881–88. 8°.

Probably continued in pt. vi., etc.

1117. †Catalogue of books, pamphlets, etc., published at Bradford. Bradford, 1895.

1118. COLLINSON, EDWARD. The history of the worsted trade and historic sketch of Bradford. London and Bradford, 1854. 12°.

A brief account.

1119. †COX, J. H. Municipal work in Bradford. Bradford, 1886. 8°.

1120. CUDWORTH, WILLIAM. Historical notes on the Bradford corporation, with records of the lighting and watching commissioners. . . . Bradford, 1881. 8°.

The best account of the municipal history of Bradford since its incorporation in 1844.

1121. †CUDWORTH, WILLIAM. Old Bradford records. *The Antiquary, the Journal of the Bradford Hist. and Antiq. Soc.*, 1890–91. Bradford, 1890–91. 8°.

1122. EMPSALL, T. T. Social life in Bradford in the 14th century. *The Antiquary, the Journal of the Bradford Hist. and Antiq. Soc.*, pt. iii. pp. 113–23. Bradford, 1884. 8°.

Contains extracts from court rolls.

In the same journal, 1890, pt. vi., is a paper by Empsall on †Bradford during the 15th century, also a paper by †Lister on the Charters of Bradford.

1123. HOLROYD, ABRAHAM. Collectanea Bradfordiana : a collection of papers on the history of Bradford and the neighbourhood. Collated and edited, with notes, by Abraham Holroyd. Saltaire, 1873. 8°.

1124. JAMES, JOHN. The history and topography of Bradford, in the county of York, with topographical notices of the parish. London and Bradford, 1841. 8°.

The best general history of Bradford.

"Continuation and additions to the history of Bradford and its parish," 1866.

BRECHIN.

1125. BLACK, D. D. The history of Brechin. Second edition. Edinburgh and Brechin, 1867. 8°.

1st edition, 1839.

1126. JERVISE, ANDREW. An account of the round tower, cathedral, castle, and town of Brechin ; also of the Maules of Panmure. From " Memorials of Angus and the Mearns." n. p. n. d. 4°.

Ch. v. of his *Memorials* (No. 799).

BRECKNOCK OR BRECON.

See Nos. 571, 571a.

1127. Charter of Brecknock. *Cambrian Archæol. Assoc.*, Archæologia Cambrensis, Third Series, viii. 19–42. London, 1862. 8°.

Charter to the burgesses, 2 & 3 Philip & Mary.

1128. Translation (The) of an attested copy of the charter [2 & 3 Philip & Mary] of the borough of Brecon and the town of Lluell, obtained from the Rolls Chapel, September,1832. [By Joseph Joseph.] Brecon, 1866. 4°.

BRIDGNORTH.

1129. BELLETT, GEORGE.   The antiquities of Bridgnorth; with some historical notices of the town and castle.   Bridgnorth, 1856. 8°.

A brief account.

1130. Bridgnorth. — Representation of the borough.   Corporation records.   Royal charters.   Bailiffs.   *The Salopian and West-Midland Monthly Illustrated Journal,* July—Aug. 1875, Jan. 1876.   Shrewsbury, 1875–76.   8°.

1131. Salopian shreds and patches. . . . (Reprinted with additions, from " Eddowes's Shrewsbury Journal "), 1887–88, vol. viii. Shrewsbury, 1889.   4°.

For Bridgnorth mayors, bailiffs, members of Parliament, etc., see the index, p. i.

BRIDGWATER.

1132. Case respecting the Bridgewater election of the exclusive right claimed by capital burgesses.   [London, 1769.]   f°.

1133. JARMAN, S. G.   A history cf Bridgwater.   London and St. Ives, 1889.   8°.

1134. ODGERS, J. E.   A short report on some MS. accounts of the commonalty of Bridgwater.   *Somerset. Archæol. and Nat. Hist. Soc.,* Proceedings, xxiii. 38–48.   Taunton, 1878.   8°.

BRIDPORT.

1135. HUTCHINS, JOHN.   The history and antiquities of the town and borough of Bridport . . . being a section from The history and antiquities of Dorset, by John Hutchins.   Third edition, corrected, augmented, and improved by William Shipp and James W. Hodson. Blandford, 1865.   f°.

See No. 594.

1136. MASKELL, JOSEPH.   The history and topography of Bridport, Dorset.   A lecture delivered before the members and friends of the Bridport Young Men's Institute, in the Town Hall, April 26th, 1855.   Bridport, 1855.   12°.

A brief sketch.

H

BRIGHTON.

1137. Ancient and modern history of Lewes and Brighthelmston, in which are compressed the most interesting events of the county at large. . . . [By William Lee.] Lewes, 1795. 8°.

1138. Borough of Brighton. Copies of the deeds relating to the division of the tenantry lands in the parish of Brighthelmston, in the year 1822, together with extracts from the minutes of the proceedings of, and copies of reports to, the late town commissioners and the town council, with reference to the portions of the same lands dedicated to public uses. Printed by order of the town council. Brighton, 1878. 8°.

1139. ERREDGE, J. A. History of Brighthelmston or Brighton as I view it and others knew it with a chronological table of local events. Brighton, 1862. 8°.

Ch. vi. contains ancient customs of Brighton, compiled in 1580 and 1618.

1140. MARTIN, HENRY. The history of Brighton and its environs. Brighton, 1871. 8°.

The best history of Brighton since its incorporation in 1854.
2nd edition, 1871.

1141. TURNER, EDWARD. The early history of Brighton, as illustrated by the " customs of the ancient fishermen of the town." *Sussex Archæol. Soc.*, Collections, ii. 38–52. London, 1849. 8°.

BRISTOL.

a. Town Records, Nos. 1142–1150.
b. General Histories, Nos. 1151–1162.
c. Gilds, Nos. 1163–1166.
d. Miscellaneous, Nos. 1167–1182.

The most important records in the town archives are Ricart's Kalendar (No. 1150), the Little Red Book, the Great Red Book, and the Great White Book. Of these the two Red Books are the most valuable. The Little Red Book contains charters and laws of Bristol, ordinances of crafts, etc., 1344–1574; the Great Red Book contains rents, agreements, acts of council, ordinances of crafts, etc., chiefly in the reigns of Henry VI. and Edward IV. ; the Great White Book contains expenses of officers, charters, etc., 1496–1590. For some account of these records, see Miss Smith's edition of Ricart's Kalendar (No. 1150), pp. xxi.–xxvi.

The best histories of Bristol are Nicholls and Taylor's, and Seyer's (Nos. 1159, 1161).

a. **Town Records.**

See No. 1172.

1142. Bristol. The city charters: containing the original institution of mayors, recorders, sheriffs, town-clerks, and all other officers whatsoever, as also of a common-council, and the ancient laws and customs of the city, diligently compar'd with, and corrected according to the Latin originals. To which are added the bounds of the city by land, with the exact distances from stone to stone, all around the city. Bristol, 1736. 4°.

Contains only a translation of the charters, etc.

1143. —— An abstract of the city charter: containing the institution of mayors, recorders, sheriffs, town clerks, and all officers whatsoever, as also of a common council. To which is added, by way of appendix, a brief historical account of the antient lords, constables, and wardens of Bristol Castle. Second edition. Bristol, 1792. 8°.

1144. BURT, JOSEPH. Contributions to the history of the city of Bristol. From documents preserved in the Chapter House, Westminster. *Archæological Institute,* Memoirs, etc. of Bristol (Bristol meeting, 1851), 80–98. London, 1853. 8°.

Contains a French document recording complaints against the mayor by inhabitants of Bristol, 16 Edw. II.

1145. BUSH, HENRY. Bristol town duties. A collection of original and interesting documents intended to explain and elucidate the above important subject. Bristol, 1828. 8°.

Most of the documents are of the 14th, 15th, and 16th centuries.

1146. Charters (The) and letters patent granted by the kings and queens of England to the town and city of Bristol, newly translated and accompanied by the original Latin. By the Rev. Samuel Seyer. Bristol, 1812. 4°.

1147. NICHOLLS, J. F. The early Bristol charters and their chief object. *Royal Hist. Soc.,* Transactions, i. 88–95. Second edition. London, 1875. 8°.

1148. Notes or abstracts of the wills contained in the volume entitled, The Great Orphan Book and Book of Wills, in the Council House at Bristol [1381–1605.] By T. P. Wadley. *Bristol and Glouc. Archæol. Soc.* Bristol, [1882–86.] 8°.

1149. Original documents relating to Bristol and the neighbourhood [1125–1505.] By W. de Gray Birch. *Brit. Archæol. Assoc.*, Journal, xxxi. 289–305. London, 1875. 8°.

1150. RICART, ROBERT. The maire of Bristowe is kalendar, by R. Ricart. . . . Edited by Miss L. T. Smith. *Camden Society.* [Westminster,] 1872. 4°.

Ricart was elected town clerk in 1479 and held the office at least 27 years. The first three parts of the Kalendar contain brief historical notes concerning England and Bristol ; the last three parts contain local customs and laws (including extracts from the laws of London, pp. 93–113). The MS. is preserved in the town archives of Bristol. Extracts from the Kalendar are also printed in Smith's *English Gilds* (No. 537), 413–31.

b. General Histories.

1151. BARRETT, WILLIAM. The history and antiquities of the city of Bristol, compiled from original records and authentic manuscripts in public offices or private hands. Illustrated with copper-plate prints. Bristol, [1789.] 4°.

Should be used with caution ; largely based on Chatterton's forgeries.

1152. CORRY, JOHN, and EVANS, JOHN. The history of Bristol, civil and ecclesiastical ; including biographical notices of eminent and distinguished natives. [Vol. i. by Corry ; vol. ii. by Evans.] 2 vols. Bristol, 1816. 4°.

Unreliable.

1153. DALLAWAY, JAMES. Antiquities of Bristow in the middle centuries ; including the topography by William Wyrcestre, and life of William Canynges. Bristol, 1834. 4°.

1154. EVANS, JOHN. A chronological outline of the history of Bristol, and the stranger's guide. . . . Bristol, 1824. 8°.

1155. [HEATH, GEORGE.] The new history, survey, and description of the city and suburbs of Bristol. . . . Bristol, 1794. 8°.

2nd edition, "The history, antiquities, survey, and description of the city," etc., 1797 ; 7th edition, "Mathews's Complete Bristol guide," 1828.

1156. HUNT, WILLIAM. Bristol. [Historic Towns. Edited by E. A. Freeman and W. Hunt.] London, 1887. 8°

A good short account.

1157. LATIMER, JOHN. The annals of Bristol in the eighteenth century. [London,] 1893. 8°.

1158. —— The annals of Bristol in the nineteenth century. Bristol, 1887. 8°.

1159. NICHOLLS, J. F., and TAYLOR, JOHN. Bristol, past and present. An illustrated history of Bristol and its neighbourhood. 3 vols. Bristol, 1881–82. 4°.

One of the best histories of Bristol.

1160. PRYCE, GEORGE. A popular history of Bristol, antiquarian, topographical, and descriptive, from the earliest period to the present time. . . . Bristol, 1861. 8°.

1161. SEYER, SAMUEL. Memoirs, historical and topographical, of Bristol and its neighbourhood, from the earliest period down to the present time. 2 vols. Bristol, 1821–23. 4°.

This is the best history of Bristol; an excellent specimen of the better class of local histories of its day.

1162. TAYLOR, JOHN. A book about Bristol, historical, ecclesiastical, and biographical, from original research. London and Bristol, 1872. 8°.

Gilds, 226–39.
Rise of the municipal constitution, 239–52.
A good short account.

c. Gilds.

1163. FOX, [F. F.] The history of the guilds of Bristol [especially the bakers' guild.] *Bristol and Glouc. Archæol. Soc.*, Transactions, iii. 90–98. Bristol, [1878.] 8°.

1164. —— Some account of the ancient fraternity of merchant tailors of Bristol, with transcripts of ordinances and other documents. [Privately printed; 50 copies only.] Bristol, 1880. 4°.

1165. † FOX, F. F., and TAYLOR, JOHN. Some account of the guild of weavers in Bristol. Bristol, 1889. 4°.

1166. ROGERS, HENRY. The calendars of Al-Hallowen, Brystowe. An attempt to elucidate some portions of the history of the priory or ffraternitie of calendars. . . . Bristol, 1846.   12°.

d. Miscellaneous: Municipal Reform, etc.

1167. Annals of Bristol. *The Bristol Memorialist* [edited by W. Tyson], pp. 38–44, 115–22, 189–201, 287–93.   Bristol, [1816–] 1823.   8°.

1168. Bristol and its environs, historical, descriptive, and scientific. Published under the sanction of the local executive committee of the British Association, with illustrations and maps.   London, 1875.   8°.

Section iv.   Local government and taxation, by H. Naish.   (A brief account.)

1169. City and port of Bristol. Letters, essays, tracts and other documents, illustrative of the municipal history of Bristol and of the trade of its port.   Written, collected, and arranged by "a burgess." Bristol, 1836.   8°.

The separate tracts were issued in 1835.   Most of them deal with the question of municipal reform.

1170. † Few facts (A) relating to the present local government of Bristol, and hints for its probable improvement.   By an inhabitant. Bristol, 1831.   8°.   pp. 12.

1171. Free thoughts on the offices of mayor, aldermen, and common council of the city of Bristol; with a constitutional proposition for their annihilation.   To which is prefixed an address inscribed to his grace the Duke of Portland.   Bristol, 1792.   8°.

1172. GARRARD, THOMAS. Memoir of the municipal antiquities of the city of Bristol : comprising notices of the ancient civic offices, the muniments, seals, and regalia of the corporation.   *Archæological Institute*, Memoirs, etc. of Bristol (Bristol meeting, 1851), 1–12.   London, 1853.   8°.

1173. GUTCH, J. M. The present mode of election of the mayor, sheriffs, and common council of Bristol considered; extracted from Felix Farley's Bristol Journal.   Bristol, 1825.   8°.   pp. 50.

A brief history of the common council of Bristol.

1174. KENTISH, EDWARD. A narrative of facts relative to the Bristol election as connected with the meeting on Brandon Hill, June 13, 1818. . . . Bristol, 1818. 8°.

1175. LUCAS, SAMUEL. Illustrations of the history of Bristol and its neighbourhood. Bristol, 1853. 8°.

Various interesting papers on the medieval history of Bristol.

1176. —— Secularia : or surveys of the mainstream of history. London, 1862. 8°.

Bristol in the time of Edw. IV., 88–130.

1177. NICHOLLS, J. F. The ancient charter privileges of the Bristol freemen ; whence derived and how maintained. *Bristol and Glouc. Archæol. Soc.*, Transactions, iii. 258–76. Bristol, [1878.] 8°.

1178. SEXAGENARIAN. Great towns and their public influence. iii. Bristol. *Gentleman's Magazine*, xiii. 290–300. London, 1874. 8°.

1179. Small token (A) of admiration at the talents and acquirements of the corporation of Bristol. With an epistle dedicatory. By two schoolmasters. Bristol, 1824. 8°.

1180. TAYLOR, C. S. Bristol and its neighbourhood in Domesday. *Clifton Antiquarian Club*, Proceedings, ii. 67–82. Exeter, 1893. 8°.

1181. Thirty letters on the trade of Bristol, the causes of its decline and means of its revival, by a burgess. With notes ; extracts from the evidence given before the commissioners of corporate enquiry in this city ; additional information relative to its commercial and municipal history. . . . Bristol, 1834. 12°.

Chs. ii.–vi. The municipal corporation.
See No. 60.

1182. Two Bristol calendars. Communicated by H. E. Hudd. *Bristol and Glouc. Archæol. Soc.*, Transactions, xix. 105–41. Bristol, [1895.] 8°.

Two lists of mayors and bailiffs, 1216–1609, with brief historical notes.

BUCKINGHAM.

1183. Case (The) of the borough of Buckingham [concerning the election of M. P.'s.] n. p. [circa 1708.] f°. pp. 4.

Without title-page.

1184. † ROUNDELL, H. Some account of the town of Buckingham : a lecture read before the members of the Buckingham Literary and Scientific Institution, on Tuesday, January 27th, 1857. Buckingham, 1857. 8°.

1185. WILLIS, BROWNE. The history and antiquities of the town, hundred, and deanery of Buckingham. . . . London, 1755. 4°.

Willis prints the Latin text of the charter granted to Buckingham, 36 Charles II., in his *Notitia Parliamentaria*, 2nd edition, vol. i. app. (See above, No. 315.)

BURFORD.

1186. FISHER, JOHN. A history of the town of Burford, Oxford-shire. Cheltenham, 1861. 8°.

A brief account.

1187. MONK, W. J. History of Burford. Burford and London, 1891. 8°.

BURTON-ON-TRENT.

1188. BLACK, W. H. Ancient charters relating to the abbey and town of Burton-on-Trent. *Brit. Archæol. Assoc.*, Journal, vii. 421–28. London, 1852. 8°.

1189. MOLYNEUX, WILLIAM. Burton-on-Trent : its history, its waters, and its breweries. London and Burton-on-Trent, [1869.] 8°.

Of little value for municipal history.

BURY.

1190. BARTON, B. T. History of the borough of Bury and neigh-bourhood, in the county of Lancaster. Bury, [1874.] 8°.

BURY ST. EDMUND'S.

The best history is that of Yates (No. 1200).

1191. Account (An) of the proceedings at the election of members for the borough of Bury St. Edmund's, Dec. 13 and 14, 1832, being the first election for the borough since the passing of the "Act for the amending the representation of the people." Bury St. Edmund's, 1833. 8°.

1191a. † BARKER, H. R. History of Bury St. Edmund's. Bury, 1885. 8°. pp. 104.

1192. BATTELY, JOHN. Johannis Battely S. T. P. Archidiaconi Cantuariensis opera posthuma, viz. Antiquitates Rutupinæ et Antiquitates S. Edmundi Burgi ad annum 1272 perductæ. Oxon., 1745. 4°.

Written in Latin. Some of the documents are important for municipal history.

1193. BRAKELOND, JOCELIN DE. Chronica Jocelini de Brakelonda, de rebus gestis Samsonis abbatis monasterii Sancti Edmundi, nunc primum typis mandata curante J. G. Rokewode. *Camden Society.* London, 1840. 4°.

Another edition in " Memorials of St. Edmund's Abbey" (No. 1198), i. 209–336.

Translated by T. E. Tomlins: " Monastic and Social Life in the Twelfth Century," etc., London, 1844; 2nd edition, [1845.]

Valuable for the medieval history of the borough.

1194. CARLYLE, THOMAS. Past and present. [Carlyle's Collected Works, vol. ix.] London, 1864. 8°.

Book ii. The ancient monk. (Based on the Chronicle of Jocelin de Brakelond.)

1195. Charter (The) for incorporating the burgh of Bury St. Edmund's, newly and carefully translated. By an inhabitant. Bury, 1810. 8°.

1196. GILLINGWATER, EDMUND. An historical and descriptive account of St. Edmund's Bury, in the county of Suffolk. . . . St. Edmund's Bury, 1804. 12°.

A brief account, of little value for municipal history.

1197. GREEN, J. R. Stray studies from England and Italy. London, 1876. 8°.

Abbot and town, 187–209.

1198. Memorials of St. Edmund's abbey. Edited by Thomas Arnold. *Rolls Series.* 3 vols. London, 1890–96. 8°.

See the index, iii. 384, for references to passages relating to municipal affairs in the 13th and 14th centuries.

1199. Monasticon Anglicanum. By W. Dugdale. New edition, by J. Caley, H. Ellis, and B. Bandinel. 6 vols. London, 1817–30. f°.

Conflicts between the burgesses and the abbots, 1264–1381, iii. 107–12.

Charter granted by Abbot Sampson to the burgesses, 1182–1211, iii. 153–4.

1200. YATES, RICHARD. An illustration of the monastic history and antiquities of the town and abbey of St. Edmund's Bury, with views . . . by . . . W. Yates. 2 pts. London, 1805. 4°.

A new title-page, with the words " second edition," and some additional sheets were published in 1843.
Ch. v. Contests with townsmen.
The appendix of the edition of 1843 contains the Latin text of the royal charters of 1606, 1608, and 1614.
The best history of the town.

CAERLEON.

1201. Historical traditions and facts relating to Newport and Caerleon. By a member of the Caerleon and Monmouthshire Antiquarian Society. Pts. i.–v. Newport, 1880–1885. 8°.

Pt. i.   Prehistoric and Roman periods.
Pt. ii.   Saxon period.
Pt. iii. Norman and Early English periods.
Pt. iv.   Edw. III. to Mary.
Pt. v.   Civil war in Montgomeryshire.

CAERWYS.

1202. OWEN, EDWARD. The place of Caerwys in Welsh history. *Cambrian Archæol. Assoc.*, Archæologia Cambrensis, Fifth Series, viii. 166–84. London, 1891. 8°.

CALNE.

1203. Short history (A) of the borough of Calne, with reference to the elective franchise. Calne, 1830. 8°.

CAMBRIDGE.

1204. Charters of King John and Henry III. to the town of Cambridge. [T. Hearne's edition of Morins' Chronicon sive annales prioratus de Dunstaple, pp. 729–31. Oxford, 1733. 8°.]

1205. COOPER, C. H. Annals of Cambridge. Vols. i.–v. Cambridge, 1842[–53.] 8°.

The best history of Cambridge.

1205a. NEWTON, S. The diary of Samuel Newton, alderman of Cambridge (1662–1717). Edited by J. E. Foster. *Cambridge Antiq. Soc.* Cambridge, 1890. 8°.

1206. † PRYME, G.   A letter to the freemen . . . of . . . Cambridge, on the state of the borough.   Cambridge, 1823.   8°.

1207. † Reflections on the contention and disorder of the corporation of Cambridge.   London, 1789.   8°.

Relates to the election of borough officers, including " A few thoughts on the inutility of corporations."

CAMELFORD.

1208. WILKINSON, J. J.   Notices of the borough of Camelford. *Royal Institution of Cornwall,* Journal, Oct. 1865, pp. 83–8.   Truro, 1865.   8°.

Contains a charter of Henry III.

CANONGATE.

1209. Extracts from the records of the burgh of the Canongate near Edinburgh, 1561–1588.   *Maitland Club,* Miscellany, ii. 281–359.   Edinburgh, 1840.   4°.

Extracts from the " Liber Consilii burgi . . . ac Registri Cartarum communitatis ejusdem.

1210. MACKAY, JOHN.   History of the burgh of Canongate, with notices of the abbey and palace of Holyrood.   Second edition.   Edinburgh, 1886.   8°.

Contains extracts from the town records in the 16th century, etc.
A good little book.
1st edition, 1879.

1211. † Notices of various Scottish local records, with extracts. Communicated to the Society of Antiquaries of Scotland [by Thomas Thomson.]   Edinburgh, 1859.   4°.

Contains a list of the protocol books, with some notice of the other records of the burgh of Canongate and the royalty and barony of Broughton, Edinburgh.

CANTERBURY.

a.   Town Records, Nos. 1212–1216.
b.   General Histories, etc., Nos. 1217–1224.

The city archives contain some valuable unpublished records.   The proceedings in the burghmote court, which begin in Edward III.'s reign, throw much light upon municipal affairs.   The chamberlains' accounts extend almost without a break from Richard II.'s reign to the present day.

There is need of a good history of this city; Brent, Hasted, and Somner (Nos. 1217, 1220, 1223) are useful but not satisfactory.

a. Town Records.

1212. Accounts of the churchwardens of St. Dunstan's, Canterbury, 1484–1580. Communicated by J. M. Cowper. *Kent Archæol. Soc.*, Archæologia Cantiana, xvi. 289–321; xvii. 77–149. London, 1886–87. 8°.

1213. CIVIS. Minutes, collected from the ancient records and accounts in the chamber of Canterbury, of transactions in that city from A. D. 1234. . . . [Canterbury, 1801–1802.] f°.

A valuable collection of extracts from the city muniments. The ordinances of several craft gilds are given in full.

This seems to be a reprint of a series of papers published in the *Kentish Gazette* by Alderman C. R. Bunce: see Smith's *Bibliotheca Cantiana*, 124. The work has also been ascribed to William Welfitt.

1214. Translation (A) of the several charters, etc., granted by Edward IV., Henry VII., James I., and Charles II. to the citizens of Canterbury; also a list of the bailiffs and mayors . . . and many curious particulars never before published. By a citizen [C. R. Bunce]. Canterbury, 1791. 8°.

1215. WRIGHT, THOMAS. On the municipal archives of the city of Canterbury. *Soc. of Antiq. of London*, Archæologia, xxxi. 198–211. London, 1846. 4°.

1216. —— The archives of Canterbury, *Brit. Archæol. Assoc.*, Proceedings at Canterbury, Sept. 1844, pp. 316–28. London, 1845. 8°.

b. General Histories, etc.

1217. BRENT, JOHN. Canterbury in the olden time, from the municipal archives and other sources. Second edition, enlarged. London, 1879. 8°.

1st edition, 1860.

1218. CLIFFORD, HENRY. A report of the two cases of controverted elections of the borough of Southwark . . . 37 George III.;

with notes and illustrations. To which are added an account of the two subsequent cases of the city of Canterbury and an appendix. . . . London, 1797. 8°.

Another edition, 1802.

1219. GODFREY-FAUSSETT, T. G. Canterbury till Domesday. *Archæol. Journal,* xxxii. 369–93. London, 1875. 8°.

1220. HASTED, EDWARD. The history of the antient and metropolitical city of Canterbury, civil and ecclesiastical. . . . Second edition. 2 vols. Canterbury, 1801. 8°.

1st edition, 1799, f°.

1221. [ROCH, THOMAS.] Charters destructive to liberty and property; demonstrated by the principles and practices of corporation patriots. London, 1776. 8°.

" The following pages contain a few of the notorious abuses committed on the inhabitants of this city by a set of men who were appointed to protect them in peculiar privileges."

1222. —— Proceedings of the corporation of C—y, shewing the abuse of corporation government. London, 1760. 8°.

Throws light upon the constitution of the surviving Canterbury companies.

1223. SOMNER, WILLIAM. The antiquities of Canterbury: or a survey of that ancient citie, with the suburbs and cathedrall. . . . Second edition, revised and enlarged by N. Battely. 2 pts. London, 1703. f°.

The most elaborate history of Canterbury.
1st edition, 1640, 4°.

1224. SUMMERLY, FELIX [HENRY COLE]. Felix Summerly's Handbook for Canterbury: its historical associations and works of art. A new edition, revised, with additions, by John Brent. . . . Canterbury and London, 1860. 8°.

A brief account.
1st edition, 1843.

CARDIFF.

1225. Growth of Cardiff from 1875 to 1880; with some particulars of Cardiff in the last century. Reprinted from the "South Wales Daily News" and "Cardiff Times." Cardiff, 1880. 12°.

1226. JENKINS, W. L.   A history of the town and castle of Cardiff, and a descriptive account of the churches, chapels, public buildings, and institutions. . . . Cardiff, 1854.   8°.

A brief account.

CARLISLE.

a. Town Records, Nos. 1227–1230.
b. General Histories, etc., Nos. 1231–1241.

There is no good detailed history of Carlisle.   Ferguson's works (especially Nos. 321, 1229–30, 1233) are the most valuable, and Creighton's short history (No. 1231) is useful.

a. Town Records.

1227.   Extracts from the charters of the city of Carlisle, 5 Hen. III.—13 Car. II.   [First report of royal commission on market rights. *Parl. Papers*, 1888, liii. 89–90.   London, 1889.   f°.]

1228.   FERGUSON, R. S.   An account of the "Dormont Book" belonging to the corporation of Carlisle.   [Read Aug. 3, 1882.] *Cumberl. and Westm. Antiq. and Archæol. Soc.*, Transactions, vi. 297–304.   Kendal, 1883.   8°.

1229. * Royal charters (The) of the city of Carlisle, printed at the expense of the mayor and corporation, and edited by R. S. Ferguson. *Cumberl. and Westm. Antiq. and Archæol. Soc.*   Carlisle, etc., 1894.   8°.

Contains the Latin text, with a translation.

1230. * Some municipal records of the city of Carlisle, viz., the Elizabethan constitutions, orders, provisions, articles, and rules from the Dormont Book, and the rules and orders of the eight trading guilds, prefaced by chapters on the corporation charters and guilds, illustrated by extracts from the court leet rolls and from the minutes of the corporation and guilds.   Edited by R. S. Ferguson and W. Nanson. *Cumberl. and Westm. Antiq. and Archæol. Soc.*   Carlisle and London, 1887.   8°.

A valuable collection of records of the 16th, 17th, and 18th centuries.

b. General Histories, etc.

1231.   CREIGHTON, M[ANDELL].   Carlisle.   [Historic Towns.   Edited by E. A. Freeman and W. Hunt.]   London, 1889.   8°.

1232. FERGUSON, R. S.   The armorial bearings of the city of Carlisle.   [Communicated Aug. 18, 1880.]   *Cumberl. and Westm. Antiq. and Archæol. Soc.*, Transactions, vi. 1–14.   Kendal, 1883. 8°.

1233. —— Handbook to the principal places to be visited by the Royal Archæological Institute of Great Britain and Ireland . . . in the vicinity of Carlisle.   Carlisle, 1882.   8°.

Ch. iv.   Carlisle and its corporation, a lecture delivered before the Carlisle Scientific Society, March, 7, 1882. This lecture was also separately printed, [Carlisle, 1882.] 4°. It contains an excellent sketch of the constitutional history of Carlisle. Its substance was reprinted in Ferguson's *History of Cumberland* (No. 585), ch. xiii.

1234. —— Municipal offices: Carlisle.   *The Antiquary*, xiv. 17–22, 118–22, 154–62.   London, 1886.   4°.

Reprinted in app. iii. of No. 1229.

1235. FREEMAN, E. A.   The place of Carlisle in English history. [Read Aug. 1, 1882.]   *Cumberl. and Westm. Antiq. and Archæol. Soc.*, Transactions, vi. 238–71.   Kendal, 1883.   8°.

Reprinted in No. 899.

1236. Historical and descriptive guide to Carlisle and district. Originally published as "Arthur's Guide to Carlisle." Fourth edition, revised and extended.   Carlisle, 1881.   8°.

Ch. vi.   Ancient charters and modern government.

1237. History of Carlisle, past and present, and guide to strangers. With a new plan of the city by Mr. Asquith.   Carlisle, 1855.   12°.

A brief sketch.

1238. History (The) and antiquities of Carlisle. . . . Carlisle, 1837.   8°.

1239. History (The) and antiquities of Carlisle; with an account of the castles . . . in the vicinity. . . . [By Samuel Jefferson.] Carlisle and London, 1838.   8°.

The account of municipal history is not detailed.

1240. HUTCHINSON, WILLIAM.   The history and antiquities of the city of Carlisle and its vicinity.   Carlisle, 1796.   4°.

A reprint of his *History of Cumberland* (No. 586), ii. 585–681.

1241. NANSON, W[ILLIAM]. On the customary tenure at Carlisle called "cullery tenure." [Read Aug. 3, 1882.] *Cumberl. and Westm. Antiq. and Archæol. Soc.*, Transactions, vi. 305–18. Kendal, 1883. 8°.

CARMARTHEN.

1242. †Calendar (A) of all the high-sheriffs for the county of Carmarthen, and of all the mayors, bailiffs, and sheriffs of the corporation of Carmarthen from 1400 to 1818, and also a correct list of all the present burgesses of the borough. Carmarthen, 1818. 8°.

1243. †Charter of the borough of Carmarthen, 4 Geo. III. Carmarthen, 1765. 8°.

1244. Royal charters and historical documents relating to the town and county of Carmarthen, and the abbeys of Talley and Tygwyn-ar-Daf. By J. R. Daniel-Tyssen. Edited and annotated by Alcwyn C. Evans. Carmarthen, 1878. 8°.

Latin, with a translation.

1245. SPURRELL, WILLIAM. Carmarthen and its neighbourhood. Notes, topographical and historical. Second edition. Carmarthen, 1879. 8°.

1st edition, 1860.

CARNARVON.

See No. 1042.

1246. J., H. L. Charter granted by Edward I. to the town of Caernarvon, A. D. 1284. *Cambrian Archæol. Assoc.*, Archæologia Cambrensis, Third Series, iii. 173–8. London, etc., 1857. 8°.

1247. JONES, W. H. Old Karnarvon. A historical account of the town of Carnarvon, with notices of the parish churches of Llanbeblig and Llanfaglan. Carnarvon, [1882.] 8°.

CARRICKFERGUS.

1248. McSKIMIN, SAMUEL. The history and antiquities of the county of the town of Carrickfergus, from the earliest records to the present time. . . . Third edition. Belfast, 1829. 8°.

Other editions, 1811, 1823.

CASHEL.

1249. †WHITE, J. D. Cashel of the kings: being a history of the city of Cashel. 1863.

CASTLE RISING.

1250. †BELOE, E. M. Castle Rising: its castle and borough. *Norfolk and Norwich Archæol. Soc.,* Norfolk Archæology, xii. 164–89. Norwich, 1895. 8°.

1251. Some records of the Ashstead estate, and of its Howard possessors; with notices of Elford, Castle Rising, Levens, and Charlton. [Not published.] Lichfield, 1873. 4°.

App. v. Members of Parliament for the borough of Castle Rising, 1557–1832.

1252. TAYLOR, WILLIAM. The history and antiquities of Castle Rising, Norfolk. Lynn and London, [1850.] 4°.

CHARD.

1253. GREEN, EMANUEL. On the history of Chard. *Somerset. Archæol. and Nat. Hist. Society,* Proceedings, xxviii. [pt. ii.] 28–78. Taunton, 1883. 8°.

1254. PULMAN, G. P. R. The book of the Axe: containing a piscatorial description of the stream, and historical sketches of all the parishes and remarkable places upon its banks, with nearly one hundred illustrations and a map. London, etc., 1875. 8°.

Chard, 455–525.

CHESTER.

a. Town Records, Nos. 1255–1258.
b. General Histories, Nos. 1259–1267.
c. Miscellaneous, Nos. 1268–1275.

The city archives contain mayors' books (pleas in the portmote, etc.), 16 Rich. II.—4 Wm. IV.; assembly books, or minutes of the common council since 1539; and other valuable muniments. Many records of the old trade companies are also still extant; and much material relating to the history of Chester will be found in the Randle Holme Collections in the British Museum (see Index of the Harley MSS., ii. 376–539).

The best histories are Hemingway's and Morris's (Nos. 1260, 1263).

a. Town Records.

See No. 1265.

1255. BROWN, C. Epitome of the charters of the city of Chester, from 1120 to 1836. *Archæol. Journal,* xliii. 358–63. London, 1886. 8°.

1256. Charter (The) of Charles the Second to the city of Chester. Chester, 1788. 8°.

1257. Charter (The) of the city of Chester, granted by King Henry VII.[th], with a confirmation thereof by Queen Elizabeth. Now first published from a faithful translation made before the civil wars. Chester, 1772. 4°.

1258. SCOTT, S. C. Lectures on the history of St. John Baptist church and parish in the city of Chester. Chester, 1892. 8°.

Contains extracts from churchwardens' accounts in 17th and 18th centuries, etc.

b. General Histories.

1259. †FENWICK, G. L. A history of the ancient city of Chester. Chester, 1896. 4°.

1260. HEMINGWAY, JOSEPH. History of the city of Chester, from its foundation to the present time. . . . 2 vols. Chester, 1831. 8°.

The best of the older histories of Chester.

1261. History of the city of Chester, from its foundation to the present time, collected from public records, private manuscripts, and other authentic sources . . . and a chronological register of important events to the year 1815. [By J. M. B. P.] Illustrated with five etchings by G. Cuitt. Chester, 1815. 8°.

1262. History (An) and description of the city of Chester, containing every useful information for the antiquarian, stranger, and resident. Chester, 1808. 12°.

A brief sketch.

1263. * MORRIS, R. H. Chester in the Plantagenet and Tudor periods. [Chester, 1893.] 8°.

Contains copious extracts from the town records.
The best history of Chester.

1264. MORTIMER, W. W. The history of the hundred of Wirral, with a sketch of the city and county of Chester, compiled from the earliest authentic sources. London and Birkenhead, 1847. 4°.

1265. Political history (The) of the city of Chester, the charter of King Henry VII., with the confirmation thereof by Queen Elizabeth, and the various papers issued at the election of mayor, aldermen, etc. of the said city, October 22, 1813. Chester, 1814. 8°.

A brief but valuable contribution to the municipal history of the city.

1266. †Sketch of the political history of the city of Chester. Chester, 1790. f°.

1267. Stranger (The) in Chester : giving an accurate sketch of its local history, with chronological arrangements of the most interesting events connected therewith. Written and compiled from the most authentic sources, including the records of the corporation. [By J. H. Hanshall.] Chester, [1816.] 12°.

There is quite a detailed account of municipal history in his history of the county (No. 578).

c. Miscellaneous.

1268. Chester corporation charities. From the Chester Courant of June 9th, 1829. [Chester, 1829.] 12°.

Without title-page.

1269. Chester election, 1818. The complete poll book. . . . Together with a collection of addresses, papers, squibs, etc., issued by the respective candidates and their friends; and a preface, giving a history of the several contested elections for members of Parliament and civic officers, from the year 1568 to 1818, comprising a period of nearly 300 years. Now first arranged and published. By the editor of the Chester Chronicle [J. Hemingway]. Chester, 1818. 12°.

1270. Earl (The) of Warrington's speech upon his being sworn mayor of Chester, 7 Nov., 1691. With a letter to his worship from one of the freemen of that city. [Chester, 1791.] 4°.

Without title-page. The letter deals with the city charter, etc.

1271. EDDOWES, R. State of facts relating to the franchises of the city of Chester and of all other corporations in the kingdom. Chester, Oct. 28, 1788. f°.

A single sheet; it relates to a contest between the corporation and citizens.

1272. † HIBBERT, F. A.   The gild history of Chester.   *Archæol. and Hist. Soc. of Chester and N. Wales,* Journal, v. 1–15.   Chester, 1894.   8°.

1273. PENNANT, THOMAS.   Tours in Wales, by Thomas Pennant ; with notes . . . by the editor, John Rhys.   3 vols.   Caernarvon, 1883.   8°.

Chester, i. 139–255.
1st edition, 1778, 4°.

1274. Report (A) of the proceedings and evidence before a committee of the honourable House of Commons appointed to decide upon the merits of the late controverted election for the city of Chester.   Chester, 1819.   8°.

1275. Whole proceedings (The) in several informations in the nature of a quo warranto, the king against Mr. T. Amery, one of the aldermen, and Mr. J. Monk, one of the common councilmen of the city of Chester, on the relation of R. Eddowes, of the said city, merchant.   Chester, 1791.   8°.

The question at issue was whether the citizens and commonalty could participate in the election of aldermen and common councilmen.   The arguments on both sides are given in full.

Valuable for the modern history of Chester.
See Nos. 189, 1271.

CHESTERFIELD.

1276. HALL, GEORGE.   The history of Chesterfield and its charities ; to which is added an historical description of Chatsworth, Hardwick, and Bolsover, in the county of Derby.   Chesterfield, 1823.   8°.

A brief account of municipal history.

1277. History (The) of Chesterfield, with particulars of the hamlets contiguous to the town, and accounts of Chatsworth, Hardwick, and Bolsover.   [By Thomas Ford.]   London, etc., 1839.   8°.

The best history of Chesterfield.
Ford was assisted in the compilation of this work by T. Adams, G. J. Stevenson, and R. Wallace.   It is Hall's book (No. 1276) much enlarged.

1278. Old and new Chesterfield : its people and steeple.   By Tatler [John Pendleton].   Chesterfield, etc., 1882.   8°.

A brief account.

1279. Records of the borough of Chesterfield: being a series of extracts from the archives of the corporation of Chesterfield and of other repositories; collected by [J.] Pym Yeatman. Chesterfield and Sheffield, 1884. 8°.

Contains many documents printed in full, with a translation.
The records are valuable, but are not well edited.
See also Yeatman's *Feudal History* (No. 591).

1280. YEATMAN, [J.] PYM. Some observations upon the law of ancient demesne; with suggestions as to the origin of the families of Brewer, Brito, Hardwick, and Cavendish, the ancient lords of the manor of Chesterfield, in the county of Derby, arising upon an examination of the archives of the borough. Sheffield and London, 1884. 8°.

CHICHESTER.

1281. HAY, ALEXANDER. The history of Chichester . . . with an appendix, containing the charters of the city at three different times. . . . Chichester, 1804. 8°.

The appendix contains the Latin charters of King Stephen and Henry II., with a translation; and a translation of the charter of James II., 1685.

1282. TURNER, EDWARD. The merchant guild of St. George at Chichester. *Sussex Archæol. Soc.*, Collections, xv. 165–77. Lewes, 1863. 8°.

CHIPPENHAM.

1283. DANIELL, J. J. The history of Chippenham. London, etc., 1894. 8°.

1283a. † GOLDNEY, F. H. Records of Chippenham. London, 1889. 8°.

1284. GOMME, G. L. Chippenham as a village community. *Archæol. Review*, i. 102–108, 203–210. London, 1888. 8°.

See No. 105.

1285. JACKSON, J. E. On the history of Chippenham. *Wilts. Archæol. and Nat. Hist. Soc.*, Magazine, iii. 19–46. Devizes and London, 1857. 8°.

A brief sketch.

CHIPPING CAMPDEN.

1286. BARTLETT, S. E. The manor and borough of Chipping Campden. *Bristol and Glouc. Archæol. Soc.*, Transactions, ix. 134–95, 354–5. Bristol, [1885.] 8°.

CHIPPING NORTON.

1287. BALLARD, A. Notes on the history of Chipping Norton. . . . Oxford, 1893. 8°.

A brief account.

CHRISTCHURCH.

1288. † Case (The) of Mr. Richard Holoway, one of the burgesses of Christchurch, in the county of Southampton. . . . [Christchurch, 1727.] 8°.

1289. FERREY, BENJAMIN. The antiquities of the priory of Christ Church, Hants. . . . together with some general particulars of the castle and borough. The literary part by E. W. Brayley. London, 1834. 4°.

2nd edition, revised by J. Britton, 1841.

CILGERRAN.

1290. PHILLIPS, J. R. The history of Cilgerran . . . including the topography of the parish; with copies of charters and other MSS. London, 1867. 8°.

CIRENCESTER.

1291. BEECHAM, K. J. History of Cirencester and the Roman city of Corinium. Cirencester, [1886.] 8°.

Untrustworthy.

1292. FULLER, E. A. Cirencester: the manor and the town. *Bristol and Glouc. Archæol. Soc.*, Transactions, ix. 298–344. Bristol, 1885. 8°.

1293. —— Cirencester guild merchant. *Ibid.*, xviii. 32–74, 175–6. Bristol, [1895.] 8°.

Contains some valuable documents of the year 4 Henry IV.

1294. —— Tenures of land by the customary tenants in Cirencester. *Ibid.*, ii. 285–319. Bristol, [1878.] 8°.

1295. History of the antient town of Cirencester. . . . [By S. Rudder.] Third edition. Cirencester, 1814. 8°.

1st edition, "The history and antiquities of Cirencester," 1780; 2nd edition, 1800. The material is taken mainly from Rudder's history of the county (No. 605).

1296. †History of the town of Cirencester, in the county of Gloucester with an account of the public buildings, institutions. . . . Cirencester, 1858. 8°.

1297. History (The) and antiquities of the town of Cirencester, in the county of Gloucester, with views of the town, tesselated pavements, and other Roman remains. Cirencester, [1842.] 8°.

CLARE.

1298. ARMSTEAD, J. B. Some account of the court leet of the borough of Clare, with extracts from the verdicts of the headboroughs [1612–1782.] *Suffolk Institute of Archæology*, Proceedings, ii. 103–112. Lowestoft, 1859. 8°.

CLITHEROE.

1299. HARLAND, JOHN. Ancient charters and other muniments of the borough of Clithero. . . . With translations and notes by J. Harland. Printed for the corporation. Manchester, 1851. 4°. pp. 52.

1300. —— On some ancient charters and grants to the borough of Clithero. *Brit. Archæol. Assoc.*, Journal, vi. 425–37. London, 1851. 8°.

1301. WHITAKER, T. D. An history of the original parish of Whalley and honor of Clitheroe, in the counties of Lancaster and York. Fourth edition, revised and enlarged by J. G. Nichols and P. A. Lyons. 2 vols. London, 1872–76. 4°.

Borough of Clitheroe, ii. 68–100.
Other editions, 1 vol., 1801, 1806, 1818.

CLONAKILTY.

1302. TOWNSHEND, DOROTHEA. Notes on [i. e. from] the Council Book of Clonakilty. Municipal records of Clonakilty, 1675–1802. *Cork Hist. and Archæol. Soc.*, Journal, Second Series, vols. i.–ii. Cork, 1895–96. 8°.

CLOYNE.

1303. Rotulus pipæ Clonensis, ex originali in registro ecclesiæ cathedralis Clonensis asservato, nunc primum editus . . . opera et studio Ricardi Caulfield, B. A.   Corcagiæ, 1859.   4°.

This roll was probably begun in 1364, but many older documents were afterwards included.   It contains findings of juries and deeds relating to the temporalities of the see of Cloyne.
Charter of Daniel, Bishop of Cloyne, to the citizens of Cloyne, 36–7.

CLUN.

1304. [SALT, THOMAS.]   A concise account of ancient documents relating to the honor, forest, and borough of Clun, in Shropshire, with copies of some of them, and observations on the custom of amobyr formerly existing there.   Read at the meeting of the Archæological Institute, at Shrewsbury, in August, 1855.   [Shrewsbury,] 1858.   4°.

1305. —— Ancient documents relating to the honor, forest, and borough of Clun.   *Shropsh. Archæol. and Nat. Hist. Soc.*, Transactions, xi. 244–71.   Shrewsbury and Oswestry, 1888.   8°.

COGGESHALL.

1306. BEAUMONT, G. F.   A history of Coggeshall, in Essex. . . . London and Coggeshall, 1890.   8°.

Contains some information about the crafts of the town.

1307. DALE, BRYAN.   The annals of Coggeshall, otherwise Sunnendon, in the county of Essex.   Coggeshall, 1863.   8°.

COLCHESTER.

a. Town Records, Nos. 1308–1314.
b. General Histories, etc., Nos. 1315–1323.

The best history is Cromwell's (No. 1315).

a. Town Records.

1308. †Charter (The new) granted to the mayor and commonalty of Colchester, 1763 ; with recitals of the old charters confirmed by the present.   [Colchester,] 1764.   8°.

1309. †Charter (The) granted to the free burgesses of the borough of Colchester by George III.; with a copious index. Colchester, 1818. 8°.

1310. Colchester charter (The) of 1662. *The Essex Notebook and Suffolk Gleaner,* January, 1885, i. 37–8. London and Colchester, 1885. 4°.

An abstract of its contents.

1311. †Constitutions of the burgh of Colchester, edited by B. Strutt. [Colchester,] 1822. 8°.

1312. HARROD, HENRY. Calendar of the court rolls of the borough of Colchester; with lists of bailiffs and mayors to the present year, 1865. Colchester, [1865.] 4°.

1313. —— Repertory of the records and evidences of the borough of Colchester, 1865. Colchester, [1865.] 4°.

1314. —— Report on the records of the borough of Colchester, 1865. Colchester, [1865.] 4°.

b. General Histories, etc.

1315. CROMWELL, THOMAS. History and description of the ancient town and borough of Colchester, in Essex. Illustrated with engravings. 2 vols. London and Colchester, 1825. 8°.

Vol. ii. ch. v. deals with municipal affairs.
The best history of Colchester.

1316. CUTTS, E. L. Colchester. [Historic Towns. Edited by E. A. Freeman and W. Hunt.] London, 1888. 8°.

1317. Guild (The) : a poem. Colchester, [1820.] 8°.

A satire directed against the town government of Colchester.

1318. History (The) and antiquities of Colchester, in the county of Essex : containing a general account of the place . . . privileges, charters, half-year lands, bounds, and extent of its liberties. Government of the corporation. . . . Selected from the most approved authors. Colchester, 1789. 8°.

1319. History (The) and antiquities of the borough of Colchester, in the county of Essex. Selected from the most approved authors [chiefly from Morant]. Colchester, 1810. 12°.

A brief account.

1320. History (The) and description of Colchester . . . with an account of the antiquities of that most ancient borough. [By Benjamin Strutt.] 2 vols. Colchester, 1803. 8°.

1321. MORANT, PHILIP. The history and antiquities of . . . Colchester . . . in three books; with an appendix of original papers. 3 pts. London, 1748. f°.

See his history of the county (No. 601).

1322. ROUND, J. H. The Domesday of Colchester. *The Antiquary*, v. 244–50; vi. 5–9, 95–100, 251–6. London, 1882. 4°.

An account of the survey of Colchester in Domesday Book.

1323. —— Municipal offices: Colchester. *The Antiquary*, xii. 188–92, 240–45; xiii. 28–30. London, 1885–86. 4°.

COLERAINE.

1324. Transactions relative to the corporation and borough of Coleraine, in Ireland. [London, 1830.] 8°.

Describes the struggle between the select governing body and the townsmen in 1830.

COLINSBURGH.

1325. DICK, ROBERT. Annals of Colinsburgh, with notes on church life in Kilconquhar parish. Edinburgh, 1896. 8°.

Ch. iv. The burgh of barony.

CONGLETON.

1326. HEAD, ROBERT. Congleton, past and present. A history of this old Cheshire town. Congleton, 1887. 8°.

The best history of Congleton.

1327. YATES, SAMUEL. An history of the ancient town and borough of Congleton; with an appendix. . . . Congleton, 1820. 8°.

CONWAY.

See No. 1042.

1328. OWEN, EDWARD. Conway municipal records. *Cambrian Archæol. Assoc.*, Archæologia Cambrensis, Fifth Series, vii. 226–33. London, 1890. 8°.

1329. WILLIAMS, ROBERT. The history and antiquities of the town of Aberconwy and its neighbourhood; with notices of the natural history of the district. Denbigh, 1835. 8°.

CORFE CASTLE.

1330. BOND, THOMAS. History and description of Corfe Castle, in the Isle of Purbeck, Dorset. London and Bournemouth, 1883. 8°.

CORK.

The best history is Gibson's (No. 727). See also No. 728.

1331. * Council Book (The) of the corporation of the city of Cork, from 1609 to 1643, and from 1690 to 1800. Edited . . . by Richard Caulfield. Guildford, 1876. 4°.

1332. †Remarks upon the religion, trade, government, police, customs, manners, and maladies of the city of Cork. By Alexander the Coppersmith. Cork, 1737. 12°.

1333. †Rights (The) of the freemen of the city of Cork asserted, and the several abuses and usurpations on the constitution pointed out. Cork, 1759.

1334. Some unpublished records of Cork [1815–18.] By C. G. Doran. *Cork Hist. and Archæol. Soc.*, Journal, i. 48–54, 71–6; ii. 107–13, 131–4. Cork, 1893–94. 8°.

1335. WINDELE, JOHN. Historical and descriptive notices of the city of Cork and its vicinity, Gougaun-Barra, Glengariff, and Killarney. New edition. Cork, 1849. 12°.

A brief account.
1st edition, 1839.

COVENTRY.

a. Town Records, Nos. 1336–1337.
b. General Histories, Nos. 1338–1343.
c. Miscellaneous, Nos. 1344–1355.

The best books relating to Coventry are those of Poole and Whitley (Nos. 1342, 1355).

a. Town Records.

1336. †Charter (The) granted by King James I. to the city of Coventry in 1621, translated from the original record in Rolls Chapel, London. Coventry, 1816. 8°.

1337. Selected list of charters and other evidences belonging to the corporation of Coventry. [By J. Fetherston.] Printed for private distribution only. [Coventry, 1871.] 8°.

b. General Histories.

1338. DUGDALE, WILLIAM. The antiquities of Coventre, illustrated from records. . . . Coventry, 1765. 4°. pp. 59.
Reprinted from Dugdale's *Warwickshire* (No. 659).

1339. †HAWKES, H. W. History and antiquities of the city of Coventry. Coventry, 1842. 8°.

1340. †HICKLING, W. History and antiquities of Coventry. Coventry, 1846. 12°.

1341. History (The) of Coventry. [Hearne's edition of Fordun's *Scotichronicon*, app., pp. 1438–74. 5 vols. Oxonii, 1722. 8°.]

1342. POOLE, BENJAMIN. Coventry : its history and antiquities . . . illustrated by W. F. Taunton with sixty exquisite tinted etchings, facsimiles, maps, etc. London and Coventry, 1870. 4°.
The best general history of Coventry.

1343. READER, WILLIAM. The history and antiquities of the city of Coventry, from the earliest authentic period to the present time. . . . Coventry, [1810.] 12°.

c. Miscellaneous.

1344. †Coventry. Case of the controverted election. Coventry, 1784. 8°.

1345. FRETTON, W. G. The fullers' guild, Coventry. Read at the annual meeting of the Warwickshire Naturalists' and Archæologists' Field Club . . . March 4th, 1879.

Without title-page.

1346. —— Municipal regalia, seals, and coinage of the city of Coventry. A paper read . . . March the 2nd, 1880, at the annual meeting of the Warwickshire Naturalists' and Archæologists' Field Club. Coventry, [1880.] 12°.

1347. HARRIS, M. D. Laurence Saunders, citizen of Coventry. *English Hist. Rev.*, ix. 633–51. London, 1894. 8°.

1348. Mayors, bailiffs, and sheriffs of Coventry. [Coventry, 1830.] 12°.

Without title-page.

1349. †Memorial of the visit of the Archæological Institute to Coventry, giving new particulars in reference to the early history of the town. Coventry, 1864. 4°.

1350. READER, WILLIAM. The origin and description of Coventry Show Fair and Peeping Tom; together with the history of Leofric, earl of Mercia, and his Countess Godiva, from authentic records. Coventry, [1824?]. 12°.

1351. SHARP, THOMAS. A dissertation on the pageants, or dramatic mysteries, anciently performed at Coventry by the trading companies of that city. . . . Coventry, 1825. 4°.

1352. —— Illustrative papers on the history and antiquities of the city of Coventry . . . from original and mostly unpublished documents. By Thomas Sharp. Carefully reprinted from an original copy, with corrections, additions, and a brief memoir of the author, by William George Fretton. [Birmingham,] 1871. 4°.

The papers deal mainly with the various churches of Coventry.

1353. [——] The pageant of the company of sheremen and taylors in Coventry, as performed by them on the festival of Corpus Christi; together with other pageants exhibited on occasion of several royal visits to that city; and two specimens of ancient local poetry. Coventry, 1817. 4°.

1354. SHARP, THOMAS. The Presentation in the Temple, a pageant as originally represented by the corporation of weavers in Coventry. Now first printed from the books of the company. With a prefatory notice. *Abbotsford Club.* Edinburgh, 1836. 4°.

1355. * WHITLEY, T. W. The parliamentary representation of the city of Coventry, from the earliest times to present date. . . . Coventry, 1894. 8°.

CRAWFURDSDYKE.

See No. 1706.

1355a. WILLIAMSON, GEORGE. Old Cartsburn: being a history of the estate from the year 1669 downwards. . . . Paisley, etc., 1894. 4°.

Ch. xi. deals with the burgh of Crawfurdsdyke.

CRICKLADE.

1356. [PETRIE, SAMUEL.] Report of the Cricklade case [1781–82]: comprehending the whole of the proceedings in the courts of law before the select committee of the commons, and in both houses of Parliament. London, 1785. 8°.

CROYDON.

1357. †ELBOROUGH, C. M. Croydon a borough: the charter and first election. Croydon, 1883. 8°.

Croydon was incorporated in 1883.

CULLEN.

1358. CRAMOND, WILLIAM. The annals of Cullen: being extracts from records relating to the affairs of the royal burgh of Cullen, 961–1887. Second edition. Buckie, [1888.] 8°.

" In the preparation of this little work every document now in the custody of the town council has been carefully examined:" Preface.

1st edition, Banff, 1880.

1359. —— Inventory of the charters, burgh court books, books of sasines, etc., belonging to the burgh of Cullen . . . together with copy of the charter of the burgh and translation thereof. . . . Banff, 1887. 8°.

CULROSS.

1360. BEVERIDGE, DAVID. Culross and Tulliallan: or Perthshire on Forth, its history and antiquities, with elucidations of Scottish life and character from the burgh and kirk-session records of that district. 2 vols. Edinburgh and London, 1885. 8°.

CUPAR.

1361. Charters and other muniments belonging to the royal burgh of Cupar [1363–1595.] Translated from the originals by George Home, Edinburgh, in 1812. Cupar-Fife, 1882. 4°. pp. 19.

1362. Forfar district of burghs. Statement of proceedings regarding the election of a delegate at Cupar, etc., etc., December, 1830. Edinburgh, 1831. 8°.

DARLINGTON.

1363. LONGSTAFFE, W. H. D. The history and antiquities of the parish of Darlington. . . . Darlington and London, 1854. 4°.

DAVENTRY.

1364. †Reasons for refusing to purchase the freedom of the burgh of Daventry. By J. D. Daventry, 1825.

1365. †Report (A) of the trial in which an action was brought by the corporation of Daventry against John Dickins for refusing to purchase the freedom of the borough. Birmingham, 1825.

For this and No. 1364, see *Northamptonshire Notes and Queries,* ii. 110.

DEAL.

See No. 687.

1366. CHAPMAN, H. S. Deal, past and present: a full and comprehensive history of this neighbourhood. . . . London, 1890. 4°.

A brief account.

1367. PRITCHARD, STEPHEN. The history of Deal and its neighbourhood. . . . Deal, 1864. 8°.

The best history of Deal.

DENBIGH.

1368. Account (An) of the castle and town of Denbigh. [By Richard Newcome.] Denbigh, 1829. 8°.

A brief account.

1369. Original charter preserved amongst the records of the corporation of Denbigh. *Cambrian Archæol. Assoc.*, Archæologia Cambrensis, Third Series, i. 185–90. London and Tenby, 1855. 8°.

Anglo-Norman charter of Henry de Lacy to the burgesses of Denbigh.

1370. PENNANT, THOMAS. Tours in Wales, by Thomas Pennant; with notes, prefaces, and copious index by the editor, John Rhys. 3 vols. Caernarvon, 1883. 8°.

Denbigh, ii. 151–68.
1st edition, 1778, 4°.

1371. WILLIAMS, JOHN. Ancient and modern Denbigh : a descriptive history of the castle, borough, and liberties. Denbigh, 1856. 8°.

The best general history of Denbigh.

1372. —— The mediæval history of Denbighshire. The records of Denbigh and its lordship. . . . Vol. i. Wrexham, 1860. 8°.

Ch. v.   The municipal history of Denbigh : corporate records, etc.
Ch. xii. Original charter of 1290, etc.
Ch. xiii. Corporate records continued (brief extracts, 1600–1831), etc.

DERBY.

Yeatman's history of the county (No. 591) contains valuable material relating to the history of the borough of Derby.

1373. BEMROSE, H. A. The Derby company of mercers. *Derbyshire Archæol. and Nat. Hist. Soc.*, Journal, xv. 113–160. London and Derby, 1893. 8°.

Contains copious extracts from the company's records, 17th and 18th centuries. Separately printed, Derby, 1893.

1374. GLOVER, STEPHEN. The history of the borough of Derby. Derby, 1843. 8°. pp. 88.

A brief account.

1375. HUTTON, WILLIAM. The history of Derby, from the remote ages of antiquity to the year 1791. . . . Second edition with additions. London, 1817. 8°.

Contains a brief account of municipal history, with lists of mayors and M. P.'s. 1st edition, 1791.

1376. SIMPSON, ROBERT. A collection of fragments illustrative of the history and antiquities of Derby, compiled from authentic sources. 2 vols. Derby, 1826. 8°.

Translation of the charters of Charles II., i. 117–55.

DEVIZES.

1377. History (A), military and municipal, of the ancient borough of the Devizes, subordinately of the entire hundred of Potterne and Cannings, in which it is included. London and Devizes, 1859. 8°.

The best history of Devizes.

1378. KITE, EDWARD. The guild of merchants, or three trading companies formerly existing in Devizes. *Wilts. Archæol. and Nat. Hist. Soc.*, Magazine, iv. 160–74. Devizes, [1858.] 8°.

1379. WAYLEN, JAMES. Chronicles of the Devizes : being a history of the castle, parks, and borough of that name. . . . London, 1839. 8°.

Much attention is devoted to municipal history.

DEVONPORT.

1380. †Charter of the borough of Devonport, with notes. By J. W. W. Ryder. Devonport, 1837. 8°.

The town was incorporated in 1837.

1381. Correct copy (A) of the charter of incorporation of the borough of Devonport, granted by her majesty, Victoria the First ; together with a list of the first council elected. . . . To which is added an appendix containing notes, forms, etc., relating to the Municipal Incorporation Act. Devonport, 1838. 12°.

1382. WORTH, R. N. History of the town and borough of Devonport, sometime Plymouth Dock. Plymouth, 1870. 8°.

I

1383. WORTH, R. N. The three towns [Plymouth, Devonport, and Stonehouse] bibliotheca : a catalogue of books, pamphlets, papers, etc., written by natives thereof, published therein, or relating thereto ; with brief biographical notices of the principal authors. [Plymouth, 1871.] 8°.

DEWSBURY.

1384. †Incorporation (The) of Dewsbury. Dewsbury, 1861. 8°.
Dewsbury was incorporated in 1862.

DONCASTER.

1385. †Acts of Parliament relating to Doncaster. Doncaster, 1756. f°.

1386. HUNTER, JOSEPH. South Yorkshire. The history and topography of the deanery of Doncaster, in the diocese and county of York. 2 vols. London, 1828–31. f°.
The parish of Doncaster, i. 1–51.
Contains an account of municipal affairs, especially in the 16th and 17th centuries.

1387. MILLER, EDWARD. The history and antiquities of Doncaster and its vicinity ; with anecdotes of eminent men. Doncaster, [1804.] 4°.
In the body of the work little attention is paid to municipal history, but the appendix contains a translation of the various town charters.

1388. SHEARDOWN, WILLIAM. The corporation of Doncaster, of the first régime. Communicated to the Doncaster Gazette, May 9, 1862. Doncaster, [1862.] 8°.
Contains a sketch of municipal history, a list of mayors, etc.

1389. —— The marts and markets of Doncaster : their rise and progress and sources of supply. [From the Doncaster Gazette.] Doncaster, [1872.] 8°.
Sheardown wrote several other sketches relating to Doncaster, but they do not deal with municipal history.

1390. TOMLINSON, JOHN. Doncaster, from the Roman occupation to the present time. Doncaster, 1887. 4°.
Contains many extracts from the town records.
A valuable work ; the best history of Doncaster.

DORCHESTER.

1391. †HALLIWELL, J. O. On the municipal archives of Dorchester. Dorchester, Weymouth, and Portland. n. d. 8°.

See Mayo, *Bibliotheca Dorsetiensis* (No. 23), 150.

1392. HUTCHINS, JOHN. The history and antiquities of the town and borough of Dorchester . . . being a section from The history and antiquities of Dorset, by John Hutchins. Third edition, corrected, augmented, and improved by W. Shipp and J. W. Hodson. Blandford, 1865. f °.

See No. 594.

1393. SAVAGE, JAMES. Dorchester and its environs during the British, Roman, Saxon, and Norman periods, illustrated and described from the best authorities ; with an account of its present state. Dorchester, 1832. 8°.

Another edition, [1833,] 12°.

1394. YOUNG, E. W. Dorchester : its ancient and modern history, principal buildings and institutions, and its neighbourhood. Dorchester, 1886. 8°.

A meagre sketch.

DOUNE.

1395. Local notes and queries. Reprinted from " The Stirling Observer." Edited by W. B. Cook. Vol. i. Stirling, 1883. 8°.

Burgh of barony of Doune, by N. A., 152–6.

DOVER.

The best history is Lyon's (No. 1401).

1396. BATCHELLER, W. A new history of Dover, and of Dover Castle, during the Roman, Saxon, and Norman governments ; with a short account of the Cinque Ports, compiled from ancient records and continued to the present time. . . . Dover, 1828. 8°.

1397. BURT, NATHANIELL. For every individuall member of the House of Commons, concerning the major, magistracy, and officers of Dover. [London,] 1649. 4°.

Without title-page.

1398. KNOCKER, EDWARD. On the municipal records of Dover. *Kent Archæol. Society*, Archæologia Cantiana, vol. x. pp. cxxxiv.–cl. Canterbury, 1876. 8°.

1399. —— A lecture on the archives of Dover. Dover, 1879. 8°.

1400. —— The archives of the borough of Dover. *Brit. Archæol. Assoc.*, Journal, xl. 1–14. London, 1884. 8°.

1401. * LYON, JOHN. The history of the town and port of Dover, and of Dover Castle ; with a short account of the Cinque Ports. 2 vols. Dover, 1813–14. 4°.

Contains copious extracts from the town records, including the whole of the medieval customal.
The best history of Dover.

1402. Report (A) on the corporation of Dover, copied from the report of the municipal corporation commissioners ; with a brief history of Dover harbour, and the proceedings of the harbour commissioners. Dover, 1835. 4°.

See No. 60.

1403. Short historical sketch (A) of the town of Dover and its neighbourhood : containing a concise history of the town, from the earliest accounts to the present time. To which is added a description of the villages near Dover, within the distance of six miles. New edition. Dover, 1807. 12°.

1st edition, 1799; 6th edition, 1828.

1404. SIMS, R. Dover records in the British Museum. *Brit. Archæol. Assoc.*, Journal, xl. 129–32. London, 1884. 8°.

DROGHEDA.

1405. D'ALTON, JOHN. The history of Drogheda, with its environs ; and an introductory memoir of the Dublin and Drogheda railway. 2 vols. Dublin, 1844. 8°.

DROITWICH.

1406. †STANTON, G. K. Historical and other notices relating to St. Andrew's church, Droitwich, together with a sketch of the history of the borough of Droitwich. [Reprinted from the Bromsgrove, Droitwich, and Redditch Weekly Messenger, 1883.]

DUBLIN.

 a. Town Records, etc., Nos. 1407–1413.
 b. General Histories, Nos. 1414–1418.
 c. Miscellaneous : Political Tracts, Nos. 1419–1443.

The city archives contain a rich collection of records, the most important of which are : the charters, beginning in 1171 ; the White Book, begun in the 13th century, containing miscellaneous documents; the Chain Book, begun in the 14th century, containing town ordinances, etc.; and the assembly rolls, from 1447 onward. The Calendar edited by Gilbert (No. 1407) is very valuable.

There is no good account of the municipal history of Dublin. The best general history is Gilbert's (No. 1415). The political tracts throw much light on municipal affairs in the 18th century.

a. Town Records, etc.

See No. 1438.

1407. * Calendar of ancient records of Dublin, in the possession of the municipal corporation of that city. By John T. Gilbert. . . . Published by authority of the municipal council. 6 vols. Dublin and London, 1889–96. 8°.

A valuable collection of extracts from the town records, 1171–1716.

1408. Chartularies of St. Mary's Abbey, Dublin ; with the register of its house at Dunbrody, and annals of Ireland. Edited by John T. Gilbert. *Rolls Series.* 2 vols. London, 1884. 8°.

For early Dublin charters, etc., see i. 266–73, 296–9, 530, etc.

1409. Lucas, Charles. The great charter of the liberties of the city of Dublin, transcribed and translated into English ; with explanatory notes. . . . Dublin, 1749. 8°.

The Latin text, with an English translation.

1410. †Macalister, A., and McNab, W. R. British Association meeting in Dublin, 1878. Guide to the county of Dublin ; its geology, industries, flora, and fauna. 2 pts. Dublin, 1878. 8°.

Pt. ii. contains a paper by W. G. Carroll on the municipal records of the city.

1411. Precedence of Edinburgh and Dublin: proceedings in the Privy Council in the question as to the precedence of the corporations of Edinburgh and Dublin in presenting addresses to the sovereign. [By J. D. Marwick.]   Edinburgh, 1865.   4°.

Contains an abstract of charters and other documents relating to these cities.

1412. Standing rules (The) and orders of the common council of the city of Dublin.   Dublin, 1778.   12°.

1413. —— The standing rules and orders of the commons of the common-council of the city of Dublin; to which is prefixed a list of the aldermen, sheriffs, and commons, and of the several committees, and the oath of a common-council-man and freeman.   Dublin, 1799.   16°.

b. General Histories.

1414. FERRAR, JOHN.   A view of ancient and modern Dublin, with its improvements to the year 1796. . . . Second edition.   Dublin, 1807.   12°.

A brief account.
1st edition, 1796, 8°.

1415. GILBERT, J. T.   A history of the city of Dublin.   3 vols. Dublin, etc., 1854–59.   8°.

Devotes little attention to municipal history.

1416. HARRIS, WALTER.   The history and antiquities of the city of Dublin, from the earliest accounts. . . . London, 1766.   8°.

Another edition, 1766.

1417. WARBURTON, J., WHITELAW, J., and WALSH, R.   History of the city of Dublin, from the earliest accounts to the present time: containing its annals, antiquities, ecclesiastical history, and charters. . . . 2 vols.   London, 1818.   4°.

Made up largely of inaccurate reprints of various earlier publications, including the whole of Harris's work (No. 1416).

1418. WRIGHT, G. N.   An historical guide to ancient and modern Dublin, illustrated by engravings after drawings by George Petrie. Second edition.   London, 1825.   12°.

A meagre account.
1st edition, 1821, 8°.

c. Miscellaneous: Political Tracts.

For various tracts, not mentioned below, see Catalogue of Trinity College Library, ii. 719–21.

1419. †Abstract of a few grievances of the citizens of Dublin. [Dublin, 1750.] 8°.
Without title-page.

1420. Briton (A). A history of the Dublin election in the year 1749, with a sketch of the present state of parties in the kingdom of Ireland. By a Briton. London, 1753. 8°.

1421. Brother (A). The state of the incorporated constitution of the city of Dublin, addressed to the free-citizens thereof by a brother. Dublin, 1755. 8°.

1422. BUTT, ISAAC. Irish Corporation Bill. A speech delivered at the bar of the House of Lords, on Friday, the 15th of May, 1840, in defence of the city of Dublin, on the order for going into committee on the Irish Corporation Bill. London, 1840. 8°.

1423. Case (The) of the city of Dublin, in relation to the election of the lord-mayor and sheriffs of the said city. [Dublin, 1711.] 16°.

1424. Case (The) of the city of Dublin. The speeches delivered by counsel at the bar of the House of Lords, in defence of the city of Dublin, on the motion for going into committee on the Irish Municipal Reform Bill. Dublin, 1840. 8°.

1425. Citizen (A). The present constitution of the city of Dublin, addressed to the citizens of Dublin. By a citizen. Dublin, 1758. 8°.

1426. FLINT, JOHN. The Dublin police and the police system. Dublin, 1847. 4°.

1427. Her majesty's prerogative in Ireland, the authority of the government and Privy-Council there, and the rights, laws, and liberties of the city of Dublin asserted. . . . London, 1712. 8°.

1428. †HOLMES, HENRY. Alphabetical list of the freeholders and freemen who voted on a late election of a member to represent the

city of Dublin in Ireland [13–30 Dec., 1773]. . . . Also an account
of the elections for the said city from 1749 to 1773. Dublin, 1773.
8°.

1429. Instructions (The) of the corporation of barbers and chir-
urgeons, apothecaries and periwig-makers, or guild of St. Mary
Magdalene, within the city of Dublin, to their representatives in
common council. Dublin, 1844. 8°.

The representatives are instructed to defend the commons against the en-
croachments of the aldermen.

1430. †Letter to the masters, wardens, and brethren of Trinity
guild, on their late reconciliation and the approaching election.
[Dublin,] 1749. 8°.

1431. Letter (A second) to a member of the honourable House of
Commons of Ireland, containing a scheme for regulating the corporation of the city of Dublin. Dublin, 1760. 8°.

1432. LUCAS, CHARLES. The complaints of Dublin, humbly offered
to his excellency William, Earl of Harrington, lord lieutenant general
and general governor of Ireland. By Charles Lucas. In behalf of
himself and the rest of the citizens and inhabitants of the said city.
[Dublin,] 1747. 8°.

Another edition, 1749.

1433. —— Divelina libera: an apology for the civil rights and
liberties of the commons and citizens of Dublin; containing an account of the foundation and constitution of this city, some remarks
on the new rules. . . . Addressed to the free citizens, and all lovers
of truth and liberty. Dublin, 1744. 8°.

Another edition, 1748–49.

1434. —— The liberties and customs of Dublin asserted and
demonstrated upon the principles of law, justice, and good policy;
with a comparative view of the constitutions of London and Dublin,
and some considerations on the customs of intrusion and quarterage.
Dublin, 1768. 8°.

1435. —— A remonstrance against certain infringements on the
rights and liberties of the commons and citizens of Dublin. Dublin,
1743. 8°.

1436. [LUCAS, CHARLES.]   A seventeenth address, etc. [to the free citizens and freeholders of the city of Dublin.]   [Dublin, Aug. 9, 1749.]   8°.

Without title-page.

The eighteenth and twentieth addresses, published in the same year, also discuss the constitution of the city of Dublin.

1437. Memoirs concerning the city of Dublin in 1755 and [17]56. Printed in the year 1757.   8°.

Deals with proposed changes in the constitution of Dublin.

1438. Proceedings of the sheriffs and commons of the city of Dublin in the years 1742 and 1743; with the several reports and messages passed between them and the lord mayor and board of aldermen relating to certain controverted matters in the city.   Dublin, 1744.   8°.   pp. 199.

Deals especially with the mode of election of town officers. Contains many extracts from the town records of the 17th century.

1439. †Serious and seasonable address (A) to the citizens and freemen of Dublin.   Dublin, 1749.   8°.

1440. Short abstract (A) of a few grievances of the citizens of Dublin.   [Dublin, 1750.]   8°.

Without title-page.

1441. Short state (A) of the case of the corporation of Trinity guild, Dublin; with an alphabetical list of the freemen, and also of the council of the house belonging to the corporation, who are all freemen thereof.   Dublin, 1749.   8°.

Briefly points out the relations of this gild to the corporation of Dublin.

1442. Strictures on the metropolis [Dublin].   Dublin, 1805.   12°.

1443. †Vindication of the rights and powers of the board of aldermen.   Addressed to C. L. [Charles Lucas], and offered to the consideration of the majority of the commons of Dublin.   Dublin, 1744.   4°.

DUMBARTON.

The best account of the history of this burgh will be found in Irving's *Book of Dumbartonshire* (No. 796).

1444. Dumbarton burgh records, 1627–1746.   Dumbarton, 1860. 4°.

1445. GLEN, JOHN.   History of the town and castle of Dumbarton, from the earliest period to the present time.   Dumbarton, 1847.   12°.

1446. IRVING, J[OSEPH].   Dumbarton sixty years since : being a chapter of local history, illustrative of certain manners and customs prevailing in a provincial town about the close of the eighteenth century.   Printed for private circulation.   [Glasgow,] 1857.   4°.

A reprint of ch. xvii. of his *History of Dumbartonshire* (No. 796).

1447. MACLEOD, DONALD.   Macleod's History of the castle and town of Dumbarton.   Second edition.   Dumbarton, [1877.]   8°.

1st edition, 1877.

1447a. †—— Ancient records of Dumbarton.   Dumbarton.   n. d.   8°.

1448. —— Dumbarton, Vale of Leven, and Loch Lomond : historical, legendary, industrial, and descriptive.   Dumbarton, etc., [1884.]   8°.

1448a. †—— Dumbarton, ancient and modern.   Glasgow, 1893.   4°.

DUMFRIES.

1449. McDIARMID, JOHN.   Picture of Dumfries and its environs. . . . With copious historical and descriptive notices.   Edinburgh, 1832.   4°.

A brief account.

1450. McDOWALL, WILLIAM.   History of the burgh of Dumfries ; with notices of Nithsdale, Annandale, and the western border.   Second edition.   Edinburgh, 1873.   8°.

The best history of Dumfries.
1st edition, 1867.

DUNBAR.

1451. MILLER, JAMES.   The history of Dunbar, from the earliest records to the present period ; with a description of the ancient castles and picturesque scenery on the borders of East Lothian.   Dunbar, 1830.   12°.

Another edition, 1859, 8°.

DUNDALK.

1452. D'ALTON, JOHN, and O'FLANAGAN, J. R. The history of Dundalk and its environs, from the earliest historic period to the present time ; with memoirs of its eminent men. Dublin, 1864. 8°.

Contains a translation of the town charters ; little attention is paid to municipal history.

DUNDEE.

> *a.* Town Records, Nos. 1453–1455.
> *b.* General Histories, Nos. 1456–1462.
> *c.* Gilds, Nos. 1463–1467.
> *d.* Miscellaneous, Nos. 1468–1472.

Dundee is well supplied with town histories ; the works of Maxwell, Beatts, and Thomson (Nos. 1459, 1461, 1462) are all valuable. A good collection of town records has been published (No. 1453), and we have an excellent account of the gilds by Warden (No. 1467).

a. Town Records.

See Nos. 1459, 1461, 1462.

1453. * Charters, writs, and public documents of the royal burgh of Dundee, the hospital and Johnston's bequest, 1292–1880. . . . [Edited by William Hay.] Dundee, 1880. 4°.

1454. Report of a committee of the burgesses of Dundee, appointed at a general meeting of the burgesses on the 29th October, 1817, to arrange, with a committee of the town-council, a new set or constitution for the borough. With an appendix, containing copies of the different sets proposed and other important documents. Dundee, 1818. 8°.

1455. †Translation of the charter by King Charles I. in favour of the town of Dundee. Dundee, 1829. 12°.

b. General Histories.

1456. Dundee delineated : or a history and description of that town, its institutions, manufactures, and commerce. . . . Dundee, 1822. 12°.

A brief account.

1457. History (The) of Dundee; with a view of its present state. Dundee, 1804. 12°.

A brief account.

1458. MACKIE, CHARLES. Historical description of the town of Dundee . . . with twelve engravings on steel by Joseph Swan. Glasgow and London, 1836. 4°.

Little attention is devoted to municipal history; but the appendix contains the burgh charters.

1459. MAXWELL, ALEXANDER. The history of old Dundee [from the Reformation to 1653], narrated out of the town council register, with additions from contemporary annals. Edinburgh and Dundee, 1884. 4°.

Valuable.

1460. —— Old Dundee, ecclesiastical, burghal, and social, prior to the Reformation. Edinburgh and Dundee, 1891. 4°.

Deals with the period 1520–70.
Valuable.

1461. Municipal history (The) of the royal burgh of Dundee. Compiled from original and authentic documents and records in the archives of the town, and other sources ; and embellished by plans of ancient and modern Dundee and harbour, engraved views of public buildings, and facsimiles of historical documents hitherto unpublished. [By J. M. Beatts.] Improved edition. Dundee, 1878. 8°.

Sect. iii. Transcripts of old acts and minutes of council, 1562–1668.
Appendix. Copies of ancient documents, 1325–1642.
A valuable book.
1st edition, 1873.

1462. * THOMSON, JAMES. The history of Dundee : being an account of the origin and progress of the burgh from the earliest period ; embracing a description of its antiquities . . . municipal, educational, and charitable institutions, with biographical sketches of eminent men. A new and enlarged edition of the work published in 1847 by James Thomson ; edited and continued to the present time, with map and illustrations, by James Maclaren. Dundee, 1874. 8°.

Contains a good short account of the municipal history, with extracts from the burgh records.
1st edition, 1847.

c. Gilds.

1463. † Abstract or inventory of charters and other writings belonging to the corporation of weavers of the royal burgh of Dundee. Drawn up in the year 1825. Dundee, 1881. 4°.

1464. Notes by the sub-committee of the guildry of Dundee; reporting to the guildry committee the result of an attempt made to settle the disputes between the magistrates and town-council and the guildry, Dec., 1816. Dundee, 1816. 8°.

1465. Report on the guildry of Dundee, by a committee appointed to ascertain the rights of that ancient body, and especially its right to elect its own officers and to manage its own funds. Dundee,1815. 8°.

1466. TALBOT, JOHN C. Report of the case of the Forfar, etc. district of burghs, tried before a committee of the House of Commons, December 3, 1830. Edinburgh, 1831. 8°.

Concerning the gildry, etc. of Dundee.

1467. * WARDEN, A. J. Burgh laws of Dundee, with the history, statutes, and proceedings of the guild of merchants and fraternities of craftsmen. London, 1872. 8°.

d. Miscellaneous.

1468. †BEATTS, J. M. Reminiscences of an old Dundonian: or sketches and incidents of and relating to the town of Dundee in the early part of the nineteenth century. Dundee, 1882. 12°.

1469. LAMB, A. C. Dundee: its quaint and historic buildings. Dundee, 1895. f°.

The account of the municipal history is brief. Contains a facsimile of the earliest town charter, valuable old maps, plans, and many other illustrations.

1470. NORRIE, W. Dundee celebrities of the nineteenth century: being a series of biographies of distinguished or noted persons. . . . Dundee, 1873. 8°.

1471. Roll of eminent burgesses of Dundee, 1513–1886. Published by order of the provost, magistrates, and town council. [Edited by A. H. Miller.] Dundee, 1887. 4°.

1472. SMALL, ROBERT. A statistical account of the parish and town of Dundee in the year 1792. Dundee, [1793.] 8°.

DUNFERMLINE.

The best history is Henderson's.

1473. CHALMERS, PETER. Historical and statistical account of Dunfermline. 2 vols. Edinburgh and London, 1844–59. 8°.

The account of municipal history is brief.

1474. FERNIE, JOHN. A history of the town and parish of Dunfermline. Dunfermline, 1815. 8°.

The account of municipal history is brief.

1475. HENDERSON, EBENEZER. The annals of Dunfermline and vicinity, from the earliest authentic period to the present time, A. D. 1069–1878. Interspersed with explanatory notes, memorabilia, and numerous illustrative engravings. Glasgow, 1879. 4°.

The best history of Dunfermline.

1476. MERCER, A[NDREW]. The history of Dunfermline, from the earliest records down to the present time. . . . Dunfermline, 1828. 12°.

The appendix contains the charter granted by Abbot Robert to the burgh of Dunfermline, and the sett of the burgh.

1477. ROSS, WILLIAM. Burgh life in Dunfermline in the olden time. A lecture by the Rev. Wm. Ross, Aberdeen, delivered in the Music Hall, Dunfermline, 8th February, 1864, at the request of the Literary Society of that town. Edinburgh, 1864. 8°.

Based upon the burgh minutes of the 15th century.

1478. STEWART, ALEXANDER. Reminiscences of Dunfermline and neighbourhood, illustrative of Dunfermline life sixty years ago. With chronological appendix, 1064–1880. Edinburgh and London, 1886. 8°.

DUNKELD.

1479. Dunkeld : its straths and glens, historical and descriptive. Compiled, arranged, and original. New and extended edition. Dunkeld, 1865. 8°.

A brief account.
Another edition, 1879.

DUNMOW, GREAT.

1480. SCOTT, W. T. Antiquities of an Essex parish: or pages from the history of Great Dunmow. London, 1873. 8°.

DUNSTAPLE.

1481. Annales prioratus de Dunstaplia [to 1297.] By Richard de Morins. [Annales Monastici, vol. iii.] Edited by R. H. Luard. *Rolls Series.* London, 1866. 8°.

For the borough of Dunstaple, see vol. v. (1869) index, 113-4. Hearne's edition (Oxford, 1733), pp. xxxviii.-xl., contains the undated "Veredictum juratorum super consuetudinibus quibusdam burgi de Dunstaple."

See also *Bibliotheca Topographica Britannica* (1790), iv. 57-252; *Monasticon Anglicanum* (1830), vi. 239-42.

1482. Dunno's originals: containing a sort of real, traditional, and conjectural history of the antiquities of Dunstaple and its vicinity. 5 pts. Dunstaple, 1821–22. 12°.

Contains very little concerning municipal history.
Reprinted in 1855.

DUNWICH.

1483. GARDNER, THOMAS. An historical account of Dunwich, antiently a city, now a borough. . . . London, 1754. 4°.

Ch. xiv. Mayors and bailiffs.
Ch. xv. Members of Parliament.
Ch. xviii. Charters.

There is also a good account of the history of Dunwich in Suckling's *Suffolk* (No. 652).

DURHAM.

A good history of Durham is needed. The best accounts of municipal development will be found in the county histories of Hutchinson and Surtees (Nos. 596, 599).

See No. 2436.

1484. Brief sketch (A) of Durham, for the use of visitors and others. Eighth edition. Durham, [1870.] 12°.

A meagre account.
1st edition, 1863.

1485. †Charter (The) granted by Hugh Pudsey, bishop of Durham, to the burgesses of the city of Durham [1179 or 1180.] G. Allan's Darlington Press. n. d. 4°.

1486. †Confirmation of Bishop Pudsey's charter to the burgesses of Durham, by Pope Alexander III. [Latin and English.] G. Allan's Darlington Press. n. d. 4°.

1487. Historical and descriptive view of the city of Durham and its environs. To which is added a reprint of Hogg's Legend of St. Cuthbert, from the edition of the late George Allan, Esq. Durham, [1824.] 12°.

A brief account.
Another edition, 1847, 8°.

1488. List (A) of the knights and burgesses who have represented the county and city of Durham in Parliament. [By Cuthbert Sharp.] Second edition. Sunderland, 1831. 4°.

1489. Memorials of St. Giles's, Durham : being grassmen's accounts and other parish records. . . . [Edited by J. Barmby.] *Surtees Society.* Durham, etc., 1896. 8°.

Grassmen's accounts (1579–1790), 1–122.
Extracts from churchwardens' accounts (1664–1778), 186–94.

1490. ORNSBY, GEORGE. Sketches of Durham : being an attempt to indicate to the stranger some of the most prominent objects of interest in that place and neighbourhood ; illustrated by historical, biographical, and architectural notices. Durham and London, 1846. 8°.

Contains no account of municipal history ; but there is a useful " Bibliographical List relating to the City and County of Durham " on pp. 217–9.

1491. Proceedings and addresses at the Durham city election ; with the poll at the election of two citizens to serve in Parliament . . . August, 1830 ; also the Poll Book. . . . To which are annexed the bye-laws of the corporation of 1728 ; the charter granted by Bishop Egerton, 1780 ; and a list of the members who have served in Parliament for the city of Durham. . . . Second edition. Durham, 1830. 4°.

The by-laws and charter are taken from Hutchinson's history of the county (No. 596).

DURSLEY.

1492. †Ancient history (The) of Dursley ; with notes, and a list of the bailiffs for a period of two hundred years. Second edition. Dursley, 1854. 8°. pp. 12.

1493. BLUNT, J. H. Chapters of parochial history. Dursley and its neighbourhood : being historical memorials of Dursley, Beverston, Cam, and Uley. London and Dursley, 1877. 8°.

1494. Dursley, with original information supplied by an old inhabitant and others ; also an interesting description of the various objects in thirteen counties as seen from Stinchcombe Hill. . . . Dursley, 1882. 8°.

DYSART.

1495. MUIR, WILLIAM. The antiquities of Dysart. [A lecture read Dec. 13, 1853.] Kirkcaldy, 1855. 8°.

1496. —— Gleanings from the records of Dysart, 1545–1796. Edinburgh, 1862. 4°.

1497. [——] Notices of the burgh, church and ministers, school and teachers of Dysart. Edinburgh, 1831. 12°.

1498. [——] Notices from the local records of Dysart [1510–1697.] *Maitland Club.* Glasgow, 1853. 4°.

Extracts from the minutes of the town council, 1534–38 ; extracts from a protocol book, 1540–56 ; extracts from the burgh court records, 1678–97, etc.

EDINBURGH.

    a. Town Records, Nos. 1499–1508.
    b. General Histories, Nos. 1509–1519.
    c. Gilds, Nos. 1520–1532.
    d. Parliamentary Representation, Nos. 1533–1537.
    e. Miscellaneous : Municipal Reform, etc., Nos. 1538–1549.

The histories of Edinburgh by Arnot and Maitland (Nos. 1510, 1516) have not yet been superseded, though these writers made little use of the stores of original material now accessible in the five volumes of records edited by Marwick (Nos. 1501, 1502). There is no good history of the gildry and incorporated trades ; the most useful books on this subject are those of Colston (Nos. 1521, 1522).

a. Town Records.

See No. 1546.

1499. Acts, statutes, and other proceedings of the provost, bailies, and council of the burgh of Edinburgh, from the year 1529 to the year 1531. *Maitland Club*, Miscellany, ii. 75–120. Edinburgh, 1840. 4°.

Extracts from the " Liber Statutorum Burgi de Edinburgh."

1500. †Charters and documents relating to the collegiate church and hospital of the Holy Trinity, and Trinity hospital, Edinburgh, A. D. 1460–1661. [Edited by J. D. Marwick.] Edinburgh, 1871. 4°.

1501. *Charters and other documents relating to the city of Edinburgh, A. D. 1143–1540. [Edited by J. D. Marwick.] *Scottish Burgh Records Society*. Edinburgh, 1871. 4°.

The Latin text of the charters, with a translation.

1502. *Extracts from the records of the burgh of Edinburgh . . . A. D. 1403–1589. [Edited by J. D. Marwick.] 4 vols. *Scottish Burgh Records Society*. Edinburgh, 1869–82. 4°.

Contains acts and ordinances made by the civic authorities, extracts from the burgh accounts, etc.

1503. Inventory of selected charters and documents from the Charter House of the city of Edinburgh, proposed to be temporarily deposited for safe keeping in the General Register House. [Edinburgh,] July, 1884. f°.

1504. †Minutes of the town council of Edinburgh. Edinburgh, 1875–97. f°.

Published annually.

1505. Precedence of Edinburgh and Dublin: proceedings in the Privy Council in the question as to the precedence of the corporations of Edinburgh and Dublin in presenting addresses to the sovereign. [Edited by J. D. Marwick.] Edinburgh, 1865. 4°.

Contains an abstract of charters and other documents relating to these cities.

1506. Rolls of superiorities belonging to the lord provost, magistrates, and council of the city of Edinburgh; showing the accounting for the feu-duties in the year ended at 1st of August, 1876. Edinburgh, 1877. f°.

A rental of the property belonging to the city. A revised edition has appeared annually since 1877.

Abstracts of the accounts of the corporation of the city of Edinburgh are also published annually.

1507. Sett (The), or decreet arbitral of King James the 6th of blessed memory [May 25, 1583], deciding all differences betwixt merchants and trades, anent the government of the city of Edinburgh, as it is registrat in the books of council and session and ratified in Parliament. Together with the acts of the town council, determining the time of the continuation of the provost, dean of gild, and thesaurer, to be no longer than one or two years together at one time. 2 pts. Edinburgh, 1683. 12°.

Other editions, 1700, 1726, 1742, 1783.
See Nos. 1510, 1512, 1513.

1508. Society (The) of trained bands of Edinburgh. Edited by William Skinner. Edinburgh, 1889. 8°.

Extracts from their minute books, 1676–1874.

b. General Histories.

1509. ANDERSON, JOHN. A history of Edinburgh, from the earliest period to the completion of the half century 1850, with brief notices of eminent or remarkable individuals. Edinburgh and London, 1856. 8°.

Contains the decreets-arbitral of 1583 and 1729, and the charters of 1603 and 1636. The account of municipal history is somewhat brief.

1510. ARNOT, HUGO. The history of Edinburgh, from the earliest accounts to the year 1780. With an appendix containing Creech's fugitive pieces . . . and the set of the city. Fourth edition. Edinburgh, 1818. 8°.

Earlier editions, 1779, 1789, 1816.

1511. GRANT, JAMES. Cassell's Old and new Edinburgh : its history, its people, and its places. 3 vols. London, Paris, and New York, [1881–83.] 4°.

Does not contain much concerning municipal history.

1512. Historical sketch (An) of the municipal constitution of the city of Edinburgh, including the set of the burgh as established in 1583 and amended in 1730; with the acts of Parliament and council relating thereto. . . . To which is added an historical account of the Blue Blanket, or the craftsmen's banner . . . by A. Pennecuik. Edinburgh, 1826. 12°.

Valuable.

1513. †History (The) of the good town of Edinburgh, from the year 1583 to the present year 1763 ; wherein the private management as well as the public transactions of that city are clearly related. To which is added a proposal for a new set of the town. . . . Edinburgh, [1763.] 4°.

1514. KINCAID, ALEXANDER. The history of Edinburgh, from the earliest accounts to the present time ; by way of guide to the city and suburbs. . . . Edinburgh, 1787. 12°.

This work is now of little value.

1515. MACKAY, JOHN. History of the barony of Broughton (now the new town of Edinburgh). . . . Edinburgh, 1867. 8°.

2nd edition, 1869.

1516. MAITLAND, WILLIAM. The history of Edinburgh, from its foundation to the present time . . . together with the antient and present state of the town of Leith. . . . In nine books. Edinburgh, 1753. f°.

Bks. iii.–iv. contain valuable documents relating to municipal history.

1517. STEVENSON, R. H. Annals of Edinburgh and Leith : embracing a minute and comprehensive development of their ecclesiastical, municipal, literary, and charitable institutions. . . . Edinburgh, 1839. 12°.

Brief notes, of little value.

1518. —— The chronicles of Edinburgh, from its foundation in A. D. 617 to A. D. 1851. Embellished with plans and several views. . . . Edinburgh, [1851.] 8°.

A brief account.

1519. WILSON, DANIEL. Memorials of Edinburgh in the olden time. Second edition. 2 vols. Edinburgh and London, 1891. 4°.

Of little value for municipal history.
Other editions, 1848, 1872.

c. Gilds.

See No. 1536.

1520. †Act of the town council of Edinburgh, commonly called the seal of cause, in favour of the surgeons and barbers of Edinburgh [July 1, 1505.] n. p. n. d. f°.

1521. COLSTON, JAMES. The guildry of Edinburgh: is it an incorporation? With introductory remarks concerning "gilds," and an appendix. Edinburgh, 1887. 4°.

The appendix contains the Statuta Gildæ of Berwick; constitutions of the gild court of Edinburgh, 1584; extracts from the dean of gild's accounts, 1554–1744; extracts from the burgh records of Aberdeen, 1399–1526, as furnished to the committee of the House of Commons in 1793 (No. 768).

1522. —— The incorporated trades of Edinburgh, with an introductory chapter on the rise and progress of municipal government in Scotland. Edinburgh, 1891. 4°.

1523. Faction displayed: or a genuine relation of the representation of the trades and of the late political contentions in the city of Edinburgh. [Edinburgh, 1777.] 4°.

Deals with contentions between the gildry and the trades.

1524. Historical notes regarding the merchant company of Edinburgh, and the Widow's Scheme and hospitals. [By A. Kirk Mackie.] Edinburgh, 1862. 4°.

Printed with A. K. Johnston's *Geographical Distribution of Material Wealth*, in one volume, at the private press of Peter Lawson and Son.

1525. LITTLE, W. C. Observations on the hammermen of Edinburgh [1582–1774.] *Soc. of Antiq. of Scotland*, Archæologia Scotica, i. 170–83. Edinburgh, 1792. 4°.

1526. Memorial for the united incorporations of Mary's Chapel, and for Alexander Miller, glazier, deacon, duly elected by them, of the incorporation of masons, pursuers, against Alexander Nicholson, the pretended deacon of the said incorporation, and the magistrates and town-council of Edinburgh, and others, defenders. [Edinburgh, 1764.] 4°.

Without title-page. Considers the history of the civic trade regulations, etc.

1527. † MILLER, R. The Edinburgh dean of guild court: a manual of history and procedure. With chapters on the guildry of Edinburgh and the dean of guild. Edinburgh, 1896. 8°.

1528. PENNECUIK, ALEXANDER. An historical account of the Blue Blanket, or crafts-men's banner . . . with the powers and prerogatives of the crafts of Edinburgh, etc. Edinburgh, 1722. 8°.

Other editions, 1780 and 1832; reprinted in *Historical Sketch* (No. 1512) and in Colston's *Incorporated Trades* (No. 1522).

1529. Proceedings of the guildry of Edinburgh, at the meeting of the incorporation, in the Freemason's Hall, Niddry Street, on Tuesday, December 16, 1817; including some documents connected with that meeting. Edinburgh, 1818. 8°.

Considers the general history of the gildry of Edinburgh, etc.

1530. Query (The), Can the city of Edinburgh be hurt by the proposed alteration of the set in favour of the trades? [Edinburgh, July 11, 1763.] f°.

A single sheet.

1531. Report (The) and representation of the united committees of the company of merchants, and of the other incorporated societies of the city of Edinburgh. [Edinburgh, Sept. 12, 1763.] 4°.

The committees were appointed to oppose a presentation to a vacant church and to promote an alteration in the sett or constitution of the burgh, with regard to the manner of electing the deacons of the fourteen incorporations.

1532. True state (The) of the case betwixt the majority of the town-council on the one hand, the general-sessions, the merchant-company, almost all the corporations, and several members of the said council, on the other; in a letter to a friend. [Edinburgh, 1763.] 4°.

Without title-page.
Throws light upon the struggle for municipal reform in Edinburgh.

d. Parliamentary Representation.

See No. 1538.

1533. [Cockburn, Henry.] Considerations submitted to the householders of Edinburgh, on the state of their representation in Parliament. Edinburgh, 1823. 8°.

1534. —— An explanation of the state of the case of the Edinburgh representation in Parliament. Edinburgh, 1826. 8°.

1535. Examination of the considerations submitted [by H. Cockburn] to the householders of Edinburgh, on the state of their representation in Parliament. Edinburgh, 1824. 8°.

See No. 1533.

1536. † Protests taken in the council of Edinburgh, at the election of a member to serve in parliament for this city. With a memorial presented to the lawiers, and their opinion thereupon, touching the rights of the trades. [Edinburgh, 1741.] 8°.

1537. ZENO. The letters of Zeno to the citizens of Edinburgh, on the present mode of electing a member of Parliament for that city. To which is prefixed a letter to the right hon. William Pitt, chancellor of the exchequer, on the political state of the Scottish burghs. . . . [Edinburgh,] 1783. 8°.

Points out the evils of election by a select body.

e. Miscellaneous : Municipal Reform, etc.

See Nos. 851, 853.

1538. Address to the burgesses inhabitants of Edinburgh : observing the defects of the old sett, and proposing the plan of a bill to Parliament for an act to restore and establish a town-council and magistracy for the city, and to ascertain the right and manner of electing its members to Parliament. . . . Edinburgh, 1746. 8°.

1539. Address (An) to the citizens and inhabitants of Edinburgh upon the constitution of the borough. [Edinburgh, 1780.] 4°.

1540. BLACK, WILLIAM. The privileges of the royal burrows. . . . With an appendix containing the privileges and jurisdictions of the cities of Edinburgh and Aberdeen. Edinburgh, 1707. 8°.

1541. CHAMBERS, ROBERT. Edinburgh papers. Edinburgh merchants and merchandise in olden times. [A lecture.] Edinburgh, 1859. 8°.

1542. CIVIS. An appeal to the citizens of Edinburgh on the recent election of Mr. Thomas Henderson to be chamberlain of the city ad vitam aut culpam ; and on the general constitution of that office. Edinburgh, 1810. 8°.

1543. COCKBURN, HENRY. Memorials of his time. Edinburgh, 1856. 8°.

Contains a vivid description of the old town council of Edinburgh, pp. 87–99, 350–55, etc.

1544. Examination (An) of the principles and conduct of the town-council of Edinburgh, from the commencement of Mr. Laurie's administration to the present time; with remarks on the set or constitution of the city. By a burgess and guild-brother. Edinburgh, 1776. 8°.

1545. GREIG, JOHN. Report on the statements of the lord provost and Mr. A. Bruce respecting the affairs of the city of Edinburgh, humbly submitted to the committee of the guildry. . . . With an appendix containing abstracts of the city's income and expenditure for 12 years preceding Martinmas, 1818; also a detailed account of the items of last year, and various other statements. Edinburgh, 1819. 8°.

1546. MARWICK, J. D. Sketch of the history of the high constables of Edinburgh; with notes on the early watching, cleaning, and other police arrangements of the city. Edinburgh, 1865. 4°.

The appendix contains extracts from the burgh records, 1609-1861.
Valuable.

1547. Modern Athens (The) : a dissection and demonstration of men and things in the Scotch capital. By a modern Greek [G. Mudie]. London, 1825. 8°.

Of little value.

1548. †SOMMERS, THOMAS. Observations on the meaning and extent of the oath taken at the admission of every burgess in the city of Edinburgh, as comprehending the duties of religion, allegiance to the king, respect and submission to the authority of the civil magistrate, and the relative duties which burgesses owe to each other. Edinburgh, 1794. 8°.

1549. Statements relative to the city of Edinburgh, shewing the practicability and necessity of, and containing proposals for, the extension of the royalty, popular election of the town council, erection of additional parish churches. . . . Edinburgh, 1833. 8°.

EGREMONT.

1550. Charters (The) of the borough of Egremont. Translated by the Rev. Canon Knowles. *Cumberl. and Westm. Antiq. and Archæol. Soc.*, Transactions, i. 282–7. Kendal, 1874. 8°.

ELGIN.

1551. * YOUNG, ROBERT.   Annals of the parish and burgh of Elgin, from the twelfth century to the year 1876 ; with some historical and other notices illustrative of the subject.   Elgin, 1879.   8°.

Contains many extracts from the town records since 1540; also an appendix of documents.

ELLESMERE.

1552.   Charters of Ellesmere [1343–1656.]   *Salopian Shreds and Patches*, vol. ix.   Shrewsbury, 1891.   8°.

1553.   †PEAKE, JOHN.   Ellesmere, Shropshire.   Shrewsbury, 1889. 8°.

EVESHAM.

1554.   MAY, GEORGE.   The history of Evesham : its Benedictine monastery . . . municipal institutions, parliamentary occurrences. . . . Evesham, 1834.   8°.

1555. —— A descriptive history of the town of Evesham, from the foundation of its Saxon monastery ; with notices of the ancient deanery of Vale.   Evesham, 1845.   8°.

Contains a good short account of its municipal and parliamentary history, a translation of the town charter of 1605, the constitutions of the borough in the time of Charles II., the by-laws of 1839, etc.
The best history of Evesham.

1556.   RUDGE, E. J.   A short account of the history and antiquities of Evesham.   Evesham, 1820.   8°.

1557.   TINDAL, WILLIAM.   The history and antiquities of the abbey and borough of Evesham, compiled chiefly from MSS. in the British Museum.   Evesham, 1794.   4°.

The appendix contains the constitutions of the borough in Charles II.'s time and a translation of the town charter of 1605.

EXETER.

    a. Town Records, Nos. 1558–1563.
    b. General Histories, Nos. 1564–1571.
    c. Gilds, Nos. 1572–1574.
    d. Miscellaneous, Nos. 1575–1582.

There is no good account of the municipal history of Exeter.   The most useful work is Oliver's (No. 1570).   In the town archives there exists the unpublished MS. of John Hoker's (or Vowell's) Annals of Exeter, from which Izacke and others freely borrowed much material. The town archives are also well stored with old records; these are well arranged and calendared, but no good collection has been printed.

a. Town Records.

1558. COTTON, W., and WOOLLCOMBE, H. Gleanings from the municipal and cathedral records relating to the history of the city of Exeter. Exeter, 1877. 8°.

Most of the extracts relate to the 16th and 17th centuries, and do not deal with municipal government.

1559. Exeter city muniments. *Notes and Gleanings . . . of Devon and Cornwall,* vols. ii.–v. Exeter, 1889–92. 4°.

A calendar of the records in the town archives.

1560. Letters and papers of John Shillingford, mayor of Exeter, 1447–50. Edited by S. A. Moore. *Camden Society.* [London,] 1871. 4°.

The letters and papers relate to a suit brought against the city by Edmund Lacy, bishop of Exeter. The quarrel turned upon the respective jurisdictions of the municipal corporation and the church.

1561. Translation (A) of a charter granted to the inhabitants of Exeter by King Charles the First. . . . By a citizen of Exeter [William Holmes]. Exeter, 1785. 4°.

1562. VOWELL, alias HOOKER, JOHN. Orders enacted for orphans and for their portions within the citie of Excester. . . . London, [1575?]. 4°.

1563. WRIGHT, THOMAS. The municipal archives of Exeter. *Brit. Archæol. Assoc.,* Journal, xviii. 306–17. London, 1862. 8°.

b. General Histories.

1564. Antient history (The) and description of the city of Exeter: containing the antient history, etc. of the city. . . . To which are added the offices and duties (as of old) of the sworn officers of the city. Compiled and digested from the works of Hooker, Izacke, and others. Exeter, [1765.] 8°.

1565. †BRICE, THOMAS. History and description, ancient and modern, of the city of Exeter. Exeter, 1802. 8°.

Not completed.

1566. FREEMAN, E. A. Exeter. [Historic Towns. Edited by E. A. Freeman and W. Hunt.] London, 1887. 8°.

Ch. v. Municipal Exeter, 1225–1688.

1567. IZACKE, RICHARD. Antiquities of the city of Exeter. . . . London, 1677. 8°.

Other editions, 1681, 1723, 1724, 1731, 1734, 1741, and 1757.

Izacke was town clerk of Exeter, 1681–98. The most valuable parts of his book were pilfered from the unpublished work of Hoker, or Vowell. See T. N. Brushfield, *Richard Izacke*, in Transactions of Devon. Assoc. for Advancement of Science, 1893, xxv. 449–69.

1568. JENKINS, ALEXANDER. The history and description of the city of Exeter and its environs, ancient and modern, civil and ecclesiastical. . . . Exeter, 1806. 8°.

†2nd edition, " The civil and ecclesiastical history of the city of Exeter and its environs," 1841. Freeman (*Exeter*, p. vi.) says that this edition is inferior to the first.

1569. NORTHY, T. J. Illustrated popular history of the city of Exeter, from the earliest times. Exeter, 1886. 8°.

The appendix contains lists of mayors, members of Parliament, etc.
Of little value.

1570. OLIVER, GEORGE. The history of the city of Exeter. . . . With a short memoir of the author, and an appendix of documents and illustrations. [Edited by E. Smirke.] Exeter, 1861. 8°.

Index by J. S. Attwood, Exeter, 1884.

The appendix contains the charter of Charles I.; abstract of a court roll, 26–27 Edw. III.; abstract of a compotus roll, 42–43 Edw. III., etc.

The best history of Exeter.

1st edition, 1821.

1571. VOWELL, alias HOKER, JOHN. The antique description and account of the city of Exeter, in three parts. Part i. Containing the ancient history. . . . Part ii. Containing a large and curious account of the antiquity, foundation, and building of the cathedral church. . . . Part iii. Contains the offices and duties (as of old) of those particular sworn officers. . . . [Edited by Andrew Brice.] Exon, 1765. 4°.

> Pts. i.–ii. are of little value for municipal history; pt. iii. is a reprint of " A pamphlet of the offices," etc. (No. 1582).

c. Gilds.

See No. 537.

1572. COTTON, WILLIAM. An Elizabethan guild of the city of Exeter: an account of the proceedings of the society of merchant adventurers during the latter half of the sixteenth century. Exeter, 1873. 4°.

1573. —— Some account of the ancient guilds of the city of Exeter. *Devon. Assoc. for Advancement of Science,* Transactions, v. 117–38. Plymouth, [1872.] 8°.

1574. ROWSELL, P. F. The ancient companies of Exeter. *The Western Antiquary,* iv. 187–9. Plymouth, 1885. 4°.

d. Miscellaneous.

1575. †DYMOND, ROBERT. Exeter in the last century. Exeter, 1877. 8°.

1576. —— The history of the parish of St. Petrock, Exeter, as shown in its churchwardens' accounts and other records. *Devon. Assoc. for Advancement of Science,* Transactions, xiv. 402–92. Plymouth, 1882. 8°.

> Also separately printed, 1882.
> Contains extracts from the churchwardens' accounts, 1425–1692.

1577. GIDLEY, B. C. On the distinctive style and title of the corporation of the city of Exeter. A paper read at the quarterly meeting of the council, 12th May, 1875. Exeter, 1875. 8°.

1578. †HOLMES, WILLIAM. Tract on bodies corporate generally, those in Exeter specially. Exeter, 1800. 8°.

1579. OLIVER, GEORGE, and JONES, PITMAN. Description of the Guildhall, Exeter. [With lists of mayors, recorders, etc.] Exeter, 1853. 12°.

1580. Rights and priviledges of the freemen of Exeter, with an account of all legacies left to the poor of the said city [1164–74]. . . . [By Richard Izacke.] London, 1751. 12°.

First printed, with a different title, in 1736; other editions, 1757, 1785, 1820.

1581. ROUND, J. H. Feudal England: historical studies of the 11th and 12th centuries. London, 1895. 8°.

William the Conqueror at Exeter (a criticism of Freeman's views), 431–55.

1582. VOWELL, alias HOKER, JOHN. A pamphlet of the offices and duties of euerie particular sworne officer of the citie of Exeter. London, 1584. 4°.

See No. 1571.

FALMOUTH.

1583. †THOMAS, RICHARD. History and description of the town and harbour of Falmouth. Falmouth, 1827. 12°.

Another edition, 1828, 8°.

1584. †TREGONING, E. S. History of Falmouth and its vicinity. . . . Falmouth, 1865. 8°. pp. 114.

FARNHAM.

1585. MILFORD, R. N. Farnham and its borough: being the substance of a lecture. . . . London and Farnham, [1859.] 8°.

Contains brief extracts from the town records.

1586. SMITH, W. C. The history of Farnham and the ancient Cistercian abbey of Waverley. Farnham, 1829. 8°

A meagre account of municipal history.

FAVERSHAM.

1587. Charter of the mayor of Faversham, 1582 [to a baron of the Cinque Ports, forming his credentials for asserting his privileges when absent from home.] *Kent Archæol. Soc.*, Archæologia Cantiana, vi. 321–2. London, 1866. 8°.

1588. COWPER, J. M. Notes from the records of Faversham, 1560–1600. *Royal Hist. Soc.*, Transactions, i. 218–38. Second edition. London, 1875. 8°.

Reprinted, [London, 1871,] 8°.

1589. GIRAUD, F. F.   Faversham town accounts, anno 33 Edw. I. [and temp. Hen. VIII.]   *Kent Archæol. Soc.*, Archæologia Cantiana, x. 221–41.   London, 1876.   8°.

1590. —— Faversham town charters.   *Ibid.*, vol. ix. pp. lxii.–lxx. London, 1874.   8°.

1591. —— Municipal archives of Faversham, A. D. 1304–24. *Ibid.*, xiv. 185–205.   London, 1882.   8°.

1592. —— The service of shipping of the barons of Faversham. *Ibid.*, xxi. 273–83.   London, 1895.   8°.

1593. GIRAUD, F. F., and DONNE, C. E.   A visitor's guide to Faversham : containing a concise history of the town and brief notices of the adjoining villages.   Faversham, 1876.   8°.

1594. JACOB, EDWARD.   The history of the town and port of Faversham in the county of Kent.   London, 1774.   8°.

FERMANAGH.

1595. †BELMORE, Earl of.   Parliamentary memoirs of Fermanagh, county and borough, from 1613 to 1885.   Dublin, 1885.   8°.

See No. 734.

FLINT.

1596. TAYLOR, HENRY.   Historic notices, with topographical and other gleanings descriptive of the borough and county-town of Flint. London, 1883.   8°.

FOLKESTONE.

1597. JENKINS, R. C.   Gossip from the municipal records of Folkestone [1464–1660.]   *Kent Archæol. Soc.* Archæologia Cantiana, vol. x. pp. lxix.–lxxxv.   London, 1876.   8°.

1598. MACKIE, S. J.   A descriptive and historical account of Folkestone and its neighbourhood.   Second edition, with gleanings from the municipal records, reprinted from the Folkestone Express. Folkestone, [1883.]   8°.

There is a separate title-page for the "Gleanings."
1st edition, 1856.

FORDWICH.

1599. BRYAN, BENJAMIN. Some account of the ancient borough of Fordwich, in Kent. *The Reliquary*, xviii. 65–70. London, 1877. 8°.

1600. WOODRUFF, C. E. Fordwich municipal records. *Kent Archæol. Soc.*, Archæologia Cantiana, xviii. 78–102. London, 1889. 8°.

1601. * —— A history of the town and port of Fordwich, with a transcription of the 15th century copy of the custumal. Canterbury, [1895.] 8°.

Contains many extracts from the town records.

FRODSHAM.

1602. BEAMONT, WILLIAM. An account of the ancient town of Frodsham, in Cheshire. Warrington, 1881. 8°.

GAINSBOROUGH.

1603. STARK, ADAM. The history and antiquities of Gainsburgh. . . . Second edition, much enlarged. London, 1843. 8°.

Contains a translation of the town charters, and various documents relating to the municipal constitution in modern times.
1st edition, 1817.

GALWAY.

1604. HARDIMAN, JAMES. The history of the town and county of the town of Galway, from the earliest period. . . . To which is added a copious appendix, containing the principal charters and other original documents. Dublin, 1820. 4°.

Pt. ii. contains by-laws, 1496–1779. The appendix contains the town charter 20 Eliz., with a translation ; and the charter of 20 Charles II.
A good book.

GARSTANG.

1605. Extracts from the records of the ancient corporation of Garstang. *Preston Guardian*, July 15—Sept. 9, 1876.

Contains the town charter of 1680, town oaths, standing orders of 1735, corporation accounts, etc.

1606. FISHWICK, HENRY. The history of the parish of Garstang, in the county of Lancaster. *Chetham Society.* 2 pts. [Manchester,] 1878–79. 4°.

GATESHEAD.

See Brand's *Newcastle* (No. 2418), i. 461–505, 661–71; and Nos. 2422, 2424.

1607. †Collections relating to St. Edmund's hospital at Gatesheved . . . together with several charters, grants, etc. concerning the said town and church of Gateside. . . . Printed in the year 1769. G. Allan's Darlington Press. n. d. 4°. pp. 56.

1608. †Investigation by his majesty's commissioners into the state of the borough of Gateshead. Gateshead, 1833. 8°.

See No. 60.

1609. Local collections: or records of remarkable events connected with the borough of Gateshead, 1837–1839. Gateshead, 1840. 4°.

Similar collections for the years 1840 and 1844 appeared in 1841 and 1845; perhaps collections for the intervening years were also published.

1610. LONGSTAFFE, W. H. D. The trade companies of Gateshead. *Gentleman's Magazine,* xiii. 164–6. London, 1862. 8°.

1611. Refutation (A) of the objections made in the committee upon the Reform Bill to the proposition for enabling Gateshead to send a member to Parliament; with a statement of the claims of the county of Durham to an increased representation. To which is added an appendix, containing a correct report of the debate on that occasion, with notes, the preamble of the act of Edward VI. for uniting Gateshead to Newcastle. . . . Newcastle, 1831. 8°.

GLAMORGAN.

1612. C[LARK], G. T. Glamorgan charters. *Cambrian Archæol. Assoc.,* Archæologia Cambrensis, Fourth Series, iii. 33–6. London, 1872. 8°.

Charter of Richard Nevill, 2 Edw. IV.

GLASGOW.

a. Town Records, Nos. 1613-1626.
b. General Histories, Nos. 1627-1644.
c. Gilds, Nos. 1645-1658.
d. Miscellaneous, Nos. 1659-1676.

There is no dearth of books relating to Glasgow, but there is still room for a good history of the burgh. The elaborate works edited by Gordon and Pagan (Nos. 1635, 1636) contain much undigested material. One of the best accounts of municipal history is furnished by MacGregor (No. 1638), and for recent times the work of Bell and Paton (No. 1627) is excellent. The records edited by Marwick (Nos. 1617, 1620) are of great value, and the Memorabilia (No. 1623) are useful. Among the histories of gilds those of most importance are Campbell's *Cordiners*, Crawfurd's *Trades' House*, and Hill's *Merchants' House* (Nos. 1648, 1649, 1658).

a. Town Records.

1613. Abstracts of protocols of the town clerks of Glasgow. [Edited by Robert Renwick.] Vol. i. First protocol book of William Hegait, 1547–55. Vol. ii. William Hegait's protocols, 1555–60; with appendix, 1503–1610. Vol. iii. William Hegait's protocols, 1561–8. 3 vols. Glasgow, 1894–96. 4°.

Many of the protocols relate to property in Glasgow.

1613a. †Acts of Parliament relating to the Glasgow police. Glasgow, 1891. 8°.

1614. Burgh records of the city of Glasgow, 1573–1581. [Edited by John Smith.] *Maitland Club.* Glasgow, 1832. 4°.

Contains the transactions of the town council.
Valuable.

1615. BURNETT, JOHN. The Glasgow Police and Statute Labour Act, vi. and vii. Vict., cap. 99, passed 17th August, 1843; with an introduction containing a narrative of the previous Police and Statute Labour Acts for Glasgow; and an appendix. . . . Glasgow, 1843. 8°.

1616. Charter by King Charles I. to the royal burgh of Glasgow . . . 1636, and confirmed . . . 1690. Glasgow, 1863. 8°.

K

1617. * Charters and other documents relating to the city of Glasgow, A. D. 1175–1649. Pt. ii. Edited by J. D. Marwick. *Scottish Burgh Records Society.* Edinburgh, 1894. 4°.

Pt. i. not yet published.

1618. Clyde navigation. Extracts from the records of the burgh of Glasgow [1611–1777], relating to the river Clyde. Reprinted for the trustees of the Clyde navigation. [Glasgow,] 1878. 4°.

Contains some material illustrating the relations of the gildry to the town council.

1619. EWING, JAMES. Act of the magistrates and council of Glasgow, abolishing the burgess oath; with a report illustrative of its history, principles, and impolicy. Second edition. Glasgow, 1819. 8°.

1620. *Extracts from the records of the burgh of Glasgow, A. D. 1573–1642, 1630–62. [Edited by J. D. Marwick.] *Scottish Burgh Records Society.* 2 vols. Glasgow, 1876–82. 4°.

Extracts from the council records, burgh accounts, etc.

1621. HILL, LAURENCE. Archium Glascuense : notes to the hon. the lord provost of Glasgow as to ancient documents in the archives of that city. The title to mill on Molendinar Burn. . . . Translated by Laurence Hill. No. 1. [Glasgow,] 1856. 8°.

1622. IRVING, JOSEPH. The west of Scotland in history : being brief notes concerning events, family traditions, topography, and institutions. Glasgow, 1885. 4°.

Glasgow burgh records, Glasgow chamber of commerce, 192–213.

1623. Memorabilia of the city of Glasgow, selected from the minute books of the burgh, 1588–1750. Printed for private circulation. Glasgow, 1835. 4°.

The selection was made by James Hill, and was communicated to the *Glasgow Courier* by William Motherwell.
Another edition, edited by W. W. Watson, 1868; "Index to a private collection of notices, entituled Memorabilia," etc., by John Smith, Maitland Club, 1836.

1624. †Records (The) of the Glasgow chamber of commerce, and other authentic documents; with facsimile signatures of early correspondents. Glasgow, 1883. 4°.

1625. Registrum Episcopatus Glasguensis. Munimenta ecclesie metropolitane Glasguensis, a sede restaurata seculo ineunte xii. ad reformatam religionem. [Edited by Cosmo Innes.] *Bannatyne Club.* 2 vols. Edinburgh, 1843. 4°.

Contains many documents relating to the burgh : see especially numbers 40, 51, 134, 135, 248, 353, 410, 453, 523.

1626. TURNER, A. An abridgement of the act (passed 7th May, 1821,) entitled " An act to continue the term, and amend and enlarge the powers of two acts of his late majesty, for paving, lighting, and cleansing the streets, and for regulating the police of the city of Glasgow." Glasgow, 1821. 8°.

b. General Histories.

1627. BELL, JAMES, and PATON, JAMES. Glasgow : its municipal organization and administration. Glasgow, 1896. 4°.

Deals mainly with municipal affairs in recent times and at the present day ; chs. iii.–iv. contain a short account of the early history of the municipality.
A valuable book.

1628. †Chronicles (The) of Gotham : or the facetious history of official proceedings. Illustrated. Glasgow, 1856. 12°.

1629. Chronicles of Saint Mungo : or antiquities and traditions of Glasgow. Glasgow, 1843. 8°.

A brief account, with a list of lord provosts.

1630. CLELAND, JAMES. Annals of Glasgow : comprising an account of the public buildings, charities, and the rise and progress of the city. 2 vols. Glasgow, 1816. 8°.

Ch. vi. gives an account of the sett or constitution of the burgh ; ch. xvii., an abstract of its charters.

1631. —— Abridgment of the annals of Glasgow. . . . Glasgow, 1817. 8°.

Ch. ii. contains documents relating to the sett.

1632. —— The rise and progress of the city of Glasgow : comprising an account of its public buildings, charities, and other concerns. Glasgow, 1820. 8°.

Of little value for municipal history. It is briefer than his *Abridgment.*

1633. DENHOLM, JAMES. An historical account and topographical description of the city of Glasgow and suburbs. Glasgow, 1797. 12°.

Contains a brief account of municipal affairs.
2nd edition, "The history of the city of Glasgow," etc., 1798; 3rd edition, 1804; and other later editions.

1634. GIBSON, JOHN. The history of Glasgow, from the earliest accounts to the present time. . . . Glasgow, 1777. 8°.

The appendix contains some valuable documents.

1635. Glasghu Facies; a view of the city of Glasgow: or an account of its origin, rise, and progress, with a more particular description thereof than has been hitherto known. Containing . . . the erection of the town into a royal burgh, with the subsequent grants from the crown thereto . . . the sett of the merchants' and deacon-conveners' houses. . . . By John McUre, alias Campbel [1736]. . . . Comprising also every history hitherto published. Edited by J. F. S. Gordon. 2 pts. Glasgow, [1873.] 8°.

Badly arranged. Does not devote much space to municipal history.

1635a. †Glasgow and its environs. . . . London, 1891. 4°.
Of little value.

1636. Glasgow, past and present: illustrated in dean of guild court reports, and in the reminiscences and communications of Senex, Aliquis, J. B., etc. [Edited by James Pagan.] 3 vols. Glasgow, 1851–56. 8°.

Another edition, edited by D. R. [David Robertson], 1884, 4°. In this edition is also incorporated Reid's *Old Glasgow* (No. 1642). The three volumes contain a series of papers dealing mainly with social history.

1637. MACGEORGE, ANDREW. Old Glasgow: the place and the people, from the Roman occupation to the eighteenth century. Third edition. London, 1888. 8°.

An excellent work. Little attention is paid to municipal affairs; particular stress is laid upon ecclesiastical and social history.
1st edition, 1880, 4°.

1638. MACGREGOR, GEORGE. The history of Glasgow, from the earliest period to the present time. Glasgow and London, 1881. 8°.

Devotes considerable attention to the history of municipal government.
A good book.

1639. †MACKENZIE, PETER. Reminiscences of Glasgow and the west of Scotland. 3 vols. Glasgow, 1865–68. 8°.

1640. McURE, alias CAMPBELL, JOHN. A view of the city of Glasgow : or an account of its origin, rise and progress. . . . Glasgow, 1736. 8°.

This work is now in large part antiquated; it contains the letter of gildry of 1605.

New edition, " The history of Glasgow," 1830.

1641. PAGAN, JAMES. Sketch of the history of Glasgow. Glasgow, 1847. 8°.

A brief account.

1642. SENEX. Old Glasgow and its environs, historical and topographical. By Senex [Robert Reid]. Glasgow, 1864. 8°.

Vol. iii. of No. 1636 (edition of 1884) is a new edition of Reid's book. It does not deal in detail with municipal history.

1643. STEWART, GEORGE. Progress of Glasgow : a sketch of the commercial and industrial increase of the city during the last century, as shown in the records of the Glasgow chamber of commerce and other authentic documents. Glasgow, 1883. 4°.

Deals with industrial and commercial rather than with municipal history.

1644. WALLACE, ANDREW. A popular sketch of the history of Glasgow, from the earliest to the present time. . . . With a frontispiece. Glasgow, 1882. 8°.

c. Gilds.

See No. 1618.

1645. †Acts and charters of the incorporation of coopers of Glasgow. Glasgow, 1885. 8°.

1646. Annals of the skinners' craft in Glasgow, from its incorporation in 1516 to the year 1616. .Presented to the craft by William Whyte, Esq., deacon, 1870. [By William H. Hill.] Glasgow, 1875. 4°.

1647. Bye-laws and regulations of the incorporation of coopers of Glasgow [made in 1879] ; with appendix. Glasgow, 1880. 8°.

1648. CAMPBELL, WILLIAM. History of the incorporation of cordiners in Glasgow ; with appendix. Glasgow, 1883. 8°.

A valuable contribution to the municipal history of Glasgow. The appendix contains the letter of gildry of 1605, the charter of Charles I. to Glasgow, etc.

1649. CRAWFURD, GEORGE. A sketch of the rise and progress of the trades' house of Glasgow, its constitution, funds, and bye-laws. Glasgow, 1858. 8°.

Valuable for the history of craft gilds.

1650. DOUIE, ROBERT. Chronicles of the maltmen craft in Glasgow, 1605–1879 ; with appendix, containing the constitution of the craft recognized and established by letter of guildry, Parliament, town councils, and archbishop's charter, etc. Glasgow, 1879. 4°.

1651. HILL, LAURENCE. On the letter of guildry, and the merchants' and trades' houses. *Glasgow Archæol Soc.*, Transactions, vol. i. pt. i. 29–37. Glasgow, 1859. 8°.

1652. †Incorporation (The) of bonnetmakers and dyers of Glasgow. Glasgow, 1886. 8°.

Another edition, 1896.

1653. Incorporation (The) of wrights in Glasgow. Glasgow, 1889. 8°.

1654. Laws and regulations of the incorporation of hammermen of Glasgow [adopted July 10, 1877] ; with appendix containing list of members, as at 21st September, 1877. Glasgow, 1878. 4°.

1655. Merchants' House (The) of Glasgow : its regulations . . . and an abbreviate of the jurisdiction of the dean of guild court. Glasgow, 1874. 4°.

1656. MITCHELL, ROBERT. Sketches of a Glasgow incorporation [the maltmen] in the seventeenth century. *Glasgow Archæol. Soc.*, Transactions, i. 420–37. Glasgow, 1868. 8°.

1657. View of the history, constitution, and funds of the guildry and merchants' house of Glasgow. [By James Ewing.] Glasgow, 1817. 8°.

1658. * View of the merchants' house of Glasgow : containing historical notices of its origin, constitution, and property, and of the charitable foundations which it administers. [By W. H. Hill and A. Scott.] Presented to the house by Archibald Orr Ewing, esquire, of Ballikinrain, lord dean of guild, 1866. Glasgow, 1866. 4°.

An important work, containing copious extracts from the old records, 1604–1866. The selection of extracts from the minutes of the house from 1791 onward was made by Andrew Scott. On pp. 1–14 is a general sketch of the history of the gild merchant in England and Scotland. The preliminary chapters were written by W. H. Hill.

d. Miscellaneous.

See No. 852.

1659. Biographical sketches of the hon. the lord provosts of Glasgow; with appendix. Glasgow, 1883. 4°.

1660. CLELAND, JAMES. Statistical tables relative to the city of Glasgow, with other matters therewith connected. Third edition, with additions. Glasgow, 1823. 8°.

1661. FISHER, GARRETT. Glasgow: a model municipality. *Fortnightly Review*, lxiii. 607–22. London, 1895. 8°.

1662. †Glasgow register (The) : being an exact list of the magistrates and other office-bearers in that city, from the most ancient records down to the present year. Glasgow, 1781. 8°.

1663. Information for John Anderson of Dowhill, provost, and the remanent magistrats and town-council of the city of Glasgow. [Glasgow, 1700.] f°.

Without title-page.
Considers the chartered rights of Glasgow.

1664. Information for the magistrats and town-council of Glasgow, against George Lockhart, merchant there, and his adherents, merchants inhabitants of the said burgh. [Glasgow, 1700.] f°.

Without title-page.
Contains the confirmation charter of 1690, and discusses important questions relating thereto.

1665. Letter (A) from —— to his friend, concerning the state of the town of Glasgow's business, etc. [Glasgow, 1700.] 4°.

Without title-page.
Considers certain charges brought against the magistrates and town council regarding their management of the town finances.
See No. 1674.

1666. Letter (A) from a citizen of Glasgow to his friend at Edinburgh, containing some modest animadversions on a late printed letter concerning the affairs of that city. [Glasgow,] 1700. 4°.

See No. 1674.

1667. Loyal Reformers' Gazette (The). Glasgow, 1831–41. 8°.

Its attacks are particularly directed against the borough-mongers in Glasgow and elsewhere.
See No. 839.

1668. [MACGEORGE, ANDREW.] An inquiry as to the armorial insignia of the city of Glasgow. Glasgow, 1866. 4°.

1669. Memoirs and portraits of one hundred Glasgow men who have died during the last thirty years, and in their lives did much to make the city what it now is. 2 vols. Glasgow, 1886. 4°.

1670. NESTOR. Rambling recollections of old Glasgow. By "Nestor" [Hugh Barclay]. Glasgow, 1880. 8°.

1671. NICOL, JAMES. Vital, social, and economic statistics of the city of Glasgow, 1881–1885, with observations thereon. [Published by order of the town council.] Glasgow, 1885. 8°.

The same, 1885–91, Glasgow, 1891.

1672. Observations on the heads of a bill for extending the royalty of the city of Glasgow over certain adjoining lands, etc. [Glasgow.] n. d. 8°.

Without title-page.

1673. Political letters by Lucius Verus. London, 1831. 8°.

On burgh reform, especially in Glasgow.

1674. Reflexions on two late letters concerning the affairs of the city of Glasgow; by a citizen thereof in answer to his friend at Edinburgh, who desired an impartial account of that matter. [Glasgow, 1700.] 4°.

Without title-page.
See Nos. 1665, 1666.

1675. SMART, WILLIAM. The municipal work and finance of Glasgow. *Economic Journal*, v. 35–49. London, 1895. 8°.

1676. †STRANG, JOHN. Report on the census of the parliamentary and municipal city of Glasgow for 1861. Glasgow, 1861. 8°.

GLASTONBURY.

1677. WARNER, RICHARD.   An history of the abbey of Glaston, and of the town of Glastonbury.   Bath, 1826.   4°.

Of little value for municipal history.

GLOUCESTER.

> *a.* Town Records, Nos. 1678-1682.
> *b.* General Histories, etc., Nos. 1683–1692.

The most important documents in the town archives are ancient deeds. Apart from these and the town charters, few of the medieval records have been preserved.

The most useful history is Fosbroke's (No. 1687).   The two works edited by Stevenson (Nos. 1678, 1682) are valuable.

a. Town Records.

See No. 1690.

1678. Calendar of records of the corporation of Gloucester.   Compiled by W. H. Stevenson.   Issued under the authority of the corporation.   Gloucester, 1893.   8°.

Abstract of royal charters and letters (1155–1672), 3–69.
Abstract of local deeds and charters (1175–1667), 70–454.
Rolls, council books, etc. (1272 to the present time), 455–66.
A valuable work, well edited.

1679. Charter (The) granted by King Charles the Second to the city of Gloucester, 1672.   [By John Webb.]   Gloucester, 1834.   4°.

Latin, with an English translation.   The preface is dated July, 1831.

1680. FRYER, K. H.   The archives of the city of Gloucester. *Bristol and Glouc. Archæol. Soc.*, Transactions, i. 59–68.   Gloucester, [1876.]   8°.

Contains brief extracts from the archives.

1681. †Gloucester Corporation Act, 1894 : 57 & 58 Vict., ch. xci. Gloucester, 1894.   4°.

1682. Rental of all the houses in Gloucester, A. D. 1455, from a roll in the possession of the corporation of Gloucester, compiled by Robert Cole.   Edited, with a translation, by W. H. Stevenson.

Issued under the authority of the corporation of Gloucester. Gloucester, 1890. 4°.

Well edited.

The object of compiling this rental was to facilitate the collection of the landgavel.

b. General Histories, etc.

1683. BAZELEY, WILLIAM. The guilds of Gloucester. *Bristol and Glouc. Archæol. Soc.*, Transactions, xiii. 260–70. Bristol, [1889.] 8°.

1684. BOND, FREDERICK. The history of Gloucester; and descriptive account of the same city and its suburbs. . . . Gloucester, 1848. 12°.

A meagre sketch.

1685. Case (The) of the citizens of Gloucester as respects the suspension of their electoral franchise. Gloucester, 1861. 8°.

1686. COUNSEL, G. W. The history and description of the city of Gloucester, from the earliest period to the present time. . . . Gloucester, 1829. 12°.

Of little value for municipal history.

1687. FOSBROKE, T. D. An original history of the city of Gloucester, almost wholly compiled from new materials . . . including also the original papers of the late R. Bigland. London, 1819. 4°.

The fullest account of the history of Gloucester.
Reissued in 1819.

1688. History (The) and antiquities of Gloucester: including the civil and military affairs of that antient city . . . from the earliest period to the present time. [By S. Rudder.] Cirencester, 1781. 8°.

A reprint of portions of Rudder's history of the county (No. 605).
The charter of Charles II. to the city of Gloucester is given in full in app. i.

1689. HOPE, W. H. ST. JOHN. The seals of the city of Gloucester. *Bristol and Glouc. Archæol. Soc.*, Transactions, xiii. 384–92. Bristol, [1889.] 8°.

1690. †New guide (A) to the city of Gloucester . . . and a correct copy of the charter of the city. . . . Gloucester, [1820?]. 8°.

1691. POWELL, JOHN J. Gloucestriana : or papers relating to the city of Gloucester. Gloucester, [1890.] 8°.

1692. RUDGE, THOMAS. The history and antiquities of Gloucester from the earliest time ; including an account of the abbey. . . . Gloucester, 1811. 8°.

Reissued after 1814 with a new title-page.

GODMANCHESTER.

1693. FOX, ROBERT. The history of Godmanchester, in the county of Huntingdon : comprising its antient, modern, municipal, and ecclesiastical history. London, 1831. 8°.

Contains a translation of the town charters.

GOWRAN.

1694. PRIM, J. G. A. Documents connected with the ancient corporation of Gowran [1608–44.] *Royal Hist. and Archæol. Assoc. of Ireland,* Journal, Fourth Series, i. 535–52. Dublin, 1871 [1878]. 8°.

GRAMPOUND.

1695. Speech of Lord John Russell in the House of Commons on December 14th, 1819, on moving resolutions relative to corrupt boroughs. With extracts from the evidence on the Grampound bribery indictments. London, 1820. 8°.

See Hansard's *Debates,* xli. 1091–1107.

GRANTHAM.

1696. MARRAT, WILLIAM. An historical description of Grantham, containing a list of burgesses in Parliament, also of the succession of aldermen. Lincoln, 1816. 12°.

A brief sketch.

1697. STREET, BENJAMIN. Historical notes on Grantham and Grantham church. Grantham, 1857. 8°.

Pp. 105–26 are devoted to municipal history ; the fullest account.

1698. TURNOR, EDMUND. Collections for the history of the town and soke of Grantham. . . . London, 1806. 4°.

A brief account.

GRAVESEND.

1699. †Charter (The) of Gravesend, with all the laws relating to the watermen using the ferry between that town and London. Gravesend. n. d. 4°.

1700. CRUDEN, R. P. The history of the town of Gravesend in the county of Kent and of the port of London. London, 1843. 8°.

The best history of Gravesend.

1701. History (The) of the incorporated town and parishes of Gravesend and Milton. . . . [By Robert Pocock.] Gravesend, 1797. 4°.

Translation of the charter of 7 Charles I., 183–212.

1702. †Mask (The) pull'd off, or the dissection of a whiggish corporation : being the late curate of Gravesend's vindication from a villanous and libelling letter inserted some time ago in the Observator. 1712. 8°.

GREENOCK.

1703. CAMPBELL, DUGALD. Historical sketches of Greenock, with an account of the struggles in 1828 and 1880 regarding the harbour constitution ; also a short description of the feuds between the reds and the blues. [Vol. ii.] Greenock, 1881. 8°.

A detailed account of municipal affairs in the present century.
Vol. i., with a different title, 1879.

1704. Journal of proceedings at the election of a magistrate, treasurer, and three councillors for the town of Greenock, in 1825. To which is prefixed the charter of erection. Greenock, 1825. 8°.

1705. WEIR, DANIEL. History of the town of Greenock. Greenock, etc., 1829. 8°.

1706. WILLIAMSON, GEORGE. Old Greenock, from the earliest times to the early part of the nineteenth century ; with some account of the burgh of Cartsburn and burgh of barony of Crawfurdsdyke. Paisley and London, 1886. 4°.

The best history of Greenock.
The second series, which appeared in 1888, is devoted mainly to ecclesiastical and literary history.

GREENWICH.

1707. HOWARTH, WILLIAM. Some particulars relating to the ancient and royal borough of Greenwich. Compiled from the best authorities. Greenwich, 1882. 8°.

1708. —— Greenwich, past and present. Greenwich, [1886.] 8°.
Neither work contains much concerning municipal history.

GRIMSBY, GREAT.

1709. OLIVER, GEORGE. [First charter granted to Grimsby.] *Gentleman's Magazine,* vol. xcix. pt. ii. 507–10. London, 1829. 8°.

1710. —— The monumental antiquities of Great Grimsby. An essay towards ascertaining its origin and population. . . . Hull, 1825. 8°.

1711. —— Yᵉ byrde of Gryme : an apologue. Grimsby, 1866. 8°.
Pt. iv. Municipal history.

1712. WILD, J. Ancient Grimsby. [A paper read before the Lincoln Diocesan Architectural Society, 1878.] *Associated Architectural Societies,* Reports and Papers, xiv. 203–19. Lincoln, [1878.] 8°.
A brief sketch of its history.

GRINSTEAD, EAST.

1713. STENNING, J. C. Notes on East Grinstead. *Sussex Archæol. Soc.,* Collections, xx. 132–74. Lewes, 1868. 8°.

GUILDFORD.

1714. Guildford : a descriptive and historical view of the county town of Surrey. Embellished with engravings on wood by Thompson, from original drawings by C. C. Pyne. Guildford, etc., 1845. 8°.

1715. Handbook (A) to Guildford and its environs. . . . Third edition. Guildford, 1871. 8°.
Contains a brief account of municipal history.

1716. History (The) of Guildford, the county-town of Surrey : containing its antient and present state, civil and ecclesiastical ; collected from public records and other authorities. With some account of the country three miles round. Guildford, 1801. 8°.

> Contains a translation of Edward III.'s charter, and many interesting extracts from the town records, Edw. III. — James II.
> The best history of Guildford.
> 1st and 2nd editions: "The history and description of Guildford," etc., 1777, and [1800].

1717. SMITH, W. C. Rambles round Guildford, with a topographical and historical description of the town. Guildford, 1828. 12°.

> A brief account, of little value.
> New edition, published anonymously, 1857.

1718. STEVENS, D. M. The records and plate of the borough of Guildford. *Surrey Archæol. Soc.*, Collections, ix. 317–35. London, 1888. 8°.

> Contains brief extracts from the minute books, 20 Hen. VIII. — 1835.

HADDINGTON.

1719. BARCLAY, GEORGE. Account of the parish of Haddington. *Soc. of Antiq. of Scotland*, Transactions, i. 40–121. Edinburgh, 1792. 4°.

1720. MARTINE, JOHN. Reminiscences of the royal burgh of Haddington and old East Lothian agriculturists. Edinburgh and Glasgow, 1883. 8°.

1721. MILLER, JAMES. The lamp of Lothian: or the history of Haddington, in connection with the public affairs of East Lothian and of Scotland, from the earliest records to the present period. Haddington, 1844. 8°.

> Pt. iii. contains a good short account of municipal history.
> The best history of Haddington.

1722. † Notices of various Scottish local records, with extracts. Communicated to the Society of Antiquaries of Scotland. Edinburgh, 1859. 4°.

> Contains a description of the oldest council books and other records of the town of Haddington, with copious extracts, by Thomas Thomson.

1722a. † ROBB, JAMES. History of . . . Haddington. . . . Haddington, [1891.] 8°.

HADLEIGH.

1723. Brief description (A) of the town of Hadleigh, in the county of Suffolk : its history and antiquities. . . . Hadleigh, 1853. 12°.

1724. PIGOT, HUGH. Hadleigh : the town, church, and the great men who have been born in, or connected with the parish. *Suffolk Institute of Archæology*, Proceedings, iii. 1–290. Lowestoft, 1863. 8°.

HALIFAX.

There is no good history of Halifax since the time of its incorporation in 1848. Crabtree (No. 1725) gives a brief account of its parliamentary representation from 1832 to 1836. Watson's book (No. 1728) is the best general history.

1725. CRABTREE, JOHN. A concise history of the parish and vicarage of Halifax, in the county of York. Halifax and London, 1836. 8°.

1726. Halifax and its gibbet-law placed in a true light ; together with a description of the town. . . . London, 1708. 12°.

Other editions, 1712, [1761, 1789]. The dedication is signed by William Bently, but the real author was Samuel Midgley.

1727. History (The) of the town and parish of Halifax : containing a description of the town. . . . Halifax, [1789.] 8°.

1728. WATSON, JOHN. The history and antiquities of the parish of Halifax, in Yorkshire. Illustrated with copper-plates. London, 1775. 4°.

2nd edition, by F. A. Leyland, [1869], f°, not completed.

1729. WRIGHT, THOMAS. The antiquities of the town of Halifax, in Yorkshire. . . . Leeds, 1738. 12°.

Reprinted by J. H. Turner, 1884, 8°.

HANLEY.

1730. †Byelaws and regulations for the borough of Hanley. Hanley, [1859.] 8°.

1731. † CRAPPER, J. S. A history of the ancient corporation of Hanley, including a notice of their centenary festival; to which is added a succinct account of the municipal corporation. Hanley, 1882. 12°. pp. 48.

2nd edition, 1882.

HARLECH.

1732. Documents relating to the town and castle of Harlech [Edw. I. — 1650.] By W. W. E. W. *Cambrian Archæol. Assoc.*, Archæologia Cambrensis, i. 246–67 ; iii. 49–55. London and Tenby, 1846–48. 8°.

HARTLEPOOL.

1733. SHARP, CUTHBERT. History of Hartlepool, by the late Sir Cuthbert Sharp, knight; being a re-print of the original work published in 1816, with a supplemental history to 1851, inclusive. Hartlepool, 1851. 8°.

Extracts from the ordinances or "orders" made in 1599, pp. 75–9.

The appendices contain the earlier town charters; also a translation of the charter of 1593; and the charter of 1850.

HARWICH.

1734. Charters granted to the borough of Harwich by King James I. and King Charles II., translated from the original Latin, by order of the corporation, in the year 1797. London, 1798. 4°.

1735. TAYLOR, SILAS. The history and antiquities of Harwich and Dovercourt, topographical, dynastical, and political. First collected by Silas Taylor, alias Domville . . . and now much enlarged . . . by Samuel Dale. London, 1730. 4°.

A brief account.

2nd edition, 1732.

HASTINGS.

See No. 691.

1736. COOPER, W. D. Hastings : rape, castle, and town. *Sussex Archæol. Soc.*, Collections, ii. 161–8. Lewes, 1849. 8°.

1737. COOPER, W. D., and ROSS, T. Notices of Hastings and its municipal institutions. Reprinted from Sussex Archæological Collections, vol. xiv. Lewes, 1862. 8°.

Contains the medieval customal in full.

1738. Moss, W. G. The history and antiquities of the town and port of Hastings. Illustrated by a series of engravings from original drawings. London, 1824. 8°.

The best history of Hastings.

1739. Ross, Thomas. Hastings documents. *Sussex Archæol. Soc.*, Collections, xxiii. 85–118. Lewes, 1871. 8°.

Contains churchwardens' accounts, 1598–1762.

HAVERFORDWEST.

1740. Haverfordwest and its story; with old Pembrokeshire parishes, their traditions, histories, and memories. Haverfordwest, 1882. 8°.

1740a. Phillips, J. Haverfordwest in 1572. *Cambrian Archæol. Assoc.*, Archæologia Cambrensis, Fifth Series, xiii. 193–211. London, 1896. 8°.

HAWICK.

1741. Edgar, James. Hawick common-riding. By James Edgar. With appendix containing Drumlanrig's charter [1537.] Hawick, 1886. 8°.

1742. *Wilson, James. Annals of Hawick, A. D. 1214–A. D. 1814; with an appendix of illustrative documents. Edinburgh, 1850. 8°.

Made up mainly of valuable extracts from the burgh records.

1743. —— Hawick and its old memories; with an appendix. . . . Edinburgh and Hawick, 1858. 8°.

Excerpts from the town treasurers' books, 1721–1805, pp. 67–80.

1744. Wilson, Robert. The history of Hawick, including some account of the inhabitants; with occasional observations. To which is appended a short memoir of the author. Second edition, corrected and considerably enlarged. Hawick, 1841. 12°.

1st edition, 1825.

HEDON.

1745. * Boyle, J. R. The early history of the town and port of Hedon, in the east riding of the county of York. Hull and York, 1895. 8°.

The appendix of records fills 209 pages, and is very valuable.

1746. Park, G. H.   The history of the ancient borough of Hedon, in the seigniory of Holderness, and east-riding of the county of York. Hull, 1895.   8°.

Contains the town charter of 1348, with a translation ; the ancient ordinances of Hedon ; the ordinances of the tailors, 1637 ; also a detailed account of parliamentary history.

A good book.

HELENSBURGH.

1747. [Battrum, William.]   Battrum's Guide to Helensburgh and neighbourhood.   Helensburgh, 1864.   8°.

Extracts from the burgh records, 1807-23, pp. 9-11.

1748. Macleod, Donald.   A nonogenarian's reminiscences of Garelochside and Helensburgh, and the people who dwelt thereon and therein.   Helensburgh, etc., 1883.   8°.

Contains brief allusions to municipal history.

HELSTON.

1749.   †Appeal case (An) before the House of Lords between John Hoblyn, Thomas Arundell and others, James Burrow and others against the crown, respecting the rights of Heleron [Helston.]   1780?.   f°.

See No. 189.

1750. Boase, G. C.   The guild of cordwainers of Helston, Co. Cornwall.   *The Reliquary*, xx. 143-4.   London and Derby, 1880.   8°.

Contains regulations of the cordwainers, made about 1459.

HENLEY-ON-THAMES.

1751. Burn, J. S.   A history of Henley-on-Thames, in the county of Oxford.   London, etc., 1861.   4°.

Ch. ii. contains an abstract of the by-laws made in 1593, and extracts from the corporation minutes, 1422-1805.

A good book.

HEREFORD.

The best books on the history of Hereford are Duncumb's and Johnson's (Nos. 613, 1757).

1752. Black, W. H., and Hills, G. M.   The Hereford municipal records and the customs of Hereford.   *Brit. Archæol. Assoc.*, Journal, xxvii. 453-88.   London, 1871.   8°.

An interesting series of extracts from the town records. The "customs" are municipal regulations, drawn up probably in the 14th century.

Another text will be found in Duncumb's *Collections* (No. 613), and in Johnson's work (No. 1757). A portion of the customs in the original Latin is printed in the *Record of Caernavon* (No. 146), 130, and in W. Wotton's *Leges Wallicæ* (London, 1730), 517–18.

1753. Catalogue of and index to MS. papers, proclamations, and other documents selected from the municipal archives of the city of Hereford, after examination by W. D. Macray. . . . Hereford, [1894.] f°.

1754. Charter (The) of the city of Hereford, granted by King William III. Hereford, 1820. 4°.

See No. 1760.

1755. Devlin, J. D. Helps to Hereford history, civil and legendary, in an account of the ancient cordwainers' company of the city, The Mordiford Dragon, and other subjects. London and Hereford, 1848. 16°.

Contains extracts from the records of the company.
"The Mordiford Dragon" forms a distinct volume, with a separate title-page.

1756. Johnson, Richard. A lecture on the ancient customs of the city of Hereford. . . . Hereford, 1845. 8°.

1757. *——— The ancient customs of the city of Hereford, with translations of the earlier city charters and grants; also some account of the trades of the city, and other information relative to its early history. Second edition. London, 1882. 4°.

1st edition, 1868.
See No. 1752.

1758. Price, John. An historical account of the city of Hereford. . . . Hereford and London, 1796. 8°.

Of little value.

1759. Proceedings (The) of the citizens of Hereford in the delivering up of their charter and renewing of it; vindicated from the scurrilous imputations of Richard Janeway. By a lover of the king, the government, and the city. In a letter to a friend. [London, 1662]. f°.

Without title-page.

1760. Translation (A) of the charter granted to the city of Hereford by King William the Third, June 14, 1697 [1696]. [By John Allen.] Hereford, 1820. 4°.

HERTFORD.

1761. TURNOR, LEWIS. History of the ancient town and borough of Hertford. Illustrated with engravings. Hertford, 1830. 8°.

Ch. iii. The borough, Queen Mary's charter, etc.
Ch. iv. The corporate body.
Ch. v. Representative history.

HIGHAM FERRERS.

1762. COLE, JOHN. The history and antiquities of Higham Ferrers, with historical notices of Rushden and Irthlingborough in the county of Northampton. Wellingborough, 1838. 12°.

A brief sketch.

HINCKLEY.

1763. NICHOLS, JOHN. The history and antiquities of Hinckley in the county of Leicester. Second edition. London, 1813. f°.

A brief account.
1st edition in Nichols's *Bibliotheca Topographica Britannica* (London, 1790), vol. vii.
See No. 624.

1764. THOMPSON, JAMES. Ancient Hinckley. *Leicestershire Archit. and Archæol. Soc.*, Transactions, ii. 313–21. Leicester, 1870. 8°.

A brief account.

HINDON.

1765. The borough-broker, or the nobleman tricked : being a detail of facts adapted to the approaching election. By a lady. London, 1774. 8°.

Relates to the proposed sale of the borough of Hindon to Ralph, 2nd Earl of Verney.

HONITON.

1766. FARQUHARSON, A. The history of Honiton. Exeter, [1868.] 4°.

HORSHAM.

1767. COOPER, W. D.   Guild [of St. John the Baptist, founded 36 Henry VI.] and chantries in Horsham.   *Sussex Archæol. Soc.*, Collections, xxii. 148–59.   Lewes, 1870.   8°.

1768. COPLEY, J. S.   Report of the proceedings before the select committee of the House of Commons, appointed the 8th of January, 1807, in the case of a double return for the borough of Horsham, in the county of Sussex.   London and Dublin, 1808.   8°.

1769. Horsham : its history and antiquities.   With illustrations. London, 1868.   8°.

HULL.

The most valuable books relating to Hull are those of Frost, Hadley, Lambert, and Sheahan (Nos. 1770, 1774, 1776, 1778).

1770. FROST, CHARLES.   Notices relative to the early history of the town and port of Hull. . . . London, 1827.   4°.

Valuable.

1771. GAWTRESS, WILLIAM.   A report of the inquiry into the existing state of the corporation of Hull, taken at the Guild-Hall before F. Dwarris and S. A. Rumball, two of his majesty's commissioners ; also the proceedings relative to the Trinity House.   With an appendix, containing many valuable and authentic documents.   Hull, 1834. 8°.

See No. 60.

1772. GENT, THOMAS.   Annales Regioduni Hullini : or the history of the royal and beautiful town of Kingston-upon-Hull. . . . York, etc., 1735.   8°.

Reprinted, Hull, 1869.

1773. GUNNELL, W. A.   Sketches of Hull celebrities : or memoirs and correspondence of alderman Thomas Johnson (who was twice mayor of Kingston-upon-Hull) and four of his lineal descendants, from the year 1640 to 1858.   The whole compiled and arranged for publication by Mr. William A. Gunnell, from ancient MSS. furnished him by the last surviving member of the Johnson family.   Hull, 1876. 8°.

Contains some valuable material relating to municipal affairs.

1774. HADLEY, GEORGE. A new and complete history of the town and county of the town of Kingston-upon-Hull. . . . Kingston-upon-Hull, 1788. 4°.

Ch. xxv. contains the laws and orders made in the time of Henry IV., and other extracts from later town records.
One of the most detailed histories of Hull.

1775. Hull letters (The), printed from a collection of original documents found among the borough archives in the Town Hall, Hull, 1884 . . . 1625–1646. Selected and edited by T. T. Wildridge. Hull, [1887?]. 8°.

Letters to the mayor or corporation from divers persons, relating mainly to the political and military affairs of the kingdom.

1776. * LAMBERT, J. M. Two thousand years of gild life . . . together with a full account of the gilds and trading companies of Kingston-upon-Hull, from the 14th to the 19th century. Hull and London, 1891. 8°.

Contains the ordinances of various gilds of Hull, especially craft and merchant gilds. Most of these ordinances belong to the 16th and 17th centuries.

1777. PARSON, WILLIAM. The directory, guide, and annals of Kingston-upon-Hull. . . . By William White & Co. Edited by William Parson. Leeds, 1826. 12°.

A brief account.

1778. SHEAHAN, J. J. General and concise history and description of the town and port of Kingston-upon-Hull. London and Beverley, 1864. 8°.

2nd edition, " History of the town and port of Kingston-upon-Hull," Beverley, [1866.]

1779. TICKELL, JOHN. The history of the town and county of Kingston-upon-Hull, from its foundation in the reign of Edward the First to the present time. . . . Hull, 1798. 4°.

Contains a translation of the town charters, etc.

1780. TODD, C. S. Incidents in the history of Kingston-upon-Hull, from the accession of Edward II. to the death of Richard III. A lecture . . . before the Literary and Philosophical Society, 1st January, 1867. London and Kingston, 1867. 8°.

Another lecture on the same subject, from the accession of Henry VII.

to the death of Henry VIII., was delivered before the same society in 1868 (London and Hull, 1869).

These two lectures contain only a few brief references to internal municipal affairs.

1781. WILDRIDGE, T. T.   Hull's honour roll : being a list of all the municipal dignitaries and officers of the borough, from its establishment to the present time. . . . Hull, 1891.   4°.

1782. WOOLEY, WILLIAM.   A collection of statutes relating to the town of Kingston upon Hull, the county of the same town, and the parish of Sculcoates, in the county of York ; with a chronological table of acts of Parliament relating to the same places, from the earliest period to the end of the reign of George IV. ; and a copious index. London and Hull, 1830.   8°.

HUNTINGDON.

1783. [CARRUTHERS, ROBERT.]   The history of Huntingdon, from the earliest to the present times ; with an appendix, containing the charter of Charles I. . . . Huntingdon, 1824.   8°.

1784. GRIFFITH, EDWARD.   A collection of ancient records relating to the borough of Huntingdon, with observations illustrative of the history of parliamentary boroughs in general.   London, 1827.   8°.

Contains translations of extracts from the public records and town archives, Wm. I. — Wm. III.

HYTHE.

1785. Hythe churchwardens' accounts [1412–13.]   By W. A. S. Robertson.   *Kent Archæol. Soc.*, Archæologia Cantiana, x. 242–58. London, 1876.   8°.

1785a. WILKS, GEORGE.   The barons of the Cinque Ports, and the parliamentary representation of Hythe [1265–1892.]   Folkestone, [1892.]   4°.

Valuable for the parliamentary history of Hythe.

INVERNESS.

1786. History (A) and description of the town of Inverness : its principal buildings, public institutions, etc. . . . [By George Cameron.]   Inverness, 1847.   16°.

A brief account.

1787. MACKINTOSH, C. FRASER. Antiquarian notes : a series of papers regarding families and places in the Highlands. Inverness, 1865. 8°.

No. 63. Sett of the burgh of Inverness, 1675.
See also ibid., Nos. 17, 22-25, 34, 62, 63, 78, 88, 89.

1788. —— Invernessiana : contributions towards a history of the town and parish of Inverness, from 1160 to 1599. Inverness, 1875. 8°.

Chs. i.–iii., xciii.–xciv., deal with the burgh charters. " The Golden Charter " of 1591 is printed in full.

INVERURIE.

1789. †[DAVIDSON, C. B.] Burgh of Inverurie. A retrospect, 1863–88. Aberdeen, 1888. 8°.

1790. DAVIDSON, JOHN. Inverurie and the earldom of the Garioch : a topographical and historical account of the Garioch, from the earliest times to the revolution settlement. . . . Edinburgh and Aberdeen, 1878. 4°.

Contains brief extracts from the burgh records, 1605–60.
Another edition, with the old title-page, and with a few additional pages headed " Addenda, 1881."

IPSWICH.

a. Town Records, Nos. 1791–1799.
b. General Histories, etc., Nos. 1800–1807.

The borough of Ipswich has a rich collection of muniments, the most valuable of which are the following : court rolls, 39 Hen. III. — Eliz.; Domesday, 19 Edw. I. (No. 1793) ; Great Domesday, 12 Hen. VIII. (No. 1795) ; assembly books and general court books, from the reign of Elizabeth to the present time ; chamberlains' accounts, Philip & Mary — Geo. III.

The best history of Ipswich is Wodderspoon's (No. 1807). The Domesday of Ipswich and Bacon's *Annals* (Nos. 1793, 1801) are also valuable.

a. Town Records.

See No. 1801.

1791. † Accounts of the chamberlains of the borough of Ipswich for the year 1555. Edited by W. S. Fitch. [Ipswich.] n. d. 8°.

1792. Ancient and modern perambulations; and extracts from charters, trials, and other records relative to the liberties of Ipswich by land and water, intended as a companion to the maps of those jurisdictions. Ipswich, 1815. 8°.

The extracts relate to the admiralty jurisdiction of Ipswich.

1793. * Domesday (Le) de Gippewyz. [Printed in vol. ii. of The Black Book of the Admiralty or Monumenta Juridica, edited by Sir Travers Twiss. *Rolls Series.* London, 1873. 8°.]

Contains the ancient usages or ordinances compiled 19 Edw. I.

1794. Extracts from the churchwardens' books of accounts, St. Matthew's, Ipswich, A. D. 1574–1676. *East Anglian,* New Series, vol. iv. London, 1891–92. 8°.

1795. Great Domesday Book (The) of Ipswich, liber sextus; with an introduction . . . by the Rev. C. H. Evelyn White. Ipswich, 1885. 4°. pp. 36.

This Domesday Book was compiled by Richard Percival, 12 Hen. VIII., but it contains many old laws, etc., made at an earlier time. Of its seven "books," the sixth is the least interesting for municipal history; it contains taxes paid by every town in Suffolk, 32 Hen. VI., lists of knights' fees, etc.

1796. LAYTON, W. E. Notices from the great court and assembly books of Ipswich [17th century.] *East Anglian,* New Series, vols. i.–v. Ipswich, 1885–93. 8°.

1797. Oaths (The) of office of the chief magistrates, subordinate officers, and free burgesses of the corporation of Ipswich. Edited by and for G. Jermyn. Woodbridge and Colchester, 1794. 4°.

1798. Principal charters (The) which have been granted to the corporation of Ipswich in Suffolk, translated [by Richard Canning.] London, 1754. 8°.

1799. WHITE, C. H. E. The Ipswich Domesday Books. *Suffolk Institute of Archæology,* Proceedings, vi. 195–219. Lowestoft, 1888. 8°.

b. General Histories, etc.

1800. Account (An) of the gifts and legacies that have been given and bequeathed to charitable uses in the town of Ipswich; with some account of the present state and management, and some proposals for

the future regulation of them.   [By Richard Canning.]   Ipswich,
1747.   8°.

1801. * BACON, NATHANIEL.   The annalls of Ipsw^che.   The lawes,
customes, and govern^mt of the same. . . . By Nath^ll Bacon . . .
1654.   Edited by William H. Richardson.   Ipswich, 1884.   4°.

Contains numerous extracts from the court rolls, accounts, and other town
records.   These extracts are more numerous and more copious than those given
by Wodderspoon.

1802.   † Collection of papers relating to the election of bailiffs of
Ipswich, 8 Sept., 1754.   [Ipswich, 1754.]   8°.

1803.   FITCH, W. S.   Notices of the Corpus Christi guild, Ipswich.
Suffolk Institute of Archæology, Proceedings, ii. 151–63.   Lowestoft,
[1855] 1859.   8°.

1804.   GLYDE, JOHN.   The moral, social, and religious condition of
Ipswich in the middle of the nineteenth century ; with a sketch of its
history, rise, and progress.   Ipswich, 1850.   12°.

Of little value.

1804a.   † GRIMSEY, B. P.   Freemen of the borough of Ipswich.   Pt. i.
Ipswich, 1892.   8°.

1804b.   † —— Members of the council of Ipswich since 1835.
Ipswich, 1892.   8°.

1805.   History (The) and description of the town and borough
of Ipswich. . . . [By G. R. Clarke.]   Ipswich, etc., [1830.]   8°.

Devotes much attention to municipal history, especially to the election of
bailiffs.

1806.   WODDERSPOON, JOHN.   A new guide to Ipswich : containing notices of its ancient and modern history, antiquities, buildings, institutions, social and commercial condition.   Ipswich, 1842.   8°.

1807.   * —— Memorials of the ancient town of Ipswich, in the
county of Suffolk.   Ipswich and London, 1850.   4°.

Contains extracts from the court rolls, town accounts, etc.
The best history of Ipswich.

IRVINE.

1808. * Muniments of the royal burgh of Irvine. [Edited by John Shedden-Dobie.] *Ayrshire and Galloway Archæol. Assoc.* 2 vols. Edinburgh, 1890–91. 4°.

A valuable collection of charters, extracts from the burgh accounts, council book, etc., 1205–1783.

KELSO.

1809. HAIG, JAMES. A topographical and historical account of the town of Kelso, and of the town and castle of Roxburgh. . . . Edinburgh and London, 1825. 8°.

A meagre account.

1810. MASON, JOHN. Kelso records : being traditions and recollections of Kelso. Edinburgh, 1839. 8°.

A meagre account.

KENDAL.

1811. Boke (A) off recorde or register containing all the acts and doings in or concerning the corporation within the town of Kirkbie-kendall, beginning [in 1575.] . . . To which are added the several charters granted by Q. Elizabeth, K. Charles I., and K. Charles II. Edited by R. S. Ferguson. *Cumb. and Westm. Antiq. and Archæol. Soc.* Kendal and Carlisle, 1892. 8°.

Contains much valuable material relating to the history of the town
The best book for the study of the municipal history of Kendal.

1812. Local chronology : being notes of the principal events published in the Kendal newspapers since their establishment [1811.] Compiled by the editors. London and Kendal, 1865. 4°.

The "preliminary chapter" contains extracts from ancient records, 1575–85, etc.

1813. NICHOLSON, CORNELIUS. The annals of Kendal : being a historical and descriptive account of Kendal. . . . Second edition. London and Kendal, 1861. 8°.

The best general history.
1st edition, Kendal, 1832.

1814. —— History and incidents connected with the grants of the three royal charters of incorporation of the borough of Kendal. London, 1875. 8°.

1815. WHARTON, ROBERT. A chronological table of the chief magistrates of the burgh of Kirkby-in-Kendal from its first incorporation in 1575, and of the most remarkable events, chiefly in the town and neighbourhood. First published to the year 1724, by Robert Wharton, and continued to the year 1802, by William Pennington, and from thence with notes and additions to 1823, by Mr. John Taylor. *Lonsdale Magazine*, ii. 286–9. Kirkby Lonsdale, 1821. 8°.

Also printed, with a continuation to 1861, in Nicholson's *Annals* (No. 1813), 2nd edition, 284–305.

Contains a list of aldermen and mayors, with brief historical notes.

KENFIG.

1816. Kenfig charters (The). *Cambrian Archæol. Assoc.*, Archæologia Cambrensis, Fourth Series, ii. 172–90, 243–56, 313–19. London, 1871. 8°.

Contains ancient town charters, town ordinances of 1330, survey of 1660: Latin texts, with a translation.

KIDDERMINSTER.

1817. BURTON, J. R. A history of Kidderminster, with short accounts of some neighbouring parishes. London, 1890. 4°.

Ch. iv. contains a good account of municipal history.

KIDWELLY.

1818. CADE, JOHN. The state of the town of Kidwillie in South Wales in the reign of Queen Elizabeth, with a plan for its improvement. Addressed to the right worshipfull Sir George Carewe, knight marshall, by John Cade, a native of that town. [J. Leland's Collectanea, i. 679–700. Editio altera, by T. Hearne. 6 vols. London, 1770. 8°.]

1819. Kidwelly charters [1357–1619.] *Cambrian Archæol. Assoc.*, Archæologia Cambrensis, Third Series, ii. 273–81 ; iii. 1–22. London and Tenby, 1856–57. 8°.

Translation only.

KILKENNY.

1819a. † HEALY, WILLIAM. History and antiquities of Kilkenny (county and city). . . . 2 vols. Kilkenny, 1893, etc. 8°.

1820. HOGAN, JOHN. The three tholsels of Kilkenny. *Royal Hist. and Archæol. Assoc. of Ireland,* Journal, Fourth Series, v. 236–52. Dublin, 1882.   8°.

1821. PRIM, J. G. A. The corporation insignia and olden civic state of Kilkenny. *Royal Hist. and Archæol. Assoc. of Ireland,* Journal, Fourth Series, i. 280–305.   Dublin, [1870] 1878.   8°.

1822. —— Documents connected with the city of Kilkenny militia in the seventeenth and eighteenth centuries. *Kilkenny and South-East of Ireland Archæol. Soc.,* Proceedings, iii. 231–74.   Dublin, 1856.   8°.

1823. —— Muniments of the corporation of Kilkenny. *Kilkenny Archæol. Soc.,* Transactions, i. 427–32.   Dublin, 1853.   8°.

KILMACLENINE.

1824. Rotulus pipae Clonensis. . . . Corcagiae, 1859.   4°.

Contains the charter granted to Kilmaclenine by Daniel, Bishop of Cloyne, A. D. 1251, and other documents relating to the town, 15–22, 54, etc. See No. 1303.

KILMARNOCK.

1825. McKAY, ARCHIBALD. The history of Kilmarnock, from an early period to the present time. . . . Fourth edition. Kilmarnock, 1880.   8°.

Other editions, 1848, 1858, 1864.

KILMAURS.

1826. Charters (The) of Kilmaurs, from the original deeds, with translations of the most important. Kilmarnock, 1874.   4°.

Only 50 copies printed.

KILPATRICK.

1827. BRUCE, JOHN. History of the parish of West or Old Kilpatrick and of the church and certain lands in the parish of East or New Kilpatrick. Glasgow, 1893.   8°.

Ch. ix. Burgh of barony.

KILSYTH.

1827a. † ANTON, PETER. Kilsyth. . . . Glasgow, 1893.   8°.

KINGHORN.

1828. Act of the town council of Kinghorn, for regulating the management of the common good, to which is prefixed a notice and report. Edinburgh, 1818. 8°.

KINGSTON-UPON-THAMES.

1829. ANDERSON, A. History and antiquities of Kingston upon Thames: containing an account of all the most remarkable occurrences . . . also an account of the charters, donations. . . . Kingston, 1818. 8°.

A brief account. Contains some extracts from the town records.

1830. BIDEN, W. D. The history and antiquities of the ancient and royal town of Kingston-upon-Thames, compiled from the most authentic documents. Kingston, 1852. 8°.

A brief account.

1831. Charters (The) of the town of Kingston-upon-Thames, translated into English, with occasional notes. By George Roots. London, 1797. 8°.

1832. LYSONS, DANIEL. Environs of London. . . . 4 vols. and supplement. London, 1792–1811. 4°.

Kingston-upon-Thames, i. 212–56.
Contains extracts from the chamberlains' and churchwardens' accounts, 19 Hen. VII.—1670.

1833. MEASOR, H. P. The antiquities of Kingston. A lecture delivered . . . on Tuesday, the 19th of February, 1861, at the Wood Street schoolroom, Kingston. Kingston, 1861. 8°.

A brief historical sketch.

KINSALE.

1834. * Council Book (The) of the corporation of Kinsale, from 1652 to 1800. . . . Edited from the original, with annals and appendices compiled from public and private records. By Richard Caulfield. Guildford, 1879. 4°.

1835. Narrative (A) of the dispute in the corporation of Kinsale. In a letter from a buff at Kinsale to his friend in Dublin. Dublin, 1756. 8°.

KINTORE.

1836. WATT, ALEXANDER. The early history of Kintore; with an account of the rights and privileges belonging to the heritors and community of the burgh; extracted from old records and charters. [Aberdeen,] 1865. 8°.

KIRKHAM.

1837. FISHWICK, HENRY. The history of the parish of Kirkham, in the county of Lancaster. *Chetham Society.* [Manchester,] 1874. 4°.

KIRKINTILLOCH.

1838. WATSON, THOMAS. Kirkintilloch: town and parish. Glasgow, 1894. 8°.

Contains the charter granted to the town by William, Earl of Wigton, in 1670.

KIRKWALL.

1839. MACKINTOSH, W. R. Glimpses of Kirkwall and its people in the olden time (taken principally from the official records of the burgh). Kirkwall, 1887. 8°.

Contains a vivid account of municipal affairs and of daily life since the latter part of the 17th century.

A good little book.

1840. —— Curious incidents from the ancient records of Kirkwall (taken principally from the official records of the burgh). Kirkwall, 1892. 8°.

The extracts relate to parliamentary elections, the craft incorporations, etc., mainly in the 17th and 18th centuries.

1841. PETERKIN, ALEXANDER. Rentals of the ancient earldom and bishoprick of Orkney. . . . 6 numbers. Edinburgh, 1820. 8°.

Charters and other records of Kirkwall, app., 42–85.

KNARESBOROUGH.

1842. CALVERT, M. The history of Knaresbrough: comprising an accurate and detailed account of the castle, the forest, and the several townships included in the said parish. Knaresbrough, 1844. 12°.

1843. GRAINGE, WILLIAM.   An historical and descriptive account of the castle, town, and borough of Knaresborough.   Knaresborough, [1865.]   8°.

Parliamentary representation, 93–104.

KNUTSFORD.

1844. GREEN, HENRY.   Knutsford, its traditions and history; with reminiscences, anecdotes, and notices of the neighbourhood.   London, etc., 1859.   8°.

A brief account.

LAMBETH.

1845. HILL, GEORGE.   The electoral history of the borough of Lambeth since its enfranchisement in 1832.   London, 1879.   8°.

LAMPETER.

1846. DAVEY, W. H.   Charters connected with Lampeter and Llanbadarn Fawr.   *Cambrian Archæol. Assoc.*, Archæologia Cambrensis, Fifth Series, ix. 308–14.   London, 1892.   8°

LANARK.

1847. COWAN, W. A.   History of Lanark and guide to the surrounding scenery.   Lanark, 1867.   16°.

A brief account.

1848. DAVIDSON, W.   History of Lanark, and guide to the scenery; with list of roads to the principal towns.   Lanark, 1828.   12°.

A brief account.

1849. * Extracts from the records of the royal burgh of Lanark; with charters and documents relating to the burgh, 1150–1722. [Edited by R. Renwick.]   Glasgow, 1893.   4°.

LANCASTER.

The best history is Simpson's (No. 1855).

1850. Charter (The) of the borough of Lancaster, dated the 7th day of August, 1819.   Lancaster, 1819.   12°.   pp. 32.

1851. Historical and descriptive account (An) of the town of Lancaster; collected from the best authorities. Second edition. Lancaster, 1811. 8°.

A meagre account.
1st edition, 1807.

1852. JOHNSON, THOMAS. An address to the freemen of Lancaster on the subject of their charter. London, 1817. 8°.

" Postscript to an Address to the freemen of Lancaster," London, 1818, 8°.

1853. † Lancaster records, or leaves from local history : comprising an authentic account of the progress of the borough of Lancaster during the period of half-a-century, 1801–1850. Lancaster, 1869. 8°.

" This volume contains an immense amount of information " : Fishwick, *Lancashire Library* (No. 31), 81.

1854. ROPER, W. O. The charters of Lancaster. *Historic Soc. of Lanc. and Cheshire,* Transactions, xxxv. 1–14. Liverpool, 1886. 8°.

1855. SIMPSON, ROBERT. The history and antiquities of the town of Lancaster, compiled from authentic sources. Lancaster, 1852. 8°.

Ch. ix. contains a translation of the early town charters, and the constitutions and orders made in 1362, 1652, and 1708.
The best history of Lancaster.

LAUNCESTON.

1856. PETER, R., and PETER, O. B. The histories of Launceston and Dunheved, in the county of Cornwall. Plymouth, 1885. 8°.

Contains many extracts from the town accounts, court rolls, and other borough records.
The best history of Launceston.

1857. ROBBINS, A. F. Launceston, past and present : a historical and descriptive sketch. Launceston, 1888. 8°.

The preface is dated February, 1883.
A useful book.

LAURENCEKIRK.

1858. FRASER, W. R. History of the parish and burgh of Laurencekirk. Edinburgh and London, 1880. 8°.

Chs. xviii.-xxi. contain a good short account of the history of the burgh government.

L

LEEDS.

The best history is Wardell's (No. 1863).

1859. Acts of Parliament relating to the borough of Leeds in the county of York ; with such portions of the Consolidation Clauses Acts as are incorporated therein. Leeds, 1851. 8°.

1860. —— Copies of all the local acts of Parliament for the town and borough of Leeds, from the reign of George II. down to the present period ; to which are added English copies of the corporation charter, and the charter under which the soke of the king's mills in Leeds at present exists. . . . Leeds, 1822. 8°.

1861. ATKINSON, D. H.   Ralph Thoresby, the topographer : his town [Leeds] and times. 2 vols. Leeds, etc., 1885–87. 8°.

For notes on the history of the corporation, see i. 13, 21, 41, 223, etc. Thoresby's " Ducatus Leodensis, or the Topography of the ancient and populous Town of Leeds " (London, 1715 ; second edition, by T. D. Whitaker, Leeds, 1816) wholly neglects the municipal history.

1862. SHAW, J. D.   Civic life in bygone centuries. *The Antiquary*, iv. 147–51. London, 1881. 4°.

1863. WARDELL, JAMES.   The municipal history of the borough of Leeds. . . . Including numerous extracts from the court books of the corporation [1662–1807], and an appendix containing copies and translations of charters and other documents relating to the borough. London and Leeds, 1846. 8°.

The best history of Leeds.

1864. WHITAKER, T. D.   Loidis and Elemete : or an attempt to illustrate the districts described in these words by Bede. . . . Leeds, 1816. f°.

Charter of Maurice Poinell, with translation, 7–11.
Charter of Charles II., with translation, app., 40–59.
An elaborate work.

LEEK.

1865. SLEIGH, JOHN.   A history of the ancient parish of Leek in Staffordshire. . . . Second edition. London, etc., [1883.] 4°.

1st edition, Leek, 1862.

LEICESTER.

a. Town Records, Nos. 1866–1875.
b. General Histories, etc., 1876–1888.

The town archives contain one of the most valuable collections of municipal records in England. The earliest charters belong to the 12th century; the gild rolls begin with the reign of Richard I.; the chamberlains' accounts extend from 1587 to 1785; and the medieval borough Chartulary contains much interesting matter relating to the history of Leicester in the 13th and 14th centuries.

The best history of Leicester is Thompson's (No. 1885). The works of Nichols and Throsby (Nos. 624, 1888) are still useful.

a. Town Records.

1866. Account [compotus] (An) of the borough of Leicester for the year 1517–1518. *The Midland Counties Historical Collector,* ii. 55–8, 84–6. Leicester, 1856. 8°.

1867. Accounts (The) of the churchwardens of S. Martin's, Leicester, 1489–1844. Edited by Thomas North. Leicester, 1884. 4°.

1868. Accounts (The) of the churchwardens of St. Mary, Leicester, 1490–1491, 1652–1729. [By W. G. D. Fletcher and Colonel Bellairs.] *Leicestershire Archit. and Archæol. Soc.,* Transactions, vi. 229–68, 353–94; vii. 39–124, 153–9. Leicester, 1887–90. 8°.

The accounts of 1490–91 in vol. vii. are printed in full.

1869. Charters (The) of the borough of Leicester. [Bibliotheca Topographica Britannica, edited by John Nichols, viii. 931–68, 1347–8. London, 1790. 4°.]

Latin charters of King John, Count Robert of Leicester, Simon de Montfort, Edward III., Edward IV., Henry VII., Henry VIII., Elizabeth, James I., Charles II.

Valuable.

1870. JEAFFRESON, J. C. An index to the ancient manuscripts of the borough of Leicester. . . . Westminster, [1878.] 8°.

Several charters granted to Leicester in the 13th century are printed in full.

1871. KELLY, WILLIAM. Ancient records of Leicester. A paper read before the Leicester Literary and Philosophical Society on the

24th Feb., 1851. Reprinted from the Transactions of the society. Leicester, 1855. 8°.

This is incorporated in Kelly's work on the drama (No. 1877).

1872. ROUND, J. H. The true story of the Leicester inquests (1253). *The Antiquary*, xi. 25–30, 63–8. London, 1885. 4°.

1873. THOMPSON, JAMES. The ancient accounts [compotus] of the borough of Leicester. *The Midland Counties Historical Collector*, i. 102–8. Leicester, 1855. 8°.

1874. —— On the archives of the borough of Leicester. *Brit. Archæol. Assoc.*, Transactions at Winchester, 70–84. London, 1846. 8°.

Deals with the gild merchant of Leicester, etc.

1875. —— The rolls of the mayors of Leicester. A paper read at the general summer meeting of the Leicestershire Archit. and Archæol. Society, held in the Guildhall, Leicester, on the 8th of Sept., 1874. *Associated Architectural Societies*, Reports and Papers, xii. 261–74. Lincoln, [1874.] 8°.

b. General Histories, etc.

1876. KELLY, WILLIAM. The great mace and other corporation insignia of the borough of Leicester. *Royal Hist. Soc.*, Transactions, iii. 295–345. London, 1874. 8°.

Separately printed, 1875.
The appendix treats of "corporate emblems and insignia in England and Wales."

1877. —— Notices illustrative of the drama and other popular amusements, chiefly in the sixteenth and seventeenth centuries. . . . extracted from the chamberlains' accounts and other manuscripts of the borough of Leicester. . . . London, 1865 [1864]. 4°.

" Leicester in the olden time " is the outer title.

1878. NORTH, THOMAS. A chronicle of the church of S. Martin in Leicester. . . . with some account of its minor altars and ancient guilds. London and Leicester, 1866. 4°.

The Corpus Christi gild, 179–245.

1879. NORTH, THOMAS. The letters of alderman Robert Heyricke, of Leicester, 1590–1617. A contribution to the Transactions of the Leicestershire Architectural and Archæological Society. (For private circulation.) Leicester, 1880. 8°.

Contains references to municipal affairs.

1880. PAUL, J. D. The origin of the corporation of Leicester. A lecture delivered before the Leicester Literary and Philosophical Society; with an appendix containing a selection from the borough charters. London, 1885. 8°.

1881. READ, ROBERT. Modern Leicester : jottings of personal experience and research, with an original history of corporation undertakings. . . . London and Leicester, 1881. 8°.

Relates mainly to the 19th century.

1882. STOREY, JOHN. Historical sketch of some of the principal works and undertakings of the council of the borough of Leicester since the passing of the Municipal Corporations Reform Act; with a complete list of mayors, magistrates, aldermen, councillors, and head officials, down to the present day. Leicester, 1895. 8°.

1883. —— A list of the mayors, magistrates, aldermen, and councillors of the borough of Leicester since the passing of the Municipal Corporation Reform Act (5 & 6 Wm. IV., c. 76). With an introduction. Leicester, 1879. 8°.

1884. Struggle (The) for municipal liberty [between the corporation and the Earl of Huntingdon] : the local law courts. *The Midland Counties Historical Collector*, ii. 243–52. Leicester, 1856. 8°.

1885. * THOMPSON, JAMES. The history of Leicester, from the time of the Romans to the end of the seventeenth century. Leicester and London, 1849. 8°.

This, with its continuation (No. 1886), is the best history of Leicester.

1886. —— The history of Leicester in the eighteenth century. Leicester, 1871. 8°.

1887. —— The nature of the municipal franchises of the Middle Ages, illustrated by documents from the archives of the town of Leicester. *Gentleman's Magazine*, xxxv. 260–63, 596–99 ; xxxvi. 244–9. London, 1851. 8°.

1888. THROSBY, JOHN. History and antiquities of the ancient town of Leicester. Leicester, 1791. 4°.

In sect. ii. the municipal history is considered in detail.

LEITH.

See Nos. 1516, 1517.

1889. CAMPBELL, ALEXANDER. The history of Leith, from the earliest accounts to the present period ; with a sketch of the antiquities of the town. Leith and Edinburgh, 1827. 8°.

Contains an account of the incorporated trades of Leith.

1890. GRANT, JAMES. Cassell's Old and new Edinburgh. . . . 3 vols. London, etc., [1883.] 4°.

Leith, iii. 164–289.

1891. † History of Leith. Extracts. 1896. Selected and printed for the town council of Leith. Leith, 1896. f°.

1892. HUTCHISON, WILLIAM. Tales and traditions of Leith, with notices of its antiquities. Leith, 1853. 8°.

Revised edition, "Tales, traditions, and antiquities of Leith," etc., 1865. (Anon.)

LEOMINSTER.

1893. PRICE, JOHN. An historical and topographical account of Leominster and its vicinity ; with an appendix. Ludlow, 1795. 8°.

A brief account. The appendix contains a translation of the charter granted by Queen Mary to the town.

1894. TOWNSEND, G. F. The town and borough of Leominster ; with illustrations of its ancient and modern history. By G. F. Townsend. Also a chapter on the parish church and priory, by E. A. Freeman. Leominster and London, [1863.] 8°.

Contains many extracts from the chamberlains' books and the leet rolls in the 16th, 17th, and 18th centuries.

A good book.

LEWES.

1895. Ancient and modern history of Lewes and Brighthelmston, in which are compressed the most interesting events of the county at large. . . . [By William Lee.] Lewes, 1795. 8°.

Ch. viii., which deals with the municipal constitution of Lewes, contains the town ordinances of 1595, etc.

1896. HORSFIELD, T. W. The history and antiquities of Lewes and its vicinity. . . . 2 vols. Lewes, 1824–27. 4°.

Contains the town ordinances of 1595, and brief extracts from other records. The best history of Lewes.

A brief supplement was issued in 1832.

1897. Incorporation (The) of Lewes. *Sussex Daily News*, June 23, 1881.

Contains a sketch of the history of the town government, and the charter of Queen Victoria, 1881, in full.

1898. Provincial history. Lewes. *The Gleaner's Portfolio, or Provincial Magazine*, 11–15, 120–21, 157–8, 217–8. Lewes, 1819. 8°.

A brief sketch.

1899. TURNER, EDWARD. The ancient merchant guild of Lewes, and the subsequent municipal regulations of the town. *Sussex Archæol. Soc.*, Collections, xxi. 90–107. Lewes, 1869. 8°.

LICHFIELD.

The best history is Harwood's (No. 1901).

1900. CROFTON, H. T. Manchester gilds and the records of the Lichfield corvisors. *Lanc. and Cheshire Antiq. Soc.*, Transactions, x. 1–24. Manchester, 1893. 8°.

Extracts from the records of the Lichfield gild of corvisors, 1561–1870.

1901. HARWOOD, THOMAS. The history and antiquities of the church and city of Lichfield : containing its ancient and present state, civil and ecclesiastical ; collected from various public records and other authentic evidences. Gloucester, 1806. 4°.

The best history of Lichfield.

1902. JACKSON, JOHN. History of the city and cathedral of Lichfield ; chiefly compiled from ancient authors, etc. London, 1805. 8°.

A brief account of municipal history.

An earlier work by the same writer : "History of the city and county of Lichfield," Lichfield, [1795]; 2nd edition, 1796. (Anon.)

1903. RUSSELL, W. H. The laws of the mercers' company of Lichfield [1623.] *Royal Hist. Soc.*, Transactions, New Series, vii. 109–26. London, 1893. 8°.

1904. Short account (A) of the ancient and modern state of the city and close of Lichfield. . . . Lichfield and London, 1819. 8°.

LIMERICK.

See No. 729.

1905. FERRAR, JOHN. The history of Limerick, ecclesiastical, civil, and military, from the earliest records to the year 1787 ; illustrated by fifteen engravings. To which are added the charter of Limerick and an essay on Castle Connell Spa. . . . Limerick, 1787. 8°.

An earlier work by the same writer: "An history of the city of Limerick," 1767, 12°.

1906. LENIHAN, MAURICE. Limerick : its history and antiquities, ecclesiastical, civil, and military, from the earliest ages. . . . Dublin, 1866. 8°.

The best history of Limerick.

1907. Report from the select committee on the Limerick election. . . . *Parl. Papers,* 1820, vol. iii. [London,] 1820. f°.

Contains many details regarding the municipal government early in the 19th century.

LINCOLN.

The registers, which contain civic ordinances, etc., form the most valuable series of records in the town archives ; they extend from 1421 to the present time, with some breaks between 1421 and 1511.

There is no good history of Lincoln.

1908. Civitas Lincolnia, from its municipal and other records. [By John Ross.] Lincoln, 1870. 8°.

Contains abstracts of royal charters, notices of the earlier volumes of the borough registers, etc.

1909. † Copy of the charter of the city of Lincoln granted by Charles I., with memorandums of occurrences within that city, 1794 and 1795. Lincoln, 1793–95. 8°.

1910. History (The) of Lincoln; with an appendix, containing a list of the members returned to serve in Parliament, as also of the mayors and sheriffs of the city. [By Adam Stark.] Lincoln, 1810. 12°.

A brief account.

1911. History (The) of Lincoln : containing an account of the antiquities, edifices, trade, and customs of that ancient city. . . . To which is added an appendix comprising the charter [1628] and a list of mayors and sheriffs. Lincoln, 1816. 8°.

Ch. iii. The civil history.
This is the best history of Lincoln, but it does not give a detailed account of municipal development.

1912. History (The) of Lincoln ; and guide to its curiosities and antiquities. Lincoln, 1818. 18°.

A brief account.
Contains a translation of the charter granted to Lincoln by Charles I.

1913. History (The) of Lincoln : containing an account of its antiquities, edifices, trade, and customs ; and a description of the cathedral. Lincoln, 1825. 8°.

Of little value for municipal history.

1914. Names of the mayors, bailiffs, sheriffs, and chamberlains of the city of Lincoln, since the year of our Lord 1313 . . . together with a concise abridgement of the city charter. . . . Lincoln, [1787.] 12°.

LINLITHGOW.

1915. McALPINE, JAMES. Linlithgow and its vicinity. Falkirk, 1890. 8°.

A brief account.

1916. WALDIE, GEORGE. A history of the town and palace of Linlithgow ; with notices, historical and antiquarian, of places of interest in the neighbourhood. Linlithgow, 1858. 16°.

Ch. viii. Decay of the old burghal system.
A good short history.
2nd and 3rd editions, 1868, 1879.
His "Sketch of the history of Linlithgow," 1843 (2nd edition, 1845), is less valuable.

LISBURN.

1917. BAYLY, HENRY. A topographical and historical account of Lisburn. . . . Belfast, 1834. 12°.

Brief and of little value.
Translation of the charter of Charles II., 19–22.

LISKEARD.

1918. ALLEN, JOHN. History of the borough of Liskeard and its vicinity. London and Liskeard, 1856. 8°.

Contains brief extracts from the mayors' accounts, 1443–1815; and from the court rolls, 1487–1804. The appendix contains an abstract of the charters granted to Liskeard, 1240–1685.

LIVERPOOL.

> *a.* Town Records, Nos. 1919–1929.
> *b.* General Histories, Nos. 1930–1939.
> *c.* Parliamentary History, Nos. 1940–1944.
> *d.* Miscellaneous, Nos. 1945–1958.

The best history of Liverpool is Picton's (No. 1935). His two collections of records (Nos. 1923, 1924) are also valuable.

a. Town Records.

1919. Authentic copies of the several acts of parliament which have been passed at different times relative to the docks, port, and harbour of Liverpool, and the light-houses, etc., thereto belonging. Liverpool, 1804. 8°.

1920. Charter (The) granted to the burgesses of Liverpool by William III., with notes and explanatory remarks on the same; also the charter of George II. . . . To which is added a summary of the proceedings of the burgesses and common council from the reign of Elizabeth to the present time, with an epitome of the two trials at Lancaster between the corporation and the common council. Liverpool, 1810. 8°.

See Nos. 1925, 1926.

1921. City of Liverpool. Copies of charters, etc., etc. Liverpool, [1881.] 4°.

Contains a facsimile of the charter of John; grant of arms, 1797; facsimile of the charter of Victoria, 1880.

1922. City of Liverpool. Report on the records and documents relating to the city of Liverpool, now in the possession of the corporation. [By J. A. Picton.] Liverpool, 1881. 8°. pp. 17.

This report, on pp. 8–10, refers to the following works:

Printed book, containing documents relative to the disputes in the corporation, 1756–59.

Red Book, containing printed copies of various documents connected with the history of the corporate estate ; also an index to valuable documents produced in the trial in 1830–32, the corporation *v.* Bolton and others. Pt. ii. of printed documents supplementary to the above.

1923. * City of Liverpool. Selections from the municipal archives and records, from the 13th to the 17th century inclusive. Extracted and annotated by Sir James A. Picton. Liverpool, 1883. 4°.

1924. * —— City of Liverpool. Municipal archives and records, from A. D. 1700 to the passing of the Municipal Reform Act, 1835. Extracted and annotated by Sir James A. Picton. Liverpool, 1886. 4°.

1925. Correct translation (A) of the charter of Liverpool [granted by William III.], with remarks and explanatory notes. By Philodemus [Joseph Clegg]. Liverpool, [1757.] 4°.

1926. —— A correct translation of the charter granted to the burgesses of Liverpool by King William the Third, with remarks and explanatory notes. [By Philodemus.] To which are added the charter granted by King George the Second, the order of the common council, and the petition for obtaining that charter; with the report of the attorney and solicitor-general thereon. Liverpool, 1783. 8°.

1927. HANCE, E. M., and MORTON, T. N. The burgess rolls of Liverpool during the 16th and 17th centuries. *Historic Soc. of Lanc. and Cheshire*, Transactions, xxxv. 147–86; xxxvi. 129–58. Liverpool, 1886–87. 8°.

1928. PICTON, J. A. Notes on the charters of the borough of Liverpool. *Historic Soc. of Lanc. and Cheshire*, Transactions, xxxvi. 53–128. Liverpool, 1887. 8°.

Also printed separately. Some of the charters are printed in full, with a translation.

1929. Town-Hall Liverpool Oath Book. List of oaths. Liverpool, 1824. f°.

Contains the mayor's oath and fifteen other oaths.

b. General Histories.

1930. AIKIN, J. Description of the country from thirty to forty miles round Manchester. . . . London, 1795. 4°.

Liverpool, 331–83, 597–615.

1931. BAINES, THOMAS. History of the commerce and town of Liverpool, and of the rise of manufacturing interests in the adjoining counties. London and Liverpool, 1852. 8°.

1932. ENFIELD, WILLIAM. An essay towards the history of Leverpool, drawn up from papers left by the late Mr. George Perry, and from other materials since collected. Second edition. London, 1774. f°.

Of little value for municipal history.
1st edition, Warrington, 1773.

1933. General and descriptive history (A) of the antient and present state of the town of Liverpool. . . . [By James Wallace.] Second edition. Liverpool and London, 1797. 8°.

Ch. xi. The government.
1st edition, 1795.

1934. History (The) of Liverpool from the earliest authentic period down to the present time. . . . [By Thomas Troughton.] Liverpool, 1810. 4°.

Ch. xii. Charters granted to Liverpool by Charles II., etc.

1935. PICTON, J. A. Memorials of Liverpool, historical and topographical, including a history of the Dock Estate. [Vol. i. Historical. Vol. ii. Topographical.] Second edition. 2 vols. London and Liverpool, 1875. 8°

Valuable.
1st edition, 1873.

1936. SMITHERS, HENRY. Liverpool, its commerce, statistics, and institutions; with a history of the cotton trade. Liverpool, 1825. 8°.

A brief account.

1937. STONEHOUSE, JAMES. A new and complete hand-book for the stranger in Liverpool: its annals, commerce, shipping, institutions. . . . New edition. Liverpool, [1850.]   8°.

A good short account of the history of Liverpool.
1st edition, " Pictorial Liverpool: its annals," etc., 1845.

1938. Stranger (The) in Liverpool: or an historical and descriptive view of the town of Liverpool and its environs. Ninth edition, with corrections and copious additions. Liverpool, 1829.   12°.

Extracts from the early town records, app., pp. i.–xliii.
1st edition, 1807; 12th edition, 1839; reprinted in 1840, 1841, 1848, and 1850.

1939. WALTHEW, J. M. A lecture on the rise and progress of Liverpool. Liverpool, 1865.   8°.

c. Parliamentary History.

1940. BENNETT, RICHARD. A record of elections, parliamentary and municipal, for Liverpool [1832–78]. . . . Liverpool, 1878.   8°.

1941. Case (The) of the Liverpool Disfranchisement Bill. London, 1834.   8°.

1942. GOTHAM, M. Parliamentary elections in Liverpool during the past 141 years; from the time of George II. (1727) to the present time. *Liverpool Telegraph and Shipping Gazette*, Nov. 19, 1868.

A brief account.

1943. History of the election for members of Parliament for the borough of Liverpool, 1806, containing the addresses of the different candidates, with a list of the freemen's names who voted. To which are prefixed observations on the importance of the representative system, with hints on the necessity of a reform in that branch of the constitution. Liverpool, [1806.]   8°.

1944. Report from the select committee appointed to inquire into the petition on Liverpool borough [complaining of corruption at elections.] *Parl. Papers*, 1833, vol. x. [London,] 1833.   f°.

d. Miscellaneous.

1945. BROOKE, RICHARD. Liverpool as it was during the last quarter of the eighteenth century, 1775 to 1800. Liverpool and London, 1853.   8°.

The introduction contains charters of John and Henry III., with a translation.
List of principal acts of Parliament relating to Liverpool, 442–50.

1946. CLEGG, JOSEPH. [Letter to the corporation of Liverpool concerning a petition for a new charter. Liverpool, 1751. 4°. pp. 23.]

Without title-page.

1947. —— [Letter to Richard Hughes, Esq., mayor of Liverpool ; with report of a conference relating to the constitutional charter laws of Liverpool. Liverpool, 1757. 4°. pp. 23.]

Without title-page.

For other letters, etc., written by Clegg, concerning the municipal affairs of Liverpool, see Catalogue of Liverpool Public Library, pt. iii. (1892) 147–8.

1948. DAVIES, R. W. Municipal history of Liverpool : being a concise historical chart of the municipal elections in the borough [1835–67.] Liverpool, [1868.] 4°.

1949. Inquiry (An) into the origin of the Liverpool town dues. London, 1857. 8°.

1950. Liverpool a few years since. By an old stager [James Aspinall]. London and Liverpool, 1852. 8°.

Ch. xviii. The old corporation, etc.

A brief account.

1951. Municipal government in Liverpool : a series of [twelve] articles, reprinted from the " Liverpool Mercury." [By J. Lovell.] Liverpool, 1885. 8°. pp. 112.

Deals especially with taxation, and the management of the corporate estate.

1952. Municipal reform. Report of special committee [appointed by the Liverpool Liberal Association.] Thomas Cope, chairman. Liverpool, 1877. 8°. pp. 24.

Deals with municipal reform in general, and especially in Liverpool.

1953. Proceedings in an action at law, brought by the mayor, bailiffs, and burgesses of the borough of Liverpool [v. Golithly] for the recovery of a penalty under a by-law made by them in common hall assembled. Containing the arguments of the counsel, as well at nisi prius as upon the motion for a new trial in the court of King's Bench ; the proceedings on the second trial at Lancaster ; and on a motion in the court of King's Bench for a third trial, with the reasons at large of the hon. the justices of the said court for granting the same. Taken in short hand by Mr. Gurney. Liverpool, 1796. 8°.

" The following proceedings, if they answer no other purpose, will at least transmit to future times a record of this memorable struggle made by the burgesses [against the common council] for the recovery of their privileges."

An important contribution to municipal history.

1954. Report of the proceedings of the associated merchants of Liverpool who have recently resisted the payment of the town's dues. . . . London, 1835. 8°.

1955. Report (A copious) of the inquiry into the affairs of the corporation of Liverpool, before his majesty's commissioners, George Hutton Wilkinson and Thomas Jefferson Hogg, commenced on the 4th and ended on the 30th November, 1833. In the Sessions Rooms, Chapel Street. Liverpool, 1833. 4°.

1956. —— A report of the proceedings of a court of inquiry into the existing state of the corporation of Liverpool, held in the court room, in the Sessions House, in Chapel Street, Liverpool, before Geo. Hutton Wilkinson and Thos. Jefferson Hogg, two of his majesty's commissioners appointed to inquire into municipal corporations in England and Wales, in the month of November, 1833. Liverpool, [1834.] f°.

The appendix contains the charters of Liverpool in full, with an English translation.

See No. 60.

1957. Report of the special committee appointed by the council on the 5th day of June, 1850, and reappointed on the 9th day of November, 1850, for the purpose of inquiring into the respective duties of all the paid officers of the corporation. . . . Liverpool, 1851. 8°. pp. 225.

1958. SEXAGENARIAN. Great towns and their public influence. iv. Liverpool. *Gentleman's Magazine*, xiii. 474–84. London, 1874. 8°.

LLANFYLLIN.

1959. Llanfyllin. Some additional items of municipal history. *Powysland Club*, Collections, xxiii. 121–66. London, 1889. 8°.

Contains charters, lists of town officers, etc., Charles II.—Victoria.

1960. WILLIAMS, ROBERT. A history of the parish of Llanfyllin. *Powysland Club,* Collections, iii. 51–112. London, 1870. 8°.

Contains a translation of the charter of Elizabeth, the report of the corporations commission (above, No. 60), etc.

LLANIDLOES.

1961. HAMER, EDWARD. Parochial account of Llanidloes. *Powysland Club,* Collections, viii. 224–48 ; ix. 247–61. London, 1875–76. 8°.

Ch. vii. The report of the corporations commission (above, No. 60), list of mayors, etc.
Ch. viii. Parliamentary history.

LLANTRISSAINT.

1962. Original documents : Llantrissaint borough charter. Communicated by G. T. C[lark]. *Archæol. Journal,* xxix. 351–9. London, 1872. 8°.

The charter of 3 Henry VI., inspecting various older charters.

LOCHMABEN.

1963. GRAHAM, WILLIAM. Lochmaben five hundred years ago : or selections, historical and antiquarian, from papers collected by the late John Parker, principal extractor of the court of Session. Edinburgh, 1865. 8°.

Ch. viii. The burgh charter and burgage property.

LONDON.

a. Bibliographies, Nos. 1964–1968.
b. Town Records, Nos. 1969–1981.
c. Chronicles, Nos. 1982–1991a.
d. General Histories, Nos. 1992–2007.
e. Medieval London, Nos. 2008–2014.
f. Charters, Laws, and Privileges, Nos. 2015–2060.
g. Courts and Offices, Nos. 2061–2080.
h. Gilds and Companies, Nos. 2081–2163.
i. Municipal Reform, Nos. 2164–2238.
j. London County Council, Nos. 2239–2258.
k. Miscellaneous, Nos. 2259–2272.

From the vast array of books and pamphlets relating to London, only the more valuable have been selected. Many other titles will be found in the bibliographies mentioned below, especially in the Catalogue of the Guildhall Library.

a. Bibliographies.

See also the general bibliographies mentioned above, especially those of Anderson, Gough, Smith, and Upcott (Nos. 1, 5, 14, 15); and the British Museum Catalogue of Printed Books (1889), under " London."

1964. Catalogue of the Guildhall library of the city of London, with additions to June, 1889. London, 1889. 8°.

1965. CLARKE, JOHN. Bibliotheca legum. . . . New edition. London, 1819. 8°.

Charters, customs, etc. of London, 45-58.

1966. TYRRELL, EDWARD. Catalogue of the valuable and singularly curious library of Edward Tyrrell, late city remembrancer . . . sold by auction by Messrs. Sotheby, Wilkinson & Hodge . . . on Monday, 4th April, 1864, and four following days. London, [1864.] 8°.

1967. WELCH, CHARLES. Bibliography of the livery companies of London. *The Library,* ii. 301-7. London, 1890. 8°.

A brief account of the principal works relating to the companies.

1968. ——— Notes on London municipal literature, and a suggested scheme for its classification. A paper read before the Bibliographical Society on 10 June, 1894. London, 1895. 4°.

b. Town Records.

Delpit (No. 1974), p. cii., comments as follows upon the richness of the city archives : " C'est certainement une grande gloire pour la commune de Londres de posséder des archives non-seulement plus complètes que celles d'aucune autre ville, mais que ces archives renferment on peut dire les titres de la nation elle-même."

The principal series of records are: the letter books, 1275–1590, containing historical memoranda of ordinances, charters, etc.; journals of the common council, from 1416 to the present time; repertories of the court of aldermen, from 1495 to the present time; rolls of pleas and memoranda, Edw. II.—Rich. III.; Remembrancia, copies of correspondence between the civic authorities and distinguished persons, relating to the affairs of London, 1579–1664; Liber Albus, Liber Custumarum, etc. (No. 1979).

For collections of charters, see Nos. 2020, 2032, 2035, 2043.

1969. Analytical index to the series of records known as the Re-membrancia, preserved among the archives of London, A. D. 1579–1664. Prepared by the authority of the corporation of London, under the superintendence of the library committee. [By W. H. and H. C. Overall.] London, 1878. 8°.

Earlier edition, "Analytical indexes to volumes ii. and viii. of the series of records known as the Remembrancia," 1870.

1970. Calendar of letters from the mayor and corporation of the city of London, circa A. D. 1350–1370, enrolled and preserved among the archives of the corporation at the Guildhall. Edited, with an introduction, by Reginald R. Sharpe. Printed by order of the corporation. . . . London, 1885. 8°.

These letters throw light mainly on the intercourse of London with the chief municipalities of Flanders and England.

1971. Calendar of wills proved and enrolled in the court of Hust-ing, London, A. D. 1258 – A. D. 1688, preserved . . . at the Guildhall. Edited, with introduction, by R. R. Sharpe. Published by order of the corporation. . . . 2 vols. London, 1889–90. 8°.

An elaborate work, well edited.

1972. Corporation records. Report to the court of common council from the library committee, presented 16th December, 1869. [London, 1869.] f°.

1973. —— Further report . . . 24th November, 1870. [London, 1870.] f°.

These two reports describe the records of the corporation.

1974. DELPIT, JULES. Collection générale des documents fran-çais qui se trouvent en Angleterre. Tome premier. Archives de la mairie de Londres. . . . Paris, 1847. 4°.

For a description of the records in the Guildhall of London, with extracts, see pp. xliii.–cii.

1975. FRESHFIELD, EDWIN. A discourse on some unpublished records of the city of London. London, 1887. 4°. pp. 35.

Deals particularly with the parish records.

1976. HUGO, THOMAS. "The Liber Albus," and other records of the corporation of London. . . . *London and Middlesex Archæol. Soc.*, Transactions, i. 245–58. London, 1860. 8°.

1977. [JUNGHANS, WILHELM.] Bericht des Herrn Dr. Junghans. *Sybel's Historische Zeitschrift*, Band iv., Beilage, 23–39. München, 1860. 8°.

A good account of the contents of the archives in Guildhall.

1978. * Memorials of London and London life, in the 13th, 14th, and 15th centuries [to 1419] : being a series of extracts, local, social, and political, from the early archives of the city of London, A. D. 1276–1419. Selected, translated, and edited by H. T. Riley. Published by order of the corporation. . . . London, 1868. 8°.

Contains extracts from the letter books.

1979. * Munimenta Gildhallæ Londoniensis : Liber Albus, Liber Custumarum, et Liber Horn. Edited by H. T. Riley. *Rolls Series*. 4 vols. London, 1859–62. 8°.

Vol. i. Liber Albus, by John Carpenter, 1419.
Vol. ii. (2 pts.). Liber Custumarum, circa 1320.
Vol. iii. Translations of the Anglo-Norman passages in Liber Albus; glossaries, etc.
Liber Horn, 1311, probably compiled by Andrew Horn; not published.

These volumes contain valuable documents illustrating the social, legal, and constitutional history of London, especially during the 13th and 14th centuries.

1980. —— Liber Albus : the White Book of the city of London, compiled A. D. 1419 by John Carpenter, common clerk, Richard Whitington, mayor. Translated from the original Latin and Anglo-Norman by H. T. Riley. London, 1861. 8°.

1981. ORRIDGE, B. B. The corporation of London and their records. *Macmillan's Magazine*, xx. 562–7. London, 1869. 8°.

Of little value.

c. Chronicles.

Most of these chronicles were written by citizens of London. The events are arranged under the names of the mayors and sheriffs; more attention is given to the political occurrences of the kingdom than to municipal affairs.

See No. 2017.

1982. Chronicle of the Grey Friars of London [1189–1556.] Edited by John Gough Nichols. *Camden Society*. [London], 1852. 4°.

Deals mainly with the reigns of Henry VIII. and Edward VI. See No. 3089.

1983. Chronicle (A) of London from 1089 to 1483, written in the fifteenth century, and for the first time printed from MSS. in the British Museum; to which are added numerous contemporary illustrations, consisting of royal letters, poems, and other articles descriptive of public events, or of the manners and customs of the metropolis. [Edited by E. Tyrrell.]   London, 1827.   4°.

Written in English about 1442; continued to 1483.

1984. Chronicles of the mayors and sheriffs of London, A. D. 1188 to A. D. 1274; translated from the original Latin and Anglo-Norman of the "Liber de antiquis legibus" . . . attributed to Arnald Fitz-Thedmar, alderman of London in the reign of Henry the Third.   The French chronicle of London, A. D. 1259 to A. D. 1343; translated from the original Anglo-Norman of the "Croniques de London." . . . With notes and illustrations by H. T. Riley.   London, 1863.   4°.

1985. Chronicles of the reigns of Edward I. and Edward II. Edited by William Stubbs.   *Rolls Series.*   2 vols.   London, 1882–83. 8°.

Vol. i.   Annales Londonienses, 1194–1330, and Annales Paulini, 1307–1341.

1986. Croniques de London, depuis l'an 44 Hen. III. jusqu'à l'an 17 Edw. III.   Edited from a MS. in the Cottonian Library by G. I. Aungier.   *Camden Society.*   London, 1844.   4°.

Translated by Edmund Goldsmid: "The Chronicles of London from 44 Hen. III. to 17 Edw. III.," 3 vols., Edinburgh, 1885–86, 8°.   See No. 1984. Contains little concerning the municipal affairs of London.

1987. * De antiquis legibus liber : cronica maiorum et vicecomitum Londoniarum et quedam que contingebant temporibus illis ab anno 1178 ad annum 1274; cum appendice.   Nunc primum typis mandata curante T. Stapleton.   *Camden Society.*   London, 1846.   4°.

See No. 1984.

1988. FABYAN, ROBERT. The new chronicles of England and France, in two parts, by Robert Fabyan; named by himself the concordance of histories.   Reprinted from Pynson's edition of 1516; the first part collated with the editions of 1533, 1542, and 1559, and the second with a manuscript of the author's own time, as well as the subsequent editions; including the different continuations.   To which are

added a biographical and literary preface and an index, by Henry
Ellis. London, 1811. 4°.

Fabyan was an alderman of London, who died in 1512.

1989. Historical collections (The) of a citizen of London in the
fifteenth century. . . . iii. William Gregory's Chronicle of London
[1189–1469.] Edited by James Gairdner. *Camden Society.* [Lon-
don,] 1876. 4°.

1990. London chronicle during the reigns of Henry VII. and
Henry VIII. Edited from the original MS. in the Cottonian library
by Clarence Hooper. *Camden Society,* Miscellany, iv. 1–18. London, 1859. 4°.

A brief chronicle from 1500 to 1545.

1991. Three fifteenth-century chronicles, with historical memoranda by John Stowe. Edited by James Gairdner. *Camden Society.*
[London,] 1880. 4°.

Pp. 1–80 contain a London chronicle in English, probably written in the reign
of Edward IV. It extends from the earliest time to 4 Edward IV. Down to the
reign of Henry V. it is of little value.

1991a. WRIOTHESLEY, CHARLES. A chronicle of England during
the reigns of the Tudors, from A. D. 1485 to 1559. Edited . . . by
W. D. Hamilton. *Camden Society.* 2 vols. [London,] 1875–77.
4°.

Written during the reigns of Henry VIII. and Elizabeth.
Based upon Arnold (No. 2017) down to 1522.

d. General Histories.

The most useful works are those of Loftie, Maitland, Noorthouck,
Norton, and Stow (Nos. 1999, 2001, 2002, 2003, 2006). A good account
of the constitutional history of London is still needed.

1992. ALLEN, THOMAS. The history and antiquities of London,
Westminster, Southwark, and parts adjacent. 4 vols. London, 1827–
29. 8°.

1993. CHAMBERLAIN, HENRY. A new and compleat history and survey of the cities of London and Westminster, the borough of Southwark, and parts adjacent . . . their laws, charters, customs, privileges,
immunities, government, trade, and navigation. . . . By a society of

gentlemen. Revised, corrected, and improved by Henry Chamberlain, of Hatton-Garden. London, [1769.] f°.

1994. DE LAUNE, THOMAS. Angliæ metropolis: or the present state of London; with memorials comprehending a full and succinct account of the ancient and modern state thereof, its original government, rights, liberties, charters. . . . First written by the late ingenious Thomas De Laune, Gent., and continu'd to this present year by a careful hand [S. W.]. London, 1690. 12°.

1995. ENTICK, JOHN. A new and accurate history and survey of London, Westminster, Southwark, and places adjacent. . . . With the charters, laws, customs, rights, liberties, and privileges of this great metropolis. . . . 4 vols. London, 1766. 8°.

1996. HARRISON, WALTER. A new and universal history, description, and survey of the cities of London and Westminster, the borough of Southwark, and their adjacent parts. . . . London, [1775.] f°.

1997. HUGHSON, DAVID [EDWARD PUGH]. London: being an accurate history and description of the British metropolis and its neighbourhood, to thirty miles extent, from an actual perambulation. 6 vols. London, 1806-9. 8°.

1998. LAMBERT, B. The history and survey of London and its environs, from the earliest period to the present time. 4 vols. London, 1806. 8°.

1999. LOFTIE, W. J. A history of London. With maps and illustrations. Second edition. 2 vols. London, 1884. 8°.

1st edition, and supplement, 1883-84.

2000. —— London. [Historic Towns. Edited by E. A. Freeman and W. Hunt.] London, 1887. 8°.

A good short account.

2001. MAITLAND, WILLIAM. The history of London, from its foundation by the Romans to the present time. . . . London, 1739. f°.

Other editions, 2 vols., f°, London, 1756, 1760, 1769, 1772, 1775.

2002. NOORTHOUCK, JOHN. A new history of London, including Westminster and Southwark. To which is added a general survey of the whole. . . . London, 1773. 4°.

The appendix contains a translation of the charters of London, and other documents.

2003. * NORTON, GEORGE. Commentaries on the history, constitution, and chartered franchises of the city of London. Third edition, revised. London, 1869. 8°.

Bk. i. Historical account.
Bk. ii. The charters.
The best constitutional history of London.
1st edition, 1829.

2004. ORRIDGE, B. B. Some account of the citizens of London and their rulers, from 1060 to 1867. London, 1867. 8°.

2005. SHARPE, R. R. London and the kingdom : a history derived mainly from the archives at Guildhall, in the custody of the city of London. 3 vols. London, 1894–95. 8°.

Deals mainly with the political history of London, i. e. its relations with the king and the kingdom.

2006. STOW, JOHN. A survey of the cities of London and Westminster and the borough of Southwark : containing the original, antiquity, increase, present state, and government of those cities. Written at first in the year 1698 [1598] by John Stow, citizen and native of London ; corrected, improved, and very much enlarged in the year 1720 by John Strype. . . . Sixth edition. 2 vols. London, 1754–55. f°.

Vol. ii. contains Fitz-Stephen's *Description* (No. 2008) ; tracts on the privileges of London, etc.

Earlier editions, 1598, 1603, 1618, 1633, 1720: see Upcott's *Bibliographical Account* (No. 15), ii. 605-17. Later editions : 1842, by William J. Thoms ; 1890, by Henry Morley.

2007. WELCH, CHARLES. Modern history of the city of London : a record of municipal and social progress from 1760 to the present day. London, 1896. 4°.

e. Medieval London.

For two documents of the 10th and 11th centuries relating to London, see Thorpe, *Laws* (No. 95), 97–103, 127–9, and Schmid, *Gesetze* (No. 96), 157–72, 218–20.

2008. FITZ-STEPHEN, WILLIAM. Fitz-Stephen's Description of the city of London, newly translated from the Latin original ; with a neces-

sary commentary. . . . By an antiquary [Samuel Pegge]. London,
1772. 4°.

Contains the Latin text, with a translation.
The text, which was written in the second half of the 12th century, is also
printed in Stow's *Survey* (No. 2006), vol. ii. app. 9; Leland's *Itinerary*, edited by
Hearne, vol. viii.; *Materials for the History of Becket* (Rolls Series, 1877, iii. 2–13;
Liber Custumarum (No. 1979), 2–15.
See No. 2014.

2009. GOMME, G. L.   On the early municipal history of London.
London and Middlesex Archæol. Soc., Transactions, vi. 520–59.
London, 1885. 8°.

Tries to show that the Anglo-Saxon invaders occupied the lower part of the
ruined city, while "the Roman traders kept to their old bounds."
See also his *Village Community* (No. 105), ch. viii.

2010. PALGRAVE, FRANCIS.   Truths and fictions of the Middle
Ages.   The merchant and the friar.   Second edition, revised and
corrected.   London, 1844. 8°.

Ch. iii. throws light on the medieval constitution of London.
1st edition, 1837.

2011. PAULI, REINHOLD.   Bilder aus Alt-England.   Zweite Ausgabe.
Gotha, 1876. 8°.

Ch. xii.   London im Mittelalter.
1st edition, 1860.

2012. * ROUND, J. H.   Geoffrey de Mandeville: a study of the
anarchy.   London, 1892. 8°.

The administration of London in the 12th century, 347–73.

2013. SIMPSON, W. S.   St. Paul's cathedral and old city life: illustrations of civil and cathedral life from the 13th to the 16th centuries.
London, 1894. 8°.

2014. WALFORD, EDWARD.   Londoniana.   2 vols.   London, 1879.
8°.

London from Fitz-Stephen's point of view, ii. 18–34.

f. Charters, Laws, and Privileges.

The principal collections of charters are those of Birch and Luffman
(Nos. 2020, 2043).   Maitland, Noorthouck, and Stow (Nos. 2001, 2002,
2006) also give translations of most of the charters.   The quo warranto

proceedings of the years 1681–83 are set forth in Nos. 178–187, 195, 2024–2026, 2029, 2030, 2033, 2050, 2055, 2059. Two of the best works on the laws and privileges of London are Norton's and Pulling's (Nos. 2003, 2053).

See No. 1150.

2015. Abridgement (The) of the charter of the city of London : being every freeman's privilege. Exactly translated from the original record. . . . London, 1680. 4°.

2016. † Ancient customes (The) and approved usages of the honourable city of London. [London,] 1639. 4°.

2017. ARNOLD, RICHARD. The customs of London, otherwise called Arnold's Chronicle. . . . Reprinted from the first edition [circa 1503], with the additions included in the second [circa 1521.] London, 1811. 4°.

Contains a list of civic officers, charters, municipal regulations, and other documents.

2018. BELLAMIE, JOHN. A plea for the commonalty of London : or a vindication of their rights (which hath been long with-holden from them) in the choice of sundry city officers ; as also a justification of the power of the court of common-councell, in the making of acts, or by-laws, for the good and profit of the citizens, notwithstanding the negative votes of the lord major and aldermen. . . . In a speech delivered in common-councell, on Munday the 24th of February, 1644. London, 1645. 8°. pp. 36.

2nd edition, 1645 ; reprinted, 1727.

2019. —— Lysimachus enervatus, Bellamius reparatus : or a reply to a book entitled, A full answer to a plea for the commonaltie of London. . . . London, 1645. 8°.

See No. 2044.

2020. BIRCH, WALTER DE GRAY. The historical charters and constitutional documents of the city of London. Revised edition, with an introduction, appendix, and copious index. London, 1887. 8°.

Besides the charters, of which a translation only is printed, this book contains various acts of the common council, etc., 1666–1750 ; a large part of the work is taken from Noorthouck's *History* (No. 2002).

1st edition, " by an antiquary," 1884.

2021. BRANDON, WOODTHORPE. An inquiry into the freedom of the city of London in connection with trade, and into the laws and ordinances within the city respecting wholesale and retail traders, and the power of the corporation over persons carrying on trade within the city not being free. London, 1850. 8°.

2022. BRYDALL, JOHN. Camera regis, or a short view of London : containing the antiquity, fame . . . officers, courts, customs, franchises, etc., of that renowned city. . . . London, 1676. 8°

Another edition, "Camera regis, or the present state of London," etc., 1678. (Anon.)

2023. CALTHROP, HENRY. The liberties, usages, and customes of the city of London, confirmed by especiall acts of Parliament, with the time of their confirmation ; also divers ample and most beneficiall charters granted by King Henry the 6th, King Edward the 4th, and King Henry the 7th, not confirmed by Parliament as the other charters were. London, 1642. 4°. pp. 25.

Contains extracts from Liber Albus. Reprinted in 1674, and in Somers's Tracts (1811), v. 520–34.

2024. Case (The) of the charter of London stated : shewing i. What a corporation is ; ii. Whether a corporation may be forfeited ; iii. Whether the mayor, commonalty, and citizens have done any act in their common council whereby to forfeit their corporation and franchises. London, 1683. f°.

2025. Case (The) of the quo warranto against the city of London : wherein the judgement in that case, and the arguments in law touching the forfeitures and surrenders of charters, are reported. London, 1690. f°.

2026. Citizens' loss (The) when the charter of London is forfeited, or given up. The last will and testament of the charter of London, anno 1683. [Somers's Tracts, viii. 385–95. London, 1812. 4°.]

2027. Citizen's pocket chronicle (The) : containing a digested view of the history, antiquity, and temporal government of the city of London ; its laws, customs . . . charters, courts, companies. . . . London, 1827. 12°.

2028. City law (The), shewing the customes, franchises, liberties, priviledges, and immunities of the famous city of London ; together with the . . . severall courts ; as also the titles . . . of the severall officers and offices in London. . . . London, 1658.   8°.

2029. City (The) of London's plea to the quo warranto, (an information) brought against their charter in Michaelmas term, 1681 ; wherein it will appear that the liberties, priviledges, and customs of the said city cannot be forfeited or lost by the misdemeanor of any officer or magistrate thereof . . . also how far the commons of the said city have power of chusing and removing their sheriffs. London, 1682.   f°.

The Latin text, with a translation.

2030. City (The) of London's rejoinder to Mr. Attorney General's Replication in the quo warranto brought by him against their charter. . . . [By Sir Robert Sawyer.]   London, 1682.   f°.

The Latin text, with a translation.
See Nos. 2055, 2059.

2031. COOTE, H. C.   London notes : a lost charter ; the tradition of London Stone. *London and Middlesex Archæol. Soc.*, Transactions, v. 282–92. London, 1877.   8°.

2032. E[VELYN], J[OHN].   The charters of the city of London which have been granted by the kings and queens of England since the Conquest . . . and an abstract of the arguings in the case of the quo warranto.   London, 1745.   8°.

Translation only.
1st edition, 1738.

2033. Forfeitures (The) of London's charter : or an impartial account of the several seisures of the city charter . . . now seasonably published for the satisfaction of the inquisitive, upon the late arrest made upon the said charter by writ of quo warranto.   London, 1682.   4°.   pp. 36.

2034. Freemen (The) of London's necessary and useful companion : or the citizen's birth-right. . . . [Containing an account of] customs, grants, privileges, trades . . . proceedings in the city courts. . . . London, 1707.   12°.

Another edition, 1741.

2035. G., S. The royal charter of confirmation granted by King Charles II. to the city of London, wherein are recited verbatim all the charters to the said city. . . . London, 1680. 8°.

Translation only.

An earlier edition seems to have appeared in 1664.

2036. HUGHSON, DAVID [EDWARD PUGH]. An epitome of the privileges of London, including Southwark, as granted by royal charters. . . . London, 1816. 12°.

2037. [JACOB, GILES.] City-liberties, or the rights and privileges of freemen : being a concise abridgment of all the laws, charters, by-laws, and customs of London. . . . London, 1732. 8°.

Reprinted in 1738.

2038. Laws (The) and customs, rights, liberties, and privileges of the city of London : containing the several charters granted to the said city . . . the magistrates and officers thereof . . . the laws and customs of the city . . . several courts in London ; and the acts of Parliament. . . . Second edition. London, 1774. 12°.

1st edition, 1765.

2039. Lawyer (The) outlaw'd : or a brief answer to Mr. Hunt's defence of the charter ; with some useful remarks on the commons proceedings in the last Parliament at Westminster. In a letter to a friend. [London,] 1683. 4°.

See No. 180.

2040. LILBURNE, JOHN. The charters of London : or the second part of London's liberty in chains discovered. . . . London, 1646. 4°.

Contains the confirmation charter of Henry V., with a translation.

2041. List (A) of the by-laws of the city of London, unrepealed. Turner, mayor. A common council holden in the chamber of the Guildhall of the city of London, on Thursday the 26th day of October, 1769. It is ordered that the list of by-laws of this city, unrepealed, as prepared by the town-clerk, be printed, and a copy thereof sent to every member of the court. [Signed] Hodges. London, 1769. 8°.

2042. London's liberties : or a learned argument of law and reason . . . [Dec. 1650] before the lord mayor, court of aldermen, and common-council . . . [between counsel for the liverymen and counsel for the freemen.] Wherein the freedom of the citizens of London in their elections of their chief officers is fully debated; the most ancient charters and records examined. . . . London, 1651. 4°. pp. 38.

Reprinted, 1682; 2nd edition, 1683.

2043. LUFFMAN, JOHN. The charters of London complete; also Magna Charta and the Bill of Rights. With explanatory notes and remarks. London, 1793. 8°.

Translation only.

2044. LYSIMACHUS, IRENÆUS (pseud.). Bellamius enervatus: or a full answer to a book entitled, A plea for the commonalty of London. . . . Refuted by Irenæus Lysimachus. London, 1645. 4°.

See No. 2019.

2045. † More reflections on the city charter and writ of quo warranto. London, 1682. 4°.

2046. NEWELL, JOSEPH. Evidence and arguments before the committee for general purposes, in support of the elective franchise of the resident freemen of London: shewing that the exclusive exercise of that right by the liverymen is contrary to ancient custom and the principles of our constitution. . . . London, 1830. 8°.

2047. NORTON, GEORGE. An exposition of the privileges of the city of London in regard to claims of non-freemen to deal by wholesale within its jurisdiction. [London,] 1821. 8°.

2048. OKE, G. C. London laws. Reference to statutes and sections relating exclusively to procedure and to subjects cognizable by the magistracy of the city of London and other parts of the metropolis, and within the metropolitan police district. London, 1872. 8°.

2049. PAYNE, WILLIAM. A treatise on municipal rights . . . from the earliest period of British history to the institution of corporations in general, and that of London in particular. . . . London, 1813. 8°.

2050. Pleadings (The) and arguments and other proceedings in the court of King's Bench upon the quo warranto [34 Car. II.] touching the charter of the city of London; with the judgment

entred thereupon. The whole pleadings faithfully taken from the
record. London, 1690. f°.

Another edition, 1696.

2051. Priviledges (The) of the citizens of London, contained in
the charters granted to them by the several kings of this realm, and
confirmed by sundry Parliaments; comprehending the whole charter,
only words of form left out. . . . London, 1682. 4°.

2052. Privilegia Londinensis [Londini] : or the laws, customs, and
priviledges of the city of London; wherein are set forth all the
charters from King William I. to his present majesty King William
III.; all their general and particular customs. . . . With an exact
table to the whole. London, 1702. 8°.

Contains only an abstract of the charters. The second half of the volume is
devoted to the practice of the various city courts.

Reprinted in 1716; and again in 1723, with additions by W. Bohun.

2053. * PULLING, ALEXANDER. The laws, customs, usages, and
regulations of the city and port of London; with notes of all the
charters, ordinances, statutes, and cases. Second edition; to which
is now added a summary of the commissioners' report on the corporation of London, 1854. . . . London, [1854.] 8°.

Earlier editions, " A practical treatise on the laws, customs," etc., 1842, 1849.
See Nos. 2218, 2222.

2054. Reflections on the city-charter and writ of quo warranto ;
together with a vindication of the late sheriffs and juries. London,
1682. 4°. pp. 32.

2055. Replication (The) to the city of London's plea to the quo
warranto brought against their charter by our sovereign lord the
king in Michaelmas term, 1681. [By Sir Robert Sawyer.] London,
1682. f°.

See Nos. 2029, 2030.

2056. † Rights (The) and authority of the commons of the city of
London, in their common hall assembled, in the choice and discharge
of their sheriffs. London, 1695. f°.

2057. Rights (The) and privileges of the city of London proved
from prescription, charters, and acts of Parliament; with a large

preface, shewing how fatal the late proceedings in Westminster-Hall in dissolving corporations were to the original constitution of the English government. London, 1689. f°. pp. 34.

Earlier edition, 1682.

2058. STONE, WILLIAM. A defence of the sole and entire corporate and deliberative rights and franchises of the lord mayor, aldermen, and livery of London, in common hall assembled. . . . Dedicated to the liverymen of the several companies. London, 1797. 8°.

2059. † Sur-rejoinder (The) of Mr. Attorney-General to the rejoinder made on the behalf of the charter of the city of London. London, 1682. f°. pp. 11.

Latin, with a translation.
See No. 2030.

2060. Whereunto is annexed divers ancient customs and usages of the said city of London. Newly re-printed. London, 1670. 8°.

g. Courts and Offices.

See Nos. 2018, 2022, 2027–2029, 2034, 2038, 2042, 2052, 2056, 2058.

2061. BESANT, WALTER, and RICE, JAMES. Sir Richard Whittington, lord mayor of London. [New Plutarch Series.] London, 1881. 8°.

Introduction. The charters of London, etc.
Ch. iii. The companies and trade of London.
App. i. Mayors of London from 1364 to 1423, etc.

2062. BRANDON, WOODTHORPE. The lord mayor's court of the city of London, and the customary law of foreign attachment; with observations on the case of Cox v. the mayor of London. London, 1876. 8°.

Earlier edition, 1863, "A review of the judgements in Cox and others v. the mayor," etc.

2063. —— Notes of practice of the mayor's court of the city of London in ordinary actions; with the mayor's court Procedure Act, and the sections of the several acts of Parliament applied by the queen in council to that court. London, 1864. 8°.

2064. BREWER, THOMAS. Memoir of the life and times of John Carpenter, town clerk of London in the reigns of Henry V. and Henry VI. London, 1856. 8°.

2065. Citizen (A). An enquiry into the nature and duties of the office of inquest jurymen of the city of London, together with the by-laws of the common council and the articles of charge. Also the law for regulating the election of constables, leet and annoyance jury, for the city of Westminster, shewing the nature and duties of their office. . . . By a citizen [Joseph Newell]. London, 1824. 8°.

2066. City law (The) : or the course and practice in all manner of juridicall proceedings in the hustings in Guild-Hall, London ; Englished out of an ancient French manuscript. Also an alphabet of all the offices disposed and given by the lord mayors of London. London, 1647. 4°.

Another edition, 1658.

2067. † City remembrancer : containing animadversions upon the oaths of the ward-officers of the city of London, and the duties and charges thereby imposed. London, 1753. 8°.

2068. COKE, EDWARD. Fourth part of the Institutes of the laws of England. Fourth edition. London, 1669. f°.

The courts and jurisdiction of the city of London, 247–53.

2069. EMERSON, THOMAS. A concise treatise on the courts of law of the city of London. London, 1794. 8°.

2070. HARRISON, O. B. C. The practice of the sheriffs' court of the city of London ; with forms of the proceedings to be used by suitors, and an appendix of the statutes and rules and orders of the court. London, 1860. 8°.

2071. History (The) of the sheriffdom of the city of London and county of Middlesex : containing the original method of electing sheriffs for the said city and county; an account of the several alterations that have happened in such elections. . . . London, 1723. 8°.

2072. LEWIS, THOMAS. On the constitution, jurisdiction, and practice of the sheriffs' courts of London ; with tables of costs of prosecuting and defending actions therein, and an appendix containing abstracts of the city charters, etc., etc.   London, 1833.   8°.

2073. Lex Londinensis, or the city law : shewing the powers, customs, and practice of the several courts belonging to the famous city of London . . . together with several acts of common council. . . . London, 1680.   8°.

2074. [NOBLE, T. C.]   The lord mayor of London : a sketch of the origin, history, and antiquity of the office.   (Reprinted from the City Press.)   London, [1860.]   16°.

A brief sketch, of little value.

2075. Recorders of the city of London, 1289–1850 [and the recorder's "othe." By J. F. Firth.]   Printed by direction of the court of aldermen.   [London, 1850.]   4°.

2076. [RILEY, H. T.]   The origin and early jurisdiction of the lord mayor's court.   [London, 1863.]   12°.

A letter to the editor of the *City Press.*

2077. ROUND, J. H.   The first mayor of London.   *The Antiquary*, xv. 107–12.   London, 1887.   4°.

2078. ——— The origin of the mayoralty of London.   *Brit. Archæol. Assoc.*, Journal, l. 247–63.   London, 1893.   8°.

2079. TORR, J. H.   A review of the origin and present position of the sheriffs' court of the city of London. . . . London, 1868.   8°.

2080. WOODCOCK, [W. and R.]   Woodcock's Lives of illustrious lords mayors and aldermen of London ; with a brief history of the city of London ; also a chronological list of the lords mayors, and sheriffs of London and Middlesex, from the earliest period to the present time.   [London, 1846.]   8°.

h. Gilds and Companies.

The most useful general works are those of Hazlitt and Herbert (Nos. 2093, 2094) and the Report of 1884 (No. 2087).   Much material relating to the medieval gilds will be found in the records edited by Riley (Nos. 1978, 1979), and there are many references to the modern companies in the Calendars of State Papers (No 170).   It is difficult to separate the history of the civic corporation from that of the livery companies ; the cry for reform

M

has been directed against both: see especially Nos. 2170, 2187, 2191, 2203, 2221, 2222.

Welch (No. 1967) gives a brief account of the works relating to particular companies. Most of them are privately printed, and even the Guildhall Library has not all of them.

See Nos. 2046, 2058.

General.

2081. Ancient guilds (The) of London. *Temple Bar*, xv. 293–303. London, 1865. 8°.

Considers their early history.

2082. ARUNDELL, THOMAS. Historical reminiscences of the city of London and its livery companies. London, 1869. 8°.

Deals with their feasts, holidays, ceremonials, etc.; not a systematic history of the companies.

2083. BLAKESLEY, G. H. The London livery companies' commission: a comment on the majority report. London, 1885. 8°. pp. 63.

See No. 2087.

2084. Chartered guilds (The) of London. *Westminster Review*, New Series, lii. 1–30. London, 1877. 8°.

2085. City companies (The). *British Quarterly Review*, lxx. 130–57. London, 1879. 8°.

2086. City companies (The) and their property: a plea for fair play. London, 1886. 8°.

2087. * City of London livery companies' commission. Report and appendix. *Parl. Papers*, 1884, vol. xxxix. 5 pts. London, 1884. f°.

For discussions of this report, see Contemporary Review, xlvii. 1–24; Edinburgh Review, clxii 181–204; Macmillan's Magazine, li. 266–77; National Review, v. 268–79; Quarterly Review, clix. 40–75.

2088. COOTE, H. C. Ordinances of some secular guilds of London, from 1354 to 1496. Reprinted from the Transactions of the London and Middlesex Archæological Society [vol. iv.]. By H. C. Coote. To which are added ordinances of St. Margaret, Lothbury, 1456. . . . By J. R. Daniel-Tyssen. London, 1871. 8°.

2089. COOTE, H. C. London notes: the English gild of knights and their socn. *London and Middlesex Archæol. Soc.*, Transactions, v. 477–93. London, 1880. 8°.

2090. Corporation commission (The) and the municipal companies of London. Letters of Civis [John Coles] on the opinions of Sir James Scarlett, Mr. Follett, and Mr. Rennoll, reprinted from the Morning Chronicle. London, 1834. 8°.

2091. DIBDIN, L. T. The livery companies of London : being a review of the report of the London livery companies' commission. London, 1886. 8°.

See No. 2087.

2092. FRANKS, R. H. Corporation abuses. A letter to the right honorable lord Viscount Althorp, on the justice and necessity of reforming the livery companies of the city of London. . . . Also a copy of his petition to the House of Commons. . . . London, 1833. 8°.

See No. 2181.

2093. * HAZLITT, W. C. The livery companies of the city of London : their origin, character, development, and social and political importance. London and New York, 1892. 8°.

Contains much information relating to the various companies. The introduction contains a digest of a part of the parliamentary returns of 1884 (No. 2087).

Valuable, though not the result of original research.

2094. * HERBERT, WILLIAM. The history of the twelve great livery companies of London, principally compiled from their grants and records; with an historical essay, and accounts of each company, its origin, constitution . . . with attested copies and translations of the companies' charters. 2 vols. London, 1836–37. 8°.

The best general history of the twelve great companies.

2095. MILDMAY, WILLIAM. The method and rule of proceeding upon all elections, polls, and scrutinies, at common halls and wardmotes, within the city of London. By Sir William Mildmay. [1743; 2nd edition, 1768.] With additional notes on wardmote elections; an historical review of the city electoral franchises, and of the incorporated mysteries, with their liverymen, electors of London. By H. K. S. Causton. . . . London, 1841. 12°.

2096. PHILLIPS, J. R. The mediæval corporation and companies of the city. *Gentleman's Magazine*, xv. 717–25. London, 1875. 8°.

2097. † Royal commission (The). The London city livery companies' vindication. London, 1885. 8°.

See No. 2087.

2098. S., L. B. The city livery companies and their corporate property. London, 1885. 8°. pp. 71.

2099. SCHULTES, HENRY. An inquiry into the elective franchise of the citizens of London, and the general rights of the livery. London, 1822. 8°.

Valuable.

2100. TAYLOR, J. R. "Behold, the spoiler cometh," "Dacoitee in excelsis!" Reform your city guilds. London, 1872. 8°. pp. 36.

2101. Trade guilds (The) of the city of London. *Fraser's Magazine*, New Series, xix. 395–405. London, 1879. 8°.

Favors reform.

2101a. † WOOLACOTT, J. E. The curse of turtledom : exposé of the livery companies. London, 1894. 8°.

Armourers.

2102. MORLEY, TIMOTHY. Some account of the worshipful company of armourers and brasiers in the city of London. . . . London, 1878. 4°.

Barber-Surgeons.

2103. LAMBERT, GEORGE. The barbers' company. A paper read before the British Archæological Association . . . on Saturday, October 15th, 1881. . . . Second edition. [London, 1881.] 8°. pp. 67.

Also printed in the Transactions of the London and Middlesex Archæological Society, vi. 123–89.

2104. PETTIGREW, T. J. History of the barber-surgeons of London. *Brit. Archæol. Assoc.*, Journal, viii. 95–130. London, 1853. 8°.

2105. SOUTH, J. F. Memorials of the craft of surgery in England ; from materials compiled by John F. South. Edited by D'Arcy Power, with introduction by Sir James Paget. With coloured plates and engravings. London, 1886. 8°.

2106. * YOUNG, SIDNEY. The annals of the barber-surgeons of
London. Compiled from their records and other sources. London,
1890. 4°.

Contains ordinances, 1387–1709; extracts from court minutes, 1550–1863;
accounts, 1603–1785, etc.

Butchers.

2107. DAW, JOSEPH. A sketch of the early history of the worshipful company of butchers of London. [London,] 1869. 8°.

Carpenters.

2108. JUPP, E. B. An historical account of the worshipful company of carpenters of the city of London. Compiled chiefly from
records in their possession. London, 1848. 8°.

A detailed account of the history of the company, with extracts from its records,
1455–1886.
Other editions, 1887, 1889.

Clockmakers.

2109. ATKINS, S. E., and OVERALL, W. H. Some account of the
worshipful company of clockmakers of the city of London. [London,]
1881. 8°.

Contains a translation of its charter, 1631, the by-laws of 1632, and extracts
from other records of the company.

2110. Charter and bye-laws of the worshipful company of clockmakers of the city of London, incorporated 1631, 7th Charles I.
London, 1825. 8°.

Clothworkers.

2111. Charters (The) and letters patent granted by the kings and
queens of England to the clothworkers' company [1480–1688.]
Transcribed from the originals in the possession of the company.
London, 1881. 4°.

2112. † Ordinances of the clothworkers, fullers, and shearmen ;
with a general account of their charters and constitution from Edward
IV. to Elizabeth. n. d. 4°.

2113. Ordinances (The) of the clothworkers' company ; together
with those of the ancient guilds or fraternities of the fullers and shear-

men of the city of London [1480–1639.] Transcribed from the originals in the possession of the company. London, 1881. 4°.

2114. Towse, W. B. Selections from the rules and orders of the court of the clothworkers' company; together with the ordinances or bye-laws sanctioned by the judges in the year 1639. [London,] 1840. 8°.

Coopers.

2115. Firth, J. F. Coopers' company, London. Historical memoranda, charters, documents, and extracts from the records of the corporation and books of the company, 1396–1848. London, 1848. 8°.

Curriers.

2116. [Norris, E. S.] A short history of the curriers' company. London, 1874. 16°.

Of little value.

Cutlers.

2117. † Cheesewright, R. J. A short account of the worshipful company of cutlers. London, 1882.

Dyers.

2118. Robins, E. C. Some account of the history and antiquities of the worshipful company of dyers, London. [London, 1880.] 4°.

See Transactions of the London and Middlesex Archæological Society, 1880, v. 441–76.

Founders.

2119. Stahlschmidt, J. C. L. Notes from an old city account book. *Archæol. Journal*, xliii. 162–76. London, 1886. 8°.

Contains extracts from an account book of the company of founders, 1497–1576.

2120. Williams, William M. Annals of the worshipful company of founders of the city of London. Compiled, with notes and illustrations, by W. M. Williams, master, 1852–3 and 1853–4. [London, 1867.] 8°.

Framework-Knitters.

2121. † Overall, H. C. The framework-knitters. London, 1879.

Goldsmiths.

2122. CHAFFERS, WILLIAM. Gilda aurifabrorum : a history of English goldsmiths and plateworkers, and their marks stamped on plate copied in fac-simile. . . . Also historical accounts of the goldsmiths' company. . . . London, 1883. 8°.

Grocers.

2123. Grocers' company. Copies in fac-simile of MS. records, A. D. 1345 to 1423. Transcribed and translated by J. A. Kingdon. [London, 1883.] 4°.

Without title-page.

2124. * —— Facsimile of MS. archives of the worshipful company of grocers of the city of London, A. D. 1345–1463. . . . Edited with introduction by John Abernethy Kingdon, master of the company, 1883–4. 2 pts. London, 1886. 4°.

2125. HEATH, J. B. Some account of the worshipful company of grocers of the city of London. Second edition. London, 1854. 8°.

The appendix contains extracts from the accounts of the company, and other documents, from 1349 to 1617.
The best history of this company.
Other editions, 1829, 1869.

2126. [RAVENHILL, WILLIAM.] A short account of the company of grocers, from their original ; together with their case and condition. . . . London, 1689. 4°.

A brief account.

2127. Tentative search (A) for the source and course of the grocers' company prior to its first charter. London. n. d. 8°.

Horners.

2128. COMPTON, C. H. The history of the worshipful company of horners of London. London, 1882. 8°.

Of little value.

Ironmongers.

2129. * NICHOLL, JOHN. Some account of the worshipful company of ironmongers. Compiled from their own records and other authentic sources of information. Second edition. London, 1866. 4°.

1st edition, 1851. An appendix to the 2nd edition was published, without date.

2130. NOBLE, T. C.   A brief history of the worshipful company of ironmongers, London, A. D. 1351–1889; with an appendix containing some account of the blacksmiths' company.   London, 1889.   8°.

Leathersellers.

2131. * BLACK, W. H.   History and antiquities of the worshipful company of leathersellers of the city of London; with fac-similes of charters and other illustrations.   London, 1871.   f°.

Loriners.

2132. † Charter (The) and by-laws of the loriners' company. London, 1743.   8°.

2133. † LATCHFORD, BENJAMIN.   The loriner: opinions and observations on bridle-bits, etc.   London, 1871.

The appendix contains ordinances and other documents relating to the company of loriners.

Masons.

2134. CONDER, EDWARD.   Records of the hole crafte and fellowship of masons; with a chronicle of the worshipful company of masons of the city of London. . . .   London, 1894.   8°.

Contains extracts from the records of the company, 1619–1894.

Mercers.

2135. Charters (The), ordinances, and bye-laws of the mercers' company [1393–1808.]   London, 1881.   f°.

2136. NICHOLS, J. G.   Remarks on the mercers and other trading companies of London, followed by some account of the records of the mercers' company.   *London and Middlesex Archæol. Soc.*, Transactions, iv. 131–50.   London, 1871.   8°.

Merchant Tailors.

2137. *[CLODE, C. M.]   Memorials of the guild of merchant taylors of the fraternity of St. John the Baptist in the city of London. . . . London, 1875.   8°.

Contains copious extracts from its accounts, ordinances, etc., 1397–1873.

2138. * CLODE, C. M.　The early history of the guild of merchant taylors of the fraternity of St. John the Baptist, London . . . [to 1613.] 2 vols.　London, 1888.　8°.

The appendix contains various documents, 1327–1620.

2139. † Fac-simile of ancient deeds of the merchant taylors, 1331– 1531.　London, 1889.

2140. Free Inquirer (The) into the rights, privileges, franchises, property, bequests, funds, etc. of the fraternity of merchant tailors. . . . [Principally by R. H. Franks.]　March — Oct. 1831.　London, 1831.　8°.

A monthly periodical. The last three numbers bear the title " The Free In-quirer into the rights, privileges, gifts, and properties of the incorporated com-panies of the city of London."

Needlemakers.

2141. [PRICE, J. E.]　The worshipful company of needlemakers of the city of London ; with a list of the court of assistants and livery. London, 1876.　4°.

Pewterers.

2142. Anno quarto Henrici VIII.　These be the statutes estab-lished in divers Parliaments for the mistery of the pewterers of Lon-don . . . with the renewing and confirming of the same statutes. London, [1684.]　4°.

Poulters.

2143. The charter of the worshipful company of poulters, London ; its orders, ordinances, and constitution ; also acts granted by the cor-poration of London ; with a list of the estates . . . of the said com-pany.　[London, 1872.]　4°.

Saddlers.

2144. * SHERWELL, J. W.　A descriptive and historical account of the guild of saddlers of the city of London.　[London,] 1889.　8°.

Contains many extracts from the records of the company.

Salters.

2145. [GILLESPY, THOMAS.]　Some account of the worshipful com-pany of salters, its members and benefactors, from the earliest known

period of its history until the opening of the new hall, on the 23rd
May, 1827. Compiled from various authors by an old salter. London, 1827. 8°.

A brief account.

Shipwrights.

2146. SHARPE, R. R. A short account of the worshipful company
of shipwrights. London, 1876. 8°. pp. 26.

Skinners.

2147. WADMORE, J. F. Some account of the history and antiquity of the worshipful company of skinners, London. London,
1876. 8°.

Reprinted from the Transactions of the London and Middlesex Archæological Society, v. 92–182.

Stationers.

2148. Charter and grants of the company of stationers of the city
of London now in force, containing a plain and rational account of
the freemen's rights and privileges. . . . London, 1825. 8°. pp. 64.

Earlier edition, 1741.

2149. NICHOLS, J. G. Historical notices of the worshipful company of stationers of London ; with descriptions of their hall, pictures,
and plate, and of their ancient seal of arms. [London,] 1861. 4°.
pp. 25.

Reprinted from the Transactions of the London and Middlesex Archæological
Society, ii. 37–61.

2150. RIVINGTON, C. R. The records of the worshipful company
of stationers. Westminster, 1883. 8°.

Reprinted from the Transactions of the London and Middlesex Archæological
Society, vi. 280–340.
Second edition, 1893, in vol. v. of Arber's work (No. 2151).

2151. * Transcript (A) of the registers of the company of stationers
of London, 1554–1640. Edited by Edward Arber. 5 vols. London, 1875–94. 4°.

Contains the detailed cash accounts; vol. i. also contains the ordinances of the
company, 1678–82.

2152. [WELCH, CHARLES.]   A brief history of the worshipful company of stationers.   London, [1880.]   8°.

Reprinted from the *Stationery Trades Journal*.

Tin-Plate Workers.

2153. EBBLEWHITE, E. A.   A chronological history of the worshipful company of tin-plate workers, alias wire-workers, of the city of London . . . [1670–1895.]   London, 1896.   4°.

Tylers and Bricklayers.

2154. † The book of ordinances [begun in 1570] belonging to the company of tylers and bricklayers incorporated within the city of London. . . . London.   n. d.   4°.

Vintners.

2155. MILBOURN, THOMAS.   The vintners' company: their muniments, plate, and eminent members, with some account of the ward of vintry.   [London,] 1888.   4°.

An enlargement of the paper mentioned in No. 2159.

2156. NICHOLS, J. G.   The muniments of the vintners' company. *London and Middlesex Archæol. Soc.*, Transactions, iii. 432–47. London, 1870.   8°.

See No. 2159.

2157. OVERALL, W. H.   Some account of the ward of vintry and the vintners' company.   *London and Middlesex Archæol. Soc.*, Transactions, iii. 404–431.   London, 1870.   8°.

See No. 2159.

2158. SHONE, WILLIAM.   The laws and privileges of the vintners, incorporated by Edward III. and confirmed by Henry VI. in 1436 and in successive reigns.   Extracted from authority.   London, 1818.   8°.

2159. Vintners' company (The).   Some account of the ward of vintry and the vintners' company.   By W. H. Overall. — The muniments of the company.   By J. G. Nichols. — Biographical notices of some eminent members of the company.   By Thomas Milbourn. . . .

From the Transactions of the London and Middlesex Archæological
Society, vol. iii.   [London, 1870.]   8°.

See Nos. 2155–2157.

Watermen.

2160. HUMPHERUS, HENRY.   History of the origin and progress of
the company of watermen and lightermen of the river Thames ; with
numerous historical notes (1514–1859).   3 vols.   London, [1874–
86.]   8°.

Weavers.

2161. Facsimile of the ancient book of the weavers' company, the
original of which is in the possession of the company.   London,
[1885.]   f°.

Valuable.

Wheelwrights.

2162. SCOTT, JAMES B.   A short account of the wheelwrights' company.   London, 1884.   4°.   pp. 72.

Wiredrawers.

2163. STEWART, HORACE.   History of the company of gold and
silver wyre-drawers.   London, 1891.   4°.

The company was incorporated in 1693.

i. Municipal Reform.

The parliamentary reports, especially those of 1837, 1854, and 1884 (Nos.
2087, 2221, 2222), throw much light on this subject.   Various reform bills
have been introduced during the past fifty years, notably in the years 1852,
1856, 1858–60, 1867–70, 1875, 1880, 1884–85 ; the discussions in Parliament
are set forth in Hansard's *Debates*.   The strongest plea in favor of reform
will be found in Firth's *Municipal London* (No. 2187); and the ablest
defence of the corporation in Scott's *Vindication* (No. 2229).

See Nos. 2083–2101a.

For the periodical literature, see Poole's *Index*.

2164. ACLAND, JAMES.   Proceedings under the royal commission
of inquiry into the constitution and conduct of the corporation of the
city of London.   From the short-hand notes of Messrs. Gurney.
Edited, explained, and illustrated.   London, [1854.]   8°.

2165. ALLEN, W. F.   The corporation of London : its rights and privileges.   London, 1858.   8°.

A defence of the corporation.

2166. Annual report (First—Ninth) of the metropolitan municipal association for promoting the establishment of a London municipality. London, 1867–75.   8°.

2167. ARNOLD, ARTHUR.   Social politics.   London, 1878.   8°.

Ch. v.   The government of London.
Ch. vi.   The city.

2168. BUXTON, CHARLES.   Self-government for London : the leading ideas on which a constitution for London should be based.   A letter to the right hon. H. A. Bruce, M. P.   London, 1869.   8°.

2169. BUXTON, SYDNEY.   Handbook to political questions of the day. . . . Fifth edition.   London, 1885.   8°.

London municipal reform, 81–93.
1st edition, 1880.

2170. CARPENTER, WILLIAM.   The corporation of London, as it is and as it should be : comprising some account of the legislative and executive bodies, the incorporated companies, and municipal franchises. . . . London, 1847.   12°.

2171. CHADWICK, EDWIN.   On the evils of disunity in central and local administration, especially with relation to the metropolis. . . . London, 1885.   8°.

2172. Citizen (A).   Corporation reform : the question considered by a citizen.   London, 1883.   8°.

2173. Citizen (A).   The necessity of reforming the corporation of London demonstrated by a plain statement of facts, showing its monopoly, corruption, abuse, and profligate expenditure ; to which is added an account of the income of the corporation for 1841. . . . By a citizen.   London, 1843.   16°.

2174. Citizen (A).   Six letters on corporation reform.   By a citizen [Hume Williams].   Reprinted from the Morning Advertiser. London, 1882.   8°.   pp. 74.

2175. † City corporation (The) : an indictment.   [By O. D.] [London,] 1877.   8°.

2176. City (The) of London. "Strike but hear." London, 1884. 8°. pp. 171.

A defence of the corporation.

2177. CIVIS. The corporation of London and the government bill: a bird's eye view of the dispute between a liberal government and an ancient corporation. London, [1856.] 8°.

2178. CLARK, J. W. Concerning London government and the proposed "clean sweep" of local institutions. London, 1884. 8°. pp. 23.

A protest against reform.

2179. CLARKE, HENRY. London municipal reform. An address delivered at the Bishopsgate ward club. London, 1882. 8°.

An appendix appeared in 1884.

2180. CONINGTON, HENRY. Reform at any price? A question about the London Corporation Bill and the commissioners' report. London, 1856. 8°.

2181. Corporation commission (The). Report delivered to the committee in aid of corporate reform, November 8, 1833: containing a statement of some of the evils and abuses existing in the corporation and in the municipal trading companies of the city of London. [By R. H. Franks.] London, 1833. 8°.

See No. 2092.

2182. Decline (The) and fall of the corporation of London. *Fraser's Magazine,* xlix. 3–18, 198–209, 318–29, 453–62, 561–71, 687–97. London, 1854. 8°.

See also ibid., New Series, 1876, xiii. 769–85: "On the Government of London."

2183. DEXTER, J. T. The government of London. London, 1875. 8°. pp. 55.

A plea for reform.

2184. Elections (The) of monster municipality: a Paris lesson for London people. By a member of Parliament. [London,] 1884. 8°.

2185. Extracts from letters by "Nemesis" [A. F. Robbins]. Reprinted from the "Weekly Dispatch." *City Guilds' Reform Assoc.,* Reform Fly Sheets, Nos. 3–4. London, 1876. 8°.

2186. Facts for Londoners: an exhaustive collection of statistical and other facts relating to the metropolis; with suggestions for reform on socialist principles. [Fabian Tracts, No. 8.] London, 1889. 8°.

2187. * FIRTH, J. F. B. Municipal London: or London government as it is, and London under a municipal council. London, 1876. 8°.

The most elaborate work in favor of reform. See *Westminster Review*, 1876, l. 188–225.
Firth has a long essay on the same subject in the Cobden Club Essays (No. 218), which was also separately printed, 1882.

2188. —— Reform of London government and of city guilds. London, 1888. 8°.

2189. FORTESCUE, HUGH (Viscount EBRINGTON). Representative self-government for the metropolis. A letter to Viscount Palmerston from Viscount Ebrington. London, 1854. 8°.

2190. FRASER, WILLIAM. London self-governed. London, [1866.] 8°. pp. 103.

2191. GILBERT, WILLIAM. The city: an inquiry into the corporation, its livery companies, and the administration of their charities and endowments. London, 1877. 8°.

A bitter attack on the corporation and the companies.

2192. GOMME, G. L. The future government of London. *Contemporary Review*, lxvi. 746–60. London, 1894. 8°.

2193. Government (The) of London. *Westminster Review*, New Series, xlix. 93–123. London, 1876. 8°.

Favors reform.

2194. GRIP. The monster municipality: or Gog and Magog reformed. A dream. By "Grip." London, 1882. 8°.

2195. GUYOT, YVES. L'organisation municipale de Paris et de Londres, présent et avenir. Suivi des discours prononcés au banquet du 19 Mars. Avec six graphiques. Paris, 1883. 12°.

2196. HARE, THOMAS. London municipal reform. A reprint, with additions, of several papers thereon. London, 1882. 8°. pp. 36.

See also his paper in *Macmillan's Magazine*, 1862, vii. 441–7.

2197. HARRISON, FREDERIC. The amalgamation of London [i. e. the city and the county of London]. *Contemporary Review*, lxvi. 737–45. London, 1894. 8°.

2198. [HICKSON, W. E.] The apologists of city administration. Reprinted from the Westminster Review for June, 1844. (With an appendix upon city freedoms). London, [1844.] 8°.

2199. [———] City administration. . . . Case of the non-freemen. . . . From the Westminster Review [xliii. 193–240]. Londo [1845.] 8°.

2200. [———] The corporation of London and municipal reform. From the Westminster Review for May, 1843, No. 77. [London, 1843.] 8°.

Deals with the financial side of the question.

2201. HOBHOUSE, ARTHUR. The government of London. *Contemporary Review*, xli. 404–16. London, 1882. 8°.

Favors reform.

2202. How London is governed. *The Municipal Review and Local Government Record*, Dec. 1883—Jan. 1884. London, 1883–84.

2203. London Corporation Bill. A short statement of the proceedings before the select committee of the House of Commons upon the London Corporation Bill; with the speech of Sir W. B. Riddell, Bart., on behalf of the livery companies of London, in opposition to such bill. London, 1852. 8°.

2204. London municipal government. Opinions of the press. 6 pts. London, 1884. 8°.

2205. Londoner (A). The London Government Bill: some observations on its scope and probable working. London, 1883. 8°.

2206. MACKAY, CHARLES. The local government of the metropolis. [London, 1884.] 8°.

Without title-page.

2207. Metropolitan municipal association. Extracts from second report on municipal corporations (1837) ; from report of commissioners [of 1854, 1861, and 1866] . . . in favor of the extension of municipal institutions to the metropolis. London, 1867. 8°.

See Nos. 2221–2224.

2208. Municipal government (The) of London. *Edinburgh Review,* cxlii. 549–85. Edinburgh, 1875. 8°.

Favors reform.

2209. Municipal reform for London. *Gentleman's Magazine,* xiv. 31–42. London, 1875. 8°.

Favors reform.

2210. NORTON, GEORGE. An address to the citizens of London on the pending Corporation Bill. London, [1856.] 8°.

2211. Observations upon a bill now before Parliament, called "A bill for the better regulation of the corporation of the city of London;" addressed to the rate-payers by the lord mayor, aldermen, and common council of the city of London, in common council assembled. London, 1858. 8°.

2212. O'DONNELL, F. H. Letter on the London government. Reprinted from the "Morning Post." [London,] 1884. 12°.

2213. P., H. A. The truth about the London Government Bill. London, [1884.] 8°.

2214. PEARSON, CHARLES. The substance of an address delivered by Charles Pearson, Esq., at a public meeting [1843] . . . containing a brief history of the corporation of London. . . . London, 1844. 8°.

2215. Proceedings in the bills [21 Vict., 1857–58] for the regulation of the corporation of London. [London,] 1858. 8°.

2216. Public opinion on the London Government Bill: being extracts from the principal newspapers in London and the provinces, and from the speeches of public men. London, 1884. 8°.

2217. PULLING, ALEXANDER. The city of London corporation inquiry. London, 1854. 8°.

Reprinted from the *Law Review.*
See No. 2222.

2218. —— The London Corporation Reform Act, 1849, and the City Election Act, 1725, with introductory comments, explanatory notes, and the statutes verbatim: being a supplement to A practical treatise on the laws, customs, usages, and regulations of the city and port of London. London, 1849. 8°.

See No. 2053.

2219. PULLING, ALEXANDER. Observations on the disputes at present arising in the corporation of the city of London, and on the power of internal reform possessed by the citizens in common council. London, 1847. 8°.

2220. Remarks on the speech of A. S. Ayrton, M. P., in reference to the corporation of London; with observations on his scheme for a new and enlarged municipality. London, 1860. 8°.

2221. * Report (Second) of the commissioners appointed to inquire into the municipal corporations in England and Wales: London and Southwark; London companies. *Parl. Papers*, 1837, vol. xxv. [London,] 1837. f°.

See No. 60.

2222. * Report of the commissioners appointed to inquire into the existing state of the corporation of the city of London, and to collect information respecting its constitution, order, and government, etc.; together with minutes of evidence and appendix. *Parl. Papers*, 1854, vol. xxvi. [London,] 1854. f°.

2223. Report (First — Third) from the select committee appointed to inquire into the local taxation and government of the metropolis, and the local administration of justice therein; together with the minutes of evidence and appendix. *Parl. Papers*, 1861, vol. viii. [London,] 1861. f°.

2224. Report (First — Second) from the select committee on metropolitan local government, etc.; together with the proceedings of the committee, minutes of evidence, and appendix. *Parl. Papers*, 1866, vol. xiii. [London,] 1866. f°.

2225. Reports from the select committee on metropolitan local government. . . . *Parl. Papers*, 1867, vol. xii. [London,] 1867. f°.

2226. * Report of the commissioners appointed to consider the proper conditions under which the amalgamation of the city and county of London can be effected, and to make specific and practical proposals for the purpose ; with maps illustrative of the report [and with appendices]. 2 vols. *Parl. Papers*, 1894, vols. xvii.–xviii. London, 1894. f°.

2227. Resolutions relative to the London Corporation Reform Bill ; passed in the city of London. [London,] 1856. 8°.

Resolutions against the bill.

2228. SANGSTER, THOMAS. Political ranters : a reply to the question, " Why should London wait?" and a few words with Sir John Bennett. . . . London, 1884. 8°.

2229. SCOTT, BENJAMIN. A statistical vindication of the city of London : or fallacies exploded and figures explained. London, 1867. 8°.

An elaborate defence of the corporation.
2nd and 3rd editions, 1867, 1877.

2230. [——] Municipal government of London. [London, 1882.] 8°. pp. 32.

Reprinted from the *Contemporary Review*, 1882, xli. 308–24.
2nd edition, 1884.

2231. SEYMOUR, DANBY. Mr. Seymour's speech at St. Pancras Club. *City Guilds' Reform Assoc.*, Reform Fly Sheets, No. 1. London, 1876. 8°.

2232. SMITH, J. T. The metropolis and its municipal administration : showing the essentials of a sound system of municipal self-government, as applicable to all town populations ; and the subject-matters that come properly within the range of municipal administration. London, 1852. 8°.

2233. "Stand fast." Will the citizens consent to the surrender of their charters to a foreign body? What says Chief Baron [Fitzroy] Kelly? London, [1867.] 8°.

2234. Statement of the corporation of London, read before the commissioners of inquiry at the Privy Council Office, on Wednesday, the 11th of January, 1854. London, 1854. 8°.

2235. STEPHENSON, H. F. A letter to the rt. hon. James Abercrombie, M. P., chairman of the committee on corporations. London, 1833. 8°.

Deals especially with the trade restrictions imposed upon non-freemen. A plea for reform.

2236. TORRENS, W. M. The government of London. Reprinted from the Nineteenth Century [viii. 766–86.] London, 1884. 8°.

2237. VALLANCE, H. W. The substance of the speech of H. Wellington Vallance, Esq., at a special court of common council, on Friday, the 11th April, 1856, to consider the bill for the regulation of the corporation of London. [London,] 1856. 8°.

2238. WEBB, SIDNEY. The reform of London. Published by the Eighty Club. London, 1892. 8°. pp. 35.
Another edition, 1894.

j. London County Council.

Reports of the proceedings of the London county council have been published since 1891, and verbatim reports of the debates since 1893.
For the Act of 1888, creating county councils, see above, Pt. I. § 7 *d.*
See also Nos. 2197, 2226.

2239. ACWORTH, W. M. The London county council. *Nineteenth Century,* xxv. 418–30. London, 1889. 8°.

2240. BEACHCROFT, R. M., and HARRIS, H. P. The work and policy of the London county council. *National Review,* xxiv. 828–46. London, 1895. 8°.

2241. BUXTON, SYDNEY. Handbook to political questions of the day. Ninth edition. London, 1892. 8°.
Municipal home rule for London, 181–98.

2242. † By-laws and regulations of the London county council. London, 1894. 8°.

2243. County counsel. *Quarterly Review,* clxx. 226–56. London, 1890. 8°.

2244. † FIRTH, J. F. B., and SIMPSON, E. R. London government under the Local Government Act. London, 1889. 8°.

2245. Fox, G. L. The London county council and its work. Reprinted from the Yale Review, May, 1895. [New Haven,] 1895. 8°.

2246. GOMME, G. L. The London county council: its duties and powers, according to the Local Government Act of 1888. London, 1888. 8°.
A digest of the act.

2247. HOBHOUSE, Lord. The London county council and its assailants. *Contemporary Review*, lxi. 332–49. London, 1892. 8°.

A defence of the county council.

2248. London county council. A review of the first year's work, in a series of addresses by the Earl of Roseberry, chairman of the council, in April and May, 1890. [London, 1890.] 8°. pp. 54.

2249. London county council (The). i. The impeachment. By T. G. Fardell. ii. The defence. By Charles Harrison. *New Review*, vi. 257–72. London, 1892. 8°.

2250. London county council (The). i. Towards a commune. By John Burns. ii. Towards common sense. By R. E. Prothero. *Nineteenth Century*, xxxi. 496–524. London, 1892. 8°.

2251. LUBBOCK, JOHN. A few words on the government of London. *Fortnightly Review*, lvii. 158–72. London, 1892. 8°.

A review of the work of the county council.

2252. LUBBOCK, JOHN, and WHITMORE, C. A. London government. *National Review*, xxiv. 530–45. London, 1894. 8°.

2253. Municipal administration of London. *Edinburgh Review*, clxxv. 500–17. London, 1892. 8°.

2254. † New London : her parliament and its work. London, 1895. 4°. pp. 64.

2255. SAUNDERS, WILLIAM. History of the first London county council (1889–91). London, 1892. 8°.

A valuable detailed account.

2256. WEBB, SIDNEY. The London programme. London, 1891. 8°.

2257. —— The work of the London county council. *Contemporary Review*, lxvii. 130–52. London, 1895. 8°.

2258. WHALE, GEORGE. Greater London and its government. London, 1888. 8°.

Describes the county council, the city of London, vestries, local boards, etc.

k. Miscellaneous.

2259. † Addresses, remonstrances, and petitions to the throne . . . [from the aldermen, common council, and livery, since 1760]; with the answers thereto. London, 1865. 8°.

2260. † BUGNOTTET, G. Études administratives et judiciaires sur Londres et l'Angleterre. 2 vols. Paris, 1889–90. 8°.

2261. COCHIN, AUGUSTIN. Le régime municipal des capitales, — Paris, Londres, Berlin, Vienne, Bruxelles, Genève, New-York. *L'Académie des Sciences morales et politiques,* Séances et Travaux, xciv., 223–76. Paris, 1870. 8°.

Compares the government of London with that of other European cities, etc.

2262. FAIRHOLT, F. W. Gog and Magog, the giants in Guildhall: their real and legendary history; with an account of other civic giants, at home and abroad. London, 1859. 8°.

2263. —— Lord mayors' pageants: being collections towards a history of these annual celebrations, with specimens of the descriptive pamphlets published by the city poets. *Percy Society.* 2 pts. London, 1843–44. 8°.

2264. GNEIST, RUDOLF. Die Stadtverwaltung der City von London. Vortrag gehalten im Berliner Handwerkerverein am 17. Jan., 1867. Berlin, 1867. 8°. pp. 52.

A brief sketch of the history of the city, with a good short account of its government in 1867.

2265. [NICHOLS, J. G.] London pageants. i. Accounts of sixty royal processions and entertainments in the city of London. . . . ii. A bibliographical list of lord mayors' pageants. London, 1831. 8°

Another edition, with additions, 1837.
Nichols also printed some essays on this subject in the *Gentleman's Magazine,* 1824–25, vols. xciv.–xcv.

2266. Opinions of the officers of the corporation of the city of London, and other opinions. For the use of the committee of the whole court. [London,] 1847. 8°.

Opinions as to the body vested with the municipal government, etc. Contains many references to the old laws of London.

2267. Price, J. E.　A descriptive account of the Guildhall of the city of London: its history and association. . . . London, 1886. 4°.

Useful, but unscholarly.

2268. † Representation (The) of London and Westminster examined and considered, wherein appears the antiquity of most of the burroughs in England, shewing that Middlesex is represented but one tenth part of its due proportion.　London, 1702.　4°.

2269. Smith, J. T.　Centralization or representation?　A letter to the metropolitan sanatory commissioners. . . . Second edition.　London, 1848.　8°.

Ch. i. Constitution of the corporation of London, etc.

2270. —— The Metropolitan Local Management Act, 1855; with an introduction, copious practical notes. . . . London, 1855. 12°.

2271. —— What is the corporation of London? and who are the freemen?　London, 1850.　8°.　pp. 44.

2272. Woolrych, E. H.　The metropolis local management acts; to which is added an appendix containing other statutes relating to the powers and duties of the metropolitan board of works, vestries, and district boards of the metropolis; with table of cases, notes, and index.　Third edition, by L. Goodrich.　London, 1888.　8°.

Earlier editions, 1863, 1880.

LONDONDERRY.

2273. Hempton, John.　The siege and history of Londonderry. Edited by John Hempton.　Londonderry, etc., 1861.　12°.

Of little value for municipal history.

2274. Ordnance survey of the county of Londonderry.　Vol. i. Memoir of the city and northwestern liberties of Londonderry.　Parish of Templemore.　Dublin, 1837.　4°.

The work was compiled under the direction of Colonel T. Colby.　The historical and topographical sections were drawn up by G. Petrie, assisted by John O'Donovan.

2275. Simpson, Robert.　The annals of Derry: showing the rise and progress of the town from the earliest accounts on record to the plantation under King James I., 1613, and thence of the city of Londonderry to the present time. Londonderry, 1847. 12°.

2276. Translation of the charter granted by King Charles II. to the mayor and community and citizens of Londonderry. . . . London, 1793. 8°.

LOOE, EAST AND WEST.

2277. BOND, THOMAS. Topographical and historical sketches of the boroughs of East and West Looe. . . . London, 1823. 8°.

2278. MEREWETHER, H. A. Report of the case of the borough of West Looe, in the county of Cornwall, tried before a committee of the House of Commons, April 18, 1822. . . . London, 1823. 8°.

LOSTWITHIEL.

2278a. † F. M. H. Memorials of Lostwithiel. Truro, 1891. 8°.

LOUGHBOROUGH.

2279. FLETCHER, W. G. D. Chapters in the history of Loughborough. Loughborough, 1883. 8°.

Ch. ii.   Medieval gilds.
Ch. iv.   Churchwardens' accounts.
This little book is made up in large part of extracts from records. Loughborough received a charter of incorporation in 1888.

LOUTH.

2280. Charters (The) of the corporation of the town of Louth, Lincolnshire, and free grammar school of Edward VI. [Edited by R. Paddison and F. Wilson.] London, 1831. 8°.

2281. Louth old corporation records : being extracts from the accounts, minutes, and memoranda of the warden and six assistants [1551–1835] . . . and other ancient documents relating to the town. Compiled by R. W. Goulding. Louth, 1891. 8°.

The best book relating to Louth.

2282. Notitiæ Ludæ, or notices of Louth. [By R. S. Bayley.] Louth and London, 1834. 8°.

LUDLOW.

    a. Town Records, Nos. 2283–2288.
    b. General Histories, Nos. 2289–2292.
    c. Gilds, Nos. 2293–2296.
    d. Parliamentary History, etc., Nos. 2297–2302.

    The best general history of Ludlow is Wright's (No. 2291). There is no good account of the municipal development.

a. Town Records.

    2283. Charters of Ludlow. *Salopian Shreds and Patches,* viii. 201–62. Shrewsbury, 1889. 4°.

    2284. Churchwardens' accounts of the town of Ludlow, in Shropshire, from 1540 to the end of the reign of Queen Elizabeth. Edited, from the original manuscript, by Thomas Wright. *Camden Society.* [London,] 1869. 4°.

    2285. Churchwardens' accounts of the town of Ludlow [9 Edw. IV.—1749.] Transcribed by Llewellyn Jones. *Shropsh. Archæol. and Nat. Hist. Soc.,* Transactions, Second Series, vols. i., ii., iv., v. Shrewsbury, 1889–93. 8°.

    2286. Copies of the charters and grants to the town of Ludlow. With a mirror for the men of Ludlow, illustrating their corporate rights . . . and extracts from G. Sharp's Essay on the ancient right of election. Ludlow, [1821.] 8°.

    2287. Corporate oaths of Ludlow. *Salopian Shreds and Patches,* viii. 26–87. Shrewsbury, 1889. 4°.

    2288. Records of Ludlow. [The "computus" of the bailiffs, 1616–17.] *Shropsh. Archæol. and Nat. Hist. Soc.,* Transactions, viii. 203–28. Shrewsbury and Oswestry, [1885.] 8°.

b. General Histories.

    2289. BAKER, OLIVER. Ludlow town and neighbourhood. . . . Ludlow, 1888. 4°.

    Of little value for municipal history.

2290. History (The) and antiquities of the town of Ludlow, and its ancient castle. . . . Ludlow, 1822.   12°.

Of little value.

2291. WRIGHT, THOMAS.   The history of Ludlow and its neighbourhood : forming a popular sketch of the history of the Welsh border. Ludlow and London, 1852.   8°.

The best general history of Ludlow, but it deals briefly with municipal affairs. Earlier editions, 1826, 1841, 1843.

2292. —— Ludlow sketches : a series of papers on the scenery and antiquities of Ludlow and its neighbourhood.   Ludlow, 1867. 8°.

Contains little concerning municipal history.

c. Gilds.

2293. HILLS, G. M.   On the ancient company of stitchmen of Ludlow : their account-book [1669] and money-box.   *Brit. Archæol. Assoc.*, Journal, xxiv. 327–34.   London, 1868.   8°.

2294. JONES, LLEWELLYN.   The antiente company of smiths and others commonly called " hammermen," Ludlow.   *Shropsh. Archæol. and Nat. Hist. Soc.*, Transactions, xi. 291–324.   Shrewsbury and Oswestry, 1888.   8°.

2295. SPARROW, W. C.   The palmers' guild of Ludlow.   *Shropsh. Archæol. and Nat. Hist. Soc.*, Transactions, i. 333–94.   Shrewsbury and Oswestry, [1878.]   8°.

Contains many documents.

2296. —— A register of the palmers' guild in the reign of Henry VIII.   *Ibid.*, vii. 81–126.   Shrewsbury, etc., [1884.]   8°.

d. Parliamentary History, etc.

2297. CHARLTON, E. L.   A letter addressed to the right hon. the speaker, respecting the decisions of two several committees of the House of Commons appointed to try the merits of the Ludlow election petitions [1828], together with a report of the same, and a letter to Wm. Harrison, Esq., king's counsel, on his mode of conducting the latter.   London, [1829.]   8°.

2298. ELLIDGE, J. P. A report of the proceedings at the election of members of Parliament for the borough of Ludlow, on the 9th of June, 1826. Ludlow, 1826. 12°.

2299. † HILL, RICHARD. Letter to the author of a pamphlet entitled Observations on the election of members for the borough of Ludlow in 1780. Shrewsbury, 1782. 8°.

2300. † Observations on the election of members for the borough of Ludlow in 1780. By a burgess. London, 1782. 8°.

2301. Proceedings in the court of Chancery against the corporation of Ludlow as trustees of Mr. Foxe's charity for pulling down St. Leonard's Chapel. . . . To which are added observations on the corporate rights of the inhabitants of Ludlow [pp. 113–117], and also an essay on borough influence [pp. 117–120]. Ludlow, [1819.] 8°.

2302. WEYMAN, H. T. The members of Parliament for Ludlow. *Shropsh. Archæol. and Nat. Hist. Soc.*, Transactions, Second Series, vii. 1–54. Shrewsbury, 1895. 8°.

LYDD.

2303. STRINGER, HENRY. Lydd records. *Kent Archæol. Soc.*, Archæologia Cantiana, xiii. 250–55. Canterbury, 1880. 8°.

LYME REGIS.

2304. ROBERTS, GEORGE. The history of Lyme Regis, Dorset, from the earliest period to the present day. Sherborne and London, 1823. 8°.

2305. —— The history and antiquities of the borough of Lyme Regis and Charmouth. London and Lyme Regis, 1834. 8°.

See No. 2306.

2306. —— The municipal government of the ancient borough of Lyme Regis; and account of the corporation, with details of its internal policy, and extracts illustrating the rigid and salutary discipline observed towards all the members of the body, and a curious picture of the government of borough towns in former years. Also an

account of the great election contests, together with lists of the representatives and mayors of the borough, from the earliest times. London
and Lyme Regis, [1834.] 16°.

This little volume is made up mainly of brief extracts from the corporation
Order Book, 1490–1709.

The second of Roberts's three books on Lyme Regis is the most elaborate, but
the third is the most useful for municipal history.

2307. Rules of practice for the court of hustings of the borough
of Lyme Regis. Lyme, 1844. 12°.

LYMINGTON.

2308. GARROW, DAVID. The history of Lymington and its immediate vicinity, in the county of Southampton. . . . London, 1825.
8°.

A brief account.

2309. [KING, EDWARD.] Old times re-visited in the borough and
parish of Lymington, Hants. London and Lymington, 1879. 8°.

Contains many extracts from the town records, mainly of the 17th and 18th
centuries.
Valuable.

2310. Records of the corporation of the borough of New-Lyming-
ton, in the county of Southampton. Extracted from the muniments
in the possession of the mayor and town council, and other authorities,
in the year 1848. By Charles St. Barbe. Printed for private circulation. London, [1848.] 4°.

Contains extracts from the town records, 1574–1833.

LYNN REGIS (KING'S LYNN).

     a. Town Records, Nos. 2311–2315.
     b. General Histories, Nos. 2316–2320.
     c. Miscellaneous, Nos. 2321–2325.

The most important series of records in the town archives are: the
assembly books, which begin in 19 Edw. I.; the chamberlains' accounts,
from Edw. III. onward; and the Trinity gild rolls, 47 Edw. III.—24 Hen.
VII.

Richards (No. 2319) gives the best account of municipal history.

a. Town Records.

2311. BULWER, JAMES.   Notice of a manuscript volume among the records of the corporation of Lynn.   *Norfolk and Norwich Archæol. Soc.*, Norfolk Archæology, vi. 217–51.   Norwich, 1864.   8°.

Contains early oaths of town officers, etc.

2312. Extracts from the chamberlain's book of accounts, 14 Henry IV., in the possession of the corporation of Lynn Regis.   By G. H. Dashwood.   *Norfolk and Norwich Archæol. Soc.*, Norfolk Archæology, ii. 183–92.   Norwich, 1849.   8°.

2313. Extracts from a manuscript containing portions of the proceedings of the corporation of Lynn Regis, in Norfolk, from 1430 to 1731, taken from the hall books; communicated by Hudson Gurney in a letter addressed to Henry Ellis.   *Soc. of Antiq. of London*, Archæologia, xxiv. 317–28.   London, 1832.   4°.

2314. HARROD, HENRY.   Report on the deeds and records of the borough of King's Lynn.   King's Lynn, 1874.   4°.

2315. Subsidy roll (A) in the possession of the corporation of Lynn Regis [circa 3 Edw. I.]   Communicated by G. H. Dashwood.   *Norfolk and Norwich Archæol. Soc.*, Norfolk Archæology, i. 334–54.   Norwich, 1847.   8°.

b. General Histories.

2316. BELOE, E. M.   Our borough.   Our church.   (King's Lynn, Norfolk.)   Part i.   Our borough.   Wisbech, [1871.]   8°.

2317. MACKERELL, BENJAMIN.   The history and antiquities of the flourishing corporation of King's Lynn, in the county of Norfolk. . . . Also an account of their several charters from time to time ; with a catalogue of all the mayors of Lynn. . . . London, 1738.   8°.

2318. PARKIN, CHARLES.   The topography of Freebridge hundred and half, in the county of Norfolk : containing the history and antiquities of the borough of King's Lynn. . . . Lynn, 1762.   f°.

Also forms a part of vol. iv. of Blomefield's history of the county (No. 628).

2319. RICHARDS, WILLIAM.   The history of Lynn, civil, ecclesiastical, political, commercial, biographical, municipal, and military, from the earliest accounts to the present time. . . . 2 vols.   Lynn, 1812. 8°.

The best history, but it does not contain a detailed account of municipal development. The writer devotes much attention to the religious gilds of Lynn.

2320. TAYLOR, WILLIAM.   The antiquities of King's Lynn, Norfolk. Lynn, 1844.   8°.

Contains the ordinances of the old Trinity gild, and a few brief extracts from the town records, 1520–1657.

c. Miscellaneous.

2321. HOWLETT, RICHARD.   Tolls levied at the Lynn tolbooth in the thirteenth century.   *Norfolk Antiq. Miscellany,* edited by Walter Rye, iii. 603–18.   Norwich, 1887.   8°.

2322. LE STRANGE, HAMON.   The early mayors of Lynn.   *Norfolk and Norwich Archœol. Soc.,* Norfolk Archæology, xii. 229–33.   Norwich, 1895.   8°.

2323.   † Report of an enquiry into the affairs of the corporation of King's Lynn, in Norfolk, held before the commissioners appointed for that purpose in the Guild-Hall of that borough, November, 1833. Taken by John Thew.   Stamford, 1833.   8°.

2324.   † —— A report of the proceedings of his majesty's commissioners for enquiring into the existing state of the municipal corporations of England and Wales, at King's Lynn, on the 16–21 of November, 1833.   By Edward Mugridge.   Lynn, 1834.   8°.

See No. 60.

2325. RYE, WALTER.   The guilds of Lynn Regis.   *Norfolk Antiq. Miscellany,* i. 153–83.   Norwich, 1873 [1877].   8°.

MACCLESFIELD.

The best history is Earwaker's (No. 577).

2326. CORRY, JOHN.   The history of Macclesfield.   London and Manchester, 1817.   8°.

Contains a translation of the town charters.

2327. FINNEY, ISAAC.   Maclesfelde in ye olden time.   Reprinted from the Macclesfield Advertiser.   Macclesfield, 1873.   8°.

2328. History (The) and directory of Macclesfield and its vicinity. Manchester, 1825. 12°.

A very brief account.

2329. RENAUD, FRANK. Contributions towards a history of the ancient parish of Prestbury, in Cheshire. *Chetham Society.* [Manchester,] 1876. 4°.

Macclesfield, 161–228.

MACDUFF.

2330. † CRAMOND, WILLIAM. The making of a Banffshire burgh ; being an account of the early history of Macduff. Banff, 1893. 12°. pp. 40.

MAIDSTONE.

The best history is Russell's (No. 2340).

2331. BAVERSTOCK, J. H. Some account of Maidstone in Kent. . . . London, 1832. 4°. pp. 24.

Brief and of little value.

2332. † Copy (A) of the charter of the town and parish of Maidstone, in the county of Kent. Canterbury, 1748. 8°. pp. 36.

Reprinted, Maidstone, 1796.

2333. † Copy (A) of the charter of the king's town and parish of Maidstone, in the county of Kent. Maidstone, 1832. 8°. pp. 29.

2334. † Copy (A) of the petition of the non-freemen, being rated inhabitant householders of the town of Maidstone, presented by Edward Knatchbull, Bart., to the House of Commons, on Tuesday, the 10th of May, 1825. Maidstone, 1825. 8°. pp. 8.

2335. GILBERT, W. B. The accounts of the Corpus Christi fraternity, and papers relating to the antiquities of Maidstone, together with a list of mayors and other corporate officers, from the earliest times. . . . Maidstone, 1865. 8°.

2336. JAMES, W. R. The charters and other documents relating to the king's town and parish of Maidstone, in the county of Kent, with notes and annotations, clearly shewing the right of election of members of Parliament to be in the inhabitant householders. London, 1825. 8°.

2337. L[AMPREYS], S. C.   A brief historical and descriptive account of Maidstone and its environs.   Maidstone, 1834.   8°.

Of little value for municipal history.

2338. NEWTON, WILLIAM.   The history and antiquities of Maidstone, the county-town of Kent, from the manuscript collections of William Newton.   London, 1741.   8°.

Ch. v.   Government and privileges of Maidstone.

2339. ROWLES, WALTER.   A general history of Maidstone, the shire town for the county of Kent : containing its ancient and present state, civil, and ecclesiastical, collected from public records, etc.   London and Maidstone, 1809.   8°.   pp. 86.

A brief account.

2340. RUSSELL, J. M.   The history of Maidstone.   Maidstone, 1881.   8°.

Ch. ix. contains a good short account of municipal and parliamentary history.

2341.   † Short treatise (A) on the institution of corporations, and an enquiry into the conduct of the bench of the corporation of Maidstone, from the year 1757 to the present time ; addressed to the freemen of Maidstone by a freeman.   Maidstone, 1786.   8°.   pp. 42.

MALDON.

2342.   † STRUTT, J.   Addresses and correspondence of Col. J. Strutt respecting the charter of Maldon.   Privately printed.   1812.   8°.

MALMESBURY.

2343. GOMME, G. L.   The history of Malmesbury as a village community.   *Soc. of Antiq. of London,* Archæologia, l. 421–38.   London, 1887.   4°.

Reprinted in No. 105.

2344. MAITLAND, F. W.   The survival of archaic communities.   i. The Malmesbury case.   *Law Quarterly Review,* ix. 36–50.   London, 1893.   8°.

2345. MOFFATT, J. M.   The history of the town of Malmesbury and of its ancient abbey. . . . Tetbury, 1805.   8°.

2346. Registrum Malmesburiense: the register of Malmesbury abbey, preserved in the Public Record Office. Edited by J. S. Brewer. *Rolls Series.* 2 vols. London, 1879–80. 8°.

Contains some records relating to the internal affairs of the borough.

MALTON, NEW.

2347. A Volume of English miscellanies. [Edited by James Raine.] *Surtees Society.* Durham, etc., 1890. 8°.

Customs of the burgesses of New Malton in the 15th century, 58–63. See No. 126.

MANCHESTER.

a. Town Records, Nos. 2348–2355.
b. General Histories, Nos. 2356–2368.
c. Miscellaneous, Nos. 2369–2376.

The best histories of Manchester are Harland's and Reilly's (Nos. 2358, 2364). The court leet records (Nos. 2352–2354) are more valuable for manorial than for municipal history.

a. Town Records.

2348. † Bye-laws passed by the council of the borough of Manchester. Manchester, 1843. 16°.

2349. Constables' accounts (The) of the manor of Manchester [1612–1776]. . . . Edited by J. P. Earwaker. 3 vols. Manchester, 1891–92. 8°

2350. † HIGSON, FREDERICK. The corporator's manual: a concise treatise on municipal corporations . . . with . . . a copy of the Manchester charter. Manchester, 1839. 12°.

2351. † ORMEROD, G. W. Manual of local acts affecting the townships comprised in the boroughs of Manchester and Salford. Manchester, 1838. 8°.

2352. Volume (A) of court leet records of the manor of Manchester in the sixteenth century. Compiled and edited by John Harland. *Chetham Society.* [Manchester,] 1864. 4°.

2353. —— Continuation of court leet records of the manor of Manchester, A. D. 1586–1602. Compiled and edited by John Harland. *Chetham Society.* [Manchester,] 1865. 4°.

N

2354. —— The court leet records of the manor of Manchester [1552–1846]. . . . [Edited by J. P. Earwaker.]   12 vols. Manchester, 1884–90.   8°.

The introduction to vol. xii. contains a good account of the incorporation of the borough.

2355. WHITAKER, JOHN.   The charter of Manchester [granted by Thomas Grelle in 1301] translated ; with explanations and remarks by the Rev. John Whitaker, 1787.   Manchester, 1838.   8°.   pp. 28.

See Nos. 2356, 2358, 2359.

b. General Histories.

2356. AIKIN, J.   Description of the country from thirty to forty miles round Manchester. . . . London, 1795.   4°.

Manchester, 147–217, 584–97.
Contains Thomas Grelle's grant to the burgesses, 1301, with a translation, etc.

2357. AXON, W. E. A.   The annals of Manchester : a chronological record from the earliest times to the end of 1885.   Edited by W. E. A. Axon.   Manchester and London, 1886.   8°.

A brief analysis of the history of Manchester, chronologically arranged.

2358. HARLAND, JOHN.   Mamecestre : being chapters from the early recorded history of the barony ; the lordship or manor ; the vill, borough, or town of Manchester.   Edited by John Harland. *Chetham Society.*   3 pts.   [Manchester,] 1861–62.   4°.

Ch. xii.   Lancashire town charters (see No. 623).
Ch. xiii.   Charter of Manchester, 1301.
Valuable.

2359. HIBBERT-WARE, SAMUEL.   The ancient parish church of Manchester, and why it was collegiated.   Manchester, 1848.   4°.

Contains a good survey of the early municipal history of Manchester ; and, on pp. 70–76, a detailed account of the charter of 1301.

2360. HOLLINGWORTH, R[ICHARD].   Mancuniensis : or an history of the towne of Manchester, and what is most memorable concerning it.   [Edited by William Willis.]   Manchester, 1839.   12°.

Written in the first half of the 17th century.
Of little value for municipal history.

2361. Manchester historical recorder (The) : being an analysis of the municipal, ecclesiastical, biographical, commercial, and statistical history of Manchester from the earliest period. . . . Manchester and London, [1874.]   8°.

Brief notes, arranged chronologically.
For other editions, see No. 2363 and Fishwick's *Lancashire Library* (No. 31), 138–9.

2362. PERRIN, JOSEPH.   The Manchester handbook : an authentic account of the place and its people. . . . Manchester and London, [1857.]   8°.

Municipal history, 41–79.   (A brief account.)

2363. Records, historical, municipal, ecclesiastical, biographical, commercial, and statistical, of Manchester from the earliest period. Revised and corrected to the present time.   Manchester, 1868.   12°.

Brief notes, arranged chronologically.
See No. 2361.

2364. REILLY, JOHN.   The history of Manchester.   Vol. i.   Manchester and London, 1861.   8°.

Pp. 1–560 deal with the civil and military history to 1860, emphasizing modern parliamentary history.   The appendix contains the town charters.

2365. —— The people's history of Manchester.   11 pts.   London and Manchester, [1859–60.]   8°.

Not completed ; extends to 1832.

2366. SAINTSBURY, GEORGE.   Manchester.   London, 1887.   8°.

A good brief account.

2367. WHEELER, JAMES.   Manchester : its political, social, and commercial history, ancient and modern.   London, etc., 1836.   8°.

Pt. iv. deals with the modern municipal history.

2368. WHITAKER, JOHN.   The history of Manchester, in four books. 2 vols.   London, 1771–75.   4°.

Vol. i.   The Roman period.
Vol. ii.   The Saxon period.

Of little value for municipal history.
Vol. i., reprinted, 2 vols., 1773.

c. **Miscellaneous.**

2369. City of Manchester.   Chronicle of city council, from incorporation, Oct., 1838, to Sept., 1879.   [Manchester, 1880.]   8°.

2370. Historical account (An) of some recent enterprises of the corporation of Manchester, and of its co-operation in the completion of the Manchester ship canal.   Manchester, 1894.   4°.

The court leet records and constables' accounts, 163–72.

2371. † HORSFALL, T. C.   Government of Manchester.   Manchester, 1895.   8°.   pp. 46.

2372. † KAY, ALEXANDER.   An address delivered to the members of the town council of Manchester, on Monday, the 10th of November, 1845, previous to the election (for the eighth time) of mayor of the borough, by Alex. Kay, the retiring mayor.   London, 1845.   8°.

Gives a good account of the affairs of the corporation since 1839.

2373. MEDCALF, WILLIAM.   On the municipal institutions of the city of Manchester.   By Mr. Councillor Medcalf.   Manchester, 1854.   8°.   pp. 32.

Reprinted from the Transactions of the Manchester Statistical Society.

2374. ROBERTS, WILLIAM.   A charge to the grand jury of the court leet for the manor of Manchester [1788] : containing an account of the internal government of that town. . . . Manchester, 1788.   4°.

2nd edition, 1793, 8°.

2375. SEXAGENARIAN.   Great towns and their public influence. ii. Manchester.   *Gentleman's Magazine*, xiii. 182–91.   London, 1874.   8°.

2376. SLUGG, J. T.   Reminiscences of Manchester fifty years ago. Manchester and London, 1881.   8°.

Ch. xx.   Government of the town.   (A brief account.)

MARAZION.

2377. LACH-SZYRMA, W. S.   Notes on the borough records of the towns of Marazion, Penzance, and St. Ives.   *Brit. Archæol. Assoc.*, Journal, xxxviii. 354–70.   London, 1882.   8°.

MARLBOROUGH.

2378. CARRINGTON, F. A.   Marlborough : facts and observations as to its ancient state.   *Wilts. Archæol. and Nat. Hist. Soc.*, Magazine, vii. 1–44.   Devizes, 1860 [1862].   8°.

2379. HULME, F. E.   The town, college, and neighbourhood of Marlborough.   London, 1881.   8°.

Contains little relating to municipal history.

2380. WAYLEN, JAMES.   A history, military and municipal, of the town (otherwise called the city) of Marlborough, and more generally of the entire hundred of Selkley.   London, 1854.   8°.

Contains brief extracts from the court books, 1524–1615; by-laws made in 19 Eliz.; extracts from the chamberlains' accounts, 1553–1772, etc.
The best history of Marlborough.

MARYHILL.

2381. THOMSON, ALEXANDER.   Random notes and random recollections of . . . Maryhill, 1750–1894.   Glasgow, 1895.   8°.

Sect. x.   The burgh.

MELTON MOWBRAY.

2382. NORTH, THOMAS.   Accounts of the churchwardens of Melton Mowbray.   *Leicestersh. Archit. and Archæol. Soc.*, Transactions, iii. 180–206.   Leicester, 1874.   8°.

Contains copious extracts from these accounts, Edw. IV. — 1612.

2383. —— The constables of Melton in the reign of Queen Elizabeth.   *Ibid.*, iii. 60–79.   Leicester, 1874.   8°.

MERTHYR TYDFIL.

2384. WILKINS, CHARLES.   The history of Merthyr Tydfil.   Merthyr Tydfil, 1867.   8°.

Of little value for municipal history.

MIDHURST.

2385. COOPER, W. D.   Midhurst : its lords and inhabitants.   *Sussex Archæol Soc.*, Collections, xx. 1–33.   Lewes, 1868.   8°.

MINEHEAD.

2386. The blessings of boroughmongering : a sketch of the borough of Minehead.   Third edition.   Chard, [1835.]   8°.   pp. 8.

A brief tirade against the traffic in rotten boroughs.

MODBURY.

2387. CAWSE, G. A. Modbury. London, 1860. 16°.
A meagre sketch.

MOFFAT.

2388. TURNBULL, W. R. History of Moffat; with frequent notices of Moffatdale and Annandale. Edinburgh and Moffat, 1871. 8°.

MONAGHAN.

2389. † RUSHE, D. C. Historical sketches of Monaghan, from the earliest times to the Fenian movement. Dublin, 1895.

MONMOUTH.

2390. Charters (The) of the town and borough of Monmouth, granted in the reigns of King Edward the Sixth, King James the First, King Charles the Second. Newport, 1826. 8°.

2391. HEATH, CHARLES. Historical and descriptive accounts of the ancient and present state of the town of Monmouth. . . . Monmouth, 1804. 4°.
A brief account.

MONTGOMERY.

2392. MONTGOMERY. Ancient charters of the borough. *Powysland Club*, Collections, xxi. 1–34. London, 1887. 8°.
Five Latin charters in full, Hen. IV.—Charles II., with a translation.

MONTROSE.

2393. D. P. D. Historical sketches of Montrose, ancient and modern. Illustrated. Montrose, 1879. 8°.

2394. MITCHELL, DAVID. The history of Montrose : containing important particulars in relation to its trade, manufactures, commerce, shipping, antiquities, eminent men. . . . Montrose, 1866. 8°.
Of little value for municipal history.

MORPETH.

2395. HODGSON, JOHN. A history of Morpeth. Newcastle-upon-Tyne, 1832. 4°.
A reprint of a part of his history of Northumberland (No. 634).
The best history of Morpeth.

2396. † HODGSON, J. C. The customs of the court leet and court baron of Morpeth, with the court rolls of 1632. *Soc. of Antiq. of Newcastle*, Archæologia Aeliana, vol. xvi. pt. i. Newcastle, 1892. 4°.

2397. MACKENZIE, E. History of the parish and borough of Morpeth. Newcastle, 1825. 4°.

See No. 636.

MUSSELBURGH.

2398. PATERSON, JAMES. History of the regality of Musselburgh, with numerous extracts from the town records [of the 17th and 18th centuries.] Musselburgh, 1857. 8°.

NANTWICH.

2399. HALL, JAMES. A history of the town and parish of Nantwich, or Wich-Malbank, in the county palatine of Chester. Nantwich, 1883. 4°.

The best history of Nantwich.

2400. Historical account (An) of the town and parish of Nantwich; with a particular relation of the remarkable siege it sustained in the grand rebellion, in 1643. [By Joseph Partridge.] Shrewsbury, 1774. 8°.

A brief account.

2401. † JOHNSON, ELIZABETH. Historical facts connected with Nantwich and its neighbourhood. 1851. 8°.

2402. PLATT, J. W. The history and antiquities of Nantwich, in the county palatine of Chester. London, 1818. 8°.

A brief account, based on Partridge's work (No. 2400).

NEATH.

2403. Original charters and materials for a history of Neath and its abbey, with illustrations; now first collected by G. G. Francis. Swansea, 1845. 8°.

NEWARK-UPON-TRENT.

2404. BROWN, CORNELIUS. The annals of Newark-upon-Trent: comprising the history, curiosities, and antiquities of the borough. Illustrated. . . . London and Newark, 1879. 4°.

The best history of Newark; little attention is devoted to municipal affairs.

2405. DICKINSON, WILLIAM. The history and antiquities of the town of Newark, in the county of Nottingham (the Sidnacester of the Romans). . . . London, 1819. 4°.

The appendix contains a translation of charters granted to Newark by Charles I. and Charles II.

Other editions, 1806, 1816.

2406. SHILTON, R. P. The history of the town of Newark-upon-Trent, in the county of Nottingham : comprising an account of its antiquities, public institutions, charities, charters, etc. 2 pts. Newark, 1820. 8°.

2407. † Translation of the charters of Charles I. and Charles II. to Newark. Newark, 1790.

NEWBURGH.

2408. LAING, ALEXANDER. Lindores abbey and its burgh of Newburgh : their history and annals. Edinburgh, 1876. 8°.

Chs. xv.–xvi. Municipal history (with extracts from the burgh records, 1459–79).

Appendix. Decreet arbitral of 1501, etc.

NEWBURY.

2409. History (The) and antiquities of Newbury and its environs. . . . Speenhamland and London, 1839. 8°.

Of little value for municipal history.

2410. † MONEY, WALTER. Guild of the clothworkers of Newbury. *Brit. Archæol. Assoc.*, Journal, 1896.

A paper read Nov. 4, 1896.

2411. —— The history of the ancient town and borough of Newbury, in the county of Berks. Oxford and London, 1887. 8°.

Contains extracts from court leet rolls, 1640–77, etc.

A good book.

NEWCASTLE–UNDER–LYME.

For the manorial history of the town, see No. 2842.

2412. INGAMELLS, J[EREMIAH]. Directory of Newcastle-under-Lyme, with historical records of the ancient borough. Newcastle, 1871. 8°. pp. 104.

A brief account of the municipal history of Newcastle, but seemingly the best. 2nd edition, " Historical records and directory of Newcastle," 1881.

2413. MAYER, JOSEPH. Account of the ancient custom of electing a mock mayor in Newcastle-under-Lyme. *Historic Soc. of Lanc. and Cheshire*, Proceedings, iii. 126–31. Liverpool, 1851. 8°.

2414. † Statute laws (The) relating to the management and disposition of the Newcastle-under-Lyme burgesses' lands, and the income thereof. Newcastle, 1861. 8°. pp. 53.

NEWCASTLE–UPON–TYNE.

> *a.* Town Records, Nos. 2415–2416.
> *b.* General Histories, Nos. 2417–2424.
> *c.* Gilds, Nos. 2425–2428.
> *d.* Miscellaneous, Nos. 2429–2447.

The best history is Brand's (No. 2418). The records of the merchant adventurers (No. 2427) are valuable.

a. Town Records.

2415. Extracts from the municipal accounts of Newcastle-upon-Tyne, extending from 1561 to the revolution of 1688. [M. A. Richardson's Reprints of rare tracts, vol. iii. Newcastle, 1849. 8°.]

2416. GIBSON, J. F. The Newcastle-upon-Tyne improvement acts and bye-laws, 1837 to 1877. With an introductory historical sketch and appendices. . . . Newcastle and London, 1881. 8°.

The introduction (pp. xi.-lx.) contains a good sketch of the municipal history of Newcastle.

b. General Histories.

See Nos. 600, 637.

2417. BOURNE, HENRY. The history of Newcastle upon Tyne : or the ancient and present state of that town. Newcastle, 1736. f°.

Ch. xiv., on the government of the town, contains much crude material, extracts from records, etc.

2418. * BRAND, JOHN. The history and antiquities of the town and county of the town of Newcastle upon Tyne, including an account of the coal trade of that place, and embellished with engraved views of the publick buildings, etc. 2 vols. London, 1789. 4°.

Contains the town charters in full; considerable use is made of the town archives and the public records.

The best history of Newcastle.

Index, by William Dodd (Society of Antiquaries of Newcastle, 1881).

2419. CHARLETON, R. J.   A history of Newcastle-on-Tyne, from the earliest records to its formation as a city. ·London, [1894.]   8°.

Of little value for municipal history.
Earlier edition, " Newcastle town : an account of its rise and progress," etc., 1885.

2420. Chorographia : or a survey of Newcastle upon Tine. . . . [By William Grey.]   Newcastle, 1649.   4°.

Reprinted in the Harleian Miscellany (1809), iii. 267–84; also in 1813 and 1818. Very brief and of little value.

2421. Impartial history (An) of the town and county of Newcastle upon Tyne and its vicinity. . . . [By John Baillie.]   Newcastle, 1801.   8°.

Contains an account of the craft gilds, but does not devote much attention to municipal history, " carefully excluding copies of old, musty grants, written in uncouth Latin."

2422. MACKENZIE, E.   A descriptive and historical account of the town and county of Newcastle upon Tyne, including the borough of Gateshead.   2 vols.   Newcastle, 1827.   4°.

In vol. ii. considerable space is devoted to the history of the corporation and the old trade gilds.

2423. OLIVER, THOMAS.   A new picture of Newcastle upon Tyne : or an historical and descriptive view of the town and county of Newcastle upon Tyne, Gateshead, and environs. . . . Newcastle, 1831.   12°.

Ch. vi. contains a brief account of municipal history.
Of little value.

2424. WELFORD, RICHARD.   History of Newcastle and Gateshead in the 14th and 15th [and 16th–17th] centuries.   Edited by Richard Welford.   3 vols.   London and Newcastle, [1883]–87.   8°.

c. Gilds.

See Nos. 2421, 2422, 2435, 2440.

2425. BOYLE, J. R.   The goldsmiths of Newcastle [with extracts from their minute book, 1702–86.]   *Soc. of Antiq. of Newcastle,* Archæologia Aeliana, xvi. 397–440.   London and Newcastle, 1894. 8°.

2426. EMBLETON, DENNIS. The incorporated company of barber surgeons and wax and tallow chandlers of Newcastle-upon-Tyne [with extracts from their minute books, 1616–86.] *Soc. of Antiq. of Newcastle,* Archæologia Aeliana, xv. 228–69. London and Newcastle, 1891–92. 8°.

2427. * Extracts from the records of the merchant adventurers of Newcastle-upon-Tyne [1480–1894. Edited by F. W. Dendy.] Vol. i. *Surtees Society.* Durham, etc., 1895. 8°.

2428. WALKER, J., and RICHARDSON, M. A. The armorial bearings of the several incorporated companies of Newcastle-upon-Tyne; with a brief historical account of each company. Newcastle, 1824. 8°.

d. Miscellaneous.

2429. BOYLE, J. R. Vestiges of old Newcastle and Gateshead. Newcastle and London, 1890. 4°.

2430. BROWN, JOHN. A short account of the customs and franchises of Newcastle. With an appendix containing: 1. The charter of Elizabeth; 2. The charter of James; 3. The Town Moor Act. Newcastle, 1823. 8°.

Contains a sketch of the town constitution.

2431. [CLARK, JOSEPH.] The Newcastle freeman's pocket companion : containing a copious view of the charters granted to the town and county of the town of Newcastle upon Tyne, including a particular account of the customs and privileges peculiar to the free burgesses of the said town. By a burgess. Gateshead, 1808. 12°. pp. 100.

New edition, " Newcastle remembrancer, and freeman's pocket companion," etc., Newcastle, 1817, 8°.

2432. COLLIER, JOHN. An essay on charters, in which are particularly considered those of Newcastle; with remarks on its constitution, customs, and franchises. Newcastle, 1777. 8°.

Contains translations of the charters of 42 Eliz. and 2 James I., etc.

2433. Conservatorship (The) of the Tyne : the plea and defence of the mayor and burgesses of Newcastle-upon-Tyne, against the malevolent accusations of Gardiner, as exhibited by him before Parliament [in the year] 1653. [M. A. Richardson's Reprints of rare tracts, vol. iii. Newcastle, 1849. 8°.]

See No. 2437.

2434. Contest (The) : being an account of the matter in dispute between the magistrates and burgesses, and an examination of the merit and conduct of the candidates in the present election for Newcastle-upon-Tyne. Newcastle, 1774. 8°.

2435. † Corporation mirror (The) : containing report of proceedings at the guild of Newcastle, October, 1829.

2436. Freeman's magazine (The), or the constitutional repository : containing a free debate concerning the cause of liberty; consisting of all the papers published in the London news-papers, from Northumberland and Newcastle, or the county of Durham, from the sending of instructions to the Newcastle members of Parliament till this present time. Newcastle, 1774. 8°.

Contains letters relating to the internal affairs of Newcastle and Durham.

2437. GARDINER, RALPH. England's grievance discovered in relation to the coal-trade ; with the map of the river of Tine, and situation of the town and corporation of Newcastle, the tyrannical oppression of those magistrates, their charters and grants . . . London, 1655. 4°.

Reprinted in 1796 and 1849.
See No. 2433.

2438. HINDE, J. H. On the early municipal history of Newcastle. *Soc. of Antiq. of Newcastle,* Archæologia Aeliana, iii. 105–15. Newcastle, 1858. 8°.

2439. —— On the trade of Newcastle previous to the reign of Henry III., with a view of its relative importance as compared with other towns and the general commerce of the kingdom. *Archæol. Institute of Great Britain and Ireland,* Memoirs of Northumberland, i. 24–40. 2 vols. London, 1858. 8°.

2440. Humble petition (The) and appeal of Thomas Cliffe, a poor shipwright, inhabiting at Northshields. [M. A. Richardson's Reprints of rare tracts, vol. ii. Newcastle, 1845. 8°.]

Illustrates the narrow spirit of the Newcastle trades in the 17th century.

2441. † Newcastle corporation annual : or recollections of the first reformed town council.   Newcastle, 1836.

2442. † Newcastle corporation enquiry . . . with the official report of the commissioners.   Newcastle, 1833.   f°.

2443. † —— Report of the official investigation into the affairs of the municipal corporation of Newcastle.   Newcastle, 1834.   8°.

See No. 60.

2444. [RICHARDSON, M. A.]   Richardson's Descriptive companion through Newcastle upon Tyne and Gateshead . . . to which is prefixed an inquiry into the origin of the primitive Britons.   Newcastle, 1838.   8°.

Ch. x. contains a brief account of "municipal concerns." Reprinted, " A guide to Newcastle," 1846.

2445. SEXAGENARIAN.   Great towns and their public influence. v. Newcastle-upon-Tyne.   *Gentleman's Magazine,* xiii. 599–609. London, 1874.   8°.

2446. Three early assize rolls for the county of Northumberland, sæc. xiii.   [Edited by William Page.]   *Surtees Society.*   Durham, etc., 1891.   8°.

Contains various cases relating to Newcastle : see the index, 474.

2447. TUNBELLY, T.   The letters of Tim. Tunbelly, Gent. [W. A. Mitchell], free burgess of Newcastle upon Tyne, on the Tyne, Newcastle, corporation. . . . Vol. i.   Newcastle, 1823.   8°.

NEWNHAM.

2448. KERR, R. J.   Notes on the borough and manor of Newnham. *Bristol and Glouc. Archæol. Soc.,* Transactions, xviii. 142–74. Bristol, [1895.]   8°.

NEWPORT (MONMOUTHSHIRE).

2449. Baronia de Kemeys.   From the original documents at Bronwydd.   *Cambrian Archæol. Assoc.*   London, [1862.]   8°.

Charters, etc., of Newport, 15, 49-55, 67-8, 111-24.

2450. Historical traditions and facts relating to Newport and Caerleon. By a member of the Caerleon and Monmouthshire Antiquarian Society. Pts. i.–v. Newport, 1880–85. 8°.

Pt. i.   Prehistoric and Roman periods.
Pt. ii. The Saxon period.
Pt. iii. Norman and early English period.
Pt. iv. Edward III. to Mary.
Pt. v.   Civil war in Montgomeryshire.

2451. On the early charters of the borough of Newport in Wentloog. Communicated by Octavius Morgan. With remarks by H. S. Milman. *Soc. of Antiq. of London*, Archæologia, xlviii. 431–55. London, 1885. 4°.

Inspeximus of Humphrey, Earl of Stafford, 5 Hen. VI., with a translation.

NEWPORT (SHROPSHIRE).

2452. JONES, EDWARD. Historical records of Newport, Co. Salop. The burgesses. *Shropsh. Archæol. and Nat. Hist. Soc.*, Transactions, viii. 229–68; ix. 117–70. Shrewsbury and Oswestry, 1885–86. 8°.

NEWTOWN (MONTGOMERYSHIRE).

2453. WILLIAMS, RICHARD. Newtown : its ancient charter and its town hall. *Powysland Club*, Collections, xii. 87–108. London, 1879. 8°.

Contains various depositions taken at Newtown in 1615, giving particulars of its old town-hall and charter.

NORTHALLERTON.

2454. History (The) of North-Allerton, in the county of York. . . . [By James Langdale.] Second edition. Northallerton, 1813. 12°.

A meagre account.
1st edition, 1791, 8°.

2455. INGLEDEW, C. J. D. The history and antiquities of North-Allerton, in the county of York. London, 1858. 8°.

The borough, 126–40.

2456. Registrum honoris de Richmond. . . . [By Roger Gale.] London, 1722. f°.

Grant to the town and inquisition concerning its liberties, 7 Edw. III., 173–5.

2457. SAYWELL, J. L. The history and annals of Northallerton, Yorkshire, with notes and voluminous appendix, compiled from authentic and reliable sources. Northallerton, 1885. 8°.

NORTHAMPTON.

a. Town Records, Nos. 2458–2461.
b. General Histories, etc., Nos. 2462–2466.

The Liber Custumarum (No. 2459) is valuable. The best history is Hartshorne's (No. 2463).

a. Town Records.

See No. 2466.

2458. Charter (The) of the corporation of the town of Northampton, granted by his majesty George the Third in the 36th year of his reign [1796]. . . . Northampton, [1796.] 4°.

2459. * Liber Custumarum (The) : the book of the ancient usages and customez of the town of Northampton, from the earliest record to 1448. Edited by Christopher A. Markham. Northampton, 1895. 4°.

The text (in English, Latin, and French) was compiled about the middle of the 15th century; various rules and decisions were added later. One third of the original is here printed. This part of the work is also being published in *Northamptonshire Notes and Queries,* 1890–94, etc., vols. i., iv.–v., etc.

2460. Northampton corporation accounts, from 1795 to 1835; and the accounts of the town council from 1836 to 1839. Northampton, [1840.] f°.

2461. † Records (The) of the borough of Northampton, edited by C. A. Markham and J. C. Cox . . . and an introductory chapter on the history of the town by W. R. D. Adkins. Published by order of the corporation of the county borough of Northampton. 2 vols. Northampton, —. 8°.

Vol. i. Extracts from the public records; the whole of the early charters and the Liber Custumarum, with a translation.
Vol. ii. Extracts from the orders of assembly, 1547–1835.
Announced for publication.

b. General Histories, etc.

2462. Account (An) of the surrender of the old charter of Northampton, September the 26, and the manner of their receiving their new charter, etc.   Together with an eloquent speech made by Robert Clerk, Esq. (deputy recorder of Northampton), upon that occasion. [London, 1686.]   f°.

A single sheet.

2463. HARTSHORNE, C. H.   Historical memorials of Northampton, taken chiefly from unprinted sources.   Northampton, etc., 1848.   8°.

Contains the town charters; extracts from the Chamberlain's Book of Minutes, 1552–1687; an account of the municipal archives, etc.
A valuable little book; the best history of Northampton.

2464. History (The) of Northampton and its vicinity; brought down to the present time.   Second edition.   Northampton, 1821.   12°.

A meagre account.
1st edition, 1815, 8°.

2465. History (The) of the town of Northampton; with an account of its public buildings . . . members of Parliament, mayors and bailiffs, and the most remarkable events that have taken place in the town.   Northampton, 1817.   12°.

The list of mayors contains some brief references to municipal history.

2466.   † Report of trial to take tolls in the town of Northampton, containing copies of the principal charters in the possession of the corporation.   Northampton, 1833.

NORWICH.

a. Town Records, Nos. 2467–2471.
b. General Histories, Nos. 2472–2479.
c. Gilds, Nos. 2480–2483.
d. Miscellaneous, Nos. 2484–2497.

The following are the principal town records, with the dates when they begin : royal charters, Hen. II., etc.; court rolls, 1284; court books, 1492; assembly rolls, 1365; assembly books, 1440; chamberlains' rolls, 1375; Old Free-Book, containing admissions to the freedom, rentals, deeds, etc., Edw. II.; Domesday Book, containing rents, grants of land, etc., mainly in Henry VI.'s reign.

The best general history of Norwich is Blomefield's (No. 628). Hudson's *Leet Jurisdiction* and his other works (Nos. 2471, 2487–2491) are scholarly contributions to the history of the city. The volume on the Town Close Estate (No. 2468) is also valuable.

a. Town Records.

2467. † Abstract (An) of several acts of Parliament relating to the city of Norwich. . . . Norwich, 1730. 8°.

2468. * Evidences relating to Town Close Estate. [Documents admitted in the case of Stanley *v.* the mayor, etc. of Norwich. Norwich, 1886.] f°. pp. 116.

Contains several of the town charters in full, with extracts from others; also copious extracts from public records, the leet rolls, the assembly rolls, etc., 1086–1886. Some of these documents are very valuable; for example, the orders for the government of the city in 1415, pp. 37–43.

The work is badly edited.

2469. Extracts from the coroners' rolls and other documents, in the record-room of the corporation of Norwich [Hen. III. — Edw. I.] By H. Harrod. *Norfolk and Norwich Archæol. Soc.*, Norfolk Archæology, ii. 253–79. Norwich, 1849. 8°.

2470. Extracts from the records of Norwich. *Norfolk and Norwich Archæol. Soc.*, Norfolk Archæology, i. 1–40. Norwich, 1847. 8°.

They relate mainly to musters in the 16th century.

2471. * Leet jurisdiction in the city of Norwich during the xiii[th] and xiv[th] centuries, with a short notice of its later history and decline. From rolls in the possession of the corporation. Edited by William Hudson. *Selden Society*. London, 1892. 4°.

b. General Histories.

2472. BAYNE, A. D. A comprehensive history of Norwich. . . . London and Norwich, 1869. 8°.

Useful for the parliamentary history of Norwich in the 19th century.

2473. BROWNE, P[HILIP.] The history of Norwich, from the earliest records to the present time. . . . Norwich, 1814. 8°.

2474. Compleat history (A) of the famous city of Norwich, from the earliest account to this present year, 1728. . . . Norwich, 1728. 8°. pp. 38.

Of little value.

An appendix was published in the same year.

2475. History (The) of the city of Norwich: containing: i. A description of that city, both in its ancient and modern state. . . . vi. A list of all the mayors and sheriffs of Norwich since it had the liberty of a mayor. . . . Norwich, 1718. 8°. pp. 40.

A brief sketch, of little value.

2476. History (The) of the city and county of Norwich, from the earliest accounts to the present time. . . . 2 pts. Norwich, 1768. 8°.

Contains copious abstracts of charters, and some notices of municipal affairs.

2477. History (The) of the city of Norwich, from the earliest records to the present time. Norwich, 1869. 8°.

Of little value for municipal history.

2478. PARKIN, CHARLES. The history and antiquities of the city of Norwich, in the county of Norfolk, collected from antient records and other authentic materials. Lynn and London, 1783. 8°.

Contains brief references to municipal history.

2479. Topographical and historical account (A) of the city and county of Norwich, its antiquities and modern improvements. . . . [By John Stacy.] Norwich and Lynn, 1819. 8°.

Based mainly on Blomefield (No. 628). Contains a brief account of municipal history.

Other editions, 1819, 1832.

c. Gilds.

2480. FITCH, ROBERT. Notices of brewers' marks and trade regulations in the city of Norwich. Contributed to the Transactions of the Norfolk and Norwich Archæological Society. Norwich, 1859. 8°.

Contains extracts from the Brewers' Book, most of them in the time of Elizabeth and James I.

2481. L'ESTRANGE, JOHN, and RYE, WALTER. Norfolk guilds. *Norfolk and Norwich Archæol. Soc.*, Norfolk Archæology, vii. 105–21. Norwich, 1872. 8°.

Contains ordinances of various Norwich gilds in Richard II.'s time.

2482. [MACKERELL, BENJAMIN.] Account of the company of St. George in Norwich. From Mackerell's History of Norwich, MS., 1737. *Norfolk and Norwich Archæol. Soc.*, Norfolk Archæology, iii. 315–74. Norwich, 1852. 8°.

2483. Norwich pageants. The grocers' play. From a manuscript in possession of Robert Fitch. Norwich, 1856. 8°.

Contains also extracts from the Grocers' Book, 1534–65, relating to the pageants.

d. Miscellaneous.

2484. † BOUSSELL, JOHN. A serious address to the magistrates of Norwich and Yarmouth. Norwich, 1793. 8°.

2485. COTTON, BARTHOLOMEW. Historia Anglicana. . . . Edited by H. R. Luard. *Rolls Series.* London, 1859. 8°.

The conflict between the citizens and the monks of Norwich, 1272–76, pp. 146–54, 421–7.
See also Samuel Bentley's *Excerpta Historica* (London, 1831), 252–3; and No. 2496.

2486. † Digest of the evidence before the parliamentary commission on municipal boroughs. [Norwich,] 1833.

See No. 60.

2487. HUDSON, WILLIAM. How the city of Norwich grew into shape . . . to which is added a short description of its municipal divisions at various times. Norwich, 1896. 4°.

2488. —— Notes about Norwich before the close of the thirteenth century. *Norfolk and Norwich Archæol. Soc.*, Norfolk Archæology, xii. 25–84. Norwich, 1893. 8°.

2489. —— A revised list of the bailiffs of the city of Norwich. *Ibid.*, xi. 228–56. Norwich, 1892. 8°.

2490. *—— Traces of the early development of municipal organization in the city of Norwich. *Archæol. Journal*, xlvi. 293–330. London, 1889. 8°.

An excellent sketch of the early history of Norwich.

2491. —— The wards of the city of Norwich, their origin and history. London, 1891. 4°.

Valuable.

2492. KIRKPATRICK, JOHN. The streets and lanes of the city of Norwich. A memoir by John Kirkpatrick. . . . Edited with notes and appendices, for the Norfolk and Norwich Archæological Society, by William Hudson. . . . Norwich, 1889. f°.

2493. L'ESTRANGE, JOHN. Calendar of the freemen of Norwich, 1317–1603. Edited by Walter Rye. London, 1888. 8°.

2494. MADDERS, S. S. Rambles in an old city [Norwich] : comprising antiquarian, historical, biographical, and political associations. London, 1853. 8°.

2495. Notices and illustrations of the costume, processions, pageantry, etc. formerly displayed by the corporation of Norwich. [With plates.] Norwich, 1850. f°.

Contains many extracts from the town records (1451–1711).

2496. RYE, WALTER. The riot between the monks and citizens of Norwich in 1272. *Norfolk Antiq. Miscellany*, ii. 17–89. Norwich, 1880 [1883]. 8°.

See No. 2485.

2497. —— The town close, Norwich. *Norfolk Antiq. Miscellany*, iii. 341–93. Norwich, 1887. 8°.

Contains town ordinances of 2 Henry V., etc.

NOTTINGHAM.

    a. Town Records, Nos. 2498–2500.
    b. General Histories, Nos. 2501–2506.
    c. Miscellaneous, Nos. 2507–2513.

The town archives contain royal charters from Henry II.'s time onward; rolls of the borough court, beginning in 1303; hall books, since 1548; deeds, etc. The Red Book, containing old customs and ordinances of the town, was destroyed by a fire in 1724; and the early mayoralty rolls have been lost.

The best histories of Nottingham are Blackner's and Deering's (Nos. 2501, 2502). Stevenson's *Records* (No. 2499) is a model work of its kind; his volume of royal charters (No. 2500) is also valuable. These two publications form a good basis for a new history of the town government.

a. Town Records.

2498. HEATHCOTE, CHARLES. An English translation of the charter of Henry VI. to the burgesses of the town and county of the town of

Nottingham; confirmed by letters patent of King William and Queen Mary. To which is prefixed an introductory address to the burgesses of the said town. Nottingham, [1807.]   f°.

This is an inspeximus of the earlier charters. See Nos. 2501–2503.

2499. * Records of the borough of Nottingham [1155–1625]: being a series of extracts from the archives of the corporation of Nottingham. [Edited by W. H. Stevenson.] Published under the authority of the corporation of Nottingham. 4 vols. London and Nottingham, 1882–89.   8°.

The Latin and French texts are accompanied with a translation.

2500. Royal charters granted to the burgesses of Nottingham, 1155–1712. [Edited by W. H. Stevenson.] Issued by order of the corporation of Nottingham. London and Nottingham, 1890.   8°.

Latin texts, with an English translation.
Valuable.

b. General Histories.

See No. 639.

2501. BLACKNER, JOHN. The history of Nottingham, embracing its antiquities, trade, and manufactures, from the earliest authentic records to the present period. Nottingham, 1815.   4°.

There is quite a detailed account of municipal history on pp. 252–87, and a translation of the town charters on pp. 411–37.

2502. DEERING, CHARLES. Nottinghamia vetus et nova: or an historical account of the ancient and present state of the town of Nottingham. . . . Nottingham, 1751.   4°.

Sect. vi. contains abstracts of the town charters, etc.
The appendix contains the Latin inspeximus of 27 Henry VI.; the case of William Sacheverell, etc.

2503. † History (The), antiquities, and present state of the town of Nottingham; with an appendix, containing a translation of the charter of Henry VI. to the burgesses of Nottingham. . . . Nottingham, 1807.   12°.

2504. SUTTON, J. F. The date-book of remarkable and memorable events connected with Nottingham and its neighbourhood, 1750–1850. London and Nottingham, 1852.   8°.

2505. THROSBY, JOHN. The history and antiquities of the town and county of the town of Nottingham : containing the whole of Thoroton's account of that place [No. 640], and all that is valuable in Deering. Nottingham, 1795. 4°.

2506. WYLIE, W. H. Old and new Nottingham. London and Nottingham, 1853. 8°.

Ch. xv. Local government.
A popular history of the town.

c. Miscellaneous.

2507. Coke and Birch. The paper war carried on at the Nottingham election, 1803 : containing the whole of the addresses, songs, squibs, etc. circulated by the contending parties ; including the books of accidents and chances. Nottingham, [1803.] 8°.

2508. HINE, T. C. Nottingham : its castle, a military fortress, a royal palace, a ducal mansion, a blackened ruin, a museum and gallery of art. With [brief] notes relating to the borough of Nottingham. London and Nottingham, 1876. 4°.

A supplement appeared in 1879.

2509. Nottingham corporation. A report of the evidence given before the commissioners appointed to enquire into municipal corporations. Taken in short-hand by Thomas Cockayne. Nottingham, 1833. 8°.

See No. 60.

2510. † Nottingham election petition of 1803. Nottingham, 1803. f°.

Contains material relating to the history of Nottingham elections.

2511. † Ten letters, principally upon the subject of the late contested election at Nottingham. London, 1803. 8°.

2512. † —— Two letters, principally upon the subject of the late contested election at Nottingham. London, 1802. 8°.

2513. Tryal (The) of William Sacheverell, Esq., and several other gentlemen, for a riot committed at Nottingham, on the election of a mayor of that town ; before the lord chief justice Jefferies, at the King's-Bench bar, in Easter term, 1684. To which is added the case of the town of Nottingham, drawn up by Mr. Sacheverell.   London, 1720.   f°.

This is one of the cases which arose out of the royal attacks upon the charters of corporations.

See Nos 195, 2502.

OKEHAMPTON.

2514. BRIDGES, W. B.   Some account of the barony and town of Okehampton : its antiquities and institutions. . . . A new edition, with additional chapters, edited by W. H. K. Wright.   Tiverton, 1889.   8°.

1st edition, Plymouth, [circa 1839.]

OSWESTRY.

2515. CATHRALL, WILLIAM.   The history of Oswestry : comprising the British, Saxon, Norman, and English eras ; the topography of the borough ; and its ecclesiastical and civil history. . . . Oswestry, [1855.] 8°.

2516. History (The) of Oswestry, from the earliest period : its antiquities and customs ; with a short account of the neighbourhood. [By William Price.]   Oswestry, [1815.]   8°.   pp. 108.

Contains some extracts from the town records.

2517. Mayors of Oswestry.   Oswestry magistrates.   Oswestry charters.   Oswestry aldermen and corporation officers.   *Bye-gones relating to Wales and the Border Counties,* 1874–75, pp. 211–316.   Oswestry, [1875.]   4°.

Contains only an abstract of the charters.

2518. Oswestry charters [List of, etc.]   *Bye-gones relating to Wales and the Border Counties,* 1878–79, pp. 76, 83, 149, 154, 167 ; 1881–82, pp. 12, 301.   Oswestry, [1879–82.]   4°.

2519. Oswestry corporation records.   *Bye-gones relating to Wales and the Border Counties,* 1876–79, 1882–83.   Oswestry, [1877–83.] 4°.

Extracts from the records since the 16th century.

2520. Records (The) of the corporation of Oswestry.   Edited by Stanley Leighton.   With an account of the mayors, stewards, recorders, and town clerks, by Askew Roberts.   Reprinted from the Transactions of the Shropshire Archæological Society, 1879–83 [vols. ii.–vii.]   Oswestry, [1884.]   8°.

Contains town charters; town constitutions of 1582; by-laws of 1677; extracts from the mayor's accounts, 1674, etc.
Valuable.

OVER.

2521. RIGBY, THOMAS.   The ancient borough of Over, Cheshire. *Historic Soc. of Lanc. and Cheshire,* Proceedings, xvii. (New Series, v.) 13–22.   Liverpool, 1865.   8°.

OVERTON.

2522. HOWSON, G. J.   Overton (caullid yn auncient tyme Orton Madoc) in days gone by.   Oswestry, 1883.   8°.

Ch. iv.   Municipal and parliamentary history.

OXFORD.

a. Town Records, etc., Nos. 2523–2531.
b. General Histories, Nos. 2532–2538.
c. Miscellaneous, Nos. 2539–2541.

The most valuable works are the records edited by Ogle, Rogers, and Turner (Nos. 2527, 2528, 2530, 2531).   Nos. 2536–2538 are also useful. A good history of the municipal development is needed.

a. Town Records, etc.

2523. Cartulary (The) of the monastery of St. Frideswide at Oxford.   Edited . . . by S. R. Wigram.   *Oxford Historical Society.* 2 vols.   Oxford, 1895–96.   8°.

See his index, ii. 442–7, for references to the city of Oxford.

2524. Charters of King John and Henry III. to the town of Oxford.   [T. Hearne's edition of Morin's Chronicon sive annales prioratus de Dunstaple, 731–4.   Oxford, 1733.   8°.]

See also No. 126.

2525. MADAN, FALCONER.   Rough list of manuscript materials relating to the history of Oxford, contained in the printed catalogues of the Bodleian and college libraries; arranged according to subject, with an index.   Oxford, 1887.   8°.

2526. Munimenta academica : or documents illustrative of academical life and studies at Oxford. Edited by Henry Anstey. 2 pts. *Rolls Series.* London, 1868. 8°.

Some of the documents relate to municipal affairs: see his index, under " Mayor " and " Townsmen."

2527. OGLE, OCTAVIUS. The Oxford market. *Oxford Historical Society,* Collectanea, ii. 1–135. Oxford, 1890. 8°.

Contains many extracts from documents relating to the history of the market since the 13th century.
Valuable.

2528. Oxford city documents, financial and judicial, 1268–1665. Selected and edited by J. E. T. Rogers. *Oxford Historical Society.* Oxford, 1891. 8°.

Valuable.

2529. Parliamentary petitions relating to Oxford [1379–1496.] Edited by Lucy Toulmin Smith. *Oxford Historical Society,* Collectanea, vol. iii. Oxford, 1896. 8°.

For the petitions dealing with municipal history, see pp. 85–6.

2530. * Royal letters addressed to Oxford, and now existing in the city archives. Transcribed and edited by Octavius Ogle. Oxford, 1892. 8°.

Contains charters, letters patent, inquisitions, writs, orders in council, and letters from the crown, 1136–1684.

2531. * Selections from the records of the city of Oxford, with extracts from other documents illustrating the municipal history, Henry VIII. to Elizabeth (1509–1583). Edited by W. H. Turner. Oxford and London, 1880. 8°.

b. General Histories.

2532. BOASE, C. W. Oxford. [Historic Towns. Edited by E. A. Freeman and W. Hunt.] London, 1887. 8°.

2533. INGRAM, JAMES. Memorials of Oxford, by James Ingram. The engravings by John Le Keux, from drawings by F. Mackenzie. 3 vols. Oxford and London, 1837. 4°.

Contains a brief account of municipal history.

2534. PARKER, JAMES. The early history of Oxford, 727–1100. Preceded by a sketch of the mythological origin of the city and university. *Oxford Historical Society.* Oxford, 1885. 8°.

2535. —— On the history of Oxford during the tenth and eleventh centuries (912–1100). The material of a lecture delivered before the Oxford Architectural and Historical Society, Feb. 28, 1871. Oxford, 1871. 8°. pp. 78.

2536. WOOD, A. The antient and present state of the city of Oxford. . . . The whole chiefly collected by Mr. Anthony à Wood ; with additions by the Rev. Sir J. Peshall, Bart. London, 1773. 4°.

The charters and government of Oxford, 338–71.

2537. —— The history and antiquities of the university of Oxford, in two books, by Anthony à Wood. Now first published in English, from the original MS. in the Bodleian Library, by John Gutch. 2 vols., 3 pts. Oxford, 1792–96. 4°.

Contains much material relating to municipal affairs.

2538. —— "Survey of the city of Oxford," composed in 1661–6 by Anthony Wood. Edited by Andrew Clark. *Oxford Historical Society.* Vols. i.–ii. Oxford, 1889–90. 8°.

The third and last volume will treat of the constitution of the city.

c. Miscellaneous.

2539. GREEN, J. R. The early history of Oxford. *Macmillan's Magazine,* xxiv. 443–51 ; xxv. 32–40. London, 1871. 8°.

Also printed in his *Stray Studies* (1876), 287–308.

2540. Oxford during the last century : being two series of papers published in the Oxford Chronicle and Berks and Bucks Gazette during the year 1859. Oxford, 1859. 4°.

Contains some brief references to municipal affairs.

2541. WILSON, JOHN. The cordwainers and corvesors of Oxford. *Archæol. Journal,* vi. 146–59, 266–79. London, 1849. 8°.

Contains charters granted to the gild by Henry II., Henry III., and Edward II. ; extracts from the gild accounts, 1631–1734, etc.

PAIGNTON.

2542. LANE, JOHN. The court rolls of the manor and borough of Paignton, Devon. With some notes on the tenures of the manor. *Devon. Assoc. for Advancement of Science*, Transactions, xvi. 703–24. Plymouth, 1884. 8°.

Contains extracts from the rolls, 1664–1716.

PAISLEY.

The best history is Brown's (No. 2543).

2543. BROWN, ROBERT. The history of Paisley, from the Roman period down to 1884. 2 vols. Paisley, 1886. 8°.

Contains many extracts from the town council records, which begin in 1594.

2544. —— The history of the Paisley grammar school and academy, and of the other town's schools ; with some notices of subjects relating to the history of the town of Paisley. Paisley, 1875. 4°.

2545. LEES, J. C. The abbey of Paisley, from its foundation till its dissolution ; with . . . an appendix of illustrative documents. Paisley, 1878. 4°.

The burgh of Paisley, 146–58.

2546. MACKIE, CHARLES. Historical description of the abbey and town of Paisley. . . . Glasgow, 1835. 8°.

Extracts from town council records, 1594–1664, pp. 133–47.

2547. PARKHILL, JOHN. The history of Paisley. Paisley, 1857. 12°.

A short account of the municipal history. The appendix contains brief extracts from the town records, 1659–64, and the charter granted to the town in 1490 by George Schaw, abbot of Paisley.

2548. Registrum monasterii de Passelet, cartas, privilegia, conventiones aliaque munimenta complectens, a domo fundata A. D. 1163 usque ad A. D. 1529. . . . [*Maitland Club.*] Edinburgh, 1832. 4°.

For documents relating to the history of the burgh, 1204–1495, see pp. 20, 247, 261–74, 403–7 : the charter granted to the burgesses in 1488, etc.

2549. Semple, David. Saint Mirin : an historical account of old houses, old families, and olden times in Paisley. . . . Paisley, 1872. 4°.

Contains only brief references to the municipal history.
Two short supplements appeared in 1873 and 1874.

PEEBLES.

2550. † Charter of James VI. (1621). Perth, 1825.

2551. * Charters and documents relating to the burgh of Peebles, with extracts from the records of the burgh, A. D. 1165–1710. [Edited by William Chambers.] *Scottish Burgh Records Society.* Edinburgh, 1872. 4°.

2552. Peebles and its neighbourhood, with a run on the Peebles railway. [By William Chambers.] Edinburgh, 1856. 8°.

Of little value.

2553. Renwick, Robert. Gleanings from the records of the royal burgh of Peebles, 1604–52. Peebles, 1892. 8°.

2554. † Williamson, Alexander. Glimpses of Peebles. Selkirk, 1895.

PENRYN.

2555. † Documents relating to Peter Pender, Esq., of Penryn, who was duly chosen mayor but was ejected by the government. 1725. f°.

Said to contain much information on the history of the borough.
See No. 189.

PENZANCE.

2556. [Beard, John.] To the worshipful the mayor . . . the aldermen and commonalty of Penzance. This translation of their charter is respectfully presented by their faithful and obedient humble servant, J. B., town clerk. Penzance, [1825.] f°. pp. 22.

2557. Boase, G. C. Collectanea Cornubiensia : a collection of biographical and topographical notes relating to Cornwall. Truro, 1890. 4°.

Pt. iii. The journal of the mayor of Penzance, Henry Boase, for his year of office 1816–17, giving the details of the management of an old unreformed borough.

2558. COURTNEY, J. S. A guide to Penzance and its neighbourhood.
. . . Penzance, 1845. 8°.

Ch. i. gives a brief account of the history of Penzance. The appendix, pp.
59–71, contains extracts from the corporation accounts, 1658–1760.

2559. † —— Half a century of Penzance, 1825–1875. . . . Penzance, 1878. 8°. pp. 52.

2560. LACH–SZYRMA, W. S. Notes on the borough records of the
towns of Marazion, Penzance, and St. Ives. *Brit. Archæol. Assoc.,*
Journal, xxxviii. 354–70. London, 1882. 8°.

2561. —— A short history of Penzance, S. Michael's Mount, S.
Ives, and the Land's End district. Truro and London, 1878. 4°.

Of little value for municipal history.

2562. MILLETT, G. B. Penzance, past and present. A lecture
delivered at the Penzance Institute. . . . Penzance, 1876. 8°.

2563. —— Penzance, past and present. A second lecture. . . .
Penzance, 1880. 8°.

PERTH.

The most valuable works relating to Perth are those of Hunt and
Marshall (Nos. 2567, 2570).

2564. CANT, JAMES. The muses threnodie : or mirthful mournings
on the death of Mr. Gall. . . . By Mr. H. Adamson. Printed at
Edinburgh . . . 1638. To this new edition are added explanatory
notes and observations ; King James's charter of confirmation
[1600] ; an account of Gowrie's conspiracy ; a list of the magistrates
of Perth, with notes. . . . By James Cant. 2 vols. Perth, 1774. 8°.

Vol. ii. consists of the additions by Cant relating to Perth, and contains a
translation of the burgh charter of 1600, the decreet obtained by Perth against
Dundee in 1602, a translation of the charter granted by Queen Mary to the trades
of Perth in 1556, King James's charter to the crafts, 1581, etc.

2565. † Charter by King James VI. in favour of the town of Perth,
dated 15th November, 1600, and a translation. n. p. n. d. 4°.

2566. Chronicle (The) of Perth : a register of remarkable occurrences, chiefly connected with that city, from the year 1210 to 1668.
[Presented to the Maitland Club, as the contribution of James Maid-
ment.] *Maitland Club.* Edinburgh, 1831. 4°.

2567. HUNT, COLIN A. The Perth Hammermen Book (1518 to 1568), with an introductory sketch by Colin A. Hunt. Perth, 1889. 4°.

The introductory sketch gives a good account of the history of the Perth crafts in general. The body of the work contains the entries in the Hammermen Book from 1518 to 1568, with brief extracts from 1577 to 1687. Valuable.

2568. LAWSON, J. P. The book of Perth: an illustration of the moral and ecclesiastical state of Scotland before and after the Reformation. With introduction, observations, and notes. Edinburgh, 1847. 8°.

Deals mainly with the ecclesiastical and social history of Perth.

2569. † MARSHALL, DAVID. Notes on the record-room of Perth. *Soc. of Antiq. of Scotland,* Proceedings, Third Series, vol. vi. Edinburgh, 1897. 4°.

2570. MARSHALL, T. H. The history of Perth, from the earliest period to the present time. With a supplement, containing the "Inventory of the Gabions" and the "Muses Threnodie," by Henry Adamson. Perth, 1849. 8°.

The best general history of Perth, but it does not contain much documentary material.

2571. Memorabilia of the city of Perth: containing a guide to Perth; historical memoranda respecting Perth; charters relating to the privileges of Perth. . . . Compiled from the best sources of information; chiefly from Mr. Cant's notes to the Muses Threnodie of Adamson. Perth, 1806. 8°.

Sect. iv. contains the documents mentioned in the note of No. 2564.

2572. PEACOCK, DAVID. Perth: its annals and its archives. Perth 1849. 8°.

Municipal government (with a few brief extracts from the burgh records, 1542–1688), pp. 529–51.

2573. PENNY, GEORGE. Traditions of Perth: containing sketches of the manners and customs of the inhabitants . . . interesting extracts from old records. . . . Perth, 1836. 8°.

Contains an account of the incorporated trades, etc.

PETERBOROUGH.

2574. WHELLAN, FRANCIS.   History, topography, and directory of Northamptonshire : comprising a general survey of the county, and a history of the city and diocese of Peterborough. . . . Second edition. London, etc., 1874.   8°.

Of little value for municipal history.
1st edition, 1849.

PETERHEAD.

2575. ARBUTHNOT, JAMES.   An historical account of Peterhead, from the earliest period to the present time. . . . With an appendix, containing a copy of the original charter of erection. . . . 2 pts. Aberdeen, 1815.   8°.

2576. BUCHAN, P.   Annals of Peterhead, from its foundation to the present time : including an account of the rise, progress, improvements, shipping, manufactures, commerce, trade, wells, baths, etc. of the town. . . . Peterhead, 1819.   8°.

Of little value for municipal history.

2577.   † Constitution (The) of the burgh of Peterhead.   Aberdeen, 1833.   8°.   pp. 31.

2578.   † Observations on the constitution of the burgh of Peterhead ; and remarks on an attempt, by certain individuals, to uphold the old system of exclusive burgh government.   By Decemviri.   Aberdeen, 1833.   8°.   pp. 21.

PETERSFIELD.

2579. ATCHESON, R. S.   Report of the case of the borough of Petersfield . . . determined by two select committees of the House of Commons in 1820 and 1821.   London, 1831.   8°.

Contains charters, etc. of the borough.

PEVENSEY.

2580. LARKING, L. B.   The custumal of Pevensey, as delivered to the lord warden at Dover Castle, in 1356.   *Sussex Archæol. Soc.,* Collections, iv. 209–18.   Lewes, 1851.   8°.

The custumal is printed in full.

2581. LOWER, M. A.   Chronicles of Pevensey. . . . Third edition, enlarged.   Lewes and London, [1873.]   8°.   pp. 58.

A brief account.
Other editions, 1846, 1863.

2582. TURNER, EDWARD.   Custumal of Pevensey [1337.]   *Sussex Archæol. Soc.*, Collections, xviii. 49–52.   Lewes, 1866.   8°.

Contains an old English translation of the customal.

PITTENWEEM.

2583. [COOK, DAVID.]   Annals of Pittenweem : being notes and extracts from the ancient records of that burgh, 1526–1793.   Anstruther, 1867.   8°.

Reprinted from the *East of Fife Record.*

PLYMOUTH.

The Gildhall of Plymouth contains a rich collection of muniments.   The regular series of records begin in 1486 with the receivers' accounts, which are practically complete to the present day.   The most valuable volume of records is the Black Book, a register of by-laws, gild ordinances, and other interesting matters relating to the town, 1441–1709.   Next in importance are the White Book (used from 1560 to 1754 for the entry of town ordinances, etc.), and Simon Carswell's Book, containing proceedings of the town courts, deeds, etc., Hen. VI.—Hen. VII.

The best history of Plymouth is Worth's (No. 2590) ; his calendar of records (No. 2589) is also valuable.

2584. BARON, R. W. S.   Mayors and mayoralties : or annals of the borough (Plymouth).   [Plymouth,] 1846.   12°·

Contains brief references to municipal affairs in modern times.

2585. † —— Municipal reform : or the old guiled all and the new gilled all.   Plymouth.   n. d.

2586. † Charter (The) of the borough of Plymouth, and the case of Rock against Berry in the Queen's Bench, 1712.   Plymouth, 1813.

2587. JEWITT, LLEWELLYNN.   A history of Plymouth.   Illustrated with wood engravings.   London and Plymouth, 1873.   8°.

Contains a translation of the charters granted to the town.

2588. ROWE, J. B. Devonshire guilds: Plymouth and Totnes. *Devon. Assoc. for Advancement of Science,* Transactions, vi. 101–106. Plymouth, 1873. 8°.

Of little value.

2589. WORTH, R. N. Calendar of the Plymouth municipal records. Plymouth, 1893. 8°.

Contains many valuable extracts from the town records.

2590. —— History of Plymouth, from the earliest period to the present time. [New enlarged edition.] Plymouth, 1890. 8°.

Ch. viii.　Parliamentary representation.
Ch. ix.　Local government.
A good book.
Other editions, 1871, 1873.

2591. —— Men and manners in Tudor [and Stuart] Plymouth. *Devon. Assoc. for Advancement of Science,* Transactions, xiv. 603–30; xv. 455–75. Plymouth, 1882–83. 8°.

Contains extracts from the accounts of the receivers of Plymouth, 1486–1700.

2592. —— On the Plymouth municipal records. *Brit. Archæol. Assoc.,* Journal, xxxix. 110–18. London, 1883. 8°.

2593. —— Some notes on the earlier municipal history of Plymouth. *Devon. Assoc. for Advancement of Science,* Transactions, xvi. 725–48. Plymouth, 1884. 8°.

2594. —— The three towns [Plymouth, Devonport, and Stonehouse] bibliotheca: a catalogue of books, pamphlets, papers, etc., written by natives thereof, published therein, or relating thereto; with brief biographical notices of the principal authors. [Plymouth, 1871.] 8°.

Reprinted from the Transactions of the Plymouth Institution, iv. 191–312, 422–30.

2595. † YONGE, JAMES. Plimouth memoirs: containing a chronologicall account of that corporation, a catalogue of all the mayors, together with ye memorable occurrences in their respective yeares . . . the charter then granted by K. Charles the Second, etc. Collected by James Yonge, 1684. Edited by R. N. Worth. Plymouth, 1876. 8°. pp. 58.

o

PLYMPTON.

2596. Cotton, William. Some account of the ancient borough town of Plympton St. Maurice, or Plympton Earl, with memoirs of the Reynolds family. London and Plymouth, 1859. 8°.

The account of municipal history is meagre.

2597. Rowe, J. B. Plympton : the borough and its charters. *Devon. Assoc. for Advancement of Science*, Transactions, xix. 555–648. Plymouth, 1887. 8°.

Contains the charters in full, also the ancient ordinances of 1623, and other records.

2598. —— Plympton : its parliamentary representation. *Ibid.*, xix. 649–74. Plymouth, 1887. 8°.

PONTEFRACT.

Fox (No. 2603) gives the best account of the municipal history. Booth-royd (No. 2600) gives the fullest survey of the parliamentary history. The Booke of Entries (No. 2599) is valuable. For the town charters, see No. 351.

2599. Booke of Entries (The) of the Pontefract corporation, 1653–1726. Edited by Richard Holmes. Pontefract, [1882.] 8°.

This oldest extant record of the Pontefract corporation contains minutes of proceedings of the meetings of the burgesses.
Valuable.

2600. Boothroyd, B[enjamin]. The history of the ancient borough of Pontefract . . . chiefly drawn from manuscripts never before pub-lished. Pontefract, 1807. 8°.

The corporation, 446–57.
Parliamentary history, 458–84.
The appendix contains a translation of the town charters.

2601. Case of the borough of Pontefract, concerning the right of election of members to serve in Parliament. On behalf of the sitting members. [London, 1770.] f°.

2602. Dunniad (The) : being a collection of pieces in prose and verse that have been published during the long-contested election for members to serve in Parliament for the borough of Pontefract. . . . London, [1769.] 8°.

2603. Fox, GEORGE. The history of Pontefract, in Yorkshire. Pontefract, etc., 1827. 8°.

Contains a translation of the town charters.

2604. Mayors (The) of the borough of Pontefract from its incorporation in 1484. With partial lists of the aldermen. Pontefract, 1882. 8°.

2605. TETLOW, R. J. Historical account of the borough of Pontefract, in the county of York; and the definition of a borough in general. . . . Leeds, 1769. 12°. pp. 43.

Of little value.

POOLE.

    a. General Histories, Nos. 2606–2608.
    b. Miscellaneous : Elections, etc., Nos. 2609–2616.

The best history is Sydenham's (No. 2608).

a. **General Histories.**

2606. History (The) of the town and county of Poole; compiled from Hutchins's history of the county of Dorset. . . . With many additions and corrections. Poole, 1788. 8°. pp. 86.

A brief account.

2607. † History of the town and county of Poole, with its charter, A. D. 1568. Poole, 1791. 8°.

2608. SYDENHAM, JOHN. The history of the town and county of Poole ; collected and arranged from ancient records and other authentic documents, and deduced from the earliest period to the present time. Poole, etc., 1839. 8°.

Contains quite a detailed account of the municipal and parliamentary history ; the town ordinances of 1566; abstracts of town charters, etc.

b. **Miscellaneous : Elections, etc.**

2609. † CLARKE, W. B. A letter to George Welch Ledgard, Esq., on the subject of the poll paper recently published, and on other subjects connected with the state of politics in Poole, and with the late election in particular. Poole, 1835. 8°. pp. 50.

2610. † Facts, letters, and comments for the consideration of the electors of the borough and district of Poole.   Poole, 1835.   8°.

2611. † Minutes of evidence given before the House of Lords, on the corporation of Poole, by Joseph Barter and George Baker Billows, on the Municipal Reform Bill, on Friday, 7th of August, 1835, as taken from the reports published by order of the House of Lords; together with notes and remarks.   Poole, [1835.]   8°.   pp. 20.

2612. † Municipal Corporation Bill.   Minutes of evidence on the corporation of Poole, taken at the bar of the House of Lords, on Friday the 7th of August, 1835.   Poole, [1835.]   8°.   pp. 16.

2613. † Petition (The) of the "500 inhabitants of Poole," presented in the House of Lords, against the Poole Corporation Bill, with the signatures alphabetically arranged; also the speeches of his grace the Duke of Richmond, delivered on that occasion.   Poole, 1836.   8°.   pp. 21.

2614. † Rate Payer (A).   A concise statement of the leading facts, and some of the most important circumstances, which have contributed to bring about the present embarrassed state of the borough of Poole.   By a rate payer.   Poole, 1838.   8°.   pp. 38.

2615. Report from the select committee on Poole borough municipal election; with the minutes of evidence. . . . *Parl. Papers*, 1836, vol. xxi.   [London,] 1836.   f°.

2616. True translation (A) of the charter granted by Queen Elizabeth, at Westminster, the 23d day of June, 1568, to the mayor, bailiffs, burgesses, and commonalty of the town and county of Poole.   Poole, 1791.   8°

PORTSMOUTH.

Allen (No. 2617) gives the best account of the municipal history.

2617. ALLEN, LAKE.   The history of Portsmouth. . . . To which is added an appendix, containing many of the charters granted to the town [1194–1484.]   London, 1817.   12°.

2618. Ancient and modern history (The) of Portsmouth, Portsea, Gosport, and their environs.   Gosport and London, [1800.]   8°.
A brief account.

2619. † Charter of King Charles I. to the corporation of Portsmouth.　Portsea.　n. d.　8°.

2620. SAUNDERS, W. H.　Annals of Portsmouth [1545–1865], historical, biographical, statistical.　Including old stories retold; remarkable events; charters; coinage; list of mayors; members of Parliament; and historical local occurrences chronologically arranged. London, 1880.　8°.

Does not devote much attention to municipal history.

2621. † Short sketch (A) of the conduct of administration of the borough of Portsmouth.　Portsmouth, 1780.　4°.

Relates to a contested election for mayor of Portsmouth.

2622. † SLIGHT, HENRY.　History of Portsmouth, Southsea, Gosport, etc.　Portsmouth, 1836.　8°.

Another edition, 1844.

2623. * SLIGHT, HENRY, and JULIAN.　Chronicles of Portsmouth. London, 1828.　12°.

Second title-page : " The history, antiquities, and present state of every public edifice of the town of Portsmouth," etc.

Contains, on pp. 177–200, a brief abstract of town charters, and some papers relating to parliamentary history.

PRESTON.

　　　a. Town Records, Nos. 2624–2628.
　　　b. General Histories, Nos. 2629–2634.
　　　c. Gilds, Nos. 2635–2648.
　　　d. Parliamentary History, etc., Nos. 2649–2652.

The best histories of Preston are Hardwick's and Hewitson's (Nos. 2631, 2632).　Two of the best accounts of the gild merchant are furnished by Abram, and Dobson and Harland (Nos. 2635, 2639).

a. Town Records

See No. 2647.

2624. Charters (The) granted by different sovereigns to the burgesses of Preston, in the county palatine of Lancaster.　Printed from attested copies.　The English translations by the Rev. John Lingard. Preston, 1821.　8°.

2625. Extracts from ancient documents in the archives of the corporation of Preston, presented to the mayor, aldermen, and burgesses, at the guild of 1842. [By John Addison.] Preston, [1842.] 4°. pp. 8 and 3 facsimiles.

Contains a facsimile of the charter of King John; the undated customal of Preston; extracts from the records of the gild for the years 1397, 1542, and 1582.

2626. Extracts from the corporation records of Preston [1635–1712.] *Preston Guardian*, Sept. 18 — Oct. 16, 1875.

2627. Preston corporation: [observations on the] ancient bye-laws, etc. *Preston Guardian*, Sept. 16, 1876.

A paper by Nicholas Grimshaw, mayor of Preston in the early part of the nineteenth century, on the relation between the corporation and the gild merchant.

2628. SMITH, T. C. Records of the parish church of Preston. Preston, 1892. 4°.

b. General Histories.

2629. Brief description (A) of the burrough and town of Preston and its government and guild. Originally composed between the years 1682 and 1686. [By Richard Kuerden.] With occasional notes by John Taylor. Preston, 1818. 8°. pp. 94.

Pt. ii. Government.
Pt. iii. Gild merchant.

2630. DOBSON, WILLIAM. The story of proud Preston: being a descriptive and historical sketch of the borough of Preston, in Lancashire. Preston, 1882. 8°. pp. 54.

A brief account.

2631. HARDWICK, CHARLES. History of the borough of Preston and its environs, in the county of Lancaster. Preston and London, 1857. 8°.

Municipal and parliamentary history, 257–350.

2632. HEWITSON, ANTHONY. History (from A. D. 705 to 1883) of Preston, county of Lancaster. Preston, 1883. 8°.

2633. History of Preston in Lancashire; together with the guild merchant, and some account of the duchy and county palatine of Lancaster. With eighteen plates. London, 1822. 4°.

A brief account of municipal history, and an account of the holding of the gild merchant; the plates display the various crafts in the gild procession.

2634. WHITTLE, PETER.   A topographical, statistical, and historical account of the borough of Preston . . . including a correct copy of the charter granted in the reign of Charles II. . . . the origin of the guild merchants' fete. . . . By Marmaduke Tulket [i. e. P. Whittle]. [Vol. i.]   Preston, 1821.   12°.

Vol. ii. : " The history of the borough of Preston, in the county palatine of Lancaster," by P. Whittle, Preston, 1837, 12°.

Government of the borough, i. 194–213.

Gilda mercatoria, i. 214–51.

Preston representative history, i. 252–62.

c. Gilds.

See Nos. 2629, 2633.

2635. ABRAM, W. A.   Preston guild merchant, 1882.   Memorials of the Preston guilds, illustrating the manner in which the guild merchant has been held in the borough from the earliest on record until the last guild in 1862.   Collected from the guild rolls, order books. . . . With full English abstracts of all the charters granted to Preston. . . . Preston, 1882.   4°.

There is a list of works relating to Preston on pp. 148–9.

2636. † Carnivals (The) of a century : or the guilds of Preston for a hundred years.   An account of the guilds merchant held at Preston from 1742 to 1842. . . . Preston, [1862.]   8°.

2637. † CLARKSON, R., and DEARDEN, J.   The guild guide and handbook of Preston, with a concise history of the guilds, and the arrangements for the festival of 1862. . . . Preston, 1862.   12°. pp. 76.

2638. DOBSON, WILLIAM.   An account of the celebration of Preston guild in 1862.   Preston, [1862.]   12°.   pp. 96.

2639. DOBSON, WILLIAM, and HARLAND, JOHN.   A history of Preston guild ; the ordinances of various guilds merchant, the custumal of Preston ; the charters of the borough. . . . Preston, [1862.]   12°.

2nd and 3rd editions, 1862.

2640. Documents concerning the ancient company of mercers, drapers, grocers, salters . . . of Preston [1628–1707.]   *Preston Guardian*, April 17 and May 1, 1875.

2641. † Full and detailed account (A) of the guild merchant of Preston, as celebrated in the year 1842. . . . . Preston, [1842.] 8°. pp. 52.

2642. Guild merchant (The) of Preston ; with an extract of the original charter granted for holding the same ; an account of the processions and public entertainments. . . . Manchester, [1762.] 8°. pp. 40.

2643. † Guild merchant (The) of Preston, or Preston guild companion : being an exact representation, on nineteen copper-plates, curiously drawn and engraved, of that ancient procession, with a letter-press explanation. . . . Manchester, 1762. 8°.

2644. † LONGWORTH, D. Celebration of the Preston guild merchant of 1862. . . . Preston, 1862.

2645. POLLARD, WILLIAM. A descriptive narrative of the guild merchant of Preston, in the county palatine of Lancaster, as celebrated in the year 1882. Preston, 1883. 4°.

2646. † Preston guild hand-book (The) : a brief sketch of the borough of Preston ; origin of the guild . . . programme and arrangements for the ensuing guild, 1842. Preston, 1842.

2647. Rolls (The) of burgesses at the guilds merchant of the borough of Preston (1397–1682). Edited by W. A. Abram. *Record Soc. of Lanc. and Cheshire,* vol. ix. [London,] 1884. 8°.

2648. WILCOCKSON, I[SAAC]. Authentic records of the guild merchant of Preston, in the county palatine of Lancaster, in the year 1822 ; with an introduction, containing an historical dissertation on the origin of guilds, and a relation of all the different celebrations of the guilda mercatoria of Preston, of which any records remain. . . . Preston, [1822.] 8°. pp. 128.

d. Parliamentary History, etc.

2649. DOBSON, WILLIAM. History of the parliamentary representation of Preston during the last hundred years. Second edition. Preston, 1868. 12°.

1st edition, 1856.

2650. DOBSON, WILLIAM.   Preston in the olden time : or illustrations of manners and customs in Preston, in the seventeenth and eighteenth centuries.   A lecture. . . . Preston, 1857.   12°.

2651. Preston electioneering 115 years ago.   *Preston Guardian,* March 3, 1883—May 10, 1884.

2652. Preston parliamentary elections [since 1295.]   Illustrated by addresses, squibs, poll books, official returns, the town records, election expenses accounts, and other materials.   *Preston Guardian,* Nov. 9, 1878—Sept. 3, 1881.

A valuable contribution to the history of Preston.

PRESTWICK.

2653. † HEWAT, KIRKWOOD.   A little Scottish world as revealed in the annals of an ancient Ayrshire parish [Prestwick].   Kilmarnock, 1895 ?.

2654. Records of the burgh of Prestwick, in the sheriffdom of Ayr, 1470–1782.   With an appendix and illustrative notes.   [Edited by John Fullerton.   *Maitland Club.*]   Glasgow, 1834.   4°.

Contains extracts from court records ; statutes ; the charter granted to Prestwick in 1600, etc.

Valuable.

QUEENBOROUGH.

2655. Copy of the charter of the borough of Queenborough [2 Charles I.]   London.   n. d.   8°.

2656. Queenborough corporation.   A copy of the report made by the commissioners appointed to inquire into the affairs of the corporation of the borough of Queenborough [regarding the misapplication of funds by the corporate body.]   *Parl. Papers,* 1844, vol. xxxi. [London,] 1831.   f°.

2657. † Report of the trial of an action of debt brought by the corporation of Queenborough against Edward Key (one of the burgesses), to recover penalties for the breach of two bye-laws made by the select body of the corporation in 1822, and re-enacted in 1824.   London, 1828.   8°.   pp. 170.

RAVENSPURNE.

2658. [THOMPSON, THOMAS.] Ocellum promontorium : or short observations on the ancient state of Holderness, with historic facts relative to the sea port and market town of Ravenspurne in Holderness. Hull, 1824. 8°.

READING.

The best histories of Reading are those of Coates and Man (Nos. 2662, 2666) ; Coates is the most trustworthy authority. The Diary of the Corporation (No. 2667) is a valuable collection of records. Besides this Diary, the archives contain charters and fiscal accounts, which reach back to the reigns of Henry III. and Edward I. respectively.

2659. † Admirable speech (An) made by the maior of Reading ; with a true impartial narrative of the whole proceedings of the maior, aldermen, and priests, trying to deprive the inhabitants of their vote of chosing. Reading, 1654. 4°.

2660. Church-wardens' account book (The) for the parish of St. Giles, Reading. Transcribed from the manuscript by W. L. Nash. Part i., 1518–46, containing the accounts for the last twenty-eight years of the reign of King Henry the Eighth. [Reading, 1881.] 4°. pp. 78.

2661. Churchwardens' accounts (The) of the parish of St. Mary's, Reading, Berks, 1550–1662. Transcribed by F. N. A. Garry and A. G. Garry. Reading, 1893. 8°.

Carefully edited.

2662. COATES, CHARLES. The history and antiquities of Reading. London, 1802. 4°.

Supplement, Reading, 1810.
The best history of Reading.

2663. DITCHFIELD, J. H. The guilds of Reading. *The Reliquary*, New Series, iv. 141–50. London, 1890. 8°.

2664. [DORAN, J.] The history and antiquities of the town and borough of Reading in Berkshire, with some notices of the most considerable places in the same county. Reading, etc., 1836. 8°.

Reprinted in 1836, with Doran's name on the title-page.

2665. JONES, J. B.   Sketches of Reading, historical, archæological, and descriptive.   Reading, 1870.   8°.

A brief account, of little value.

2666. MAN, JOHN.   The history and antiquities, ancient and modern, of the borough of Reading in the county of Berks.   Reading, 1816.   4°.

Ch. xviii. contains some interesting documents relating to the corporation and to the old trade companies.

Not as reliable as Coates.

2667. * Reading records.   Diary of the corporation, 1431–1654. Edited by J. M. Guilding.   4 vols.   London and Oxford, 1892–96. 8°.

Minutes of official proceedings of the mayor and burgesses.

2668. Reminiscences of Reading.   By an octogenarian.   Reading, [1889.]   8°.

Parliamentary elections, 1807-85, pp. 129-83.
Municipal elections, 1832-50, pp. 185-211.

2669. Report of the municipal commissioners appointed to enquire into the state of corporations in England and Wales.   Date of report, October 24th, 1833. . . . Corporation of Reading.   Reading, [1833.] 8°.

See No. 60.

REIGATE.

2670. Representation of Reigate.   The election of 1863, its history and results, and the threatened contest in 1865.   With extracts from the Surrey Gazette.   Lewes, [1865.]   8°.

RENFREW.

2671. Registrum monasterii de Passelet, cartas, privilegia, conventiones aliaque munimenta complectens, a domo fundata A. D. 1163 usque ad A. D. 1529. . . . [*Maitland Club.*]   Edinburgh, 1832.   4°.

For documents relating to Renfrew, 1204-1495, see pp. 20, 247, 403-7.

RETFORD, EAST.

2672. House of Lords.   Proceedings on East Retford Disfranchisement Bill, Monday, 21 June, 1830.   n. p.   n. d.   8°.

Without title-page.

2673. House of Lords. Report of Mr. Alderson's speech in his summing up on the East Retford Disfranchisement Bill, Monday, 12 July, 1830. London, 1830. 8°.

2674. PIERCY, J. S. The history of Retford, in the county of Nottingham : comprising its ancient, progressive, and modern state. . . . Retford, 1828. 8°.

Ch. iii. Translation of the charter of James I., etc.
Ch. iv. Contested parliamentary elections, 1700–1826.

2675. Speech of Lord Durham in the House of Lords, on Monday, the 19th of July, 1830, on the second reading of the East Retford Election Bill. London, [1830.] 8°.

2676. † WRAY, CECIL. Letter to the bailiffs . . . of East Retford. 1780. 8°.

RICHMOND.

2677. CLARKSON, CHRISTOPHER. The history and antiquities of Richmond, in the county of York, with a brief description of the neighbourhood. Richmond, 1821. 4°.

Gives a full account of municipal history. The appendix contains a translation of the charter of Charles II., 1668.
An earlier work by the same writer : " The history of Richmond, in the county of York," etc., 1814, 12°. (Anon.)

2678. Registrum honoris de Richmond exhibens terrarum et villarum quae quondam fuerunt Edwini comitis infra Richmundshire descriptionem. . . . [By Roger Gale.] London, 1722. f°.

Contains charters and other valuable documents relating to the town of Richmond, 100–101, 171, 209–18.

RIPON.

The most useful work on the history of Ripon is Harrison's (No. 2681). The other books give only a brief account of municipal history.

2679. CARTER, THOMAS. Ripon : its wakemen and their ancient badge. *Archæol. Journal,* xxxii. 394–416. London, 1875. 8°.

2680. GENT, THOMAS. The antient and modern history of the loyal town of Rippon. . . . York, 1733. 8°.

2681. [HARRISON, WILLIAM.] Ripon millenary : a record of the festival and a history of the city, arranged under its wakemen and mayors from the year 1400. Ripon, 1892. 4°.

2682. History (The) of Ripon : comprehending a civil and ecclesiastical account of that ancient borough.   To which is added a description of Fountains Abbey, Studley, and Hackfall, and an appendix containing charters, etc., illustrative of the work.   Ripon, 1801.   12°.

2nd edition, 1806.

ROCHDALE.

2683. FISHWICK, HENRY.   The bibliography of Rochdale, as illustrated by the books in the local Free Public Library.   A paper read before the Manchester Literary Club, March 22, 1880.   Manchester, 1880.   8°.

ROCHESTER.

2684. Authentic copy (An) of the charter and bye-laws, etc. of the city of Rochester, in the county of Kent.   Published for the information of the members of the corporation, in the year 1749, by order of John Waite, then mayor.   London, [1749.]   f°.   pp. 55.

Other editions : [London,] 1809, 8° ; Rochester, 1816, 8°.

2685. BLENCOWE, R. W.   Rochester records [1578–80.]   *Kent Archæol. Soc.*, Archæologia Cantiana, ii. 73–84.   Canterbury, 1859. 8°.

2686. BURT, JOSEPH.   On the archives of Rochester.   *Kent Archæol. Soc.*, Archæologia Cantiana, vi. 108–19.   London, 1866. 8°.

2687. History (The) and antiquities of Rochester and its environs. . . . [By S. Denne, W. Shrubsole, and others.]   Rochester, 1772.   8°.

2nd edition [by W. Wildash], 1817, 8° ; another edition, with omissions 1833, 12°.

2688. † Rochester charters.   1797.   8°.

ROMNEY, NEW.

For the customal of Romney, see No. 682.

2689. SALISBURY, EDWARD.   Report on the records of New Romney.   *Kent Archæol. Soc.*, Archæologia Cantiana, xvii. 12–33.   London, 1887.   8°.

2690. WALKER, E. B. The town and port of New Romney. *Kent Archæol. Soc.*, Archæologia Cantiana, xiii. 201–15. Canterbury, 1880. 8°.

A brief account of some of the town records.

ROSS.

2691. Ancient Norman-French poem on the erection of the walls of New Ross, in Ireland, 1265. By Fred. Madden. *Soc. of Antiq. of London*, Archæologia, xxii. 307–22. London, 1829. 4°.

This poem is also printed, with a translation, in *Facsimiles of National MSS. of Ireland*, edited by J. T. Gilbert (London, 1879) vol. iii. p. v. and app. ii.

2692. VIGORS, P. D. Alphabetical list of the free burgesses of New Ross, Co. Wexford, 1658–1839. *Royal Hist. and Archæol. Assoc. of Ireland*, Journal, Fifth Series, i. 298–309. Dublin, 1890. 8°.

2693. —— Extracts from the books of the old corporation of Ross, Co. Wexford [1658–87.] *Royal Soc. of Antiq. of Ireland*, Journal, Fifth Series, ii. 171–6, 287–90; iv. 176–9. Dublin, 1892–94. 8°.

ROTHERHAM.

2694. GUEST, JOHN. Yorkshire. Historic notices of Rotherham, ecclesiastical, collegiate, and civil. Worksop, 1879. 4°.

Rotherham was incorporated in 1871.

RUTHERGLEN.

2695. URE, DAVID. The history of Rutherglen and East-Kilbridge. Published with a view to promote the study of antiquity and natural history. Illustrated with plates. Glasgow, 1793. 8°.

Contains various charters granted to the burgh, and the sett made in 1671.

RUTHIN.

2696. [NEWCOME, RICHARD.] An account of the castle and town of Ruthin. Second edition. Ruthin, 1836. 8°.

A brief account.
1st edition, 1829.

2697. Ruthin charters. *Bye-gones relating to Wales and the Border Counties*, 1876–77, p. 301. Oswestry, [1877.] 4°.

RUYTON.

2698. KENYON, R. L. The borough of Ruyton. *Shropsh. Archæol. and Nat. Hist. Soc.*, Transactions, Second Series, iii. 237–52. Shrewsbury, 1891. 8°.

RYE.

For the customal of Rye, see No. 682.

2699. * HOLLOWAY, WILLIAM. The history and antiquities of the town and port of Rye, in the county of Sussex ; with incidental notices of the Cinque Ports. Compiled from manuscripts and original authorities. London, 1847. 8°.

Ch. i. The charters.
Ch. ii. The customal.
Ch. iii. Parliamentary history.
The best history of Rye.

2700. † INDERWICK, F. A. Rye under the commonwealth. *Sussex Archæol. Soc.*, Collections, xxix. 1–15. Lewes, 1895. 8°.

2701. † MASTERS, J. N. Catalogue of antiquities and historical manuscripts of Rye. Rye, 1894. 8°. pp. 14.

2702. Notes on the Rye elections. London, 1830. 8°.

An attempt to prove the identity of the " commonalty " and the "inhabitants " of Rye.

2703. Trial (The) in the court of King's Bench : the king versus the mayor and jurats of Rye ; with a letter to the freemen. London, 1829. 8°.

SAFFRON WALDEN.

2704. [GRIFFIN,] RICHARD (Lord BRAYBROOKE). The history of Audley End. To which are appended notices of the town and parish of Saffron Walden, in the county of Essex. London, 1836. 4°.

Contains a good account of the ancient town government ; extracts from the corporation accounts, 1546–1830 ; and a translation of the charter of William & Mary.

2705. PLAYER, JOHN. Sketches of Saffron Walden and its vicinity. Saffron Walden, 1845. 8°.

A brief account.

ST. ALBANS.

There is no good history of this town. The account of municipal development in Nos. 2710 and 2713 is brief. Gibbs's book (No. 2709) is the most useful.

2706. BLACK, W. H. On the town records of St. Albans. *Brit. Archæol. Assoc.*, Journal, xxvi. 143–9. London, 1870. 8°.

2707. Charter (The) and also the constitutions granted to the inhabitants of the town of St. Albans, in the county of Hertford. Translated from the original by the late E. Farrington, sergeant at law, recorder. Edited by a member of the present corporation. St. Albans, [1813.] 8°.

The charter was granted by Charles II. in the 16th year of his reign; the constitutions were confirmed by him in 1667. The latter give a comprehensive view of the town government.

2708. Chronicon Angliæ, ab anno domini 1328 usque ad annum 1388, auctore monacho quodam Sancti Albani. Edited by E. M. Thompson. *Rolls Series.* London, 1874. 8°.

The uprising of the townsmen in 1381, pp. 289–326.

2709. GIBBS, A. E. The corporation records of St. Albans; with lists of mayors, high stewards, members of Parliament, etc. St. Albans, 1890. 8°.

Contains extracts from the municipal records, 1586–1889, a reprint of articles in the *Herts Advertiser.*
A useful book.

2710. History of Verulam and St. Albans; containing an historical account of the decline of Verulam and origin of St. Albans, and of the present state of the town. . . . St. Albans, 1815. 12°.

2711. Journals of the House of Lords, 5 Geo. IV., 1824, vol. lvi. [London, 1824.] f°.

On p. 1105 there is an agreement between the abbey and the burgesses, in Edward III.'s time. Also printed in Parl. Papers, 1826, ix. 9–10.

2712. WALSINGHAM, THOMAS. Gesta abbatum monasterii Sancti Albani . . . [793–1411.] Edited by H. T. Riley. *Rolls Series.* 3 vols. London, 1867–69. 8°.

For documents, etc. relating to the burgesses, see i. 410–23, ii. 155–76, 215–64, iii. 285–372.

2713. WILLIAMS, F. L.   An historical and topographical description of the municipium of Verulam; the martyrdom of St. Alban; foundation of the monastery. . . . 2 pts.   St. Albans, 1822.   8°.

ST. ANDREWS.

2714. † ROGER, CHARLES.   History of St. Andrews, with a full account of the recent improvements in the city.   Edinburgh, 1849. 8°.

ST. IVES (CORNWALL).

2715. † Bye-laws for the good rule and government of the borough of St. Ives.   St. Ives, 1837.   8°.   pp. 20.

2716. LACH-SZYRMA, W. S.   Notes on the borough records of the towns of Marazion, Penzance, and St. Ives.   *Brit. Archæol. Assoc.,* Journal, xxxviii. 354–70.   London, 1882.   8°.

2717. —— A short history of Penzance, S. Michael's Mount, S. Ives, and the Land's End district.   Truro and London, 1878.   4°.

A brief account.

2718. MATTHEWS, J. H.   A history of the parishes of St. Ives, Lelant, Towednack, and Zennor, in the county of Cornwall.   London, 1892.   8°.

Contains the borough accounts, 1570-1776; a translation of the charter of James II., 1685, etc.

Valuable; the best history of St. Ives.

2719. Records of the borough of St. Ives [in the 17th century.] By Porthminster.   *The Western Antiquary,* v. 33–7, 77–9, etc.   Plymouth, 1885–86.   4°.

2720. † St. Ives election.   On the petition of Sir Walter Stirling, Bart., complaining of an undue return in James Robert, George Graham, Esq., and Lyndon Evelyn, Esq.   The reply of Mr. [W.] Harrison, the petitioner's counsel on the above petition.   London, 1820.   8°.   pp. 101.

ST. MONANCE.

2721. JACK, JOHN.   An historical account of St. Monance, Fifeshire, ancient and modern; interspersed with a variety of tales, incidental, legendary, and traditional.   Edinburgh, etc., 1844.   12°.

SALFORD.

2722. † BAILEY, J. E.   The first charter of Salford, Co. Lancaster [circa 1231.]   Manchester, 1882.   4°.   pp. 10.

2723. First charter (The) of Salford.   *Palatine Note-Book*, ii. 146–51, 160–61.   Manchester, [1882.]   4°.

The Latin text, with an English translation.

This charter of Ranulf de Blundeville is also printed by Harland (No. 2358), 200-202, and by Hibbert-Ware (No. 2359), 43-51.

2724. † ORMEROD, G. W.   Manual of local acts affecting the townships comprised in the boroughs of Manchester and Salford.   Manchester, 1838.   8°.

2725. † PEET, THOMAS.   Translated copy and inquiry into the date of the [first] charter of the borough of Salford, in the county palatine of Lancaster, with a chronological sketch of the history of the honour of Lancaster.   Together with the charter of incorporation for the borough of Salford, granted April 16th, 1844.   Salford, 1862.   8°. pp. 15.

Earlier editions, without Queen Victoria's charter, 1824, 1848.

2726. REILLY, JOHN.   The people's history of Manchester [and Salford.]   11 pts.   London and Manchester, [1859–60.]   8°.

Not completed ; extends to 1832.

In his *History of Manchester*, 1861 (No. 2364), i. 515–20, 553–60, he prints the charters granted to Salford by Earl Ranulf and Queen Victoria.

SALISBURY.

The only book of much value relating to the municipal history of this city is Benson and Hatcher's (No. 2729).   Swayne's extracts from the records (No. 2737) have not been published in a separate volume.

2727. Antiquitates Sarisburienses : or the history and antiquities of Old and New Sarum, collected from original records and early writers ; with an appendix.   Illustrated with two copper-plates.   [By Edward Ledwich.]   New edition.   Salisbury, 1777.   8°.

1st edition, 1771.

2728. BENSON, ROBERT.   Remarks on the office of deputy-recorder of Salisbury, in a letter addressed to the right hon. William Earl of Radnor, recorder.   London, 1831.   8°.

2729. * BENSON, ROBERT, and HATCHER, HENRY. Old and New Sarum, or Salisbury. London, 1843. f°.

Contains "orders and constitutions" made under divers mayors since 10 Henry IV.; the town charters in full; and many other extracts from the town records. The best history of Salisbury. See No. 663.

2730. Charters and documents illustrating the history of the cathedral, city, and diocese of Salisbury in the twelfth and thirteenth centuries. Selected . . . by W. R. Jones and edited by W. D. Macray. *Rolls Series.* London, 1891. 8°.

2730a. † Churchwardens' accounts (The) of SS. Edmund and Thomas, Sarum. Edited by H. J. F. Swayne. *Wilts. Record Society.* 1896.

2731. Collection (A) of remarkable events relative to the city of New Sarum, with the year and name of the mayor in whose time they occurred, being from A. D. 1356 to 1783, a period of four hundred and twenty-seven years. [By J. Easton.] New edition. Salisbury, 1817. 12°.

5th edition, "A chronology of remarkable events," etc., 1824.

2732. Correct list (A) of the bishops and mayors of Salisbury, from the earliest period to the present time. . . . [By J. Easton.] Salisbury, 1798. 12°.

2nd edition, "A correct list of the mayors of New Sarum," etc., 1826.

2733. Description (A) of that admirable structure, the cathedral church of Salisbury . . . to which is prefixed an account of Old Sarum. London, 1774. 4°.

A translation of various documents relating to municipal history, 19-32.

2734. DUKE, EDWARD. Prolusiones historicæ : or essays illustrative of the halle of John Halle, citizen and merchant of Salisbury, in the reigns of Henry VI. and Edward IV. . . . Salisbury and London, 1837. 8°.

Deals with the internal affairs of the city.

2735. HALL, PETER. A brief history of Old and New Sarum. By the Rev. Peter Hall. Three copies, in follio (sic), printed separately. Salisbury, 1834. f°.

A brief account. Seemingly reprinted from his "Picturesque memorials of Salisbury," 1834.

2736. † Medieval guilds of Salisbury.   *Wilts. Archæol. and Nat. Hist. Soc.*, 1896, vol. xxix.

2737. S[WAYNE], H. J. F.   Gleanings from the archives of Salisbury. Nos. 1–30. *Salisbury and Winchester Journal,* Nov. 25, 1882—Dec. 27, 1884.

An important collection of charters, extracts from town accounts, etc., from the 13th to the 17th centuries inclusive.

SALTASH.

2738. CARPENTER, SAMUEL.   A statement of the evidence and arguments of counsel before the committee of the House of Commons, upon the controverted election for Saltash. Together with a few annotations. London, 1808. 8°.

SANDWICH.

2739. BAKER, OSCAR.   History of the antiquities of Sandwich and Richborough Castle in Kent. With illustrations by the author. London, 1848. 8°.

Extracts from the town customal, 110–44.

2740. * BOYS, WILLIAM.   Collections for an history of Sandwich in Kent, with notices of the other Cinque Ports and members, and of Richborough. Canterbury, 1792. 4°.

Contains the customal and charter of Sandwich. For the customal, see also No. 682.

2741. DORMAN, THOMAS.   The Sandwich Book of Orphans [1589–1649.] *Kent Archæol. Soc.,* Archæologia Cantiana, xvi. 179–206. London, 1886. 8°.

SANQUHAR.

2742. BROWN, JAMES.   The history of Sanquhar. Dumfries, etc., 1891. 8°.

Ch. vii. contains a good account of the municipal history.
The best history of Sanquhar.

2743. SIMPSON, ROBERT.   History of Sanquhar. Second edition. Edinburgh, etc., 1853. 12°.

Ch. vii contains a brief account of municipal history.
1st edition, 1853.

SCARBOROUGH.

2744. BAKER, J. B.   The history of Scarborough from the earliest date.   London, 1882.   8°.

Contains a good account of its municipal and parliamentary history.
The best history of Scarborough.

2745. HINDERWELL, THOMAS.   The history and antiquities of Scarborough.   Third edition, enlarged.   Scarborough, 1832.   8°.

Municipal and parliamentary history, 155–89, 357–66.
1st and 2nd editions, 1798, 1811.

2746. Yorkshire inquisitions of the reigns of Henry III. and Edward I.   *Yorkshire Archæol. and Topog. Soc.*, Record Series, vol. xii.   Edited by William Brown.   [Worksop,] 1892.   8°.

For documents relating to Scarborough, see pp. 21, 72, 122, 163, 220, 271.

SEAFORD.

2747. LOWER, M. A.   Memorials of the town, parish, and Cinque-Port of Seaford, historical and antiquarian.   With the charter of incorporation and other documents.   London and Lewes, 1855.   8°.

A reprint from the collections of the Sussex Archæological Society (Lewes, 1854), vii. 73–150, with some additions.

2748. LOWER, M. A., and COOPER, W. D.   Further memorials of Seaford.   *Sussex Archæol. Soc.*, Collections, xvii. 141–63.   Lewes, 1865.   8°.

SHAFTESBURY.

2749. History (A) of the ancient town of Shaftesbury, from the founder, Alfred the Great ; partly selected from Hutchins [No. 594]. . . . [By Thomas Adams.]   Sherborne, [1808.]   8°.

A brief account.

2750. History of the Shaftesbury election, 1830 : containing a complete and correct account of the extraordinary contest for the liberty and independence of the borough.   To which is prefixed a supplement, containing an account of the subsequent proceedings.   By a constitutional reformer.   Shaftesbury, etc., 1830.   8°.   pp. 170.

" It is believed to furnish a fair specimen of the proceedings connected with the borough-mongering system generally."

2751. MAYO, C. H. The municipal records of the borough of Shaftesbury [with extracts]. Sherborne, 1889. 8°. pp. 87.

2752. Rejoinder (A) to "An elector" on his "Plain observations" on Mr. Knowles's address to the electors of Shaftesbury. By a student of Lincoln's Inn. Shaftesbury, 1830. 8°. pp. 26.

SHEFFIELD.

The best history is Hunter's (No. 2754).

2753. ADDY, S. O. The hall of Waltheof: or the early condition and settlement of Hallamshire. London and Sheffield, 1893. 4°.

Chs. xvi.–xvii. The burgery or corporation of Sheffield.

2754. HUNTER, JOSEPH. Hallamshire : the history and topography of the parish of Sheffield. . . . New and enlarged edition, by Alfred Gatty. London, 1869. f°.

Valuable.

1st edition, 1819.

2755. LEADER, J. D. Extracts from the earliest book of accounts belonging to the town trustees of Sheffield, dating from 1566 to 1707 ; with explanatory notes. Sheffield, 1879. 8°.

2756. —— Notes on the cutlers' company's accounts. A paper read before the Sheffield Architectural and Archæological Society [1874.] *Associated Architectural Societies*, Reports and Papers, xii. 287–306. Lincoln, [1874.] 8°.

2757. —— Some speculations and reflections suggested by Furnivall's charter [1297] and the town burgery accounts of Sheffield. [A paper read before the Sheffield Architectural and Archæological Society, 1876.] *Associated Architectural Societies*, Reports and Papers, xiii. 281–96. Lincoln, [1876.] 8°.

Mr. Leader is preparing a volume on the Burgery of Sheffield, which will contain the charter of 1297, the burgery accounts and minutes in full from 1565 to the end of the 17th century, together with extracts from these records in later times down to 1848.

2758. † MITCHELL, SAMUEL. An essay on the history of the burgery of Sheffield, commonly called the town trust. A paper read before the Literary and Philosophical Society of Sheffield, circa 1828.

Said to be valuable.

2759. PARKER, JOHN, and WARD, H. G.   Chapters in the political history of Sheffield, 1832–1849 : consisting of letters from Mr. John Parker, M. P., and Mr. Henry George Ward, M. P.   (Reprinted from the Sheffield and Rotherham Independent.)   Sheffield, 1884.   8°.

2760. Picture (The) of Sheffield : or an historical and descriptive view of the town of Sheffield, in the county of York.   Sheffield, 1824. 8°.

2761. WHITE, WILLIAM.   History, guide, and description of the borough of Sheffield, and the town and parish of Rotherham : comprising the ancient and modern history of Hallamshire. . . . Sheffield, 1833.   12°.

A brief account.

SHOREHAM.

2762. GREEN, BURTON.   New Shoreham.   *Sussex Archæol. Soc.*, Collections, xxvii. 69–109.   Lewes, 1877.   8°.

SHREWSBURY.

a. Town Records, Nos. 2763–2770.
b. General Histories, Nos. 2771–2775.
c. Gilds, Nos. 2776–2784.
d. Parliamentary History, Nos. 2785–2789.

Few boroughs have records as complete as those of Shrewsbury. Some of the oldest gild merchant rolls in England are preserved in the archives of that town; this series extends from 1209 to 1511.   The bailiffs' and mayors' accounts (beginning in 1257) and the court rolls (beginning in 1272) extend, with few breaks, to the present day.

The best general history of Shrewsbury is Owen and Blakeway's (No. 2773).   Hibbert and Leighton (Nos. 546, 2783) give good accounts of the craft gilds.

a. Town Records.

See Nos. 2777–2779.

2763. ADNITT, H. W.   The orders of the corporation of Shrewsbury, 1511–1735.   *Shropsh. Archæol. and Nat. Hist. Soc.*, Transactions, xi. 153–210.   Shrewsbury and Oswestry, 1888.   8°.

2764. Calendar of the muniments and records of the borough of Shrewsbury.   Shrewsbury, 1896.   8°.

2765. DRINKWATER, C. H.   The abbot of Shrewsbury versus the burgesses thereof in the matter of the mills.   *Shropsh. Archæol. and Nat. Hist. Soc.*, Transactions, Second Series, vi. 341–57.   Shrewsbury, 1894.   8°.

Account of a plea at Westminster, 1306-7.

2766. —— Bailiffs' accounts of Shrewsbury, 1275–7.   Edited by C. H. Drinkwater.   *Ibid.*, iii. 41–92.   Shrewsbury, 1891.   8°.

2767. FLETCHER, W. G. D.   The municipal records of Shrewsbury. *Archæol. Journal*, li. 283–92.   London, 1894.   8°.

2768. —— The poll-tax for the town and liberties of Shrewsbury, 1380.   *Shropsh. Archæol. and Nat. Hist. Soc.*, Transactions, Second Series, ii. 17–28.   Shrewsbury, 1890.   8°.

2769. Inquisition of the liberties of the town of Shrewsbury, 1515. Edited by W. G. D. Fletcher.   n. p.   [1892.]   8°.   pp. 4.

2770. Shrewsbury corporation rental in 1657.   [Edited by C. M.] *Shropshire Notes and Queries*, vols. i.–iii.   Shrewsbury, [1884]–86. 4°.

b. General Histories.

2771. Early chronicles of Shrewsbury, 1372–1606.   Transcribed and annotated by Rev. W. A. Leighton.   *Shropsh. Archæol. and Nat. Hist. Soc.*, Transactions, iii. 239–352.   Shrewsbury and Oswestry, [1880.]   8°.

To the events of each year are prefixed the names of the bailiffs of Shrewsbury.

2772. [OWEN, HUGH.]   Some account of the ancient and present state of Shrewsbury.   New edition.   London, 1810.   8°.

Of little value for municipal history.
1st edition, 1808.

2773. [OWEN, H., and BLAKEWAY, J. B.]   A history of Shrewsbury. 2 vols.   London, 1825.   4°.

Contains extracts from the bailiffs' accounts since 1457, etc.
Valuable.

2774. PHILLIPS, T[HOMAS].   The history and antiquities of Shrewsbury, from its first foundation to the present time. . . . Second edi-

tion, with continuation . . . by Charles Hulbert. 2 vols. Shrewsbury, 1837. 4°.

Vol. i. ch. viii. Abstract of town charters; and brief extracts from the town
records, 1516–1684.

Vol. i. ch. ix. Parliamentary elections, 1709–1830.

1st edition, 1779; reprinted, 1828.

2775. PIDGEON, HENRY. Memorials of Shrewsbury : being a concise description of the town and its environs. . . . Second edition,
enlarged. Shrewsbury, [1851.] 8°.

Of little value for municipal history.

1st edition, 1837.

c. **Gilds.**

See No. 546.

2776. CHAMBERS, ROBERT. The book of days. . . . 2 vols. London and Edinburgh, [1863–64.] 8°.

Shrewsbury Show [by Thomas Wright], i. 704–8.

2777. CUNNINGHAM, WILLIAM. The gild merchant of Shrewsbury.
Royal Hist. Soc., Transactions, New Series, ix. 99–118. London,
1895. 8°.

Contains two rolls of the gild merchant, 1209–10, 1219–20, transcribed by C.
H. Drinkwater.

See No. 2779.

2778. DRINKWATER, C. H. The merchants' gild of Shrewsbury.
Shropsh. Archæol. and Nat. Hist. Soc., Transactions, Second Series,
ii. 29–59. Shrewsbury, 1890. 8°.

Contains gild rolls of Edward I.'s time.

2779. † —— The merchants' gild of Shrewsbury, the two earliest
rolls, for 1209–10 and 1219–20. Translated and edited by C. H.
Drinkwater. *Ibid.*, vol. viii. Shrewsbury, 1896. 8°.

See No. 2777.

2780. —— Petition of cordwainers of the town of Salop in 1323–4.
Ibid., vi. 284–90. Shrewsbury, 1894. 8°.

2781. † —— The Shrewsbury drapers' company charter, Jan. 12,
1461–2. Edited by C. H. Drinkwater. *Ibid.*, vol. viii. Shrewsbury, 1896. 8°.

2782. DRINKWATER, C. H.   Shrewsbury trade guilds.   The glovers' company.   *Shropsh. Archæol. and Nat. Hist. Soc.*, Transactions, x. 33–95.   Shrewsbury and Oswestry, 1887.   8°.

Gives an account of the contents of the company's Register Book, 17th and 18th centuries.

2783. * LEIGHTON, W. A.   The guilds of Shrewsbury.   [Extracts from the records of the tailors and skinners, the barbers, the mercers, etc.]   *Ibid.*, iv. 193–292 ; v. 265–97 ; vii. 408–30 ; viii. 269–412. Shrewsbury and Oswestry, [1881–85.]   8°.

2784. PIDGEON, HENRY.   Ancient guilds, trading companies, and the origin of Shrewsbury Show.   *Shropsh. Archæol. and Nat. Hist. Soc.*, Transactions, vi. 183–204.   Shrewsbury, etc., [1883.]   8°.

Also printed in *The Reliquary*, 1862, iii. 61–73.

d. Parliamentary History.

2785.   † Considerations on the principles of representation, with a review of the late contest for Shrewsbury.   [Shrewsbury,] 1807.   8°.

2785a.   † FISHER, G. W.   Notes on the election of burgesses of Parliament for Shrewsbury in 1584 and 1586.   *Shropsh. Archæol. Soc.*, Transactions, Second Series, vol. ix.   Shrewsbury, 1897.   8°.

2786.   † Free thoughts on the late contested election for Shrewsbury.   By an independent voter.   [Shrewsbury,] 1806.   8°.

2787. HUGHES, W.   The poll for the borough of Shrewsbury, June 29–30, 1747.   *Shropsh. Archæol. and Nat. Hist. Soc.*, Transactions, iii. 221–38.   Shrewsbury, etc., [1880.]   8°.

2788.   † Popular rights vindicated : being free remarks in answer to a pamphlet entitled Free thoughts on the late contested election for Shrewsbury ; with an appendix containing Sir Wm. Pulteney's address to the burgesses of Shrewsbury in the year 1774.   Shrewsbury, 1806.   8°.

2789.   † Serious thoughts on the late election for Shrewsbury, in answer to a pamphlet entitled Free thoughts. . . . Shrewsbury, 1807.   8°.

SLIGO.

2790. O'RORKE, T. The history of Sligo, town and county. 2 vols. Dublin, [1889.] 8°.

Vol. i. ch. xiii. The borough of Sligo.

2791. WOOD-MARTIN, W. G. History of Sligo, county and town, from the earliest ages. . . . 3 vols. Dublin, 1882–92. 8°.

Vol. iii. ch. xx. contains a good account of the municipal history since the creation of the corporation in 1612.

The best history of Sligo.

2792. —— Sligo and the Enniskilleners, from 1688–1691. Second edition. Dublin, 1882. 8°.

Does not devote much attention to municipal affairs.

SOUTHAMPTON.

The most valuable of the old town muniments are the Oak Book of Edward II.'s time (containing municipal ordinances, etc.) and the Black Book, 16 Rich. II. — 12 Eliz. (containing deeds, ordinances, etc.).

The best history of Southampton is that of Davies.

2793. Charter (The) of the town and county of Southampton, dated the 27th of June, 1641, in the 16th year of the reign of Charles I. : being the last charter, and comprising all former grants, privileges, etc. Carefully revised. Southampton, 1810, 12°

Translation only.

2794. CLUTTERBUCK, R. H. The Black Book of Southampton. *Brit. Archæol. Assoc.*, Journal, l. 125–30. London, 1894. 8°.

2795. * DAVIES, J. S. A history of Southampton, partly from the MS. of Dr. Speed, in the Southampton archives. Southampton and London, 1883. 8°.

Contains the ancient ordinances of the gild merchant and extracts from other records.

The most valuable work relating to Southampton.

2796. † Last charter of the county of the town of Southampton, dated June 27th, 1641. [Southampton,] 1826. 12°.

2797. SHORE, T. W. Guide to Southampton and neighbourhood, written for the visit of the British Association for the Advancement of Science, 1882. Southampton, [1882.] 16°.

Contains a good short account of municipal history.

2798. SMIRKE, EDWARD. Ancient ordinances of the gild merchant of the town of Southampton. *Archæol. Journal*, xvi. 283–96, 343–52. London, 1859. 8°.

These ordinances are also printed by Davies (No. 2795) and Gross (No. 541). They are valuable for the study of municipal history.

2799. VAUX, W. S. W. Some notices of records preserved amongst the corporation archives at Southampton. *Archæol. Journal*, iii. 229–33. London, 1846. 8°.

2800. WRIGHT, THOMAS. Remarks on the municipal privileges and legislation in the Middle Ages, as illustrated from the archives of Winchester and Southampton. *Brit. Archæol. Assoc.*, Transactions at Winchester, 16–27. London, 1846. 8°.

2801. —— Report on the municipal records of Winchester and Southampton. *Ibid.*, 28–39. London, 1846. 8°.

SOUTHWARK.

See the histories of London by Allen, Chamberlain, Noorthouck, etc. (Nos. 1992–2007, 2221).

2802. † Articles (The) of lete and courte for the lyberties of South-warke. Imprinted by John Cawood. London, 1561. 4°.

2803. BOGER, C. G. Southwark and its story. London, 1881. 8°.

2804. Candid enquiry (A) into the right of the jurisdiction in the city of London over the borough of Southwark, and of the assumed power of the Surry magistrates over that borough; with the royal charter at full of Edward VI. . . . Addressed to the right hon. Thomas Sainsbury, lord mayor of the city of London. By an inhabitant of the borough of Southwark [James Hedger]. London, [1787.] 8°.

2805. CLIFFORD, HENRY. A report of the two cases of controverted elections of the borough of Southwark . . . 37 George III.; with notes and illustrations. To which are added an account of the two subsequent cases of the city of Canterbury, and an appendix. . . . London, 1797. 8°.

Another edition, 1802.

2806. CORNER, G. R. A concise account of the local government of the borough of Southwark, and observations upon the expediency of uniting the same more perfectly with the city of London, or of obtaining a separate municipal corporation. . . . Southwark, 1836. 8°. pp. 40.

2807. HUGHSON, DAVID [EDWARD PUGH]. Multum in parvo. The privileges of Southwark, comprised in the charters granted to the city of London by Edward III., Edward IV., Edward VI. . . . Southwark, [1818.] 12°. pp. 22.

2808. —— A respectful appeal to the consideration and justice of the mayor, commonalty, and citizens of London, on behalf of the rights, privileges, and franchises of . . . Southwark. London, 1816. 8°.

2809. † Humble address (An) to the right honorable the lord mayor of London, concerning the jurisdiction of the city over the borough of Southwark. London, 1760. 8°.

2810. KEMMISH, WILLIAM. Southwark rights. The various royal charters granted to the city of London by Kings Edw. III., Edw. IV., and Edw. VI., at full length, respecting the town and borough of Southwark . . . interspersed with an abstract from the Police Act, and occasional notes. Edited by William Kemmish. Southwark, 1816. 8°.

2811. RENDLE, WILLIAM. Old Southwark and its people. Southwark, 1878. 8°.

One of the best histories of Southwark, but the account of municipal government is brief.

2812. ROBERTSON, JAMES. Lectures on the history of Southwark. London, 1863. 8°.

Contains only a few brief allusions to municipal history.

2813. † Statement (The) of the inhabitants of Bridge Ward Without, in the city of London, in support of their petition to the court of common council for the election of their own aldermen and other municipal rights; with the report of the committee of general purposes thereon, and observations on the report. By an inhabitant of Southwark. London, 1836.

" Containing much curious and valuable information relating to the ancient and present state of Southwark ": Brayley's *Surrey* (new edition), iv. 355.

SOUTHWOLD.

2814. Extracts from the report of the select committee of the House of Commons, appointed to enquire into the operation of the Municipal Reform Act on the privileges and private property of the freemen of cities and boroughs in England and Wales; with the proceedings of the committee and minutes of evidence, as far as the same relate to the borough of Southwold. Southwold, 1840. 8°.

See No. 253.

2815. GARDNER, THOMAS. An historical account of Dunwich, antiently a city, now a borough; Blithburgh, formerly a town of note, now a village; Southwold, once a village, now a town corporate. . . . London, 1754. 4°.

Charter of William & Mary, inspecting older charters, Henry VII. — Charles I., 230–44.

2816. M., J. Southwold in the 16th century. *East Anglian Notes and Queries*, iii. 49–51, 62–3, 71–3. Lowestoft, 1869. 8°.

Contains by-laws of the town, 1516–86.

2817. WAKE, ROBERT. Southwold and its vicinity, ancient and modern. Yarmouth, 1839. 8°.

Chs. v.–vii. Borough and corporation.

STAFFORD.

2818. CALVERT, CHARLES. History of Stafford, and guide to the neighbourhood. Illustrated with wood engravings. Stafford, 1886. 8°.

A meagre sketch.

2819. CHERRY, J. L. Stafford in olden times: being a reprint of articles published in the "Staffordshire Advertiser," with illustrations. Stafford, 1890. 8°.

The best book on the history of Stafford, but it consists of disconnected notes and articles.

STAMFORD.

The best histories are those of Drakard and Harrod (Nos. 2822, 2823).

2820. BURTON, GEORGE. Chronology of Stamford. Compiled from Peck, Butcher, Howgrave, Harrod, Drakard, parliamentary reports, and other important works. Stamford and London, 1846. 8°.

Arranged in the form of a dictionary.

Contains a detailed account of the municipal history, pp. 117–62, etc.

2821. BUTCHER, RICHARD. The survey and antiquitie of the towne of Stamford, in the county of Lincolne ; with its ancient foundation, grants, priviledges. . . . [With notes by Francis Peck.] London, [1727.] f°.

Contains town ordinances of 6 Charles I.

Earlier editions: 1646, 4°; 1717, 8°.

2822. DRAKARD, JOHN. The history of Stamford, in the county of Lincoln : comprising its ancient, progressive, and modern state. With an account of St. Martin's, Stamford Baron, and Great and Little Wothorpe, Northamptonshire. Stamford, 1822. 8°.

Ch. iv. Translation of the charter of James II., 1685; the municipal ordinances of 1640, etc.

Ch. v. State of the representation.

2823. HARROD, W. The antiquities of Stamford and St. Martin's, compiled chiefly from the annals of the Rev. Francis Peck, with notes ; to which is added their present state, including Burghley. 2 vols. Stamford, 1785. 8°.

Contains a translation of the town charter of 1685.

2824. HOWGRAVE, FRANCIS. An essay of the ancient and present state of Stamford : its situation, erection, dissolution, and re-edification. . . . Stamford, 1726. 4°.

The author borrows much of his material from Butcher, without acknowledgment.

2825. NEVINSON, C[HARLES]. History of Stamford. Stamford and London, 1879. 8°.

A brief account.

2826. Petition (The) of the electors of Stamford to the House of Commons, 1830 [complaining that the Marquess of Exeter unlawfully interferes with the elections for M. P.'s.] London, [1830.] 8°.

2827. SIMPSON, JUSTIN. The Stamford waits and their predecessors : an historical sketch. *The Reliquary*, xxvi. 1–6. London and Derby, 1885. 8°.

Contains brief extracts from the town records, 1686–1830.

STEYNING.

2828. MEDLAND, THOMAS. Notices of the early history of Steyning and its church. *Sussex Archæol. Soc.*, Collections, v. 111–26. London, 1852. 8°.

STIRLING.

2828a. † Abstract of protocol book of the burgh of Stirling, A. D. 1469–1484. Edinburgh, 1896. 8°.

2829. † CHAMBERS, ROBERT. Picture of Stirling; with historical and descriptive notes by Robert Chambers. Stirling, 1830. 4°.

2830. * Charters and other documents relating to the royal burgh of Stirling, A. D. 1124–1705. [Compiled by Robert Renwick.] Glasgow, 1884. 4°.

The Latin records, with a translation.

2831. * Extracts from the records of the royal burgh of Stirling, A. D. 1519–1752; with appendix, A. D. 1295–1752. [Edited by Robert Renwick.] Printed for the Glasgow Stirlingshire and Sons of the Rock Society. 2 vols. Glasgow, 1887–89. 4°.

Extracts from the gildry records, ii. 378–95.

2832. General history (A) of Stirling : containing a description of the town, and origin of the castle and burgh. To which is prefixed a short view of the causes which gave rise to burghs in Europe. [By — Sutherland.] Stirling, 1794. 12°.

A good short account.

2833. History (The) of Stirling from the earliest accounts to the present time. Compiled from the best and latest authorities. . . . Third edition. Stirling, 1836. 12°.

The account of municipal history is meagre.
Earlier editions, 1812, 1817.

2834. New description (A) of the town and castle of Stirling; with an appendix, containing notices of roads. . . . Stirling, 1835. 8°.

A brief account.

STOCKPORT.

2835. Advertiser notes and queries [relating to Stockport, etc.] Reprinted from the "Stockport Advertiser." 5 vols. Stockport, 1882–85. 8°.

2836. HEGINBOTHAM, HENRY. Stockport, ancient and modern.
. . . 2 vols. London, 1882–92. 4°.

Contains a good account of the corporate and parliamentary history of Stockport; also the charters granted to the town in the 13th century, with a translation: see ii. 257–315.

Valuable.

2837. WATSON, JOHN. Memoirs of the ancient earls of Warren and Surrey, and their descendants to the present time. 2 vols. Warrington, 1782. 4°.

Latin charter granted to the town by Robert de Stockport in Henry III.'s reign, with a translation, ii. 202–10.

STOCKTON-UPON-TEES.

2838. BREWSTER, JOHN. The parochial history and antiquities of Stockton-upon-Tees; including an account of the trade of the town. . . . Second edition, with additions and alterations. Stockton, 1829. 8°.

1st edition, 1796.

2839. † Description of the town and borough of Stockton, and table of remarkable events since 1200. Stockton, 1825. 12°.

2840. HEAVISIDES, HENRY. The annals of Stockton-on-Tees; with biographical notices. Stockton-on-Tees, 1865. 8°.

Of little value for municipal history.

2841. RICHMOND, THOMAS. The local records of Stockton and the neighbourhood: or a register of memorable events, chronologically arranged, which have occurred in and near Stockton Ward and the north-eastern parts of Cleveland. Stockton and London, 1868. 8°.

Brief notes.

STOKE-UPON-TRENT.

2842. WARD, JOHN. The borough of Stoke-upon-Trent, in the commencement of the reign of her most gracious majesty Queen Victoria: comprising its history, statistics, civil polity, and traffic . . . also the manorial history of Newcastle-under-Lyme. . . . The appendix contains many ancient and curious charters and documents never before published, and the work is embellished with a variety of plates. London, 1843. 8°.

An elaborate work, but it does not contain much concerning municipal history.

P

STRATFORD.

a. Town Records, Nos. 2843–2853.
b. General Histories, etc., Nos. 2854–2856.

There is no good history of the borough of Stratford.

a. Town Records.

2843. Extenta burgi de Stratford in comitatu Warewike; facta anno quinto-decimo pontificatus domini Walteri de Cantilupo [1252.] [Middle Hill Press, 1840?.] f°.

2844. [HALLIWELL, J. O.] A brief hand-list of the records belonging to the borough of Stratford-upon-Avon, showing their general character; with notes of a few of the Shakespearian documents in the collection. [London,] 1862. 4°.

2845. [——] A brief history of the ancient records of Stratford-on-Avon, chiefly in reply to a leading article in the Stratford-on-Avon Herald. Brighton, 1884. 8°.

2846. —— A descriptive calendar of the ancient manuscripts and records in the possession of the corporation of Stratford-upon-Avon; including notices of Shakespeare and his family. . . . London, 1863. f°.

2847. —— A nominal index to J. O. Halliwell's Descriptive calendar of the ancient records of Stratford-on-Avon. London, 1865. 8°.

2848. —— Extracts from the accounts of the chamberlains of the borough of Stratford-upon-Avon, from the year 1585 to 1608. . . . London, 1866. 4°.
The same, from 1590 to 1597. London, 1866. 4°.
The same, from 1609 to 1619. London, 1867. 4°.

2849. [——] Extracts from ancient subsidy rolls [14 Hen. VIII. — 16 Charles I.], showing the values of goods and lands upon which assessments were made in respect to the inhabitants of Stratford-upon-Avon. Taken from the original records of the court of Exchequer. [London,] 1864. 4°.

2850. —— Selected extracts from the ancient registry of the causes tried in the court of record at Stratford-upon-Avon in the time of Shakespeare. . . . London, 1867. 8°.

2851. HALLIWELL, J. O. Stratford-upon-Avon in the times of the Shakespeares, illustrated by extracts from the council books of the corporation. . . . London, 1864. f°.

2852. [——] The Stratford records and the Shakespeare autotypes. A brief review of singular delusions that are current at Stratford-on-Avon. By the supposed delinquent. Brighton, 1884. 8°.

This is really a new edition of No. 2845, with additions.
Fifth edition, 1887.

2853. † HARDY, W. J. Calendar of documents of the mediæval gild of Stratford. Stratford-on-Avon, 1885.

b. General Histories, etc.

2854. FISHER, THOMAS. The gilde of the Holy Cross, etc. at Stratford-on-Avon. *Gentleman's Magazine,* New Series, iii. 162–7, 375–80 ; iv. 586–7. London, 1835. 8°.

Contains extracts from the ledger of the gild, 1411–1530.

2855. LEE, S. L. Stratford-on-Avon, from the earliest times to the death of Shakespeare. . . . London, 1885. f°.

2856. WHELER, R. B. History and antiquities of Stratford-upon-Avon. . . . Stratford, [1806.] 8°.

The account of municipal history is meagre.

SUDBURY.

2857. † Account of the vindictive conduct of the corporation party, in the borough of Sudbury. Sudbury, 1832. 8°.

2858. Original documents relating to Sudbury. [Communicated by W. S. W.] *Bury and West Suffolk Archæol. Institute,* Proceedings, i. 199–207. Bury St. Edmund's, 1857. 8°.

Three documents, dated 1397, 1576, 1577.

SUNDERLAND.

2859. BURNETT, JAMES. The history of the town and port of Sunderland, and the parishes of Bishopwearmouth and Monkwearmouth. Sunderland, 1830. 12°.

A brief account.

2860. GARBUTT, GEORGE.   A historical and descriptive view of the parishes of Monkwearmouth and Bishopwearmouth, and the port and borough of Sunderland. . . . Sunderland, 1819.   8°.

The appendix contains the charter of Hugh Pudsey; a translation of the charter of Bishop Morton, 1634; and extracts from the minute book of the vestry, 1719–34.

2861. SUMMERS, J. W.   The history and antiquities of Sunderland, Bishopwearmouth, Bishopwearmouth Panns, Burdon. . . . Vol. i. Sunderland, 1858.   8°.

Ch. iv. Bishop Pudsey's charter.
Ch. vii. Bishop Morton's charter.
The best history of Sunderland.

SUTTON COLDFIELD.

2862. † A genuine translation of the royal charter granted by King Henry VIII. to the corporation of Sutton Coldfield.   [Edited by Thomas Bonell.]   [Oxford,] 1763.   8°.   pp. 61.

SWANSEA.

2863. * Charters granted to Swansea, the chief borough of the seignory of Gower, in the marches of Wales and Co. of Glamorgan. Translated, illustrated, and edited by G. G. Francis.   [London,] 1867.   f°.

The Latin text, with a translation.

2864. DILLWYN, L. W.   Contributions towards a history of Swansea. Swansea, 1840.   8°.   pp. 72.

Ch. ii. A translation of the town charters.
Ch. iii. The laws compiled in 1569, 1584, and 1586.
Ch. vi. Selections from the corporation accounts, 1723.
A useful little book.

2865. FRANCIS, G. G.   Charter of confirmation of the borough of Swansea, by Oliver Cromwell.   Ex eleventh annual report of Royal Institution of South Wales.   Swansea, 1846.   8°.

Translation only.

2866. —— Notes on a gold chain of office presented to the corporation of Swansea in the year 1875, and a description of its design; together with a list of the gentlemen who have filled the office of mayor, from 1835 to 1875 inclusive.   Swansea, 1876.   4°.

2867. Surveys of Gower and Kilvey. By Charles Baker and G. G. Francis. Published for the Cambrian Archæological Association. London, [1870.] 8°.

Survey of Swansea in 1660, pp. 18–32.

TAIN.

2868. TAYLOR, WILLIAM. Fragments of the early history of Tain, from its origin to the middle of the sixteenth century. Tain, etc., 1865. 8°.

2869. —— Researches into the history of Tain, earlier and later. Tain, 1882. 8°.

TAMWORTH.

2870. PALMER, C. F. The history of the town and castle of Tamworth, in the counties of Stafford and Warwick. Tamworth and London, 1845. 8°.

TAUNTON.

2871. TOULMIN, JOSHUA. The history of the town of Taunton, in the county of Somerset; greatly enlarged and brought down to the present time by James Savage. Taunton, 1822. 8°.

1st edition, 1791, 4°.

TAVISTOCK.

2872. WORTH, R. N. Calendar of the Tavistock parish records. [Plymouth,] 1887. 8°.

Contains extracts from churchwardens' accounts, 1385–1714; deeds, 1287–1742, etc.

2873. —— Municipal life in Tavistock. *Devon. Assoc. for Advancement of Science,* Transactions, xxi. 305–11. Plymouth, 1889. 8°.

TENBY.

There is no good history of Tenby; all the works mentioned below are brief.

2874. Account (An) of Tenby: containing an historical sketch of the place, compiled from the best authorities. . . . Pembroke, 1818. 8°.

2875. FRANCIS, G. G.　The case of Tenby *v.* Narberth, touching a market established in the latter during the commonwealth.　Edited . . . from the originals, with notes.　[Reprinted from the Cambrian Journal.]　Tenby, 1864.　8°.

2876. HORE, H. F.　Mayors and bailiffs of Tenby.　*Cambrian Archæol. Assoc.*, Archæologia Cambrensis, New Series, iv. 114–26. London, 1853.　8°.

2877. NORRIS, CHARLES.　Etchings of Tenby; including many ancient edifices which have been destroyed. . . . With a short account of that town and of the principal buildings in its neighbourhood.　London, 1812.　4°.

2878. —— An historical sketch of Tenby, compiled from the best authorities, and a description of its present state.　Second edition, with an appendix.　Tenby, 1856.　12°.

2879. SMITH, J. B.　An historical sketch of the town of Tenby. . . . Tenby, [1855.]　8°.

TEWKESBURY.

2880. BENNETT, JAMES.　The history of Tewkesbury.　Tewkesbury, 1830.　8°.

The appendix contains a translation of the town charters granted by Robert Earl of Gloucester, Edward III., and William III.; also abstracts of the charters of Elizabeth, James I., and James II.

The best history of Tewkesbury.

An abridgement appeared in 1835.

2881. DYDE, W.　The history and antiquities of Tewkesbury. Third edition.　To which is prefixed a descriptive sketch of Glocestershire.　Tewkesbury, 1803.　12°.

Translation of the charter of William III., 189–236.

The sketch of municipal history is meagre.

Earlier editions, 1790, 1798.

2882. † Tewkesbury borough magistrates.　Copy of all correspondence relating to the appointment of additional magistrates for the borough of Tewkesbury, since January, 1864, including all representations and applications to the lord chancellor. . . . [Tewkesbury,] 1865.　f°.

The corporation of Tewkesbury had resented the appointment of additional magistrates.

THAXTED.

2883. Dixon, R. W. Thaxted. *The Antiquary*, xvii. 10–12, 57–62. London, 1888. 4°.

A brief account.

2884. Symonds, G. E. Thaxted and its cutlers' guild. *The Reliquary*, v. 65–72. London and Derby, 1864. 8°.

Also printed in the Transactions of the Essex Archæological Society, New Series, 1889, iii. 255–61.

THETFORD.

The best history is Hunt's (No. 2886) ; the other two works are also useful.

2885. Blomefield, Francis. The history of the ancient city and burgh of Thetford, in the counties of Norfolk and Suffolk; shewing its rise, increase, decrease, and present state. Fersfield, 1739. 4°.

From his *History of Norfolk* (No. 628), vol. i.

2886. Hunt, A. L. The capital of the ancient kingdom of East Anglia, " the mighty city in the east " : being a complete and authentic history of the ancient borough town of Thetford. . . . London, 1870. 8°.

Ch. xi. The corporation of the borough.
App. iii. Charter granted by Elizabeth.

2887. Martin, Thomas. The history of the town of Thetford, in the counties of Norfolk and Suffolk, from the earliest accounts to the present time. London, 1779. 4°.

Ch. xviii. The corporation.
The appendix contains some interesting documents.

THIRSK.

2888. Grainge, William. The vale of Mowbray : a historical and topographical account of Thirsk and its neighbourhood. London and Thirsk, 1859. 8°.

THOMASTOWN.

2889. Graves, James. The records of the ancient borough towns of the county of Kilkenny [especially those of Thomastown.] *Kilkenny and South-East of Ireland Archæol. Soc.*, Journal, New Series, i. 84–93. Dublin, [1856] 1858. 8°.

THORNBURY.

2890. HOWARD, E. S.   Thornbury.   *Bristol and Glouc. Archæol. Soc.*, Transactions, viii. 6–16.   Bristol, [1884.]   8°.

A brief account.

TINTAGEL.

2891. MACLEAN, JOHN.   Tintagel and Trevalga.   London and Bodmin, 1877.   4°.

This is vol. iii. pp. 185–302 of his *History of Trigg Minor* (No. 583), with distinct pagination, index, etc.

TIVERTON.

The best history is Harding's (No. 2895).

2892.   Charter (The) granted to the inhabitants of Tiverton by his majesty George the First, and such clauses of the charter of King James as are pretended to be restored by that of King George.   With a prefatory letter addressed to the inhabitant householders of Tiverton.   By a friend of local jurisdictions [G. Coles].   Exeter, [1824.] 8°.

2893.   Cursory observations on the charters granted to the inhabitants of Tiverton. . . . By a friend to local jurisdictions [G. Coles]. Tiverton, 1823.   8°.

2894. DUNSFORD, MARTIN.   Historical memoirs of the town and parish of Tiverton, in the county of Devon.   Collected from the best authorities, with notes and observations.   Second edition.   Exeter, 1790.   4°.

Contains an abstract of the charters of James I. and George I.

1st edition, Exeter, 1790 ; 3rd edition (not completed), Tiverton, 1836.

2895. HARDING, [WILLIAM].   The history of Tiverton, in the county of Devon.   2 vols.   Tiverton and London, 1845–47.   8°.

The best history of Tiverton.

2896.   † Memoirs and antiquities of the town and parish of Tiverton. . . . Faithfully collected from the ancient records.   By a gentleman, native thereof [John Blundell].   Exeter, 1712.   8°.

2897. SNELL, F. J.   The chronicles of Twyford : being a new history of the town of Tiverton.   Tiverton and London, [1892.]   8°.

Useful for the history of Tiverton in modern times.

TORQUAY.

2898. WHITE, J. T.   The history of Torquay.   Illustrated.   Torquay, 1878.   8°.

Torquay received a charter of incorporation in 1892.

TORRINGTON.

2899. COLBY, F. T.   The history of Great Torrington.   (Reprinted from the transactions of the Devonshire Association for the Advancement of Science, Literature, and Art, 1875.)   n. p.   [1875.]   8°.

Without title-page.
Brief and of little value.

TOTNES.

The best history is Cotton's (No. 2902).

2900. AMERY, J. S.   The accounts of the receiver of the corporation of Totnes in the year 1554–5.   *Devon. Assoc. for Advancement of Science*, Transactions, xii. 322–31.   Plymouth, 1880.   8°.

2901. AMERY, P. F. S.   The gild merchant of Totnes.   *Devon. Assoc. for Advancement of Science*, Transactions, xii. 179–91.   Plymouth, 1880.   8°.

2902. COTTON, WILLIAM.   A graphic and historical sketch of the antiquities of Totnes.   London, etc., 1850.   4°.

The appendix contains a translation of charters granted to Totnes by King John and Queen Elizabeth.

2903. DYMOND, R.   Ancient documents relating to the civil history of Totnes.   *Devon. Assoc. for Advancement of Science*, Transactions, xii. 192–203.   Plymouth, 1880.   8°.

2904. † Our representative system : a political history of Totnes from 1826 to 1853.   Totnes, 1853.

2905. ROWE, J. B.   Devonshire guilds : Plymouth and Totnes.   *Devon. Assoc. for Advancement of Science*, Transactions, vi. 101–6.   Plymouth, 1873.   8°.

Brief and of little value.

2906. † Translation (A) of a charter of incorporation of the borough of Totnes, granted by Queen Elizabeth, 1596. . . . With a prefatory comment.   Totnes, 1832.

2907. WINDEATT, EDWARD. An historical sketch of Totnes. *Devon. Assoc. for Advancement of Science,* Transactions, xii. 159–78. Plymouth, 1880. 8°.

2908. —— Totnes : its mayors and mayoralties. *The Western Antiquary,* vols. ix.–x. Plymouth, 1890–91. 4°.

TRURO.

2909. † Copy (A) of the charter of the borough of Truro. To which is added several cases on points of law relating to the said charter and the opinion of counsel thereon. Truro, 1815. 8°. pp. 38.

2910. Defence (A) of the corporation of Truro against the attacks of the radical press. Truro, 1835. 8°.

Relates especially to the financial administration of the town.

2911. † Mayoralty (The) of Truro, with a list of the gentlemen who have filled the office of chief magistrate in the present century. *West Briton,* Jan. 23, 1873.

2912. † Report of the committee appointed January 1st, 1836, to enquire into the duties, responsibilities, and property of the corporation of Truro to the town council. . . . Truro, 1836. 8°. pp. 12.

2913. Some account of the proceedings at the election for Truro, Aug. 3–6, 1830 . . . also a translation of the charter [1589], and a table of parliamentary patronage. London, 1830. 8°. pp. 40.

TUTBURY.

2914. MOSLEY, OSWALD. History of the castle, priory, and town of Tutbury, in the county of Stafford. London, etc., 1832. 8°.

The appendix contains some brief references to old municipal customs.

UTTOXETER.

2915. History (The) and topography of Ashbourn, the valley of the Dove, and the adjacent villages ; with biographical sketches of eminent natives. . . . Ashbourn, 1839. 8°

Uttoxeter, 300–317 : a translation of the charter granted by William de Ferrers to Uttoxeter in 1251, and brief extracts from churchwardens' accounts, 1642–72.

2916. REDFERN, FRANCIS.   History and antiquities of the town and neighbourhood of Uttoxeter ; with notices of adjoining places.   Second edition.   Hanley and London, 1886.   8°.

Of little value for municipal history.

1st edition, " History of the town of Uttoxeter," 1865.

UXBRIDGE.

2917. REDFORD, G., and RICHES, T. H.   The history of the ancient town and borough of Uxbridge, containing copies of interesting public documents. . . . Uxbridge, etc., 1818.   8°.

WAKEFIELD.

2918. BANKS, W. S.   Walks in Yorkshire : Wakefield and its neighbourhood ; with map and fifty-five woodcuts.   London and Wakefield, 1871.   8°.

Contains extracts from the accounts of the churchwardens and the constables, 1586–1829.

2919. TAYLOR, THOMAS.   The history of Wakefield, in the county of York.   The rectory manor, with biographical and other notices of some of the persons connected therewith.   Wakefield, 1886.   8°.

Contains many extracts from manorial records ; more valuable for manorial than for municipal history.

WALLINGFORD.

Few corporations in England possess archives of greater antiquity than those of Wallingford.   The burghmote rolls begin with the year 1232 ; there are several assessment rolls of Henry III.'s reign, and many deeds of the reigns of Henry III. and Edward I.

2920. * HEDGES, J. K.   The history of Wallingford, in the county of Berks, from the invasion of Julius Cæsar to the present time. . . . 2 vols.   London, 1881.   8°.

Contains many extracts from the town records.

WALSALL.

Willmore's (No. 2926) is the best history.

2921. † Ancient and modern history of the borough of Walsall, its charitable and scholastic institutions.   Walsall, 1838.   8°.

2922. † Charter (The) of the corporation of Walsall, with an account of the estates thereto belonging; to which is added a list of the donations and benefactions to the town and foreign of Walsall and Bloxwich. Wolverhampton, 1774. 12°.

2923. GLEW, E. L. History of the borough and foreign of Walsall, in the county of Stafford. . . . Walsall, 1856. 8°.

Contains town laws made in 1440, etc.

2924. PEARCE, THOMAS. History and directory of Walsall. . . . To which is added a correct account of the trial between the borough and foreign. Birmingham, 1813. 8°.

Contains a translation of the charter of the corporation, 13 Charles II., a list of mayors, etc.

2925. SIMS, RICHARD. Borough of Walsall. Calendar of the deeds and documents belonging to the corporation of Walsall in the town chest, extending from the reign of King John . . . [to 1688.] Walsall, 1882. 8°.

2926. WILLMORE, F. W. A history of Walsall and its neighbourhood. Walsall and London, 1887. 8°.

Contains a good account of the municipal history, with some extracts from the town records, including the laws made in Henry VI.'s reign.

WARRINGTON.

2927. † Charter of incorporation of Warrington, 1847. Warrington, 1847.

WARWICK.

2928. DUGDALE, WILLIAM. The antiquities of Warwick and Warwick Castle; extracted from Sir William Dugdale's Antiquities of Warwickshire. . . . Warwick, 1786. 8°.

See No. 659.

2929. [FIELD, WILLIAM.] An historical and descriptive account of the town and castle of Warwick, and of the neighbouring spa of Leamington. . . . Warwick, 1815. 8°.

A meagre account.

2930. PARKES, JOSEPH. The governing charter of the borough of Warwick . . . 1694; with a letter to the burgesses on the past and present state of the corporation. London, 1827. 8°.

The Latin text, with a translation.

2931. Report (A) of an inquiry into the present state of Warwick corporation, as given in evidence before R. Whitcombe and A. E. Cockburn, esquires, the commissioners appointed by his majesty to inquire into the existing state of the municipal corporations . . . 1833. With an appendix. Warwick, 1834. 8°.

See No. 60.

2932. [ROBINSON, G. T.] Notes on and extracts from the Black Book of Warwick. *The Warwickshire Antiquarian Magazine*, pts. ii., iii., and vi. Warwick, 1860–71. 4°.

Extracts relating to municipal history, 16th century.

Extracts from the Black Book are also printed in Nichols's *Bibliotheca Topographica Britannica* (London, 1783), vol. iv., No. 17.

WATERFORD.

The Great Parchment Book is the most important volume in the town archives; it contains charters, acts made in the civic assemblies, etc., from the 14th century to 1649.

The best histories of the city are Ryland's and Smith's (Nos. 732, 733). See also Nos. 730, 731.

2933. † Historical remarks of the city of Waterford from 873 to 1270; with a list of the mayors, bayliffs, and sherrifes from 1377 to 1735. Waterford, —.

2934. Magna charta libertatum civitatis Waterford [2 Charles I.] Timotheo Cunningham editore. Dublin, 1752. 8°.

2935. —— The great charter of the liberties of the city of Waterford. Transcribed and translated into English; with explanatory notes. Humbly inscribed to the corporation of that city. [Translation only.] By Timothy Cunningham. Dublin, 1752. 8°.

2936. † —— The great charter [translation only]. . . . With a list of the mayors, bailiffs, and sheriffs of the city of Waterford, 1377–1806. Kilkenny, 1806. 8°.

WELLS.

The Year Book of 16 Edward III., edited by L. O. Pike, 1896 (pp. xiv.–xciv. and 108–20), contains a valuable contribution to the medieval history of Wells: see No. 142.

2937. CHURCH, C. M. Chapters in the early history of the church of Wells, A. D. 1136–1333. . . . London and Taunton, 1894. 8°.

Two charters granted to the city by Bishop Reginald (1174–80), 359–64.
Charter of Bishop Savaric (circa 1201), 386–90.
Charter of King John (1201), 390–1.
These charters are also printed in the Archæologia of the Society of Antiquaries of London, 1887–88, l. 350–2, li. 103–5.

2938. SEREL, THOMAS. A lecture on the history of Wells, delivered at the Town Hall, Wells, May 3rd, 1858; with explanatory notes. Wells, [1858.] 8°.

WELSHPOOL.

2939. † HOWELL, ABRAHAM. Printed statement of the result of an examination and inquiry respecting the books, etc. relating to the borough of Pool. April, 1865.

2940. [JONES, M. C.] Welsh Pool: materials for the history of the parish and borough. *Powysland Club*, Collections, vols. vii., xii. –xv., xvii., xix., xxi., xxiv. London, 1874–90. 8°.

2941. Welshpool bailiffs. Welshpool corporation officers. *Byegones relating to Wales and the Border Counties*, 1874–75. Oswestry, [1875.] 4°.

WENLOCK.

2942. Borough of Wenlock. [Charters, privileges, extracts from the corporation records, etc.] *The Salopian and West-Midland Monthly Illustrated Journal*, March—April, Nov.—Dec., 1877; April, October, 1878; March, 1879. Shrewsbury, 1877–79. 8°.

Valuable.

2943. RANDALL, JOHN. Randall's Tourists' guide to Wenlock . . . containing a full description and history of the priory. Wenlock, 1875. 8°.

Early charters, privileges, and ancient register of the corporation, 160–83.

2944. † Translation of the charters of the corporation of Wenlock; with explanatory notes. [Wenlock,] 1820. 8°.

2945. VAUGHAN, H. F. J. Wenlock corporation records. *Shropsh. Archæol. and Nat. Hist. Soc.*, Transactions, Second Series, vi. 223–83. Shrewsbury, 1894. 8°.

Contains extracts from the records, Edw. IV. — James II.

WEOBLY.

2946. PHILLOTT, H. W.   Notes on Weobly, Herefordshire.   *Cambrian Archæol. Assoc.*, Archæologia Cambrensis, Third Series, xv. 39–55, 170–86, 265–76.   London, 1869.   8°.

WESTMINSTER.

See the histories, etc. of London by Allen, Chamberlain, Noorthouck, etc. (Nos. 1992–2007); and Nos. 2065, 2268.

2947. † Act (An) for the good government of the city and borough of Westminster.   London, 1806.   4°.

For this act of 27 Eliz. c. 31, see Statutes of the Realm (Record Com. edition), iv. 763.

2948. † Acts relating to the government of the city of Westminster. 1838.   8°.

2949. Brief account (A) of the powers given to, and exercised by, the burgess court of Westminster; and some reasons for continuing and enlarging those powers, by amending the act of the 27th of Queen Elizabeth.   [London, circa 1720.]   8°.

2950. Power (The) and practice of the court leet of the city and liberty of Westminster display'd : being a full relation of the case lately depending between the high-bailiffs and William Philips. . . . To which are added many useful and seasonable particulars concerning the constitution and authority of burgesses. . . . London, 1743. 8°.

It is supposed that the author of this tract was Sir Matthew Hale.

2951. SAYER, EDWARD.   Observations on the police or civil government of Westminster, with a proposal for a reform.   London, 1784. 4°.   pp. 72.

2952. WALCOTT, M. E. C.   The memorials of Westminster : the city, royal palaces, houses of Parliament. . . . A new edition, with an appendix and notes.   London, 1851.   8°.

Of little value for municipal history.
1st edition, " Westminster : memorials of the city," etc., 1849.

WEYMOUTH AND MELCOMBE REGIS.

2953. ELLIS, G. A. The history and antiquities of the borough and town of Weymouth and Melcombe Regis. Weymouth and London, 1829. 8°.

Contains the charter of incorporation of 1804.

2954. MOULE, H. J. Descriptive catalogue of the charters, minute books, and other documents of the borough of Weymouth and Melcombe Regis, A. D. 1252 to 1800. With extracts and some notes. Weymouth, 1883. 4°.

Valuable.

2955. † Privately printed papers (The) of Richard Tucker against the king, endeavouring to establish that he was duly elected mayor of Weymouth and Melcombe Regis. With copies of the ancient charters. Dorchester, 1742. f °.

WHITBY.

2956. ATKINSON, J. C. Memorials of old Whitby : or historical gleanings from ancient Whitby records. London, 1894. 8°.

Contains the best account of the early municipal history of Whitby. Valuable.

2957. Cartularium abbathiæ de Whiteby, ordinis S. Benedicti, fundatæ anno 1078. [Edited by J. C. Atkinson.] *Surtees Society.* 2 vols. Durham, 1879–81. 8°.

Documents relating to the borough (14th century), ii. 422–8, 501–5, 513–4, etc.

2958. CHARLTON, LIONEL. The history of Whitby and of Whitby abbey. Collected from the original records of the abbey and other authentic memoirs never before made public. . . . York, 1779. 4°.

Apart from the charter of Abbot Richard, 1185, making Whitby a borough (pp. 144–6), this work contains little concerning municipal history.

2959. ROBINSON, F. K. Whitby : its abbey and the principal parts of the neighbourhood ; or a sketch of the place in its former history and present state, with the topography and antiquities of the surrounding country. Whitby, 1860. 8°.

2960. YOUNG, GEORGE. A history of Whitby and Streoneshalh abbey; with a statistical survey of the vicinity to the distance of twenty-five miles. 2 vols. Whitby, 1817. 8°.

The most detailed general history of Whitby.

WIGAN.

The best history is Sinclair's (No. 2967).

2961. BRIDGEMAN, G. T. O. The history of the church and manor of Wigan, in the county of Lancaster. *Chetham Society.* 4 pts. Manchester, 1888–90. 4°.

2962. Charters (The) of the borough of Wigan, in Latin and English; opinions of counsel relative thereto, and observations thereon; together with an account of the manner of electing officers, and of the different proceedings, at various periods in that borough. In two parts. Warrington, 1808. 4°.

2963. FOLKARD, H. T. Wigan bibliography. A local catalogue of Wigan printed books and pamphlets and the works of authors connected with Wigan and the district, etc. Wigan, 1886. 4°.

2964. Lancashire's oldest borough and great mining centre. The case of Wigan, as affected by the Seats Redistribution Bill, 1884. Introductory note by the mayor [H. Park] and extracts from the Lancashire Press. Wigan. n. d.

2965. † MACLURE, JOHN. History of Wigan: an essay. Wigan, 1852. 12°.

2966. † ROGER, WILLIAM. History of Wigan and suburbs, compiled from the records of the Chetham Society. Wigan, 1879. 4°.

2967. * SINCLAIR, DAVID. The history of Wigan. 2 vols. Wigan, 1882–[83]. 4°.

Contains the principal town charters in full, with a translation; the proceedings of the court leet for 1742; and other records.

A good book.

WIGTOWN.

2968. FRASER, GORDON. Wigtown and Whithorn: historical and descriptive sketches, stories, and anecdotes, illustrative of the racy wit and pawky humour of the district. Wigtown, 1877. 8°.

Contains extracts from the records of the burgh of Wigtown.

WILTON.

2969. S[WAYNE], H. J. F.   The old charters of Winchester and Wilton.   *Salisbury and Winchester Journal,* July 26, 1884.

Charters of Henry I. and Henry II., with a translation.

2970. —— Wilton : its charters and its mayors.   *Salisbury and Winchester Journal,* Oct. 21, 1882, June 9, 1883, and July 26, 1884.

The article printed June 9, 1883, contains the confirmation charter of 1433 in full, with a translation.

There are also some papers in this journal beginning July, 1883, entitled, " Old times and customs " and " Our parliamentary representation."

WINCHCOMB.

2971. Landboc, sive registrum monasterii beatæ Mariæ Virginis et Sancti Cénhelmi de Winchelcumba. . . . Edente David Royce.   Vol. i. A. D. 798–1332.   Exeter, 1892.   8°.

Well edited.   The introduction contains a good account of the history of the town.

WINCHELSEA.

For the medieval customal of Winchelsea, see Lyon's *Dover* (No. 682).

2972. COOPER, W. D.   The history of Winchelsea, one of the ancient towns added to the Cinque Ports.   London and Hastings, 1850.   8°.

2973. —— Notices of Winchelsea in and after the fifteenth century.   *Sussex Archæol. Soc.,* Collections, viii. 201–34 ; xxiii. 20–35. Lewes, 1856–71.   8°.

Contains town ordinances in Henry VI.'s time, etc.

2974. INDERWICK, F. A.   The story of King Edward [I.] and New Winchelsea : the edification of a mediæval town.   London, 1892.   8°.

2975. Letter (A) to the mayor and jurats of the town of Winchelsea, respecting the choice of officers in that corporation, A. D. 1609.   Communicated by William Bray.   *Soc. of Antiq. of London,* Archæologia, xviii. 291–3.   London, 1817.   4°.

WINCHESTER.

a. Town Records, Nos. 2976–2986.
b. General Histories, Nos. 2987–2992.

The oldest roll in the town archives contains the proceedings of a borough court held in the last years of Henry III.'s reign. The Black Book of Winchester is in the British Museum (Additional MS. 6036); it contains the acts and proceedings of the corporation of Winchester from Richard II. to 5 Edward VI.

There is no good account of the municipal history. The best books are Woodward's, Kitchin's, and Milner's (Nos. 611, 2991, 2992). Among the publications of records, Nos. 537, 2976, 2981, 2984 are valuable.

a. **Town Records.**

See No. 537.

2976. Charter (A) of Edward the Third, confirming and enlarging the privileges of St. Giles Fair, Winchester, A. D. 1349. Edited by G. W. Kitchin. [Winchester Cathedral Records, No. 2.] London and Winchester, 1886. 4°.

Well edited.

2977. Corporation of Winchester [in 1798.] *The Hampshire Repository,* i. 117–24. Winchester, [1798.] 8°.

2978. Domesday-Book, seu libri censualis Willelmi Primi, regis Angliæ, additamenta ex codic. antiquiss. *Record Com.* [London,] 1816. f°.

Pp. 531–62 contain Liber Winton', i. e. two surveys of Winchester, one made between 1107 and 1128, the other in 1148.

2979. KIRBY, T. F. The ancient charters of the city of Winchester. *Soc. of Antiq. of London,* Archæologia, xlix. 213–18. London, 1885. 4°.

2980. SHENTON, F. K. J. Winchester [corporation] records. *Gentleman's Magazine,* viii. 163–84. London, 1872. 8°.

2981. SMIRKE, EDWARD. Ancient consuetudinary of the city of Winchester [13th century.] *Archæol. Journal,* ix. 69–89. London, 1852. 8°.

2982. SMIRKE, EDWARD.   Winchester in the thirteenth century. [Veredictum xii. juratorum Winton'.]   *Archæol. Journal,* vii. 374–83.   London, 1850.   8°.

2983. S[WAYNE], H. J. F.   The old charters of Winchester and Wilton.   *Salisbury and Winchester Journal,* July 26, 1884.

Contains the charter granted by Henry II. to Winchester.

2984. Transcripts from the municipal archives of Winchester, and other documents, elucidating the government, manners, and customs of the same city from the thirteenth century to the present period. By Charles Bailey.   Winchester and London, 1856.   8°.

A small but valuable collection of records.   Most of the documents printed belong to the 16th and 17th centuries.

2985. WRIGHT, THOMAS.   Remarks on the municipal privileges and legislation in the Middle Ages, as illustrated from the archives of Winchester and Southampton.   *Brit. Archæol. Assoc.,* Transactions at Winchester, 16–27.   London, 1846.   8°.

2986. —— Report on the municipal records of Winchester and Southampton.   *Ibid.,* 28–39.   London, 1846.   8°.

b. General Histories.

2987. Antiquities of Winchester; with an historical account of the city, including the cathedral. . . . [Winchester, 1850.]   12°.

Of little value.

2988. BALL, CHARLES.   An historical account of Winchester; with descriptive walks.   Winchester, 1818.   8°.

Of little value.

2989. BRAMSTON, A. R., and LEROY, A. C.   Historic Winchester, England's first capital.   Revised edition.   London, 1884.   8°.

A popular history; does not deal in detail with municipal development. 1st edition, 1882.

2990. History (The) and antiquities of Winchester : setting forth its original constitution . . . together with the charters, laws, customs, rights, liberties, and privileges of that ancient city.   2 vols.   Winton, 1773.   12°.

Contains a translation of the principal town charters.   Apart from this, little attention is devoted to municipal affairs.

2991. KITCHIN, G. W. Winchester. [Historic Towns. Edited by E. A. Freeman and W. Hunt.] London, 1890. 8°.

2992. MILNER, JOHN. The history and survey of the antiquities of Winchester. . . . With supplementary notes by F. C. Husenbeth. Third edition. 2 vols. Winchester, [1839.] 8°.

Commonly regarded as one of the best town histories, but it does not give a good account of the municipal history. The most valuable part of the work is the appendix, which contains the town charters.

Earlier editions, [1798], 1809; second appendix, 1801.

WINDSOR.

The best history of Windsor is that of Tighe and Davis (No. 3004).

2993. ASHMOLE, ELIAS. The antiquities of Berkshire. By Elias Ashmole, Esq. With a large appendix of many valuable original papers, pedigrees of the most considerable families in the said county, and a particular account of the castle, college, and town of Windsor. Reading, 1736. f°.

The sketch of municipal history is very brief.

1st edition, 3 vols., 1719, 8°; reprinted, 1723.

2994. Case (The) of the burrough of New-Windsor, in the county of Berks [Winwood v. Starkey], concerning the election of burgesses to serve in this ensuing Parliament. [Windsor, 1679.] f°.

2995. † Copy of the charter of the borough of New Windsor. Windsor, 1787. 8°.

2996. Copy (A) of the poll taken [1802] . . . at the Guildhall, in the borough of New Windsor, in the county of Berks, at an election of two representatives. . . . To which are added several new cases, tending to establish the right of voting in the borough. . . . Second edition. Windsor, 1802. 8°.

2997. DIXON, W. H. Royal Windsor. 4 vols. London, 1879–80. 8°.

Contains only brief references to the municipal history.

2998. † Election of representatives for the borough of New Windsor [April 30, 1831]. . . . With appendix containing a copy of the original charter, list of representatives. . . . Windsor, 1831. 8°. pp. 39.

2999. HAKEWILL, JAMES. The history of Windsor and its neighbourhood. London, 1813. f°.

In large part a reprint of Pote's work (No. 3001).
Contains an abstract of the town charters.

3000. LOFTIE, W. J. Windsor: a description of the castle, park, town, and neighbourhood. London, 1885. f°.

Ch. viii. contains a brief account of the history of the borough.

3001. POTE, JOSEPH. The history and antiquities of Windsor Castle . . . with an account of the town and corporation of Windsor. . . . Eton, 1749. 4°.

An appendix appeared in 1762.

3002. STOUGHTON, JOHN. Notices of Windsor in the olden time. Windsor, [1844.] 8°.

3003. —— Windsor: a history and description of the castle and the town. London, 1862. 8°.

3004. TIGHE, R. R., and DAVIS, J. E. Annals of Windsor: being a history of the castle and town; with some account of Eton and places adjacent. 2 vols. London, 1858. 8° and f°.

Contains the by-laws of the corporation made in 1474 (i. 400–3) and in 1683 (ii. 398–406), extracts from the borough accounts since Henry VIII.'s reign, and extracts from other records.
A valuable work; the best history of Windsor.

WISBECH.

3005. History (The) of Wisbech, with an historical sketch of the Fens, and their former and present aspect. Wisbech and London, 1833. 8°.

Ch. vi. The corporation.

3006. HUTCHESSON, MANN. An introduction to the charter of Wisbech. Wisbech, 1791. 4°. pp. 22.

3007. WALKER, NEIL, and CRADOCK, THOMAS. The history of Wisbech and the Fens. Wisbech, 1849. 8°.

Contains many extracts from the town records from 1580 to 1800.
The best history of Wisbech.

3008. WATSON, WILLIAM. An historical account of the ancient town and port of Wisbech, in the Isle of Ely, in the county of Cambridge. . . . With engravings. Wisbech, 1827. 8°.

Useful.

WITNEY.

3009. GILES, J. A. History of Witney, with notices of the neighbouring parishes. . . . London, 1852. 8°.

More valuable for manorial than for municipal history.

WOKINGHAM.

3010. CARRINGTON, F. A. Ancient state of the town of Wokingham. *Wilts. Archœol. and Nat. Hist. Soc.*, Magazine, xi. 50–82. Devizes, 1869. 8°.

Contains town ordinances of 1625, etc.

WOODSIDE.

3011. MORGAN, PATRICK. Annals of Woodside and Newhills, historical and genealogical. Aberdeen, 1886. 8°.

WOODSTOCK.

3012. BALLARD, ADOLPHUS. Chronicles of the royal borough of Woodstock, compiled from the borough records and other original documents. Oxford, 1896. 8°.

A good little book; the best account of the municipal history of Woodstock.

3013. MARSHALL, EDWARD. The early history of Woodstock manor and its environs, in Bladon, Hensington, New Woodstock, Blenheim; with later notices. Oxford and London, 1873. 8°.

A supplement appeared in 1874.

WORCESTER.

    a. Town Records, etc., Nos. 3014–3015.
    b. General Histories, Nos. 3016–3020.
    c. Gilds, etc., Nos. 3021–3024.

The town archives contain: the Book of Charters; chamber orders, 1522–1684; chamberlains' accounts, beginning in 1542; the Book of Ordinances, Edw. IV.—Hen. VII.; the By-Law Book, beginning early in the 17th century; the Oath's Book, 1723, etc.

The records printed by Noake (No. 3020) and the ordinances in Smith's *English Gilds* (No. 537) are valuable.

Green's (No. 3018) is the most useful history of Worcester.

a. Town Records, etc.

See Nos. 537, 3018, 3020.

3014. † Churchwardens' accounts of St. Michael's, Worcester, 1539–1603. Edited by John Amphlett. *Worcestershire Historical Society.* Oxford, 1896. 8°.

3015. WOOF, RICHARD. Catalogue of manuscript records and printed books in the library of the corporation of Worcester. . . . With an appendix of local records not in the custody of the corporation. Worcester, 1874. 8°.

b. General Histories.

3016. CHAMBERS, JOHN. A general history of Worcester. Embellished with plates. Worcester, 1820. 8°.

Ch. xi. contains a meagre sketch of municipal history.

3017. Concise history (A) of Worcester. . . . To which is added the tolls claimed by the sheriff and sword-bearer, and a copy of the charter of James I. to the city, and various extracts of other charters and bye-laws. . . . [By W. R.] Worcester, 1808. 12°.

Other editions, with different title-pages, 1816, 1829.

3018. GREEN, VALENTINE. The history and antiquities of the city and suburbs of Worcester. 2 vols. London, 1796. 4°.

Sect. xviii., which deals with "the civil government," is brief. A valuable appendix contains municipal ordinances of 12 Henry VII. ; a translation of Queen Elizabeth's charter to the clothiers ; a translation of the charter granted to the town by James I. ; and extracts from municipal ordinances, 6 Edw. IV. —1710.

An earlier work by the same writer : "A survey of the city of Worcester," etc., Worcester, 1764, 8°.

3019. History (The) of the city of Worcester : containing the ecclesiastical and civil government thereof, and the most material parts of its history. . . . Worcester, 1790. 12°.

A brief account.

3020. NOAKE, JOHN. Worcester in olden times. London, 1849. 16°.

Consists mainly of extracts from the town records, which latter begin in 1522. Contains information about the town charters, the ancient craft gilds, town elections, etc.

A valuable little book.

c. Gilds, etc.

3021. GUTCH, J. M. The clothiers' company of Worcester. *Brit. Archæol. Assoc.*, Proceedings at Worcester, Aug. 1848, pp. 243–60. London, 1851. 8°.

3022. HOOPER, J. H. The clothiers' company, Worcester. A paper read before the Worcester Diocesan Architectural and Archæological Society, on 20th Oct., 1880. *Associated Architectural Societies*, Reports and Papers, xv. 331–9. Lincoln, [1880.] 8°.

3023. NOAKE, JOHN. Ancient Worcester cordwainers' company. *Gentleman's Magazine*, iii. 317–9. London, 1857. 8°.

3024. WOOF, RICHARD. On the seals and arms of the city of Worcester. The substance of a paper read at a meeting of the Worcester Archæological Club. [Worcester, 1865.] 8°. pp. 10.

WOTTON-UNDER-EDGE.

3025. SMYTH, JOHN. Berkeley manuscripts. . . . Edited by Sir John Maclean for the Bristol and Gloucestershire Archæological Society. 3 vols. Gloucester, 1883–85. 4°.

Wotton, iii. 396–407.

3026. † WRIGHT, W. H. Historical notes relating to the borough of Wotton, and a list of the mayors of the borough from 1660. London and Wotton, 1872. 8°. pp. 48.

WYCOMBE.

The best history is Parker's (No. 3030). Rumsey's Report (No. 198) is also valuable.

3027. Charters and grants relating to the borough of Chepping Wycombe, in the county of Buckingham [5 John — 4 Eliz.] Wycombe, 1817. 4°.

Translation only.

3028. Charters granted to the borough of Chepping Wycombe, in the county of Buckingham [40 Eliz. — 15 Charles II.] London, 1817. 4°.

Translation only.

3029. KINGSTON, HENRY. The history of Wycombe; with recollections of my native town. . . . High Wycombe, [1848.] 8°.

A brief account.

3030. PARKER, JOHN. The early history and antiquities of Wycombe, in Buckinghamshire. Wycombe, 1878. 4°.

The appendix contains a translation of the town charters from 1205 to 1665. A valuable book.

YARMOUTH (HANTS).

3031. Yarmouth, in the Isle of Wight. *The Hampshire Repository*, ii. 240–48. Winchester, [1801.] 8°.

YARMOUTH, GREAT.

    a. Town Records, Nos. 3032-3034.
    b. General Histories, Nos. 3035-3043.
    c. Miscellaneous, Nos. 3044-3049.

The most valuable town records are the borough court rolls, from 1290 to 1670; they contain much information concerning municipal affairs. The archives also contain: royal charters, 9 John — 2 Anne; leet rolls, 1366–1653; the Book of Oaths and Ordinances, Edw. I. — Charles II.; assembly books, 1550–1840; books of entries, 30 Hen. VIII. — 1860; a borough chartulary, compiled in 1580, etc.

The best history of Yarmouth is Swinden's (No. 3043). Palmer's works (Nos. 3040, 3041) are also valuable.

a. Town Records.

3032. HARROD, HENRY. Notes on the records of the corporation of Great Yarmouth. *Norfolk and Norwich Archæol. Soc.*, Norfolk Archæology, iv. 239–66. Norwich, 1855. 8°.

3033. [——] Repertory of deeds and documents relating to the borough of Great Yarmouth. . . . Great Yarmouth, 1855. 4°.

3034. TENISWOOD, C. G. H. Charters relating to the government of Great Yarmouth. *Brit. Archæol. Assoc.*, Journal, xxxvi. 273–90. London, 1880. 8°.

b. General Histories.

3035. CRISP, W. F.　Chronological retrospect of the history of Yarmouth . . . including public buildings, high stewards, borough elections, bailiffs, mayors. . . . Great Yarmouth, [1871.]　8°.

Brief notes.

3036. DRUERY, J. H.　Historical and topographical notices of Great Yarmouth, in Norfolk, and its environs, including the parishes and hamlets of Lothingland, in Suffolk.　London, 1826.　8°.

Based mainly on Swinden.

3037. History (The) of Great Yarmouth; collected from antient records and other authentic materials.　[By C. Parkin.]　Lynn, 1776.　8°.

A reprint of part of Blomefield's history of the county (No. 628).

3038. [MANSHIP, HENRY.]　A booke of the foundacion and antiquitye of the towne of Greate Yermouthe; from the original manuscript written in the time of Queen Elizabeth; with notes and an appendix.　Edited by C. J. Palmer.　Great Yarmouth, 1847.　4°.

The work was probably compiled toward the close of Elizabeth's reign.

3039. MANSHIP, HENRY.　The history of Great Yarmouth, by Henry Manship, town clerk, temp. Queen Elizabeth.　Edited by C. J. Palmer.　Great Yarmouth and London, 1854.　4°.

The work was completed in 1619.

3039a. NALL, J. G.　Great Yarmouth and Lowestoft . . . with chapters on the archæology, natural history, etc. of the district. . . . London, 1866.　8°.

A brief account.

3040. PALMER, C. J.　The history of Great Yarmouth, designed as a continuation of Manship's history of that town.　Great Yarmouth and London, 1856.　4°.

Ch. i.　The charters.
Ch. ii.　Ancient customs (i. e. ordinances, 1272 and 1491).
Ch. vi.　Representation of the borough in Parliament.

A good book.

3041. PALMER, C. J. The perlustration of Great Yarmouth, with Gorleston and Southtown. 3 vols. Great Yarmouth, 1872–75. 4°.

This is a good topographical work; it also contains many references to municipal affairs.

3042. PRESTON, JOHN. The picture of Yarmouth: being a compendious history and description of all the public establishments within that borough. . . . Yarmouth, 1819. 8°.

Of little value for municipal history.

3043. * SWINDEN, HENRY. The history and antiquities of the ancient burgh of Great Yarmouth, in the county of Norfolk. Collected from the corporation charters, records, and evidences, and other the most authentic materials. Norwich, 1772. 4°.

Contains municipal ordinances temp. Hen. III., 10 Rich. II., and 1491; the town charters in full; and other valuable documents.
One of the best of England's older town histories.

c. Miscellaneous.

3044. † BOUSSELL, JOHN. Serious address to the magistrates of Norwich and Yarmouth. Norwich, 1793. 8°.

3045. Great Yarmouth corporation. A report of the investigation before his majesty's municipal commissioners, T. J. Hogg and J. Buckle . . . on the corporate affairs of this borough. Compiled by Henry Barrett. Second edition. Yarmouth, 1834. 8°.

1st edition, 1834.
See No. 60.

3046. PALMER, C. J. [On the parliamentary history of Great Yarmouth.] *The Times*, October 16, 1866, p. 9. London, 1866.

3047. † PALMER, F. D. The tolhouse at Great Yarmouth. Yarmouth, 1884. 4°.

3048. † —— The tolhouse restored. Yarmouth, 1887.

3049. † Yarmouth magistracy (The) : copy of a correspondence with H. M. Secretary for the Home Department and certain inhabitants of Yarmouth. Yarmouth, 1841. 8°. pp. 20.

YORK.

a. Town Records, Nos. 3050–3052.
b. General Histories, Nos. 3053–3060.
c. Gilds, Nos. 3061–3069.
d. Miscellaneous, Nos. 3070–3073.

There are some valuable records in the town archives which should be published: for example, a book of "memoranda" begun in the time of John Santone, mayor, 1376, containing many ordinances relating to craft gilds, etc.; minute books, from 1476 to the present time; enrollments of deeds and inquisitions, from 1340 to Charles II. (containing also ordinances of crafts).

The best history is Drake's (No. 3054), but it contains many errors. Davies's volume of records (No. 3050) is valuable.

a. Town Records.

3050. Extracts from the municipal records of the city of York, during the reigns of Edward IV., Edward V., and Richard III.; with notes illustrative and explanatory, and an appendix containing some account of the celebration of the Corpus Christi festival at York in the fourteenth, fifteenth, and sixteenth centuries. By Robert Davies. London, 1843. 8°.

The extracts are from the chamberlains' accounts and the minutes of the proceedings of the city council.

Valuable.

3051. † GENT, THOMAS. The customs and orders of the lord mayor, aldermen, sheriffs, four-and-twenty, and commons of the city of York, touching the wearing of their gowns, treats at elections, and other ancient customs. York, 1731. 12°.

3052. Subsidy roll for York and Ainsty. [15 Hen. VIII. Edited by E. Peacock.] *Yorkshire Archæol. and Topog. Assoc.,* Journal, iv. 170–201. London, 1877. 8°.

b. General Histories.

See No. 673.

3053. CAINE, CÆSAR. The martial annals of the city of York. London and York, 1893. 8°.

Contains some brief allusions to municipal history.

3054. * DRAKE, FRANCIS. Eboracum : or the history and antiquities of the city of York, from its original to the present times; together with the history of the cathedral church. . . . In two books. London, 1736. f°.

Contains the early town charters in full; extracts from town ordinances, 1519–1684, etc.

One of the best works of the old school of English topographers.

3055. Eboracum : or the history and antiquities of the city of York, from its origin to this time; together with an account of the Ainsty, or county of the same. . . . 2 vols. York, 1788. 8°.

3056. [GENT, THOMAS.] The ancient and modern history of the city of York . . . an account of the mayors and bayliffs, lord mayors and sheriffs. . . . The whole diligently collected by T. G. York and London, 1730. 8°.

Contains only a few brief notes relating to municipal history.

3057. HARGROVE, WILLIAM. History and description of the ancient city of York : comprising all the most interesting information already published in Drake's Eboracum; enriched with much entirely new matter. . . . 2 vols. York, 1818. 8°.

3058. History (The) and antiquities of the city of York, from its origin to the present times. . . . 3 vols. York, 1785. 12°.

Based on Drake.

A large part of vol. ii. is devoted to municipal history. Contains the early town charters; extracts from municipal ordinances, 1550–1650, etc.

3059. RAINE, JAMES. York. [Historic Towns. Edited by E. A. Freeman and W. Hunt.] London, 1893. 8°.

A good little book, but the account of municipal history is brief.

3060. TORR, JAMES. The antiquities of York city, and the civil government thereof; with a list of all the mayors and bayliffs. . . . Collected from the papers of Christopher Hildyard, Esq. With notes. . . . York, 1719. 8°.

Contains only brief notes concerning municipal history.

c. Gilds.

3061. Extracts from ye gild book of the barber-surgeons of York [1592–1614.] By J. T. Bent. *The Antiquary,* vi. 154–7. London, 1882. 4°.

3062. HOPE, R. C. Old English pewter. *The Reliquary*, New Series, v. 20–26, 72–80. London, 1891. 8°.

Contains a summary of the ordinances made by the pewterers of York in 1419 and 1540; and the ordinances of 1599, printed in full.

3063. KERRY, CHARLES. Discovery of the register and chartulary of the mercers' company, York [with extracts from these records, 1420–1523.] *The Antiquary*, xxii. 266–70; xxiii. 27–30, 70–73. London, 1890–91. 4°.

3064. Register (The) of the guild of Corpus Christi in the city of York; with an appendix. . . . [Edited by R. H. Skaife.] *Surtees Society*. Durham, etc., 1872. 8°.

3065. SMITH, LUCY T. The bakers of York and their ancient ordinary. *Archæol. Review*, i. 124–34, 215–28. London, 1888. 8°.

3066. —— The book of accounts of the bakers of York [with extracts, 1585–88.] *Ibid.*, i. 450–52. London, 1888. 8°.

3067. —— Ordinances of the companies of marshals and smiths of York, 1409–1443. *The Antiquary*, xi. 105–9. London, 1885. 4°.

3068. Volume (A) of English miscellanies, illustrating the history and language of the northern counties of England. [Edited by James Raine.] *Surtees Society*. Durham, etc., 1890. 8°.

Documents relating to the craft of girdlers, 1428, and the craft of masons and wrights, etc., 1417–51, pp. 11–22.

3069. York plays. The plays performed by the crafts or mysteries of York on the day of Corpus Christi in the 14th, 15th, and 16th centuries. . . . Edited, with introduction and glossary, by Lucy Toulmin Smith. Oxford, 1885. 8°.

d. Miscellaneous.

3070. Cause (The) between the city of York and the non-freemen, at the Lammas assizes, 1776, compared with the cause between the city of London and Allen Evans, Esq., on the validity of a by-law; and with the case of a non-freeman of the town of Berwick upon Tweed. London, [1776.] 8°. pp. 16.

Relates to a person who was fined for trading and keeping a shop in York, not being a freeman thereof.

3071. List (A) or catalogue of all the mayors and bayliffs . . . of Yorke, from the time of Edw. I. untill this present year, 1664. . . . [By Christopher Hildyard.] York, 1664. 4°. pp. 67.

Reprinted, London, 1715.

3072. SELLERS, MAUD. The city of York in the sixteenth century. *English Hist. Review*, ix. 275–304. London, 1894. 8°.

3073. —— York in the sixteenth and seventeenth centuries. *Ibid.*, xii. 437–47. London, 1897. 8°.

YOUGHAL.

3074. Ancient and present state (The) of Youghall : containing a natural, civil, ecclesiastical, and topographical history thereof. . . . Youghall, 1784. 12°.

A brief account, of little value.

3075. * CAULFIELD, RICHARD. The council book of the corporation of Youghal, from 1610 to 1659, from 1666 to 1687, and from 1690 to 1800. . . . Edited from the original, with annals and appendices compiled from public and private records. Guildford, 1878. 4°.

3076. [HAYMAN, SAMUEL.] The handbook for Youghal : containing an account of St. Mary's collegiate church . . . and the monastery of St. John's ; with the historical annals of the town. (Third Series.) Youghal, 1852. 8°.

3077. —— The new handbook for Youghal : containing notes and records of the ancient religious foundations, and historical annals [brief notices] of the town. (Fourth Series.) By the Rev. Samuel Hayman. Youghal, 1858. 8°.

ADDENDA.

3078. † BEAVEN, A. B.   The municipal representation of Bristol (1835–1880). . . . Bristol, 1880.   8°.   pp. 60.

3079. † Bristol.   An abstract of the city charter: containing the institution of mayors. . . . Bristol, 1832.   8°.   pp. 22.

This has the same title as No. 1143.

3080. † Bristol corporation.   An analysis of the report of the commissioners of corporate inquiry, for the city and county of Bristol. Bristol, 1835.   8°.   pp. 28.

See No. 60.

3081. † Corporation reform.   Six addresses to the citizens of Bristol on the reform of their municipal body.   By a rated burgess [J. B. Kington].   Bristol, 1836.   8°.

These addresses were published separately in 1835.   They will also be found in No. 1169.

3082. † DAWES, M.   Observations on the mode of electing representatives in Parliament for the city of Bristol, with a proposed reform. . . . Bristol, 1784.   8°.   pp. 46.

3083. FULLER, E. A.   The tallage of 6 Edward II. (Dec. 16, 1312) and the Bristol rebellion.   *Bristol and Glouc. Archæol. Soc.*, Transactions, xix. 171–278.   [Bristol, 1897.]   8°.

3084. † TAYLOR, C. S.   On the date of the earliest charter of Bristol.   *Clifton Antiquarian Club*, Proceedings, iii. 151–61.   Bristol, 1896.   8°.

3085. † Thirty letters on the trade of Bristol, which appeared in the Bristol Mercury during the year 1833, under the signature "A burgess" [J. B. Kington].   [Bristol, 1833.]   f°.

This is the first edition of No. 1181.

BURY ST. EDMUND'S.

3086. ROUND, J. H.   The first charter of St. Edmund's Bury, Suffolk [temp. Stephen.]   *American Hist. Review*, ii. 688–90.   New York, 1897.   8°.

CHIPPENHAM.

3087. GOLDNEY, F. H.   Records of Chippenham relating to the borough, from its incorporation by Queen Mary, 1554, to its reconstruction by act of Parliament, 1889 : comprising extracts from the minute books and registers of accounts of the corporation, together with copies and references from the charters, deeds, and documents in the borough chest.   London, 1889.   8°.

This is the full title of No. 1283a.   The work contains valuable documents; the greater portion of the material is of the 17th century.

COVENTRY.

3088. † WHITLEY, T. W.   The charters and manuscripts of Coventry : their story and purport.   Warwick, 1897.

LONDON.

3089. Chronicon ab anno 1189 ad 1556 ex registro fratrum minorum Londoniæ.   [Monumenta Franciscana, edited by Richard Howlett, ii. 143–260.   *Rolls Series.*   London, 1882.   8°.]

This is a revised edition of No. 1982.

SALFORD.

3090. MAKINSON, C.   On the ancient court records of the borough of Salford [1597–1669.]   *Brit. Archæol. Assoc.*, Journal, New Series, i. 314–26.   London, 1895.   8°.

YARMOUTH, GREAT.

3091. † A letter to the corporation of Great Yarmouth on the election of a recorder.   By Observator.   Yarmouth, 1831.   8°.

3092. † On the conduct of the corporation of Great Yarmouth.   In two parts.   By a freeman.   Yarmouth, 1825.   12°.

INDEX.

Numerals included within brackets refer to pages. Other numerals refer to the numbered titles. For the various kinds of gilds, companies, and records, see under "Gilds and Companies," "Public Records," and "Town Records."

Glastonbury, 58, 62, 647, 1677.
Glen, Alexander, 270–1.
— John, 1445.
— R. C., 271.
— W. C., 502, 516.
Glengariff, 1335.
Glew, E. L., 2923.
Gloucester, 59, 130, 138, 158, 330, 346, 604–5, 1678–92.
Gloucestershire, 24–5, 604–5, 2881.
Glover, Stephen, 589, 1374.
— William, 242.
Glyde, John, 1804.
Gneist, Rudolf, [16], 83–6, [53], 299, 2264.
Godalming, 58.
Godfrey-Faussett, T. G., 1219.
Godmanchester, 1693.
Godwin, G. N., 28.
Goldney, F. H., 1283a, 3087.
Gomme, G. L., 4, [18], 102–5, 901–2, 1284, 2009, 2192, 2246, 2343.
Goodnow, F. J., 272.
Goodrich, L., 2272.
Gordon, J. F. S., 806, 1635.
— James, 928.
Gore, Montague, 399–401.
Gorleston, 78.
Gorton, John, 402.
Gosport, 2618, 2622.
Gotham, M., 1942.
Goudy, H., 832.
Gougaun-Barra, 1335.
Gough, Henry, 17.
— Richard, 5, 6.
Goulding, R. W., 2281.
Gower, 2867.
Gower, G. L., 1098.
Gowran, 1694.
Graham, Robert, 833.
— William, 1963.
Grainge, William, 1843, 2888.
Grampound, 58, 582, 1695.
Grant, James (M. A.), 881.
— — (novelist), 1511, 1890.
Grantham, 58–9, 345–6, 626, 1696–8.
Grattan, Henry, 737.
Graves, James, 2889.
Gravesend, 1699–1702.
Gray, Henry, 7, 8.
Greary, Thomas, 264.
Green, Burton, 2762.
— Emanuel, 1253.
— Henry, 1844.
— J. R., [18], 106–7, 152, 1197, 2539.
— Mrs. J. R., [15, 21], 153.
— M. A. E., 170.
— Valentine, 3018.

Greenock, 1703–6.
Greenwell, William, 118.
Greenwich, 58, 1707–8.
Greg, P., 523.
Grego, Joseph, 334.
Gregory, William, 1989.
Greig, John, 1545.
Grey, Charles (2nd Earl), 390, 405.
— H. G. (3rd Earl), 360a.
— William, 2420.
Gribble, J. B., 1022.
Griffin, Richard, 2704.
Griffith, Edward, 406, 1784.
Grimsby, Great, 62, 130, 346, 355, 626, 1709–12.
Grimsey, B. P., 1804a–b.
Grinstead, East, 58, 319, 345–6, 355, 653, 657, 1713.
Grip (pseud.), 2194.
Groome, F. H., 883.
Gross, Charles, 140, 154, [83–4], 540–1, 903, 1066.
Grote, George, 407.
Guest, John, 2694.
Guildford, 58, 346, 541, 653–5, 1714–8.
Guilding, J. M., 2667.
Gunnell, W. A., 1773.
Guppy, Robert, 243.
Gurney, Hudson, 248, 2313.
Gutch, J. M., 1173, 3021.
— John, 2537.
Guyot, Yves, 2195.
Gwynedd, 317.

Hackfall, 2682.
Haddington, 350, 764, 775, 1717–22a.
Hadleigh, 1723–4.
Hadley, George, 1774.
Haig, Charles, 752.
— James, 1809.
Hailstone, Edward, 42.
Hakewill, James, 2999.
Hale, Matthew, 692, 2950.
Halifax, 667, 669–71, 674, 1725–9.
Hall, George, 1276.
— James, 2399.
— Peter, 2735.
— T. H., 523.
Hallam, Henry, 155, 171, 250.
Hallamshire, 2753–4.
Halliwell, J. O., 593, 1391, 2844–52.
Hamer, Edward, 1961.
Hamilton, H. C., 713.
— W. D., 170, 1991a.
— William, 802.
Hampshire, 26–8, 606–12.
Hance, E. M., 1927.